Self-Service Linux®

D1401155

BRUCE PERENS' OPEN SOURCE SERIES

www.phptr.com/perens

- *Java™ Application Development on Linux®*
  Carl Albing and Michael Schwarz
- *C++ GUI Programming with Qt 3*
  Jasmin Blanchette and Mark Summerfield
- *Managing Linux Systems with Webmin: System Administration and Module Development*
  Jamie Cameron
- *Understanding the Linux Virtual Memory Manager*
  Mel Gorman
- *PHP 5 Power Programming*
  Andi Gutmans, Stig Bakken, and Derick Rethans
- *Linux® Quick Fix Notebook*
  Peter Harrison
- *Implementing CIFS: The Common Internet File System*
  Christopher Hertel
- *Open Source Security Tools: A Practical Guide to Security Applications*
  Tony Howlett
- *Apache Jakarta Commons: Reusable Java™ Components*
  Will Iverson
- *Embedded Software Development with eCos*
  Anthony Massa
- *Rapid Application Development with Mozilla*
  Nigel McFarlane
- *Subversion Version Control: Using the Subversion Version Control System in Development Projects*
  William Nagel
- *Intrusion Detection with SNORT: Advanced IDS Techniques Using SNORT, Apache, MySQL, PHP, and ACID*
  Rafeeq Ur Rehman
- *Cross-Platform GUI Programming with wxWidgets*
  Julian Smart and Kevin Hock with Stefan Csomor
- *Samba-3 by Example, Second Edition: Practical Exercises to Successful Deployment*
  John H. Terpstra
- *The Official Samba-3 HOWTO and Reference Guide, Second Edition*
  John H. Terpstra and Jelmer R. Vernooij, Editors
- *Self-Service Linux®: Mastering the Art of Problem Determination*
  Mark Wilding and Dan Behman

Self-Service Linux®

Mastering the Art of Problem Determination

Mark Wilding and Dan Behman

PRENTICE HALL
Professional Technical Reference
Upper Saddle River, NJ ● Boston ●
Indianapolis ● San Francisco ● New York ●
Toronto ● Montreal ● London ● Munich ●
Paris ● Madrid ● Capetown ● Sydney ●
Tokyo ● Singapore ● Mexico City

Visit us on the Web: www.phptr.com
Library of Congress Number: 2005927150
Copyright © 2006 Pearson Education, Inc.

ISBN 0-13-147751-X
Text printed in the United States on recycled paper at R.R. Donnelley in Crawfordsville, Indiana.
First printing, September, 2005

I would like to dedicate this book to my wife, Caryna, whose relentless nagging and badgering forced me to continue working on this book when nothing else could. Just kidding... Without Caryna's support and understanding, I could never have written this book. Not only did she help me find time to write, she also spent countless hours formatting the entire book for production. I would also like to dedicate this book to my two sons, Rhys and Dylan, whose boundless energy acted as inspiration throughout the writing of this book.
Mark Wilding

Without the enduring love and patience of my wife Kim, this laborous project would have halted long ago. I dedicate this book to her, as well as to my beautiful son Nicholas, my family, and all of the Botzangs and Mayos.
Dan Behman

About Prentice Hall Professional Technical Reference

With origins reaching back to the industry's first computer science publishing program in the 1960s, and formally launched as its own imprint in 1986, Prentice Hall Professional Technical Reference (PH PTR) has developed into the leading provider of technical books in the world today. Our editors now publish over 200 books annually, authored by leaders in the fields of computing, engineering, and business.

Our roots are firmly planted in the soil that gave rise to the technical revolution. Our bookshelf contains many of the industry's computing and engineering classics: Kernighan and Ritchie's *C Programming Language*, Nemeth's *UNIX System Administration Handbook*, Horstmann's *Core Java*, and Johnson's *High-Speed Digital Design*.

PH PTR acknowledges its auspicious beginnings while it looks to the future for inspiration. We continue to evolve and break new ground in publishing by providing today's professionals with tomorrow's solutions.

PRENTICE
HALL
PTR

Contents

Contents

About the Authors

Mark Wilding is a senior developer at IBM who currently specializes in serviceability technologies, UNIX, and Linux. With over 15 years of experience writing software, Mark has extensive expertise in operating systems, networks, C/C++ development, serviceability, quality engineering, and computer hardware.

Dan Behman is a member of the DB2 UDB for Linux Platform Exploitation development team at the Toronto IBM Software Lab. He has over 10 years of experience with Linux, and has been involved in porting and enabling DB2 UDB on the latest architectures that Linux supports, including x86-64, zSeries, and POWER platforms.

Preface

Linux is the ultimate choice for home and business users. It is powerful, as stable as any commercial operating system, secure, and best of all, it is open source. One of the biggest deciding factors for whether to use Linux at home or for your business can be service and support. Because Linux is developed by thousands of volunteers from around the world, it is not always clear who to turn to when something goes wrong.

In the true spirit of Linux, there is a slightly different approach to support than the commercial norm. After all, Linux represents an unparalleled community of experts, it includes industry leading problem determination tools, and of course, the product itself includes the source code. These resources are in addition to the professional Linux support services that are available from companies, such as IBM, and the various Linux vendors, such as Redhat and SUSE. Making the most of these additional resources is called "self-service" and is the main topic covered by this book.

Self-service on Linux means different things to different people. For those who use Linux at home, it means a more enjoyable Linux experience. For those who use Linux at work, being able to quickly and effectively diagnose problems on Linux can increase their value as employees as well as their marketability. For corporate leaders deciding whether to adopt Linux as part of the corporate strategy, self-service for Linux means reduced operation costs and increased Return on Investment (ROI) for any Linux adoption strategy. Regardless of what type of Linux user you are, it is important to make the most of your Linux experience and investment.

WHAT IS THIS BOOK ABOUT?

In a nutshell, this book is about effectively and efficiently diagnosing problems that occur in the Linux environment. It covers good investigation practices, how to use the information and resources on the Internet, and then dives right into detail describing how to use the most important problem determination tools that Linux has to offer.

Chapter 1 is like a crash course on effective problem determination practices, which will help you to diagnose problems like an expert. It covers where and how to look for information on the Internet as well as how to start investigating common types of problems.

Chapter 2 covers strace, which is arguably the most frequently used problem determination tool in Linux. This chapter includes both practical usage information as well as details about how strace works. It also includes source code for a simple strace tool and details about how the underlying functionality works with the kernel through the ptrace interface.

Chapter 3 is about the /proc filesystem, which contains a wealth of information about the hardware, kernel, and processes that are running on the system. The purpose of this chapter is to point out and examine some of the more advanced features and tricks primarily related to problem determination and system diagnosis. For example, the chapter covers how to use the SysRq Kernel Magic hotkey with /proc/sys/kernel/sysrq.

Chapter 4 provides detailed information about compiling. Why does a book about debugging on Linux include a chapter about compiling? Well, the beginning of this preface mentioned that diagnosing problems in Linux is different than that on commercial environments. The main reason behind this is that the source code is freely available for all of the open source tools and the operating system itself. This chapter provides vital information whether you need to recompile an open source application with debug information (as is often the case), whether you need to generate an assembly language listing for a tough problem (that is, to find the line of code for a trap), or whether you run into a problem while recompiling the Linux kernel itself.

Chapter 5 covers intimate details about the *stack*, one of the most important and fundamental concepts of a computer system. Besides explaining all the gory details about the structure of a stack (which is pretty much required knowledge for any Linux expert), the chapter also includes and explains source code that can be used by the readers to generate stack traces from within their own tools and applications. The code examples are not only useful to illustrate how the stack works but they can save real time and debugging effort when included as part of an application's debugging facilities.

Chapter 6 takes an in-depth and detailed look at debugging applications with the GNU Debugger (GDB) and includes an overview of the Data Display Debugger (DDD) graphical user interface. Linux has an advantage over most other operating systems in that it includes a feature rich debugger, GDB, for free. Debuggers can be used to debug many types of problems, and given that GDB is free, it is well worth the effort to understand the basic as well as the more advanced features. This chapter covers hard-to-find details about debugging C++ applications, threaded applications, as well as numerous best practices. Have you ever spawned an xterm to attach to a process with GDB? This chapter will show you how—and why!

Chapter 7 provides a detailed overview of system crashes and hangs. With proprietary operating systems (OSs), a system crash or hang almost certainly requires you to call the OS vendor for help. However with Linux, the end user can debug a kernel problem on his or her own or at least identify key information to search for known problems. If you do need to get an expert involved, knowing what to collect will help you to get the right data quickly for a fast diagnosis. This chapter describes everything from how to attach a serial console to how to find the line of code for a kernel trap (an "oops"). For example, the chapter provides step-by-step details for how to manually add a trap in the kernel and then debug it to find the resulting line of code.

Chapter 8 covers more details about debugging the kernel or debugging with the kernel debugger, kdb. The chapter covers how to configure and enable kdb on your system as well as some practical commands that most Linux users can use without being a kernel expert. For example, this chapter shows you how to find out what a process is doing from within the kernel, which can be particularly useful if the process is hung and not killable.

Chapter 9 is a detailed, head-on look at Executable and Linking Format (ELF). The details behind ELF are often ignored or just assumed to work. This is really unfortunate because a thorough understanding of ELF can lead to a whole new world of debugging techniques. This chapter covers intimate but practical details of the underlying ELF file format as well as tips and tricks that few people know. There is even sample code and step-by-step instructions for how to override functions using LD_PRELOAD and how to use the global offset table and the GDB debugger to intercept functions manually and redirect them to debug versions.

Appendix A is a toolbox that outlines the most useful tools, facilities, and files on Linux. For each tool, there is a description of when it is useful and where to get the latest copy.

Appendix B includes a production-ready data collection script that is especially useful for mission-critical systems or those who remotely support customers on Linux. The data collection script alone can save many hours or even days for debugging a remote problem.

Note: The source code used in this book can be found at `http://www.phptr.com/title/013147751X`.

Note: A code continuation character, ➥, appears at the beginning of code lines that have wrapped down from the line above it.

Lastly, as we wrote this book it became clear to us that we were covering the right information. Reviewers often commented about how they were able to use the information immediately to solve real problems, not the problems that may come in the future or may have happened in the past, but real problems that people were actually struggling with when they reviewed the chapters. We also found *ourselves* referring to the content of the book to help solve problems as they came up. We hope you find it as useful as it has been to those who have read it thus far.

WHO IS THIS BOOK FOR?

This book has useful information for any Linux user but is certainly geared more toward the Linux professional. This includes Linux power users, Linux administrators, developers who write software for Linux, and support staff who support products on Linux.

Readers who casually use Linux at home will benefit also, as long as they either have a basic understanding of Linux or are at least willing to learn more about it—the latter being most important.

Ultimately, as Linux increases in popularity, there are many seasoned experts who are facing the challenge of translating their knowledge and experience to the Linux platform. Many are already experts with one or more operating systems except that they lack specific knowledge about the various command line incantations or ways to interpret their knowledge for Linux.

This book will help such experts to quickly adapt their existing skill set and apply it effectively on Linux.

This power-packed book contains real industry experience on many topics and very hard-to-find information. Without a doubt, it is a must have for any developer, tester, support analyst, or anyone who uses Linux.

ACKNOWLEDGMENTS

Anyone who has written a book will agree that it takes an enormous amount of effort. Yes, there is a lot of work for the authors, but without the many key people behind the scenes, writing a book would be nearly impossible. We would like to thank all of the people who reviewed, supported, contributed, or otherwise made this book possible.

First, we would like to thank the reviewers for their time, patience, and valuable feedback. Besides the typos, grammatical errors, and technical omissions, in many cases the reviewers allowed us to see other vantage points, which in turn helped to make the content more well-rounded and complete. In particular, we would like to thank Richard Moore, for reviewing the technical content of many chapters; Robert Haskins, for being so thorough with his reviews and comments; Mel Gorman, for his valuable feedback on the ELF (Executable and Linking Format) chapter; Scott Dier, for his many valuable comments; Jan Kritter, for reviewing pretty much the entire book; and Joyce Coleman, Ananth Narayan, Pascale Stephenson, Ben Elliston, Hien Nguyen, Jim Keniston, as well as the IBM Linux Technology Center, for their valuable feedback. We would also like to thank the excellent engineers from SUSE for helping to answer many deep technical questions, especially Andi Kleen, Frank Balzer, and Michael Matz.

We would especially like to thank our wives and families for the support, encouragement, and giving us the time to work on this project. Without their support, this book would have never gotten past the casual conversation we had about possibly writing one many months ago. We truly appreciate the sacrifices that they have made to allow us to finish this book.

Last of all, we would like to thank the Open Source Community as a whole. The open source movement is a truly remarkable phenomenon that has and will continue to raise the bar for computing at home or for commercial environments. Our thanks to the Open Source Community is not specifically for this book but rather for their tireless dedication and technical prowess that make Linux and all open source products a reality. It is our hope that the content in this book will encourage others to adopt, use or support open source products and of course Linux. Every little bit helps.

Thanks for reading this book.

OTHER

The history and evolution of the Linux operating system is fascinating and certainly still being written with new twists popping up all the time. Linux itself comprises only the kernel of the whole operating system. Granted, this is the single most important part, but everything else surrounding the Linux kernel is made up mostly of GNU free software. There are two major things that GNU software and the Linux kernel have in common. The first is that the source code for both is freely accessible. The second is that they have been developed and continue to be developed by many thousands of volunteers throughout the world, all connecting and sharing ideas and work through the Internet. Many refer to this collaboration of people and resources as the *Open Source Community*.

The Open Source Community is much like a distributed development team with skills and experience spanning many different areas of computer science. The source code that is written by the Open Source Community is available for anyone and everyone to see. Not only can this make problem determination easier, having such a large and diverse group of people looking at the code can reduce the number of defects and improve the security of the source code. Open source software is open to innovations as much as criticism, both helping to improve the quality and functionality of the software.

One of the most common concerns about adopting Linux is service and support. However, Linux has the Open Source Community, a wide range of freely available problem determination tools, the source code, and the Internet itself as a source of information including numerous sites and newsgroups dedicated to Linux. It is important for every Linux user to understand the resources and tools that are available to help them diagnose problems. That is the purpose of this book. It is not intended to be a replacement to a support contract, nor does it require one. If you have one, this book is an enhancement that will be sure to help you make the most of your existing support contract.

Best Practices and Initial Investigation

1.1 INTRODUCTION

Your boss is screaming, your customers are screaming, you're screaming ... Whatever the situation, there is a problem, and you need to solve it. Remember those old classic MUD games? For those who don't, a Multi-User Dungeon or MUD was the earliest incarnation of the online video game. Users played the game through a completely non-graphical text interface that described the surroundings and options available to the player and then prompted the user with what to do next.

```
You are alone in a dark cubicle. To the North is your boss's office, to
the West is your Team Lead's cubicle, to the East is a window opening
out to a five-floor drop, and to the South is a kitchenette containing
a freshly brewed pot of coffee. You stare at your computer screen in
bewilderment as the phone rings for the fifth time in as many minutes
indicating that your users are unable to connect to their server.

Command>
```

What will you do? Will you run toward the East and dive through the open window? Will you go grab a hot cup of coffee to ensure you stay alert for the long night ahead? A common thing to do in these MUD games was to examine your surroundings further, usually done by the look command.

```
Command> look

Your cubicle is a mess of papers and old coffee cups. The message
waiting light on your phone is burnt out from flashing for so many
months. Your email inbox is overflowing with unanswered emails. On top
of the mess is the brand new book you ordered entitled "Self-Service
Linux." You need a shower.

Command> read book "Self-Service Linux"

You still need a shower.
```

1

This tongue-in-cheek MUD analogy aside, what can this book really do for you? This book includes chapters that are loaded with useful information to help you diagnose problems quickly and effectively. This first chapter covers best practices for problem determination and points to the more in-depth information found in the chapters throughout this book. The first step is to ensure that your Linux system(s) are configured for effective problem determination.

1.2 GETTING YOUR SYSTEM(S) READY FOR EFFECTIVE PROBLEM DETERMINATION

The Linux problem determination tools and facilities are free, which begs the question: Why not install them? Without these tools, a simple problem can turn into a long and painful ordeal that can affect a business and/or your personal time. Before reading through the rest of the book, take some time to make sure the following tools are installed on your system(s). These tools are just waiting to make your life easier and/or your business more productive:

☞ **strace:** The strace tool traces the system calls, special functions that interact with the operating system. You can use this for many types of problems, especially those that relate to the operating system.

☞ **ltrace:** The ltrace tool traces the functions that a process calls. This is similar to strace, but the called functions provide more detail.

☞ **lsof:** The lsof tool lists all of the open files on the operating system (OS). When a file is open, the OS returns a numeric file descriptor to the process to use. This tool lists all of the open files on the OS with their respective process IDs and file descriptors.

☞ **top:** This tool lists the "top" processes that are running on the system. By default it sorts by the amount of current CPU being consumed by a process.

☞ **traceroute/tcptraceroute:** These tools can be used to trace a network route (or at least one direction of it).

☞ **ping:** Ping simply checks whether a remote system can respond. Sometimes firewalls block the network packets ping uses, but it is still very useful.

☞ **hexdump or equivalent:** This is simply a tool that can display the raw contents of a file.

☞ **tcpdump and/or ethereal:** Used for network problems, these tools can display the packets of network traffic.

☞ **GDB:** This is a powerful debugger that can be used to investigate some of the more difficult problems.

☞ **readelf:** This tool can read and display information about various sections of an Executable and Linking Format (ELF) file.

These tools (and many more) are listed in Appendix A, "The Toolbox," along with information on where to find these tools. The rest of this book assumes that your systems have these basic Linux problem determination tools installed. These tools and facilities are free, and they won't do much good sitting quietly on an installation CD (or on the Internet somewhere). In fact, this book will self-destruct in five minutes if these tools are not installed.

Now of course, just because you have a tool in your toolbox, it doesn't mean you know how to use it in a particular situation. Imagine a toolbox with lots of very high quality tools sitting on your desk. Suddenly your boss walks into your office and asks you to fix a car engine or TV. You know you have the tools. You might even know what the tools are used for (that is, a wrench is used for loosening and tightening bolts), but could you fix that car engine? A toolbox is not a substitute for a good understanding of how and when to use the tools. Understanding how and when to use these tools is the main focus of this book.

1.3 THE FOUR PHASES OF INVESTIGATION

Good investigation practices should balance the need to solve problems quickly, the need to build your skills, and the effective use of subject matter experts. The need to solve a problem quickly is obvious, but building your skills is important as well.

Imagine walking into a library looking for information about a type of hardwood called "red oak." To your surprise, you find a person who knows absolutely everything about wood. You have a choice to make. You can ask this person for the information you need, or you can read through several books and resources trying to find the information on your own. In the first case, you will get the answer you need right away...you just need to ask. In the second case, you will likely end up reading a lot of information about hardwood on your quest to find information about red oak. You're going to learn more about hardwood, probably the various types, relative hardness, and what each is used for. You might even get curious and spend time reading up on the other types of hardwood. This peripheral information can be very helpful in the future, especially if you often work with hardwood.

The next time you need information about hardwood, you go to the library again. You can ask the mysterious and knowledgeable person for the answer or spend some time and dig through books on your own. After a few trips to the library doing the investigation on your own, you will have learned a lot about hardwood and might not need to visit the library any more to get the answers you need. You've become an expert in hardwood. Of course, you'll use your new knowledge and power for something nobler than creating difficult decisions for those walking into a library.

Likewise, every time you encounter a problem, you have a choice to make. You can immediately try to find the answer by searching the Internet or by asking an expert, or you can investigate the problem on your own. If you investigate a problem on your own, you will increase your skills from the experience regardless of whether you successfully solve the problem.

Of course, you need to make sure the skills that you would learn by finding the answer on your own will help you again in the future. For example, a physician may have little use for vast knowledge of hardwood ... although she or he may still find it interesting. For a physician that has one question about hardwood every 10 years, it may be better to just ask the expert or look for a shortcut to get the information she or he needs.

The first section of this chapter will outline a useful balance that will solve problems quickly and in many cases even faster than getting a subject matter expert involved (from here on referred to as an *expert*). How is this possible? Well, getting an expert usually takes time. Most experts are busy with numerous other projects and are rarely available on a minute's notice. So why turn to them at the first sign of trouble? Not only can you investigate and resolve some problems faster on your own, you can become one of the experts of tomorrow.

There are four phases of problem investigation that, when combined, will both build your skills and solve problems quickly and effectively.

1. Initial investigation using your own skills.
2. Search for answers using the Internet or other resource.
3. Begin deeper investigation.
4. Ask a subject matter expert for help.

The first phase is an attempt to diagnose the problem on your own. This ensures that you build some skill for every problem you encounter. If the first attempt takes too long (that is, the problem is urgent and you need an immediate solution), move on to the next phase, which is searching for the answer using the Internet. If that doesn't reveal a solution to the problem, don't get an expert involved just yet. The third phase is to dive in deeper on your own. It will help to build some deep skill, and your homework will also be appreciated by an expert should you need to get one involved. Lastly, when the need arises, engage an expert to help solve the problem.

The urgency of a problem should help to guide how quickly you go through the phases. For example, if you're supporting the New York Stock Exchange and you are trying to solve a problem that would bring it back online during the peak hours of trading, you wouldn't spend 20 minutes surfing the Internet looking for answers. You would get an expert involved immediately.

The type of problem that occurred should also help guide how quickly you go through the phases. If you are a casual at-home Linux user, you might not benefit from a deep understanding of how Linux device drivers work, and it might not make sense to try and investigate such a complex problem on your own. It makes more sense to build deeper skills in a problem area when the type of problem aligns with your job responsibilities or personal interests.

1.3.1 Phase #1: Initial Investigation Using Your Own Skills

Basic information you should always make note of when you encounter a problem is:

☞ The exact time the problem occurred

☞ Dynamic operating system information (information that can change frequently over time)

The exact time is important because some problems are related to an event that occurred at that time. A common example is an errant cron job that randomly kills off processes on the system. A cron job is a script or program that is run by the cron daemon. The cron daemon is a process that runs in the background on Linux and Unix systems and runs programs or scripts at specific and configurable times (refer to the Linux man pages for more information about cron). A system administrator can accidentally create a cron job that will kill off processes with specific names or for a certain set of user IDs. As a non-privileged user (a user without super user privileges), your tool or application would simply be killed off without a trace. If it happens again, you will want to know what time it occurred and if it occurred at the same time of day (or week, hour, and so on).

The exact time is also important because it may be the only correlation between the problem and the system conditions at the time when the problem occurred. For example, an application often crashes or produces an error message when it is affected by low virtual memory. The symptom of an application crashing or producing an error message can seem, at first, to be completely unrelated to the current system conditions.

The dynamic OS information includes anything that can change over time without human intervention. This includes the amount of free memory, the amount of free disk space, the CPU workload, and so on. This information is important enough that you may even want to collect it any time a serious problem occurs. For example, if you don't collect the amount of free virtual memory when a problem occurs, you might never get another chance. A few minutes or hours later, the system resources might go back to normal, eliminating any evidence that the system was ever low on memory. In fact, this is so important that distributions such as SUSE LINUX Enterprise Server continuously run sar (a tool that displays dynamic OS information) to monitor the system resources. Sar is a special tool that can collect, report, or save information about the system activity.

The dynamic OS information is also a good place to start investigating many types of problems, which are frequently caused by a lack of resources or changes to the operating system. As part of this initial investigation, you should also make a note of the following:

☞ **What you were doing when the problem occurred.** Were you installing software? Were you trying to start a Web server?

☞ **A problem description.** This should include a description of what happened and a description of what was supposed to happen. In other words, how do you know there was a problem?

☞ **Anything that may have triggered the problem**. This will be pretty problem-specific, but it's worthwhile to think about it when the problem is still fresh in your mind.

☞ **Any evidence that may be relevant.** This includes error logs from an application that you were using, the system log (/var/log/messages), an error message that was printed to the screen, and so on. You will want to protect any evidence (that is, make sure the relevant files don't get deleted until you solve the problem).

If the problem isn't too serious, then just make a mental note of this information and continue the investigation. If the problem is very serious (has a major impact to a business), write this stuff down or put it into an investigation log (an investigation log is covered in detail later in this chapter).

If you can reproduce the problem at will, strace and ltrace may be good tools to start with. The strace and ltrace utilities can trace an application from the command line, or they can trace a running process. The `strace` command traces all of the system calls (special functions that interact with the operating system), and `ltrace` traces functions that a program called. The strace tool is probably the most useful problem investigation tool on Linux and is covered in more detail in Chapter 2, "strace and System Call Tracing Explained."

Every now and then you'll run into a problem that occurs once every few weeks or months. These problems usually occur on busy, complex systems, and even though they are rare, they can still have a major impact to a business and your personal time. If the problem is serious and cannot be reproduced, be sure to capture as much information as possible given that it might be your only chance. Also if the problem can't be reproduced, you should start writing things down because you might need to refer to the information weeks or months into the future. For these types of problems, it may be worthwhile to collect a lot of information about the OS (including the software versions that are installed on it) considering that the problem could be related to something else that may change over weeks or months of time. Problems that take weeks or months to resolve can span several major changes or upgrades to the system, making it important to keep track of the original conditions under which the problem occurred.

Collecting the right OS information can involve running many OS commands, too many for someone to run when the need arises. For your convenience, this book comes with a data collection script that can gather an enormous amount of information about the operating system in a very short period of time. It will save you from having to remember each command and from having to type each command in to collect the right information.

The data collection script is particularly useful in two situations. The first situation is that you are investigating a problem on a remote customer system that you can't log in to. The second situation is a serious problem on a local system that is critical to resolve. In both cases, the script is useful because it will usually gather all the OS information you need to investigate the problem with a single run.

When servicing a remote customer, it will reduce the number of initial requests for information. Without a data collection script, getting the right information for a remote problem can take many emails or phone calls. Each time you ask for more information, the information that is collected is older, further from the time that the problem occurred.

The script is easy to modify, meaning that you can add commands to collect information about specific products (including yours if you have any) or applications that may be important. For a business, this script can improve the efficiency of your support organization and increase the level of customer satisfaction with your support.

Readers that are only using Linux at home may still find the script useful if they ever need to ask for help from a Linux expert. However, the script is certainly aimed more at the business Linux user. For this reason, there is more information on the data collection script in Appendix B, "Data Collection Script" (for the readers who support or use Linux in a business setting).

Do not underestimate the importance of doing an initial investigation on your own, even if the information you need to solve the problem is on the Internet. You will learn more investigating a problem on your own, and that earned knowledge and experience will be helpful for solving problems again in the future. That said, make sure the information you learn is in an area that you will find useful again. For example, improving your skills with strace is a very worthwhile exercise, but learning about a rare problem in a device driver is probably not worth it for the average Linux user. An initial investigation will also help you to better understand the problem, which can be helpful when trying to find the right information on the Internet. Of course, if the problem is urgent, use the appropriate resources to find the right solution as soon as possible.

1.3.1.1   Did Anything Change Recently?   Everything is working as expected and then suddenly, a problem occurs. The first question that people usually ask is "Did anything change recently?" The fact of the matter is that something either changed or something triggered the problem. If something changed and you can figure out what it was, you might have solved the problem and avoided a lengthy investigation.

In general, it is very important to keep changes to a production environment to a minimum. When changes are necessary, be sure to notify the system users of any changes in advance so that any resulting impact will be easier for them to diagnose. Likewise, if you are a user of a system, look to your system administrator to give you a heads up when changes are made to the system. Here are some examples of changes that can cause problems:

☞ A recent upgrade or change in the kernel version and/or system libraries and/or software on the system (for example, a software upgrade). The change could introduce a bug or a change in the (expected) behavior of the operating system. Either can affect the software that runs on the system.

☞ Changes to kernel parameters or tunable values can cause changes to behavior of the operating system, which can in turn cause problems for software that runs on the system.

☞ Hardware changes. Disks can fail causing a major outage or possibly just a slowdown in the case of a RAID. If more memory is added to the system and applications start to fail, it could be the result of bad memory. For example, gcc is one of the tools that tend to crash with bad memory.

☞ Changes in workload (that is, more users suddenly going to a particular Web site) may push the system close to the limit of its resources. Increases in workload can consume the last bit of memory, causing problems for any software that could be running on the system.

One of the best ways to detect changes to the system is to periodically run a script or tool that collects important information about the system and the software that runs on it. When a difficult problem occurs, you might want to start with a quick comparison of the changes that were recently made on the system — if nothing else, to rule them out as candidates to investigate further.

Using information about changes to the system requires a bit of work up front. If you don't save historical information about the operating environment, you won't be able to compare it to the current information when something goes wrong. There are some useful tools such as tripwire that can help to keep a history of good, known configuration states.

Another best practice is to track any changes to configuration files in a revision control system such as CVS. This will ensure that you can "go back" to a stable point in the system's past. For example, if the system were running smoothly three weeks ago but is unstable now, it might make sense to go back to the configuration three weeks prior to see if the problems are due to any configuration changes.

1.3.2 Phase #2: Searching the Internet Effectively

There are three good reasons to move to this phase of investigation. The first is that your boss and/or customer needs immediate resolution of a problem. The second reason is that your patience has run out, and the problem is going in a direction that will take a long time to investigate. The third is that the type of problem is such that investigating it on your own is not going to build useful skills for the future.

Using what you've learned about the problem in the first phase of investigation, you can search online for similar problems, preferably finding the identical problem already solved. Most problems can be solved by searching the Internet using an engine such as Google, by reading frequently asked question (FAQ) documents, HOW-TO documents, mailing-list archives, USENET archives, or other forums.

1.3.2.1 Google When searching, pick out unique keywords that describe the problem you're seeing. Your keywords should contain the *application name* or "kernel" + *unique keywords from actual output* + *function name where problem occurs* (if known). For example, keywords consisting of "kernel Oops sock_poll" will yield many results in Google.

There is so much information about Linux on the Internet that search engine giant Google has created a special search specifically for Linux. This is a great starting place to search for the information you want - `http://www.google.com/linux`.

There are also some types of problems that can affect a Linux user but are not specific to Linux. In this case, it might be better to search using the main Google page instead. For example, FreeBSD shares many of the same design issues and makes use of GNU software as well, so there are times when documentation specific to FreeBSD will help with a Linux related problem.

1.3.2.2 USENET USENET is comprised of thousands of *newsgroups* or discussion groups on just about every imaginable topic. USENET has been around since the beginning of the Internet and is one of the original services that molded the Internet into what it is today. There are many ways of reading USENET newsgroups. One of them is by connecting a software program called a *news reader* to a USENET *news server*. More recently, Google provided *Google Groups* for users who prefer to use a Web browser. Google Groups is a searchable archive of most USENET newsgroups dating back to their infancies. The search page is found at `http://groups.google.com` or off of the main page for Google. Google Groups can also be used to post a question to USENET, as can most news readers.

1.3.2.3 Linux Web Resources There are several Web sites that store searchable Linux documentation. One of the more popular and comprehensive documentation sites is The Linux Documentation Project: `http://tldp.org`.

The Linux Documentation Project is run by a group of volunteers who provide many valuable types of information about Linux including FAQs and HOW-TO guides.

There are also many excellent articles on a wide range of topics available on other Web sites as well. Two of the more popular sites for articles are:

☞   Linux Weekly News – `http://lwn.net`
☞   Linux Kernel Newbies – `http://kernelnewbies.org`

The first of these sites has useful Linux articles that can help you get a better understanding of the Linux environment and operating system. The second Web site is for learning more about the Linux kernel, not necessarily for fixing problems.

1.3.2.4 Bugzilla Databases

Inspired and created by the Mozilla project, Bugzilla databases have become the most widely used bug tracking database systems for all kinds of GNU software projects such as the GNU Compiler Collection (GCC). Bugzilla is also used by some distribution companies to track bugs in the various releases of their GNU/Linux products.

Most Bugzilla databases are publicly available and can, at a minimum, be searched through an extensive Web-based query interface. For example, GCC's Bugzilla can be found at `http://gcc.gnu.org/bugzilla`, and a search can be performed without even creating an account. This can be useful if you think you've encountered a real software bug and want to search to see if anyone else has found and reported the problem. If a match is found to your query, you can examine and even track all the progress made on the bug.

If you're sure you've encountered a real software bug, and searching does not indicate that it is a known issue, do not hesitate to open a new bug report in the proper Bugzilla database. Open source software is community-based, and reporting bugs is a large part of what makes the open source movement work. Refer to investigation Phase 4 for more information on opening a bug reports.

1.3.2.5 Mailing Lists

Mailing lists are related closely to USENET newsgroups and in some cases are used to provide a more user friendly front-end to the lesser known and less understood USENET interfaces. The advantage of mailing lists is that interested parties explicitly *subscribe* to specific lists. When a posting is made to a mailing list, everyone subscribed to that list will receive an email. There are usually settings available to the subscriber to minimize the impact on their inboxes such as getting a daily or weekly digest of mailing list posts.

The most popular Linux related mailing list is the *Linux Kernel Mailing List* (lkml). This is where most of the Linux pioneers and gurus such as Linux Torvalds, Alan Cox, and Andrew Morton "hang out." A quick Google search will tell you how you can subscribe to this list, but that would probably be a bad idea due to the high amount of traffic. To avoid the need to subscribe and deal with the high traffic, there are many Web sites that provide fancy interfaces and searchable archives of the lkml. The main one is `http://lkml.org`.

There are also sites that provide summaries of discussions going on in the lkml. A popular one is at Linux Weekly News (`lwn.net`) at `http://lwn.net/Kernel`.

As with USENET, you are free to post questions or messages to mailing lists, though some require you to become a subscriber first.

1.3.3 Phase #3: Begin Deeper Investigation (Good Problem Investigation Practices)

If you get to this phase, you've exhausted your attempt to find the information using the Internet. With any luck you've picked up some good pointers from the Internet that will help you get a jump start on a more thorough investigation.

Because this is turning out to be a difficult problem, it is worth noting that difficult problems need to be treated in a special way. They can take days, weeks, or even months to resolve and tend to require much data and effort. Collecting and tracking certain information now may seem unimportant, but three weeks from now you may look back in despair wishing you had. You might get so deep into the investigation that you forget how you got there. Also if you need to transfer the problem to another person (be it a subject matter expert or a peer), they will need to know what you've done and where you left off.

It usually takes many years to become an expert at diagnosing complex problems. That expertise includes technical skills as well as best practices. The technical skills are what take a long time to learn and require experience and a lot of knowledge. The best practices, however, can be learned in just a few minutes. Here are six best practices that will help when diagnosing complex problems:

1. Collect relevant information when the problem occurs.
2. Keep a log of what you've done and what you think the problem might be.
3. Be detailed and avoid qualitative information.
4. Challenge assumptions until they are proven.
5. Narrow the scope of the problem.
6. Work to prove or disprove theories about the problem.

The best practices listed here are particularly important for complex problems that take a long time to solve. The more complex a problem is, the more important these best practices become. Each of the best practices is covered in more detail as follows.

1.3.3.1 Best Practices for Complex Investigations

1.3.3.1.1 Collect the Relevant Information When the Problem Occurs
Earlier in this chapter we discussed how changes can cause certain types of problems. We also discussed how changes can remove evidence for why a problem occurred in the first place (for example, changes to the amount of free memory can hide the fact that it was once low). In the former situation, it is important to collect information because it can be compared to information that was collected at a previous time to see if any changes caused the problem. In the latter situation, it is important to collect information before the changes on the system wipe out any important evidence. The longer it takes to resolve a problem, the better the chance that something important will change during the investigation. In either situation, data collection is very important for complex problems.

Even reproducible problems can be affected by a changing system. A problem that occurs one day can stop occurring the next day because of an unknown change to the system. If you're lucky, the problem will never occur again, but that's not always the case.

Consider a problem that occurred many years ago where application trap occurred in one xterm (a type of terminal window) window but not in another. Both xterm windows were on the same system and were identical in every way (well, so it seemed at first) but still the problem occurred only in one. Even the list of environment variables was the same except for the expected differences such as PWD (present working directory). After logging out and back in, the problem could not be reproduced. A few days later the problem came back again, only in one xterm. After a very complex investigation, it turned out that an environment variable PWD was the difference that caused the problem to occur. This isn't as simple as it sounds. The contents of the PWD environment variable was not the cause of the problem, although the difference in size of PWD variables between the two xterms forced the stack (a special memory segment) to slightly move up or down in the address space. Sure enough, changing PWD to another value made the problem disappear or recur depending on the length. This small difference caused the different behavior for the application in the two xterms. In one xterm, a memory corruption in the application landed without issue on an inert part of the stack, causing no side-effect. In the other xterm, the memory corruption landed on a pointer on the stack (the long description of the problem is beyond the scope of this chapter). The pointer was dereferenced by the application, and the trap occurred. This is a very rare problem but is a good example of how small and seemingly unrelated changes or differences can affect a problem.

If the problem is serious and difficult to reproduce, collect and/or write down the information from 1.3.1: Initial Investigation Using Your Own Skills.

For quick reference, here is the list:

☞ The exact time the problem occurred

☞ Dynamic operating system information

☞ What you were doing when the problem occurred

☞ A problem description

☞ Anything that may have triggered the problem

☞ Any evidence that may be relevant

The more serious and complex the problem is, the more you'll want to start writing things down. With a complex problem, other people may need to get involved, and the investigation may get complex enough that you'll start to forget some of the information and theories you're using. The data collector included with this book can make your life easier whenever you need to collect information about the OS.

1.3.3.1.2 Use an Investigation Log Even if you only ever have one complex, critical problem to work on at a time, it is still important to keep track of what you've done. This doesn't mean well written, grammatically correct explanations of everything you've done, but it does mean enough detail to be useful to you at a later date. Assuming that you're like most people, you won't have the luxury of working on a single problem at a time, which makes this even more important. When you're investigating 10 problems at once, it sometimes gets difficult to keep track of what has been done for each of them. You also stand a good chance of hitting a similar problem again in the future and may want to use some of the information from the first investigation.

Further, if you ever need to get someone else involved in the investigation, an investigation log can prevent a great deal of unnecessary work. You don't want others unknowingly spending precious time re-doing your hard earned steps and finding the same results. An investigation log can also point others to what you have done so that they can make sure your conclusions are correct up to a certain point in the investigation.

An investigation log is a history of what has been done so far for the investigation of a problem. It should include theories about what the problem could be or what avenues of investigation might help to narrow down the problem. As much as possible, it should contain real evidence that helps lead you to the current point of investigation. Be very careful about making assumptions, and be very careful about qualitative proofs (proofs that contain no concrete evidence).

The following example shows a very structured and well laid out investigation log. With some experience, you'll find the format that works best for you. As you read through it, it should be obvious how useful an investigation log is. If you had to take over this problem investigation right now, it should be clear what has been done and where the investigator left off.

```
Time of occurrence: Sun Sep 5 21:23:58 EDT 2004
Problem description: Product Y failed to start when run from a cron
job.
Symptom:

ProdY: Could not create communication semaphore: 1176688244 (EEXIST)

What might have caused the problem: The error message seems to indicate
that the semaphore already existed and could not be recreated.
```

Theory #1: Product Y may have crashed abruptly, leaving one or more IPC resources. On restart, the product may have tried to recreate a semaphore that it already created from a previous run.

Needed to prove/disprove:
☞ The ownership of the semaphore resource at the time of
the error is the same as the user that ran product Y.
☞ That there was a previous crash for product Y that
would have left the IPC resources allocated.

Proof: Unfortunately, there was no information collected at the time of the error, so we will never truly know the owner of the semaphore at the time of the error. There is no sign of a trap, and product Y always leaves a debug file when it traps. This is an unlikely theory that is good given we don't have the information required to make progress on it.

Theory #2: Product X may have been running at the time, and there may have been an IPC (Inter Process Communication) key collision with product Y.

Needed to prove/disprove:
☞ Check whether product X and product Y can use the same
IPC key.
☞ Confirm that both product X and product Y were actually
running at the time.

Proof: Started product X and then tried to start product Y. Ran "strace" on product X and got the following semget:

```
ion 618% strace -o productX.strace prodX
ion 619% egrep "sem|shm" productX.strace
semget(1176688244, 1, 0)       = 399278084
```

```
Ran "strace" on product Y and got the following semget:

ion 730% strace -o productY.strace prodY
ion 731% egrep "sem|shm" productY.strace
semget(1176688244, 1, IPC_CREAT|IPC_EXCL|0x1f7|0666) = EEXIST

The IPC keys are identical, and product Y tries to create the semaphore
but fails. The error message from product Y is identical to the original
error message in the problem description here.

Notes: productX.strace and productY.strace are under the data directory.

Assumption: I still don't know whether product X was running at the
time when product Y failed to start, but given these results, it is very
likely. IPC collisions are rare, and we know that product X and product
Y cannot run at the same time the way they are currently configured.
```

> **Note:** A semaphore is a special type of inter-process communication mechanism that provides a synchronization mechanism between processes (and/or threads). The type of semaphore used here requires a unique "key" so that multiple processes can use the same semaphore. A semaphore can exist without any processes using it, and some applications expect and rely on creating a semaphore before they can run properly. The `semget()` in the strace that follows is a system call (a special type of OS function) that, as the name suggests, gets a semaphore.

Notice how detailed the proofs are. Even the commands used to capture the original strace output are included to eliminate any human error. When entering a proof, be sure to ask yourself, "Would someone else need any more proof than this?" This level of detail is often required for complex problems so that others will see the proof and agree with it.

The amount of detail in your investigation log should depend on how critical the problem is and how close you are to solving it. If you're completely lost on a very critical problem, you should include more detail than if you are almost done with the investigation. The high level of detail is very useful for complex problems given that every piece of data could be invaluable later on in the investigation.

If you don't have a good problem tracking system, here is a possible directory structure that can help keep things organized:

```
<problem identifier>/ inv.txt
                    / data /
                    / src /
```

The problem identifier is for tracking purposes. Use whatever is appropriate for you (even if it is 1, 2, 3, 4, and so on). The inv.txt is the investigation log, containing the various theories and proofs. The data directory is for any data files that have been collected. Having one data directory helps keep things organized and it also makes it easy to refer to data files from your investigation log. The src directory is for any source code or scripts that you write to help investigate the problem.

The problem directory is what you would show someone when referring to the problem you are investigating. The investigation log would contain the flow of the investigation with the detailed proofs and should be enough to get someone up to speed quickly.

You may also want to save the problem directory for the future or better yet, put the investigation directories somewhere where others can search through them as well. After all, you worked hard for the information in your investigation log; don't be too quick to delete it. You never know when you'll hit a similar (or the same) problem again. The investigation log can also be used to help educate more junior people about investigation techniques.

1.3.3.1.3 Be Detailed (Avoid Qualitative Information) Be very detailed in your investigation log or any time when discussing the problem. If you prove a theory using an error record from an error log file, include the error record and the name of the error log file as proof in the investigation log. Avoid qualitative proofs such as, "Found an error log that showed that the suspect product was running at the time." If you transfer a problem to another person, that person will want to see the actual error record to ensure that your assumption was correct. Also if the problem lasts long enough, you may actually start to second-guess yourself as well (which is actually a good thing) and may appreciate that quantitative proof (a proof with real data to back it up).

Another example of a qualitative proof is a relative term or description. Descriptions like "the file was very large" and "the CPU workload was high" will mean different things to different people. You need to include details for how large the file was (using the output of the `ls` command if possible) and how high the CPU workload was (using `uptime` or `top`). This will remove any uncertainty that others (or you) have about your theories and proofs for the investigation.

Similarly, when you are asked to review an investigation, be leery of any proof or absolute statement (for example, "I saw the amount of virtual memory drop to dangerous levels last night") without the required evidence (that is, a log record, output from a specific OS command, and so on). If you don't have the actual evidence, you'll never know whether a statement is true. This doesn't mean that you have to distrust everyone you work with to solve a problem but rather a realization that people make mistakes. A quick cut and paste of an error log file or the output from an actual command might be all the evidence you need to agree with a statement. Or you might find that the statement is based on an incorrect assumption.

1.3.3.1.4 Challenge Assumptions

There is nothing like spending a week diagnosing a problem based on an assumption that was incorrect. Consider an example where a problem has been identified and a fix has been provided ... yet the problem happens again. There are two main possibilities here. The first is that the fix didn't address the problem. The second is that the fix is good, but you didn't actually get it onto the system (for the statistically inclined reader: yes there is a chance that the fix is bad *and* it didn't get on the system, but the chances are very slim). For critical problems, people have a tendency to jump to conclusions out of desperation to solve a problem quickly. If the group you're working with starts complaining about the bad fix, you should encourage them to challenge both possibilities. Challenge the assumption that the fix actually got onto the system. (Was it even built into the executable or library that was supposed to contain the fix?)

1.3.3.1.5 Narrow Down the Scope of the Problem

Solution (that is, a complete IT solution) -level problem determination is difficult enough, but to make matters worse, each application or product in a solution usually requires a different set of skills and knowledge. Even following the trail of evidence can require deep skills for each application, which might mean getting a few experts involved. This is why it is so important to try and narrow down the scope of the problem for a solution level problem as quickly as possible.

Today's complex heterogeneous solutions can make simple problems very difficult to diagnose. Computer systems and the software that runs on them are integrated through networks and other mechanism(s) to work together to provide a solution. A simple problem, even one that has a clear error message, can become difficult given that the effect of the problem can ripple throughout a solution, causing seemingly unrelated symptoms. Consider the example in Figure 1.1.

Application A in a solution could return an error code because it failed to allocate memory (effect #1). On its own, this problem could be easy to diagnose. However, this in turn could cause application B to react and return an error of its own (effect #2). Application D may see this as an indication that application B is unavailable and may redirect its requests to a redundant application C (effect #3). Application E, which relies on application D and serves the end user, may experience a slowdown in performance (effect #4) since application D is no longer using the two redundant servers B and C. This in turn can cause an end user to experience the performance degradation (effect #5) and to phone up technical support (effect #6) because the performance is slower than usual.

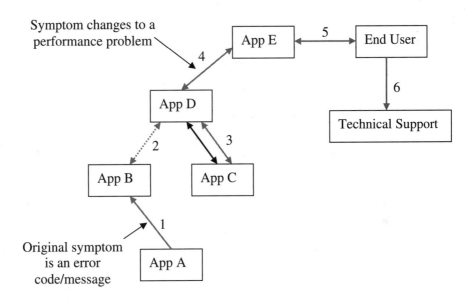

Fig. 1.1 Ripple effect of an error in a solution.

If this seems overly complex, it is actually an oversimplification of real IT solutions where hundreds or even thousands of systems can be connected together. The challenge for the investigator is to follow the trail of evidence back to the original error.

It is particularly important to challenge assumptions when working on a solution-level problem. You need to find out whether each symptom is related to a local system or whether the symptom is related to a change or error condition in another part of a solution.

There are some complex problems that cannot be broken down in scope. These problems require true skill and perseverance to diagnose. Usually this type of problem is a race condition that is very difficult to reproduce. A *race condition* is a type of problem that depends on timing and the order in which things occur. A good example is a "late read." A late read is a software defect where memory is freed, but at some point in the very near future, it is used again by a different part of the application. As long as the memory hasn't been reused, the late read may be okay. However, if the memory block has been reused (and written to), the late read will access the new contents of the memory block, causing unpredictable behavior. Most race conditions can be narrowed in scope in one way or another, but some are so timing-dependent that any changes to the environment (for the purposes of investigation) will cause the problem to not occur.

Lastly, everyone working on an IT solution should be aware of the basic architecture of the solution. This will help the team narrow the scope of any problems that occur. Knowing the basic architecture will help people to theorize where a problem may be coming from and eventually identify the source.

1.3.3.2 Create a Reproducible Test Case Assuming you know how the problem occurs (note that the word here is *how*, not why), it will help others if you can create a test case and/or environment that can reproduce the problem at will. A *test case* is a term used to refer to a tool or a small set of commands that, when run, can cause a problem to occur.

A successful test case can greatly reduce the time to resolution for a problem. If you're investigating a problem on your own, you can run and rerun the test case to cause the problem to occur many times in a row, learning from the symptoms and using different investigation techniques to better understand the problem.

If you need to ask an expert for help, you will also get much more help if you include a reproducible test case. In many cases, an expert will know how to investigate a problem but not how to reproduce it. Having a reproducible test case is especially important if you are asking a stranger for help over the Internet. In this case, the person helping you will probably be doing so on his or her own time and will be more willing to help out if you make it as easy as you can.

1.3.3.3 Work to Prove and/or Disprove Theories This is part of any good problem investigation. The investigator will do his best to think of possible avenues of investigation and to prove or disprove them. The real art here is to identify theories that are easy to prove or disprove or that will dramatically narrow the scope of a problem.

Even nonsolution level problems (such as an application that fails when run from the command line) can be easier to diagnose if they are narrowed in scope with the right theory. Consider an application that is failing to start with an obscure error message. One theory could be that the application is unable to allocate memory. This theory is much smaller in scope and easier to investigate because it does not require intimate knowledge about the application. Because the theory is not application-specific, there are more people who understand how to investigate it. If you need to get an expert involved, you only need someone who understands how to investigate whether an application is unable to allocate memory. That expert may know nothing about the application itself (and might not need to).

1.3.3.4 The Source Code If you are familiar with reading C source code, looking at the source is always a great way of determining why something isn't working the way it should. Details of how and when to do this are discussed in several chapters of this book, along with how to make use of the cscope utility to quickly pinpoint specific source code areas.

Also included in the source code is the Documentation directory that contains a great deal of detailed documentation on various aspects of the Linux kernel in text files. For specific kernel related questions, performing a search command such as the following can quickly yield some help:

```
find /usr/src/linux/Documentation -type f |
xargs grep -H <search_pattern> | less
```

where **<search_pattern>** is the desired search criteria as documented in **grep(1)**.

1.3.4 Phase #4: Getting Help or New Ideas

Everyone gets stuck, and once you've looked at a problem for too long, it can be hard to view it from a different perspective. Regardless of whether you're asking a peer or an expert for ideas/help, they will certainly appreciate any homework you've done up to this point.

1.3.4.1 Profile of a Linux Guru A great deal of the key people working on Linux do so as a "side job" (which often receives more time and devotion than their regular full-time jobs). Many of these people were the original "Linux hackers" and are often considered the "Linux gurus" of today. It's important to understand that these Linux gurus spend a great deal of their own spare time working (sometimes affectionately called "hacking") on the Linux kernel. If they decide to help you, they will probably be doing so on their own time. That said, Linux gurus are a special breed of people who have great passion for the concept of open source, free software, and the operating system itself. They take the development and correct operation of the code very seriously and have great pride in it. Often they are willing to help if you ask the right questions and show some respect.

1.3.4.2 Effectively Asking for Help

1.3.4.2.1 Netiquitte *Netiquette* is a commonly used term that refers to Internet etiquette. Netiquette is all about being polite and showing respect to others on the Internet. One of the best and most succinct documents on netiquette is RFC1855 (RFC stands for "Request for Comments"). It can be found at `http://www.faqs.org/rfcs/rfc1855.html`. Here are a few key points from this document:

☞ Read both mailing lists and newsgroups for one to two months before you post anything. This helps you to get an understanding of the culture of the group.

☞ Consider that a large audience will see your posts. That may include your present or next boss. Take care in what you write. Remember too, that mailing lists and newsgroups are frequently archived and that your words may be stored for a very long time in a place to which many people have access.

☞ Messages and articles should be brief and to the point. Don't wander off-topic, don't ramble, and don't send mail or post messages solely to point out other people's errors in typing or spelling. These, more than any other behavior, mark you as an immature beginner.

Note that the first point tells you to read newsgroups and mailing lists for one to two months before you post anything. What if you have a problem now? Well, if you are responsible for supporting a critical system or a large group of users, don't wait until you need to post a message, starting getting familiar with the key mailing lists or newsgroups now.

Besides making people feel more comfortable about how you communicate over the Internet, why should you care so much about netiquette? Well, if you don't follow the rules of netiquette, people won't want to answer your requests for help. In other words, if you don't respect those you are asking for help, they aren't likely to help you. As mentioned before, many of the people who could help you would be doing so on their own time. Their motivation to help you is governed partially by whether you are someone they want to help. Your message or post is the only way they have to judge who you are.

There are many other Web sites that document common netiquette, and it is worthwhile to read some of these, especially when interacting with USENET and mailing lists. A quick search in Google will reveal many sites dedicated to netiquette. Read up!

1.3.4.2.2 Composing an Effective Message In this section we discuss how to create an effective message whether for email or for USENET. An effective message, as you can imagine, is about clarity and respect. This does not mean that you must be completely submissive — assertiveness is also important, but it is crucial to respect others and understand where they are coming from. For example, you will not get a very positive response if you post a message such as the following to a mailing list:

```
To: linux-kernel-mailing-list
From: Joe Blow
Subject: HELP NEEDED NOW: LINUX SYSTEM DOWN!!!!!!
Message:

MY LINUX SYSTEM IS DOWN!!!! I NEED SOMEONE TO FIX IT NOW!!!! WHY DOES
LINUX ALWAYS CRASH ON ME???!!!!

Joe Blow
Linux System Administrator
```

First of all, CAPS are considered an indication of yelling in current netiquette. Many people reading this will instantly take offense without even reading the complete message.

Second, it's important to understand that many people in the open source community have their own deadlines and stress (like everyone else). So when asking for help, indicating the severity of a problem is OK, but do not overdo it.

Third, bashing the product that you're asking help with is a very bad idea. The people who may be able to help you may take offense to such a comment. Sure, you might be stressed, but keep it to yourself.

Last, this request for help has no content to it at all. There is no indication of what the problem is, not even what kernel level is being used. The subject line is also horribly vague. Even respectful messages that do not contain any content are a complete waste of bandwidth. They will always require two more messages (emails or posts), one from someone asking for more detail (assuming that someone cares enough to ask) and one from you to include more detail.

Ok, we've seen an example of how *not* to compose a message. Let's reword that bad message into something that is far more appropriate:

```
To: linux-kernel-mailing-list
From: Joe Blow
Subject: Oops in zisofs_cleanup on 2.4.21
Message:

Hello All,
My Linux server has experienced the Oops shown below three times in
the last week while running my database management system. I have
tried to reproduce it, but it does not seem to be triggered by
anything easily executed. Has anyone seen anything like this before?

Unable to handle kernel paging request at virtual address
ffffffff7f1bb800
 printing rip:
ffffffff7f1bb800
PML4 103027 PGD 0
Oops: 0010
CPU 0
Pid: 7250, comm: foo Not tainted
```

```
RIP: 0010:[zisofs_cleanup+2132522656/-2146435424]
RIP: 0010:[<ffffffff7f1bb800>]
RSP: 0018:0000010059795f10 EFLAGS: 00010206
RAX: 0000000000000000 RBX: 0000010059794000 RCX: 0000000000000000
RDX: ffffffffffffffea RSI: 0000000000000018 RDI: 0000007fbfff8fa8
RBP: 0000000037e00de R08: 0000000000000000 R09: 0000000000000000
R10: 0000000000000000 R11: 0000000000000246 R12: 0000000000000009
R13: 0000000000000018 R14: 0000000000000018 R15: 0000000000000000
FS: 0000002a957819e0(0000)  GS:ffffffff804beac0(0000)
knlGS:0000000000000000
CS: 0010 DS: 0000 ES: 0000 CR0: 000000008005003b
CR2: ffffffff7f1bb800 CR3: 0000000000101000 CR4: 00000000000006e0
Process foo (pid: 7250, stackpage=10059795000)
Stack: 0000010059795f10 0000000000000018 ffffffff801bc576
➥0000010059794000
   0000000293716a88 0000007fbfff8da0 0000002a9cf94ff8
➥0000000000000003
   0000000000000000 0000000000000000 0000007fbfff9d64
➥0000007fbfff8ed0
Call Trace: [sys_msgsnd+134/976]{sys_msgsnd+134} [system_call+119/
124]{system_call+119}
Call Trace: [<ffffffff801bc576>]{sys_msgsnd+134}
[<ffffffff801100b3>]{system_call+119}

Thanks in advance,
Joe Blow
```

The first thing to notice is that the subject is clear, concise, and to the point. The next thing to notice is that the message is polite, but not overly mushy. All necessary information is included such as what was running when the oops occurred, an attempt at reproducing was made, and the message includes the Oops Report itself. This is a good example because it's one where further analysis is difficult. This is why the main question in the message was if anyone has ever seen anything like it. This question will encourage the reader at the very least to scan the Oops Report. If the reader has seen something similar, there is a good chance that he or she will post a response or send you an email. The keys again are respect, clarity, conciseness, and focused information.

1.3.4.2.3 Giving Back to the Community The open source community relies on the sharing of knowledge. By searching the Internet for other experiences with the problem you are encountering, you are relying on that sharing. If the problem you experienced was a unique one and required some ingenuity either on your part or someone else who helped you, it is very important to give back to the community in the form of a follow-up message to a post you have made. I have come across many message threads in the past where someone posted a question that was exactly the same problem I was having. Thankfully, they responded to their own post and in some cases even prefixed the original subject with "SOLVED:" and detailed how they solved the problem. If that person had not taken the time to post the second message, I might still be looking for the answer to my question. Also think of it this way: By posting the answer to USENET, you're also very safely archiving information at no cost to you! You could attempt to save the information locally, but unless you take very good care, you may lose the info either by disaster or by simply misplacing it over time.

If someone responded to your plea for help and helped you out, it's always a very good idea to go out of your way to thank that person. Remember that many Linux gurus provide help on their own time and not as part of their regular jobs.

1.3.4.2.4 USENET When posting to USENET, common netiquette dictates to only post to a single newsgroup (or a very small set of newsgroups) and to make sure the newsgroup being posted to is the correct one. If the newsgroup is not the correct one, someone may forward your message if you're lucky; otherwise, it will just get ignored.

There are thousands of USENET newsgroups, so how do you know which one to post to? There are several Web sites that host lists of available newsgroups, but the problem is that many of them only list the newsgroups provided by a particular news server. At the time of writing, Google Groups 2 (`http://groups-beta.google.com/`) is currently in beta and offers an enhanced interface to the USENET archives in addition to other group-based discussion archives. One key enhancement of Google Groups 2 is the ability to see all newsgroup names that match a query. For example, searching for "gcc" produces about half of a million hits, but the matched newsgroup names are listed before all the results. From this listing, you will be able to determine the most appropriate group to post a question to.

Of course, there are other resources beyond USENET you can send a message to. You or your company may have a support contract with a distribution or consulting firm. In this case, sending an email using the same tips presented in this chapter still apply.

1.3.4.2.5 Mailing Lists As mentioned in the RFC, it is considered proper netiquette to not post a question to a mailing list without monitoring the emails for a month or two first. Active subscribers prefer users to *lurk* for a while before posting a question. The act of lurking is to subscribe and read incoming posts from other subscribers without posting anything of your own.

An alternative to posting a message to a newsgroup or mailing list is to open a new bug report in a Bugzilla database, if one exists for the package in question.

1.3.4.2.6 Tips on Opening Bug Reports in Bugzilla When you open a bug report in Bugzilla, you are asking someone else to look into the problem for you. Any time you transfer a problem to someone else or ask someone to help with a problem, you need to have clear and concise information about the problem. This is common sense, and the information collected in Phase #3 will pretty much cover what is needed. In addition to this, there are some Bugzilla specific pointers, as follows:

☞ Be sure to properly characterize the bug in the various drop-down menus of the bug report screen. See as an example the new bug form for GCC's Bugzilla, shown in Figure 1.2. It is important to choose the proper version and component because components in Bugzilla have individual owners who get notified immediately when a new bug is opened against their components.

☞ Enter a clear and concise summary into the *Summary* field. This is the first and sometimes only part of a bug report that people will look at, so it is crucial to be clear. For example, entering `Compile aborts` is very bad. Ask yourself the same questions others would ask when reading this summary: "How does it break?" "What error message is displayed?" and "What kind of compile breaks?" A summary of `gcc -c foo.c -O3 for gcc3.4 throws sigsegv` is much more meaningful. (Make it a part of your *lurking* to get a feel for how bug reports are usually built and model yours accordingly.)

☞ In the *Description* field, be sure to enter a clear report of the bug with as much information as possible. Namely, the following information should be included for all bug reports:

   ☞ Exact version of the software being used
   ☞ Linux distribution being used
   ☞ Kernel version as reported by `uname -a`
   ☞ How to easily reproduce the problem (if possible)
   ☞ Actual results you see - cut and paste output if possible
   ☞ Expected results - detail what you expect to see

☞ Often Bugzilla databases include a feature to attach files to a bug report. If this is supported, attach any files that you feel are necessary to help the developers reproduce the problem. See Figure 1.2.

Note: The ability for others to reproduce the problem is crucial. If you cannot easily reproduce the bug, it is unlikely that a developer will investigate it beyond speculating what the problem may be based on other known problems.

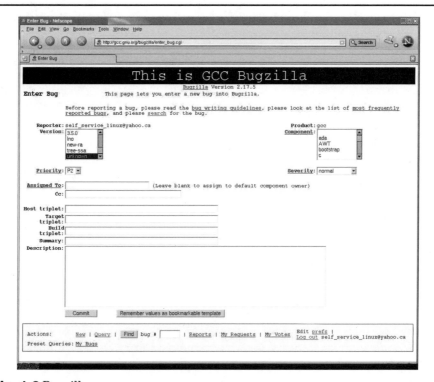

Fig. 1.2 Bugzilla

1.3.4.3 Use Your Distribution's Support
If you or your business has purchased a Linux distribution from one of the distribution companies such as Novell/SuSE, Redhat, or Mandrake, it is likely that some sort of support offering is in place. Use it! That's what it is there for. It is still important, though, to do some homework on your own. As mentioned before, it can be faster than simply asking for help at the first sign of trouble, and you are likely to pick up some knowledge along the way. Also any work you do will help your distribution's support staff solve your problem faster.

1.4 TECHNICAL INVESTIGATION

The first section of this chapter introduced some good investigation practices. Good investigation practices lay the groundwork for efficient problem investigation and resolution, but there is still obviously a technical aspect to diagnosing problems. The second part of this chapter covers a technical overview for how to investigate common types of problems. It highlights the various types of problems and points to the more in-depth documentation that makes up the remainder of this book.

1.4.1 Symptom Versus Cause

Symptoms are the external indications that a problem occurred. The symptoms can be a hint to the underlying cause, but they can also be misleading. For example, a memory leak can manifest itself in many ways. If a process fails to allocate memory, the symptom could be an error message. If the program does not check for out of memory errors, the lack of memory could cause a trap (SIGSEGV). If there is *not* enough memory to log an error message, it could result in a trap because the kernel may be unable to grow the stack (that is, to call the error logging function). A memory leak could also be noticed as a growing memory footprint. A memory leak can have many symptoms, although regardless of the symptom, the cause is still the same.

Problem investigations always start with a symptom. There are five categories of symptoms listed below, each of which has its own methods of investigation.

1. Error
2. Crash
3. Hang (or very slow performance)
4. Performance
5. Unexpected behavior/output

1.4.1.1 Error Errors (and/or warnings) are the most frequent symptoms. They come in many forms and occur for many reasons including configuration issues, operating system resource limitations, hardware, and unexpected situations. Software produces an error message when it can't run as expected. Your job as a problem investigator is to find out why it can't run as expected and solve the underlying problem.

Error messages can be printed to the terminal, returned to a Web browser or logged to an error log file. A program usually uses what is most convenient and useful to the end user. A command line program will print error messages to the terminal, and a background process (one that runs without a command line) usually uses a log file. Regardless of how and where an error is produced, Figure 1.3 shows some of the initial and most useful paths of investigation for errors.

Unfortunately, errors are often accompanied by error messages that are not clear and do not include associated actions. Application errors can occur in obscure code paths that are not exercised frequently and in code paths where the full impact (and reason) for the error condition is not known. For example, an error message may come from the failure to open a file, but the purpose of opening a file might have been to read the configuration for an application. An error message of "could not open file" may be reported at the point where the error occurred and may not include any context for the severity, purpose, or potential action to solve the problem. This is where the strace and ltrace tools can help out.

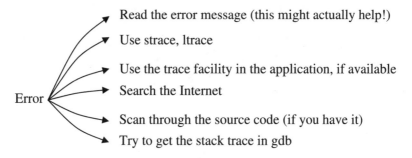

Fig. 1.3 Basic investigation for error symptoms.

Many types of errors are related to the operating system, and there is no better tool than strace to diagnose these types of errors. Look for system calls (in the strace output) that have failed right before the error message is printed to the terminal or logged to a file. You might see the error message printed via the write() system call. This is the system call that printf, perror, and other print-like functions use to print to the terminal. Usually the failing system call is very close to where the error message is printed out. If you need more information than what strace provides, it might be worthwhile to use the ltrace tool (it is similar to the strace tool but includes function calls). For more information on strace, refer to Chapter 2.

If strace and ltrace utilities do not help identify the problem, try searching the Internet using the error message and possibly some key words. With so many Linux users on the Internet, there is a chance that someone has faced the problem before. If they have, they may have posted the error message and a solution. If you run into an error message that takes a considerable amount of time to resolve, it might be worthwhile (and polite) to post a note on USENET with the original error message, any other relevant information, and the resulting solution. That way, if someone hits the same problem in the future, they won't have to spend as much time diagnosing the same problem as you did.

If you need to dig deeper (strace, ltrace, and the Internet can't help), the investigation will become very specific to the application. If you have source code, you can pinpoint where the problem occurred by searching for the error message directly in the source code. Some applications use error codes and not raw error messages. In this case, simply look for the error message, identify the associated error code, and search for it in source code. If the same error code/message is used in multiple places, it may be worthwhile to add a `printf()` call to differentiate between them.

If the error message is unclear, strace and ltrace couldn't help, the Internet didn't have any useful information, and you don't have the source code, you still might be able to make further progress with GDB. If you can capture the point in time in GDB when the application produces the error message, the functions on the stack may give you a hint about the cause of the problem. This won't be easy to do. You might have to use break points on the `write()` system call and check whether the error message is being written out. For more information on how to use GDB, refer to Chapter 6, "The GNU Debugger (GDB)."

If all else fails, you'll need to contact the support organization for the application and ask them to help with the investigation.

1.4.1.2 Crashes   Crashes occur because of severe conditions and fit into two main categories: traps and panics. A trap usually occurs when an application references memory incorrectly, when a bad instruction is executed, or when there is a bad "page-in" (the process of bringing a page from the swap area into memory). A panic in an application is due to the application itself abruptly shutting down due to a severe error condition. The main difference is that a trap is a crash that the hardware and OS initiate, and a panic is a crash that the application initiates. Panics are usually associated with an error message that is produced prior to the panic. Applications on Unix and Linux often panic by calling the `abort()` function (after the error message is logged or printed to the terminal).

Like errors, crashes (traps and panics) can occur for many reasons. Some of the more popular are included in Figure 1.4.

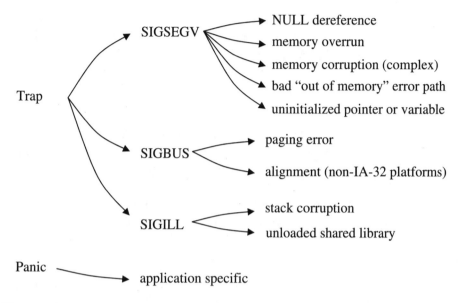

Trap

SIGSEGV
- NULL dereference
- memory overrun
- memory corruption (complex)
- bad "out of memory" error path
- uninitialized pointer or variable

SIGBUS
- paging error
- alignment (non-IA-32 platforms)

SIGILL
- stack corruption
- unloaded shared library

Panic
- application specific

Fig. 1.4 Common causes of crashes.

1.4.1.2.1 Traps When the kernel experiences a major problem while running a process, it may send a signal (a Unix and Linux convention) to the process such as SIGSEGV, SIGBUS or SIGILL. Some of these signals are due to a hardware condition such as an attempt to write to a write-protected region of memory (the kernel gets the actual trap in this case). Other signals may be sent by the kernel because of non-hardware related issues. For example, a bad page-in can be caused by a failure to read from the file system.

The most important information to gather for a trap is:

☞ **The instruction that trapped.** The instruction can tell you a lot about the type of trap. If the instruction is invalid, it will generate a SIGILL. If the instruction references memory and the trap is a SIGSEGV, the trap is likely due to referencing memory that is outside of a memory region (see Chapter 3 on the /proc file system for information on process memory maps).

☞ **The function name and offset of the instruction that trapped.** This can be obtained through GDB or using the load address of the shared library and the instruction address itself. More information on this can be found in Chapter 9, "ELF: Executable Linking Format."

☞ **The stack trace.** The stack trace can help you understand why the trap occurred. The functions that are higher on the stack may have passed a bad pointer to the lower functions causing a trap. A stack trace can also be used to recognize known types of traps. For more information on stack trace backs refer to Chapter 5, "The Stack."

☞ **The register dump.** The register dump can help you understand the "context" under which the trap occurred. The values of the registers may be required to understand what led up to the trap.

☞ **A core file or memory dump.** This can fill in the gaps for complex trap investigations. If some memory was corrupted, you might want to see how it was corrupted or look for pointers into that area of corruption. A core file or memory dump can be very useful, but it can also be very large. For example, a 64-bit application can easily use 20GB of memory or more. A full core file from such an application would be 20GB in size. That requires a lot of disk storage and may need to be transferred to you if the problem occurred on a remote and inaccessible system (for example, a customer system).

Some applications use a special function called a "signal handler" to generate information about a trap that occurred. Other applications simply trap and die immediately, in which case the best way to diagnose the problem is through a debugger such as GDB. Either way, the same information should be collected (in the latter case, you need to use GDB).

A SIGSEGV is the most common of the three *bad programming signals*: SIGSEGV, SIGBUS and SIGILL. A bad programming signal is sent by the kernel and is usually caused by memory corruption (for example, an overrun), bad memory management (that is, a duplicate free), a bad pointer, or an uninitialized value. If you have the source code for the tool or application and some knowledge of C/C++, you can diagnose the problem on your own (with some work). If you don't have the source code, you need to know assembly language to properly diagnose the problem. Without source code, it will be a real challenge to fix the problem once you've diagnosed it.

For memory corruption, you might be able to pinpoint the stack trace that is causing the corruption by using *watch points* through GDB. A watch point is a special feature in GDB that is supported by the underlying hardware. It allows you to stop the process any time a range of memory is changed. Once you know the address of the corruption, all you have to do is recreate the problem under the same conditions with a watch point on the address that gets corrupted. More on watch points in the GDB chapter.

There are some things to check for that can help diagnose operating system or hardware related problems. If the memory corruption starts and/or ends on a page sized boundary (4KB on IA-32), it could be the underlying physical memory or the memory management layer in the kernel itself. Hardware-based corruption (quite rare) often occurs at cache line boundaries. Keep both of them in mind when you look at the type of corruption that is causing the trap.

The most frequent cause of a SIGBUS is misaligned data. This does not occur on IA-32 platforms because the underlying hardware silently handles the misaligned memory accesses. However on IA-32, a SIGBUS can still occur for a bad page fault (such as a bad page-in).

Another type of hardware problem is when the instructions just don't make sense. You've looked at the memory values, and you've looked at the registers, but there is no way that the instructions could have caused the values. For example, it may look like an increment instruction failed to execute or that a subtract instruction did not take place. These types of hardware problems are very rare but are also very difficult to diagnose from scratch. As a rule of thumb, if something looks impossible (according to the memory values, registers, or instructions), it might just be hardware related. For a more thorough diagnosis of a SIGSEGV or other traps, refer to Chapter 6.

1.4.1.2.2 Panics A panic in an application is due to the application itself abruptly shutting down. Linux even has a system call specially designed for this sort of thing: abort (although there are many other ways for an application to "panic"). A panic is a similar symptom to a trap but is much more purposeful. Some products might panic to prevent further risk to the users' data or simply because there is no way it can continue. Depending on the application, protecting the users' data may be more important than trying to continue running. If an application's main control block is corrupt, it might mean that the application has no choice but to panic and abruptly shutdown. Panics are very product-specific and often require knowledge of the product (and source code) to understand. The line number of the source code is sometimes included with a panic. If you have the source code, you might be able to use the line of code to figure out what happened.

Some panics include detailed messages for what happened and how to recover. This is similar to an error message except that the product (tool or application) aborted and shut down abruptly. The error message and other evidence of the panic usually have some good key words or sentences that can be searched for using the Internet. The panic message may even explain how to recover from the problem.

If the panic doesn't have a clear error message and you don't have the source code, you might have to ask the product vendor what happened and provide information as needed. Panics are somewhat rare, so hopefully you won't encounter them often.

1.4.1.2.3 Kernel Crashes A panic or trap in the kernel is similar to those in an application but obviously much more serious in that they often affect the entire system. Information for how to investigate system crashes and hangs is fairly complex and not covered here but is covered in detail in Chapter 7, "Linux System Crashes and Hangs."

1.4.1.3 Hangs (or Very Slow Performance) It is difficult to tell the difference between a hang and very slow performance. The symptoms are pretty much identical as are the initial methods to investigate them. When investigating a perceived hang, you need to find out whether the process is hung, looping, or performing very slowly. A true hang is when the process is not consuming any CPU and is stuck waiting on a system call. A process that is looping is consuming CPU and is usually, but not always, stuck in a tight code loop (that is, doing the same thing over and over). The quickest way to determine what type of hang you have is to collect a set of stack traces over a period of time and/or to use GDB and strace to see whether the process is making any progress at all. The basic investigation steps are included in Figure 1.5.

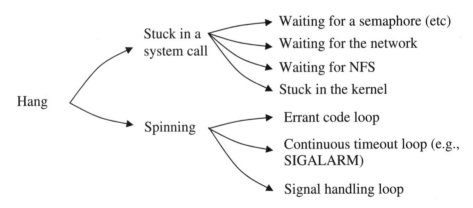

Fig. 1.5 Basic investigation steps for a hang.

If the application seems to be hanging, use GDB to get a stack trace (use the `bt` command). The stack trace will tell you where in the application the hang *may* be occurring. You still won't know whether the application is actually hung or whether it is looping. Use the `cont` command to let the process continue normally for a while and then stop it again with Control-C in GDB. Gather another stack trace. Do this a few times to ensure that you have a few stack traces over a period of time. If the stack traces are changing in any way, the process may be looping. However, there is still a chance that the process is making progress, albeit slowly. If the stack traces are identical, the process may still be looping, although it would have to be spending the majority of its time in a single state.

With the stack trace and the source code, you can get the line of code. From the line of code, you'll know what the process is waiting on but maybe not why. If the process is stuck in a semop (a system call that deals with semaphores), it is probably waiting for another process to notify it. The source code should explain what the process is waiting for and potentially what would wake it up. See Chapter 4, "Compiling," for information about turning a function name and function offset into a line of code.

If the process is stuck in a read call, it may be waiting for NFS. Check for NFS errors in the system log and use the mount command to help check whether any mount points are having problems. NFS problems are usually not due to a bug on the local system but rather a network problem or a problem with the NFS server.

If you can't attach a debugger to the hung process, the debugger hangs when you try, or you can't kill the process, the process is probably in some strange state in the kernel. In this rare case, you'll probably want to get a kernel stack for this process. A kernel stack is stack trace for a task (for example, a process) in the kernel. Every time a system call is invoked, the process or thread will run some code in the kernel, and this code creates a stack trace much like code run outside the kernel. A process that is stuck in a system call will have a stack trace in the kernel that may help to explain the problem in more detail. Refer to Chapter 8, "Kernel Debugging with KDB," for more information on how to get and interpret kernel stacks.

The strace tool can also help you understand the cause of a hang. In particular, it will show you any interaction with the operating system. However, strace will not help if the process is spinning in user code and never calls a system call. For signal handling loops, the strace tool will show very obvious symptoms of a repeated signal being generated and caught. Refer to the hang investigation in the strace chapter for more information on how to use strace to diagnose a hang with strace.

1.4.1.3.1 Multi-Process Applications
For multi-process applications, a hang can be very complex. One of the processes of the application could be causing the hang, and the rest might be hanging waiting for the hung process to finish. You'll need to get a stack trace for all of the processes of the application to understand which are hung and which are causing the hang.

If one of the processes is hanging, there may be quite a few other processes that have the same (or similar) stack trace, all waiting for a resource or lock held by the original hung process. Look for a process that is stuck on something unique, one that has a unique stack trace. A unique stack trace will be different than all the rest. It will likely show that the process is stuck waiting for a reason of its own (such as waiting for information from over the network).

Another cause of an application hang is a dead lock/latch. In this case, the stack traces can help to figure out which locks/latches are being held by finding the source code and understanding what the source code is waiting for. Once you know which locks or latches the processes are waiting for, you can use the source code and the rest of the stack traces to understand where and how these locks or latches are acquired.

> **Note**: A *latch* usually refers to a very light weight locking mechanism. A lock is a more general term used to describe a method to ensure mutual exclusion over the access of a resource.

1.4.1.3.2 Very Busy Systems Have you ever encountered a system that seems completely hung at first, but after a few seconds or minutes you get a bit of response from the command line? This usually occurs in a terminal window or on the console where your key strokes only take effect every few seconds or longer. This is the sign of a very busy system. It could be due to an overloaded CPU or in some cases a very busy disk drive. For busy disks, the prompt may be responsive until you type a command (which in turn uses the file system and the underlying busy disk).

The biggest challenge with a problem like this is that once it occurs, it can take minutes or longer to run any command and see the results. This makes it very difficult to diagnose the problem quickly. If you are managing a small number of systems, you might be able to leave a special telnet connection to the system for when the problem occurs again.

The first step is to log on to the system before the problem occurs. You'll need a root account to renice (reprioritize) the shell to the highest priority, and you should change your current directory to a file system such as /proc that does not use any physical disks. Next, be sure to unset the LD_LIBRARY_PATH and PATH environment variables so that the shell does not search for libraries or executables. Also when the problem occurs, it may help to type your commands into a separate text editor (on another system) and paste the entire line into the remote (for example, telnet) session of the problematic system.

When you have a more responsive shell prompt, the normal set of commands (starting with `top`) will help you to diagnose the problem much faster than before.

1.4.1.4 Performance Ah, performance ... one could write an entire book on performance investigations. The quest to improve performance comes with good reason. Businesses and individuals pay good money for their hardware and are always trying to make the most of it. A 15% improvement in performance can be worth 15% of your hardware investment.

Whatever the reason, the quest for better performance will continue to be important. Keep in mind, however, that it may be more cost effective to buy a new system than to get that last 10-20%. When you're trying to get that last 10-20%, the human cost of improving performance can outweigh the cost of purchasing new hardware in a business environment.

1.4.1.5 Unexpected Behavior/Output This is a special type of problem where the application is not aware of a problem (that is, the error code paths have not been triggered), and yet it is returning incorrect information or behaving incorrectly. A good example of unexpected output is if an application returned "!$#%#@" for the current balance of a bank account without producing any error messages. The application may not execute any error paths at all, and yet the resulting output is complete nonsense. This type of problem can be difficult to diagnose given that the application will probably not log any diagnostic information (because it is not aware there is a problem!).

> **Note:** An error path is a special piece of code that is specifically designed to react and handle an error.

The root cause for this type of problem can include hardware issues, memory corruptions, uninitialized memory, or a software bug causing a variable overflow. If you have the output from the unexpected behavior, try searching the Internet for some clues. Failing that, you're probably in for a complex problem investigation.

Diagnosing this type of problem manually is a lot easier with source code and an understanding of how the code is supposed to work. If the problem is easily reproducible, you can use GDB to find out where the unexpected behavior occurs (by using break points, for example) and then backtracking through many iterations until you've found where the erroneous behavior starts. Another option if you have the source code is to use printf statements (or something similar) to backtrack through the run of the application in the hopes of finding out where the incorrect behavior started.

You can try your luck with strace or ltrace in the hopes that the application is misbehaving due to an error path (for example, a file not found). In that particular case, you might be able to address the reason for the error (that is, fix the permissions on a file) and avoid the error path altogether.

If all else fails, try to get a subject matter expert involved, someone who knows the application well and has access to source code. They will have a better understanding of how the application works internally and will have better luck understanding what is going wrong. For commercial software products, this usually means contacting the software vendor for support.

1.5 TROUBLESHOOTING COMMERCIAL PRODUCTS

In today's ever growing enterprise market, Linux is making a very real impact. A key to this impact is the availability of large scale software products such as database management systems, Web servers, and business solutions systems. As more companies begin to examine their information technology resources and spending, it is inevitable that they will at the very least consider using Linux in their environments. Even though there is a plethora of open source software available, many companies will still look to commercial software to provide a specific service or need.

With a rich problem determination and debugging skill set in-house, many problems that typically go to a commercial software vendor for support could be solved much faster internally. The intention of this book is to increase that skill set and give developers, support staff, or anyone interested the right toolkit to confidently tackle these problems. Even if the problem does in fact lie in the commercial software product, having excellent problem determination skills will greatly expedite the whole process of communicating and isolating the problem. This can mean differences of days or weeks of working with commercial software support staff.

It is also extremely important to read the commercial software's documentation, in particular, sections that discuss debugging and troubleshooting. Any large commercial application will include utilities and built-in problem determination facilities. These can include but are certainly not limited to:

☞ Dump files produced at the time of a trap (or set of predefined signals) that include information such as:
  ☞ a stack traceback
  ☞ contents of system registers at the time the signal was received
  ☞ operating system/kernel information
  ☞ process ID information
  ☞ memory dumps of the software's key internal data structures
  ☞ and so on
☞ Execution tracing facilities

☞ Diagnostic log file(s)

☞ Executables to examine and dump internal structures

Becoming familiar with a commercial product's included problem determination facilities along with what Linux offers can be a very solid defense against any software problem that may arise.

1.6 CONCLUSION

The rest of the book goes into much more detail, each chapter exploring intimate details of problem diagnosis with the available tools on Linux. Each chapter is designed to be practical and still cover some of the background information required to build deep skills.

strace and System Call Tracing Explained

2.1 INTRODUCTION

In a perfect world, an error message reported by a tool or application would contain all of the information required to diagnose the problem. Unfortunately, the world is far from being a perfect place. Many, if not most, error messages are unclear, ambiguous, or only describe what happened and not why (for example, "could not open file"). Errors are often related to how a tool or application interacted with the underlying operating system. A trace of those interactions can provide a behind-the-scenes look at many types of errors. On Linux the strace utility can be used to trace the thin layer between the kernel and a tool or application. The strace tool can help to investigate an unclear error message or unexpected behavior when it relates to the operating system.

2.2 WHAT IS STRACE?

The strace tool is one of the most powerful problem determination tools available for Linux. It traces the thin layer (the system calls) between a process and the Linux kernel as shown in Figure 2.1. System call tracing is particularly useful as a first investigation tool or for problems that involve a call to the operating system.

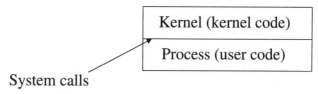

Fig. 2.1 System calls define the layer between user code and the kernel.

A system call is a special type of function that is run inside the kernel. It provides fair and secure access to system resources such as disk, network, and memory. System calls also provide access to kernel services such as inter-process communication and system information.

Depending on the hardware platform, a system call may require a gate instruction, a trap instruction, an interrupt instruction, or other mechanism to switch from the user code into the kernel. The actual mechanism is not really important for this discussion but rather that the code is switching from user mode directly into the kernel. It may help to explain this concept by comparing how a function and a system call work.

A function call is fairly simple to understand as shown in the following assembly language (bear with me if you are not familiar with IA-32 assembly language):

```
080483e8 <_Z3barv>:
 80483e8:       55              push    %ebp
 80483e9:       89 e5           mov     %esp,%ebp
 80483eb:       83 ec 08        sub     $0x8,%esp
 80483ee:       83 ec 08        sub     $0x8,%esp
 80483f1:       68 4e 61 bc 00  push    $0xbc614e
 80483f6:       6a 61           push    $0x61
 80483f8:       e8 cf ff ff ff  call    80483cc <_Z3fooi>
 80483fd:       83 c4 10        add     $0x10,%esp
 8048400:       c9              leave
 8048401:       c3              ret
```

The `call` instruction will jump to a function called `foo` (note: `foo` is mangled because it was compiled as a C++ function). The flow of execution always remains in the application code and does not require the kernel. The instructions for `foo` are just as easily examined, and a debugger can follow the call to `foo` without any issue. All instructions perform a single, specific action that is defined by the underlying hardware.

Note: In the preceding example, the arguments to function `foo` are pushed on to the stack by the function `bar` and are then subsequently used inside of `foo`. Arguments are passed into functions using a special convention called a *procedure calling convention*. The procedure calling convention also defines how return values are passed. This ensures that all of the functions for a program are using the same method to store and retrieve arguments when calling a function.

Note: For more information on assembly language and procedure calling conventions, refer to Chapter 5, "The Stack."

A system call is similar in concept to that of a function call but requires switching into the kernel to execute the actual system call instructions. Remember, a function call does not require the kernel. The method used to get into the kernel varies by platform, but on IA-32, the method used is a software interrupt as shown in the following example for the open system call:

```
ion 214% nm /lib/libc.so.6 | egrep ' open$'
000bf9b0 W open

ion 216% objdump -d /lib/libc.so.6 |less
...
000bf9b0 <__libc_open>:
  bf9b0:    53                  push   %ebx
  bf9b1:    8b 54 24 10         mov    0x10(%esp,1),%edx
  bf9b5:    8b 4c 24 0c         mov    0xc(%esp,1),%ecx
  bf9b9:    8b 5c 24 08         mov    0x8(%esp,1),%ebx
  bf9bd:    b8 05 00 00 00      mov    $0x5,%eax
  bf9c2:    cd 80               int    $0x80
  bf9c4:    5b                  pop    %ebx
  bf9c5:    3d 01 f0 ff ff      cmp    $0xfffff001,%eax
  bf9ca:    73 01               jae    bf9cd <__libc_open+0x1d>
  bf9cc:    c3                  ret
  bf9cd:    53                  push   %ebx
```

Notice the interrupt instruction: int $0x80 and the move (mov) instruction directly preceding. The move instruction moves the system call number 5 into the %eax register, and the interrupt instruction switches the current thread of execution into the kernel. This is where the actual instructions are for the open system call. A bit of grepping through the system header files shows that the system call is indeed open.

```
ion 217% egrep open /usr/include/bits/syscall.h
#define SYS_open __NR_open

ion 218% egrep __NR_open /usr/include/asm/unistd.h
#define __NR_open            5
```

It's worth noting programs that call the open system call are actually calling a function in the C library that, in turn, interrupts into the kernel to invoke the actual system call. The open *function* is a thin wrapper around the mechanism to call the open *system call*.

From the user-space point of view, the interrupt instruction (int $0x80) is silently executed and performs all of the functionality of the open system call. The contents of any memory addresses or registers that were passed into the system call may change, but from the application's point of view, it seems as if the single interrupt instruction performed the role of the system call. A normal debugger cannot follow the interrupt into the kernel but will treat it pretty much as any other instruction.

Invoking a system call follows a calling convention called a *system call calling convention*. For function calls, the calling function and called function need to use the same calling convention. For system calls, the invoking function and the kernel need to follow the same calling convention. A failure to follow the convention of either side of the function or system call will result in unexpected behavior.

> **Note:** Applications built for one operating system can run on another operating system on the same hardware if 1) the same file object type is supported (for example, ELF); 2) the function calling conventions are the same; 3) the system calling conventions are the same; and last 4) the behavior of the called functions and system calls are the same. The actual OS-supplied functions and OS-supported system calls may have completely different code under the covers, but as long as the interfaces are the same, an application won't know the difference.

The basic system call calling convention for Linux on IA-32 is simple. The arguments to a system call are stored in the following registries:

Argument #	Registry
1	EBX
2	ECX
3	EDX
4	ESI
5	EDI

The return value for a system call is stored in the EAX register from within the kernel. In other words, a system call could be represented as:

EAX = syscall(EBX, ECX, EDX, ESI, EDI) ;

If an error occurs, a negative return code will be returned (that is, EAX will be set to a negative value). A zero or positive value indicates the success of a system call.

Going back to the assembly listing for the open call in libc (the C library), it is easy to see the system call calling convention at work:

```
bf9b1:    8b 54 24 10       mov     0x10(%esp,1),%edx
bf9b5:    8b 4c 24 0c       mov     0xc(%esp,1),%ecx
bf9b9:    8b 5c 24 08       mov     0x8(%esp,1),%ebx
bf9bd:    b8 05 00 00 00    mov     $0x5,%eax
bf9c2:    cd 80             int     $0x80
bf9c4:    5b                pop     %ebx
```

```
bf9c5:        3d 01 f0 ff ff      cmp      $0xfffff001,%eax
bf9ca:        73 01               jae      bf9cd <__libc_open+0x1d
```

The three arguments to the system call are set in registers ebx, ecx, and edx
using the first three instructions. The system call number for the open system
call is set in EAX and the int $0x80 instruction makes the actual transition
into the kernel. After the system call, the EAX register contains the return
code. If the return code is negative, the absolute value is the corresponding
errno. For example a return code (in EAX) of -2 would mean an errno of 2 or
ENOENT.

> **Note:** There is another calling convention (for programs that are
> not native Linux programs (lcall7/lcall27 call gates), although this is out
> of scope for this book.
>
> **Note:** Linux actually supports up to six arguments for system calls.
> The 6th argument can be passed in with the ebp register. See _syscall6
> in asm-i386/unistd.h for more information.

2.2.1 More Information from the Kernel Side

We have discussed the application side of system calls and the system call
mechanism itself. It is worth a quick overview of the kernel side of a system
call to complete the picture. This is also a good introduction for how the strace
tool works. We've already mentioned the int 0x80 instruction, but let's take a
look at how this works in the kernel.

The int $0x80 instruction traps into the kernel and invokes 0x80 in the
IDT (interrupt descriptor table). According to include/asm-i386/hw_irq.h,
SYSCALL_VECTOR is 0x80, which matches the value after the int instruction.

```
#define SYSCALL_VECTOR              0x80
```

The actual 0x80 entry in the interrupt descriptor table is set in arch/i386/
kernel/traps.c with the following code:

```
set_system_gate(SYSCALL_VECTOR,&system_call);
```

This sets entry 0x80 in the interrupt descriptor table to the kernel entry point
system_call which is defined in entry.s. Curious readers can take a look at
what happens in the kernel when the interrupt is raised by looking at arch/
i386/kernel/entry.s in the kernel source. Among other things, this assembly

language file includes the support for calling and returning from a system call. Here is a snippet from `entry.s` that contains the assembly code that is called first by the kernel when the `int 0x80` triggered:

```
ENTRY(system_call)
        pushl %eax                              # save orig_eax
        SAVE_ALL
        GET_CURRENT(%ebx)
        testb $0x02,tsk_ptrace(%ebx)    # PT_TRACESYS
        jne tracesys
        cmpl $(NR_syscalls),%eax
        jae badsys

    ...


        call *SYMBOL_NAME(sys_call_table)(,%eax,4)
        movl %eax,EAX(%esp)             # save the return value
```

> **Note**: Some of the optional assembly language has been excluded for clarity.

The `testb` instruction tests to see whether `ptrace` is turned on. If so, the code immediately jumps to tracesys (explained in the following paragraphs). Otherwise, the code follows the normal code path for system calls. The normal code path then compares the system call number in EAX to the highest numbered system call. If it is larger, then the system call is invalid. Assuming that the system call number is in the valid range, the actual system call is called with the following instruction:

```
call *SYMBOL_NAME(sys_call_table)(,%eax,4)
```

Notice that this instruction indexes into the system call table (which explains why system calls have numbers). Without a number, it would be very expensive to find the right system call!

The strace tool works with the kernel to stop a program when it enters and when it exits a system call. The strace utility uses a kernel interface called `ptrace` to change the behavior of a process so that it stops at each system call entry and exit. It also uses `ptrace` to get information about the stopped process to find the system call, the arguments to the system call, and the return code from the system call.

The kernel support for `ptrace` is visible in the `system_call` code in `entry.s` (this is from the `ENTRY(system_call)` example previously):

```
        testb $0x02,tsk_ptrace(%ebx)    # PT_TRACESYS
        jne tracesys
```

The first instruction tests whether ptrace was used to trace system calls for this process (that is, ptrace was used with PT_TRACESYS/PTRACE_SYSCALL). The second instruction jumps to the tracesys function if the conditions from the previous instruction are met. In other words, if system calls are being traced through the ptrace facility for this process, the tracesys function is called instead of the normal system calling code.

From entry.s on IA-32:

```
tracesys:
        movl $-ENOSYS,EAX(%esp)
        call SYMBOL_NAME(syscall_trace)
        movl ORIG_EAX(%esp),%eax
        cmpl $(NR_syscalls),%eax
        jae tracesys_exit
        call *SYMBOL_NAME(sys_call_table)(,%eax,4)
        movl %eax,EAX(%esp)                   # save the return value
tracesys_exit:
        call SYMBOL_NAME(syscall_trace)
        jmp ret_from_sys_call
badsys:
        movl $-ENOSYS,EAX(%esp)
              jmp ret_from_sys_call
```

The tracesys function immediately sets the EAX to -ENOSYS (this is important for the strace tool). It then calls the syscall_trace function (explained later) to support ptrace. The tracesys function then does some validation of the system call number, calls the actual system call and then traces the exit of the system call. Notice that trace is called twice using exactly the same method [call SYMBOL_NAME(syscall_trace)], once before the system call and once after. The only way to tell the two calls apart is that EAX is set to -ENOSYS in the first trace call.

The strace call is notified whenever a traced program enters or exits a system call. In the syscall_trace function (used for both system call entry and exit), it is easy to see the expected ptrace functionality with the lines highlighted in bold:

```
asmlinkage void syscall_trace(void)
{
        if ((current->ptrace & (PT_PTRACED|PT_TRACESYS)) !=
                   (PT_PTRACED|PT_TRACESYS))
                return;
        /* the 0x80 provides a way for the tracing parent to
➥distinguish between a syscall stop and SIGTRAP delivery */
        current->exit_code = SIGTRAP | ((current->ptrace &
➥PT_TRACESYSGOOD)
                                        ? 0x80 : 0);
```

```
      current->state = TASK_STOPPED;
      notify_parent(current, SIGCHLD);
   schedule();
   /*
   * this isn't the same as continuing with a signal, but it will do
   * for normal use.  strace only continues with a signal if the
   * stopping signal is not SIGTRAP.  -brl
   */
     if (current->exit_code) {
        send_sig(current->exit_code, current, 1);
         current->exit_code = 0;
      }
}
```

The line, current->state = TASK_STOPPED; essentially stops the process/thread. The line, notify_parent(current, SIGCHLD); notifies the parent (in this case, the strace tool) that the traced process has stopped. Notice how simple the code is, and yet it supports stopping a process on system call entry and exit. The kernel is just stopping the process, but it does not actively send any information to the strace tool about the process. Most of the hard work is done by the strace tool.

Note: Tracing a process using the ptrace mechanism is almost like making the tracing process the parent of the traced process. More will be provided on this topic later in the system call tracing sample code.

Now that you have a basic understanding of how system calls work and how strace is supported in the kernel, let's take a look at how to use strace to solve some real problems.

2.2.2 When To Use It

The strace tool should be used as a first investigation tool or for problems that are related to the operating system. The phrase "related to the operating system" does not necessarily mean that the operating system is at fault but rather that it is involved in a problem. For example, a program may fail because it cannot open a file or because it cannot allocate memory. Neither is necessarily the fault of the operating system, but the system call trace will clearly show the cause of either problem. Recognizing that a problem is related to the OS becomes easier with experience, but given that strace is also useful as a first investigation tool, this isn't a problem for those just learning how to use it. Experienced users might use strace either way until they narrow down the scope of a problem.

The strace tool is rarely, if ever, useful for code logic problems because it only provides information about the system calls that were invoked by a process.

There is another utility called ltrace that provides function-level tracing, but it is rarely used compared to strace. The ltrace tool can display both function calls and system calls, but in many cases, strace is still more useful because:

☞ It produces less information without being less useful in most cases.
☞ System calls are very standard and have man pages. Not all functions do.
☞ Functions are not usually as interesting for problem determination.
☞ ltrace relies on dynamic linking to work. Statically linked programs will show no output. Also, calls within the executable object itself will not show up in ltrace.

The ltrace tool can still be useful for problem determination when more detail is needed, but strace is usually the best tool to start with.

Let's refocus back on the strace tool...

2.2.3 Simple Example

The following example uses a simple program to show how to use strace. The program attempts to open a file as "read only" and then exits. The program only contains one system call, open:

```
#include <sys/types.h>
#include <sys/stat.h>
#include <fcntl.h>

int main( )
{
  int fd ;
  int i = 0 ;

  fd = open( "/tmp/foo", O_RDONLY ) ;

  if ( fd < 0 )
    i=5;
  else
    i=2;

  return i;
}
```

There is some trivial code after the call to open, the details of which will not be shown in the strace output because the trivial code does not invoke any system calls. Here is the system call trace output:

```
ion 216% gcc main.c -o main
ion 217% strace -o main.strace main
ion 218% cat main.strace
1. execve("./main", ["main"], [/* 64 vars */]) = 0
2. uname({sys="Linux", node="ion", ...})     = 0
3. brk(0)                                     = 0x80494f8
4. mmap2(NULL, 4096, PROT_READ|PROT_WRITE, MAP_PRIVATE|MAP_ANONYMOUS,
➥-1, 0) = 0x40013000
5. open("/etc/ld.so.preload", O_RDONLY)       = -1 ENOENT (No such file
➥or directory)
6. open("/lib/i686/mmx/libc.so.6", O_RDONLY) = -1 ENOENT (No such
➥file or directory)
7. stat64("/lib/i686/mmx", 0xbfffe59c)        = -1 ENOENT (No such file
➥or directory)
8. open("/lib/i686/libc.so.6", O_RDONLY)      = -1 ENOENT (No such file
➥or directory)
9. stat64("/lib/i686", 0xbfffe59c)            = -1 ENOENT (No such file
➥or directory)
10.open("/lib/mmx/libc.so.6", O_RDONLY)       = -1 ENOENT (No such file
➥or directory)
11.stat64("/lib/mmx", 0xbfffe59c)             = -1 ENOENT (No such file
➥or directory)
12.open("/lib/libc.so.6", O_RDONLY)           = 3
13.read(3,
➥"\177ELF\1\1\1\0\0\0\0\0\0\0\0\0\3\0\3\0\1\0\0\0\300\205"...,
➥1024) = 1024
14.fstat64(3, {st_mode=S_IFREG|0755, st_size=1312470, ...}) = 0
15.mmap2(NULL, 1169856, PROT_READ|PROT_EXEC, MAP_PRIVATE, 3, 0) =
➥0x40014000
16.mprotect(0x40128000, 39360, PROT_NONE)   = 0
17.mmap2(0x40128000, 24576, PROT_READ|PROT_WRITE,
➥MAP_PRIVATE|MAP_FIXED, 3, 0x113) = 0x40128000
18.mmap2(0x4012e000, 14784, PROT_READ|PROT_WRITE,
➥MAP_PRIVATE|MAP_FIXED|MAP_ANONYMOUS, -1, 0) = 0x4012e000
19.close(3)                                   = 0
20.open("/tmp/foo", O_RDONLY)                 = -1 ENOENT (No such file
➥or directory)
21.exit(5)                                    = ?
```

> **Note:** The line numbers to the left are not actually part of the strace output and are used for illustration purposes only.

In this strace output, the vast majority of the system calls are actually for process initialization. In fact, the only system call (on line 20) from the actual program code is open("/tmp/foo", O_RDONLY). Also notice that there are no system calls from the if statement or any other code in the program because the if statement does not invoke a system call. As mentioned before, system call tracing is rarely useful for code logic problems, but it can be very useful to find a problem that relates to the interaction with the operating system.

It takes a bit of practice to understand a system call trace, but a good example can go a long way. For those who are not familiar with the standard system calls, it is quick and easy to read the man pages for the system calls for more information. For example, the first system call in the trace is `execve`. The man page can be referenced using

```
ion 225% man 2 execve
```

The arguments for a system call in the strace output should match those listed in the man page. The first argument listed in the man page for `execve` is `const char *filename`, and the documentation in the man page mentions that this system call executes the program pointed to by `filename`. The functionality of `execve` is not the point of this but rather that man pages can be used to help understand strace output for beginners.

Line #1: The `execve` system call (or one of the exec system calls) is always the first system call in the strace output if strace is used to trace a program off the command line. The strace tool forks, executes the program, and the `exec` system call actually returns as the first system call in the new process. A successful `execve` system call will not return in the calling process' code (because `exec` creates a new process).

Line #2: The `uname` system call is being called for some reason—but is not immediately important.

Line #3: The `brk` system call is called with an argument of zero to find the current "break point." This is the beginning of memory management (for example, `malloc` and `free`) for the process.

Line #4: The `mmap` call is used to create an anonymous 4KB page. The address of this page is at `0x40013000`.

Line #5: This line attempts to open the `ld.so.preload` file. This file contains a list of ELF shared libraries that are to be pre-loaded before a program is able to run. The man page for ld.so may have additional information.

Lines #6 - #12. These lines involve finding and loading the libc library.

> **Note:** If the LD_LIBRARY_PATH lists the library paths in the wrong order, process initialization can involve a lot of searching to find the right library.

Line #13: Loads in the ELF header for the libc library.

Line #14: Gets more information (including size) for the libc library file.

Line #15: This line actually loads (mmaps) the contents of libc into memory at address 0x40014000.

Line #16: This removes any protection for a region of memory at 0x40128000 for 39360 bytes.

Line #17: This line loads the data section at address 0x40128000 for 24576 bytes. The address of 0x40128000 is 0x114000 bytes from the beginning of the memory segment (0x40014000). According to the ELF layout of libc.so.6, the data section starts at 0x114920, but that section must be aligned on 0x1000 boundaries (hence the offset of 0x114000).

```
ion 722% readelf -l /lib/libc.so.6

Elf file type is DYN (Shared object file)
Entry point 0x185c0
There are 7 program headers, starting at offset 52

Program Headers:
  Type        Offset   VirtAddr   PhysAddr   FileSiz MemSiz  Flg Align
  PHDR        0x000034 0x00000034 0x00000034 0x000e0 0x000e0 R E 0x4
  INTERP      0x113610 0x00113610 0x00113610 0x00013 0x00013 R   0x1
      [Requesting program interpreter: /lib/ld-linux.so.2]
  LOAD        0x000000 0x00000000 0x00000000 0x113918 0x113918 R E
0x1000
  LOAD        0x113920 0x00114920 0x00114920 0x04f8c 0x090a0 RW 0x1000
  DYNAMIC     0x117ba4 0x00118ba4 0x00118ba4 0x000d8 0x000d8 RW  0x4
  NOTE        0x000114 0x00000114 0x00000114 0x00020 0x00020 R   0x4
  GNU_EH_FRAME 0x113624 0x00113624 0x00113624 0x002f4 0x002f4 R 0x4

ion 723% readelf -S /lib/libc.so.6
There are 53 section headers, starting at offset 0x11d170:

Section Headers:
  [Nr] Name      Type      Addr      Off     Size    ES Flg Lk Inf Al
  ...
  [16] .data     PROGBITS  00114920  113920  0031f8  00  WA  0   0 32
  ...
```

```
        [25] .bss    NOBITS      001198C0 1188C0 004100 00  WA  0   0 32
        ...
```

Line #18: Creates an anonymous memory segment for the bss section (more on this in the ELF chapter). This is a special section of a loaded executable or shared library for uninitialized data. Because the data is not initialized, the storage for it is not included in an ELF object like a shared library (there are no real data values to store). Instead, memory is allocated for the bss section when the library is loaded. One thing worth noting is that part (0x740 bytes) of the bss section is on the last page of the data section. Whenever dealing with memory at the system level, the minimum unit of memory is always a page size, 0x1000 by default on IA-32. The offset of the bss is 0x00114920, which is not on a page size boundary. The next page boundary is at 0x4012e000, which is where the rest of the memory for the bss segment is allocated. Given that the size of the bss is 0x4100 and since 0x740 of the bss is included on the last page of the data section, the rest of the bss segment is 0x39C0 (14784 in decimal) in size and is allocated as expected at 0x4012e000.

Line #19: Closes the file descriptor for libc.

Line #20: The only system call from the actual program code. This is the same open call from the source code just listed.

Line #21: Exits the process with a return code of 5.

2.2.4 Same Program Built Statically

Statically built programs do not require any external libraries for program initialization. This means there is no need to find or load any shared libraries, making the program initialization much simpler.

```
ion 230% gcc main.c -o main -static
ion 231% strace main
execve("./main", ["main"], [/* 64 vars */]) = 0
fcntl64(0, F_GETFD)                 = 0
fcntl64(1, F_GETFD)                 = 0
fcntl64(2, F_GETFD)                 = 0
uname({sys="Linux", node="ion", ...}) = 0
geteuid32()                          = 7903
getuid32()                           = 7903
getegid32()                          = 200
getgid32()                           = 200
brk(0)                               = 0x80a3ce8
brk(0x80a3d08)                       = 0x80a3d08
brk(0x80a4000)                       = 0x80a4000
```

```
brk(0x80a5000)                          = 0x80a5000
open("/tmp/foo", O_RDONLY)              = -1 ENOENT (No such file or
↪directory)
_exit(5)                                = ?
```

The strace output is quite different when the program is linked statically. There are some other system calls (the purpose of which is not important for this discussion), but note that the program does not load libc or any other library. Also worth nothing is that ltrace will not show any output for this program since it is built statically.

2.3 IMPORTANT STRACE OPTIONS

This section is not meant to be a replacement for the strace manual. The strace manual does a good job of documenting issues and options for strace but does not really describe when to use the various options. The focus of this section is to briefly describe the important strace options and when to use them.

2.3.1 Following Child Processes

By default strace only traces the process itself and not any child processes that may be spawned. There are several reasons why you may need or want to trace all of the child processes as well, including:

☞ Tracing the activity of a command line shell.

☞ Tracing a process that will create a daemon process that will continue to run after the command line tool exits.

☞ Tracing inetd or xinetd to investigate problems relating to logging on to a system or for tracing remote connections to a system (an example of this is included later in this chapter).

☞ Some processes spawn worker processes that perform the actual work while the parent process manages the worker process pool.

To trace a process and all of its children, use the -f flag. Tracing with -f will have no effect if the process does not fork off any children. However, the output will change once a child is created:

```
rt_sigprocmask(SIG_SETMASK, [INT], [INT], 8) = 0
rt_sigprocmask(SIG_BLOCK, [INT], [INT], 8) = 0
rt_sigprocmask(SIG_SETMASK, [INT], [INT], 8) = 0
rt_sigprocmask(SIG_BLOCK, [CHLD], [INT], 8) = 0
fork()                                    = 24745
[pid 14485] setpgid(24745, 24745 <unfinished ...>
```

```
[pid 24745] gettimeofday( <unfinished ...>
[pid 14485] <... setpgid resumed> )      = 0
```

In particular, the system calls are prefixed with a process ID to distinguish the various processes being traced. The grep utility can then be used to separate the strace output for each process ID.

> **Note:** As a rule of thumb, always use the -f switch unless you specifically want to exclude the output from the child processes.

2.3.2 Timing System Call Activity

The strace tool also can be used to investigate some types of performance problems. In particular, the timed tracing features can provide information about where a process is spending a lot of time.

Be very careful not to make incorrect assumptions about where the time is spent. For example, the -t switch will add a timestamp (time of day) to the strace output, but it is a timestamp between the system call entry times. In other words, subtracting two timestamps gives time for the first system call and the user code that is run between the two system calls.

There are two other ways to include a timestamp: -tt (time of day with microseconds) and -ttt (number of seconds since the epoch with microseconds).

> **Note:** The -tt option is usually the best option to capture a timestamp. It includes the time of day with microseconds.

If you're interested in getting the time between system calls, you can use the -r switch:

```
ion 235% strace -r main
0.000000 execve("./main", ["main"], [/* 64 vars */]) = 0
0.000801 fcntl64(0, F_GETFD)        = 0
0.000090 fcntl64(1, F_GETFD)        = 0
0.000055 fcntl64(2, F_GETFD)        = 0
0.000052 uname({sys="Linux", node="ion", ...}) = 0
0.000305 geteuid32()                = 7903
0.000038 getuid32()                 = 7903
0.000038 getegid32()                = 200
0.000037 getgid32()                 = 200
0.000076 brk(0)                     = 0x80a3ce8
0.000048 brk(0x80a3d08)             = 0x80a3d08
0.000040 brk(0x80a4000)             = 0x80a4000
0.000054 brk(0x80a5000)             = 0x80a5000
```

```
0.000058 open("/tmp/foo", O_RDONLY) = -1 ENOENT (No such file or
directory)
0.000092 _exit(5)                    = ?
```

Again, keep in mind that this is the time between two system call entries and includes the time for the system call and the user code. This usually has limited usefulness.

A more useful method of timing actual system calls is the -T switch. This provides the actual time spent in a system call instead of the time between system calls. It is slightly more expensive because it requires two timestamps (one for the system call entry and one for the system call exit) for each system call, but the results are more useful.

```
ion 249% strace -T main
execve("./main", ["main"], [/* 64 vars */]) = 0
fcntl64(0, F_GETFD)                  = 0 <0.000016>
fcntl64(1, F_GETFD)                  = 0 <0.000012>
fcntl64(2, F_GETFD)                  = 0 <0.000012>
uname({sys="Linux", node="ion", ...}) = 0 <0.000013>
geteuid32()                          = 7903 <0.000012>
getuid32()                           = 7903 <0.000012>
getegid32()                          = 200 <0.000011>
getgid32()                           = 200 <0.000012>
brk(0)                               = 0x80a3ce8 <0.000012>
brk(0x80a3d08)                       = 0x80a3d08 <0.000011>
brk(0x80a4000)                       = 0x80a4000 <0.000011>
brk(0x80a5000)                       = 0x80a5000 <0.000012>
open("/tmp/foo", O_RDONLY)           = -1 ENOENT (No such file or
directory) <0.000019>
_exit(5)                             = ?
```

The time spent in the system call is shown in angle brackets after the system call (seconds and microseconds).

Another useful way to time system calls is with the -c switch. This switch summarizes the output in tabular form:

```
ion 217% strace -c main
execve("./main", ["main"], [/* 64 vars */]) = 0
```

% time	seconds	usecs/call	calls	errors	syscall
40.00	0.000030	30	1	1	open
25.33	0.000019	6	3		fcntl64
16.00	0.000012	3	4		brk
5.33	0.000004	4	1		uname
4.00	0.000003	3	1		getuid32
4.00	0.000003	3	1		getegid32
2.67	0.000002	2	1		getgid32

```
2.67    0.000002    2    1    geteuid32
```
```
100.00  0.000075         13    1 total
```

It can also be useful to time both the difference between system call entries
and the time spent in the system calls. With this information, it is possible to
get the time spent in the user code *between* the system calls. Keep in mind that
this isn't very accurate unless there is a considerable amount of time spent in
the user code. It also requires writing a small script to parse the strace output.

```
ion 250% strace -Tr main
  0.000000 execve("./main", ["main"], [/* 64 vars */]) = 0
  0.000931 fcntl64(0, F_GETFD)       = 0 <0.000012>
  0.000090 fcntl64(1, F_GETFD)       = 0 <0.000022>
  0.000060 fcntl64(2, F_GETFD)       = 0 <0.000012>
  0.000054 uname({sys="Linux", node="ion", ...}) = 0 <0.000014>
  0.000307 geteuid32()               = 7903 <0.000011>
  0.000040 getuid32()                = 7903 <0.000012>
  0.000039 getegid32()               = 200 <0.000011>
  0.000039 getgid32()                = 200 <0.000011>
  0.000075 brk(0)                    = 0x80a3ce8 <0.000012>
  0.000050 brk(0x80a3d08)            = 0x80a3d08 <0.000012>
  0.000043 brk(0x80a4000)            = 0x80a4000 <0.000011>
  0.000054 brk(0x80a5000)            = 0x80a5000 <0.000013>
  0.000058 open("/tmp/foo", O_RDONLY) = -1 ENOENT (No such file or
➥directory) <0.000024>
  0.000095 _exit(5)                  = ?
```

> **Note:** Some of the time spent may not be due to a system call or user
> code but may be due to the scheduling behavior of the system. The program
> may not execute on a CPU for a small period of time on a busy system
> because other programs are competing for CPU time.

2.3.3 Verbose Mode

By default, strace does not include all of the information for every system call.
It usually provides a good balance between enough information and too much.
However, there are times when more information is required to diagnose a
problem. The verbose option -v tells strace to include full information for system
calls such as stat or uname.

```
ion 251% strace -v main
execve("./main", ["main"], [/* 64 vars */]) = 0
fcntl64(0, F_GETFD)                         = 0
fcntl64(1, F_GETFD)                         = 0
```

```
fcntl64(2, F_GETFD)                      = 0
uname({sysname="Linux", nodename="ion", release="2.4.19-64GB-SMP",
➥version="#1 SMP Mon Oct 21 18:48:05
UTC 2002", machine="i686"}) = 0
geteuid32()                              = 7903
getuid32()                               = 7903
getegid32()                              = 200
getgid32()                               = 200
brk(0)                                   = 0x80a3ce8
brk(0x80a3d08)                           = 0x80a3d08
brk(0x80a4000)                           = 0x80a4000
brk(0x80a5000)                           = 0x80a5000
open("/tmp/foo", O_RDONLY)               = -1 ENOENT (No such file or
➥directory)
_exit(5)                                 = ?
```

Notice that the `uname` system call is fully formatted with all information
included. Compare this to the preceding examples (such as the strace of the
statically linked program):

```
uname({sys="Linux", node="ion", ...})   = 0
```

Another verbose feature is `-s`, which can be useful for showing more information
for the `read` and `write` system calls. This option can be used to set the maximum
size of a string to a certain value.

```
ion 687% strace dd if=strace.strace of=/dev/null bs=32768 |& tail
➥-15 | head -10
write(1, "DATA, 30354, 0xbfffe458, [0x2e6f"..., 32768) = 32768
read(0, "ETFD, FD_CLOEXEC\"", 30) = 30\nptra"..., 32768) = 32768
write(1, "ETFD, FD_CLOEXEC\"", 30) = 30\nptra"..., 32768) = 32768
read(0, "ed) —\nrt_sigprocmask(SIG_BLOCK"..., 32768) = 32768
write(1, "ed) —\nrt_sigprocmask(SIG_BLOCK"..., 32768) = 32768
read(0, ") && WSTOPSIG(s) == SIGTRAP], 0x"..., 32768) = 7587
write(1, ") && WSTOPSIG(s) == SIGTRAP], 0x"..., 7587) = 7587
read(0, "", 32768)                       = 0
write(2, "7+1 records in\n", 157+1 records in
)          = 15
```

Of course, this shows very little information about the contents that were read
or written by dd. In many cases, an investigation requires more or all of the
information. Using the switch `-s 256`, the same system call trace will show 256
bytes of information for each read/write:

```
ion 688% strace -s 256 dd if=strace.strace of=/dev/null bs=32768 | &
tail -15 | head -10
➥write(1, "DATA, 30354, 0xbfffe458, [0x2e6f732e]) =
0\nptrace(PTRACE_PEEKDATA, 30354, 0xbfffe45c, [0xbfff0031]) =
```

```
0\nwrite(2, \"open(\\\"/home/wilding/sqllib/lib/l\"..., 54) =
54\nptrace(PTRACE_SYSCALL, 30354, 0x1, SIG_0) = 0\n- SIGCHLD (Child
exited) -\nrt_sigprocmask(SI"..., 32768) = 32768
➥read(0, "ETFD, FD_CLOEXEC\", 30) = 30\nptrace(PTRACE_SYSCALL,
30354, 0x1, SIG_0) = 0\n- SIGCHLD (Child exited) -
\nrt_sigprocmask(SIG_SETMASK, [], NULL, 8) = 0\nwait4(-1,
[WIFSTOPPED(s) && WSTOPSIG(s) == SIGTRAP], 0x40000000, NULL) =
30354\nrt_sigprocmask(SIG_BLOCK, ["..., 32768) = 32768
➥write(1, "ETFD, FD_CLOEXEC\", 30) = 30\nptrace(PTRACE_SYSCALL,
30354, 0x1, SIG_0) = 0\n- SIGCHLD (Child exited) -
\nrt_sigprocmask(SIG_SETMASK, [], NULL, 8) = 0\nwait4(-1,
[WIFSTOPPED(s) && WSTOPSIG(s) == SIGTRAP], 0x40000000, NULL) =
30354\nrt_sigprocmask(SIG_BLOCK, ["..., 32768) = 32768
➥read(0, "ed) -\nrt_sigprocmask(SIG_BLOCK, [HUP INT QUIT PIPE TERM],
NULL, 8) = 0\nptrace(PTRACE_PEEKUSER, 30354, 4*ORIG_EAX, [0x4]) =
0\nptrace(PTRACE_PEEKUSER, 30354, 4*EAX, [0xffffffda]) =
0\nptrace(PTRACE_PEEKUSER, 30354, 4*EBX, [0x1]) =
0\nptrace(PTRACE_PEEKUSER, "..., 32768) = 32768
➥write(1, "ed) -\nrt_sigprocmask(SIG_BLOCK, [HUP INT QUIT PIPE
TERM], NULL, 8) = 0\nptrace(PTRACE_PEEKUSER, 30354, 4*ORIG_EAX,
[0x4]) = 0\nptrace(PTRACE_PEEKUSER, 30354, 4*EAX, [0xffffffda]) =
0\nptrace(PTRACE_PEEKUSER, 30354, 4*EBX, [0x1]) =
0\nptrace(PTRACE_PEEKUSER, "..., 32768) = 32768
➥read(0, ") && WSTOPSIG(s) == SIGTRAP], 0x40000000, NULL) = 30354\n-
SIGCHLD (Child exited) -\nrt_sigprocmask(SIG_BLOCK, [HUP INT QUIT
PIPE TERM], NULL, 8) = 0\nptrace(PTRACE_PEEKUSER, 30354, 4*ORIG_EAX,
[0x4]) = 0\nptrace(PTRACE_PEEKUSER, 30354, 4*EAX, [0xffffffda]"...,
32768) = 7587
➥write(1, ") && WSTOPSIG(s) == SIGTRAP], 0x40000000, NULL) =
30354\n- SIGCHLD (Child exited) -\nrt_sigprocmask(SIG_BLOCK, [HUP
INT QUIT PIPE TERM], NULL, 8) = 0\nptrace(PTRACE_PEEKUSER, 30354,
4*ORIG_EAX, [0x4]) = 0\nptrace(PTRACE_PEEKUSER, 30354, 4*EAX,
[0xffffffda]"..., 7587) = 7587
➥read(0, "", 32768)                              = 0
➥write(2, "7+1 records in\n", 157+1 records in" )         = 15
```

The amount of information shown in the strace output here is pretty
intimidating, and you can see why strace doesn't include *all* of the information
by default. Use the -s switch only when needed.

2.3.4 Tracing a Running Process

Sometimes it is necessary to trace an existing process that is running, such as
a Web daemon (such as apache) or xinetd. The strace tool provides a simple
way to attach to running processes with the -p switch:

```
ion 257% strace -p 3423
```

Once attached, both the strace tool and the traced process behave as if strace ran the process off of the command line. Attaching to a running process establishes a special parent-child relationship between the tracing process and the traced process. Everything is pretty much the same after strace is attached. All of the same strace options work whether strace is used to trace a program off of the command line or whether strace is used to attach to a running process.

2.4 EFFECTS AND ISSUES OF USING STRACE

The strace tool is somewhat intrusive (although it isn't too bad). It will slow down the traced process, and it may also wake up a sleeping process if the process is waiting in the `pause()` function. It is rare that strace actually causes any major problems, but it is good to be aware of the effects.

The strace tool prints its output to stderr, which makes it a bit easier to separate the output from the traced tool's output (if tracing something off of the command line). For csh or tcsh, you can use something like (`strace /bin/ ls > /dev/null`) | `& less` to see the actual strace output without the output from the traced program (/bin/ls in this case). Other shells support separating stdout and stderr as well, although it is usually just easier to send the output to a file using the `-o` switch to strace. This also ensures that the strace output is completely clean and without any stderr output from the traced process.

When a setuid program is run off of the command line, the program is run as the user of the strace program, and the setuid does not take place. There are also security protections against tracing a running program that was setuid. Even if a running setuid-root program changes its effective user ID back to the real user ID, strace will not be able to attach to the process and trace it. This is for security reasons since the process may still have sensitive information in its memory from when it was running as root.

If a program is setuid to root, strace requires root privileges to properly trace it. There are two easy ways to trace a setuid-root program, both of which require root privileges. The first method is to strace the setuid program as root. This will ensure the setuid-root program is also straced as root, but the real user ID will be root and not a mortal user as would normally be the case. The other method is to trace the shell as root using the `-f` switch to follow the setuid-root program and its invocation. The latter method is better, although it is a bit less convenient.

2.4.1 strace and EINTR

If you are using strace on a program that does not handle interrupted system calls properly, the target program will very likely experience a problem. Consider the following source code snippet:

```
result = accept(s, addr, &addrlen);

if (result < 0)
{
  perror( "accept" ) ;
  return (SOCKET) INVALID_SOCKET;
}
else
 return result;
```

This function does *not* handle interruptions to the accept() call properly and is not safe to strace. If you were to strace this process while it was waiting on accept(), the process would pop out of the accept call and return an error via perror(). The error code (errno) received when a system call is interrupted is EINTR. Because the process does not handle EINTR error codes, the process will not recover, and the process may even exit altogether.

A better (and more robust) way to write this code would be

```
do
{
    result = accept(s, addr, &addrlen);
} while ( result < 0 && errno == EINTR )

if (result < 0)
{
  perror( "accept" ) ;
  return (SOCKET) INVALID_SOCKET;
}
else
 return result;
```

The new code will still pop out of accept() if strace attaches to it, although the while loop will call accept() again when it receives the EINTR error code. In other words, when strace attaches, the code loop will see the EINTR error code and restart the accept() system call. This code is robust with respect to interrupts (that are caused by signals).

2.5 Real Debugging Examples

The best way to learn about any tool is to roll up your sleeves and try to solve some real problems on your own. This section includes some examples to get you started.

2.5.1 Reducing Start Up Time by Fixing LD_LIBRARY_PATH

The LD_LIBRARY_PATH environment variable is used by the run time linker to find the depended libraries for an executable or library. The `ldd` command can be used to find the dependent libraries:

```
ion 201% ldd /bin/ls
        librt.so.1 => /lib/librt.so.1 (0x40024000)
        libacl.so.1 => /lib/libacl.so.1 (0x40035000)
        libc.so.6 => /lib/libc.so.6 (0x4003b000)
        libpthread.so.0 => /lib/libpthread.so.0 (0x40159000)
        libattr.so.1 => /lib/libattr.so.1 (0x4016e000)
        /lib/ld-linux.so.2 => /lib/ld-linux.so.2 (0x40000000)
```

When a program is first run, the run time linker must locate and load all of these libraries before the program can execute. The run time linker runs inside the process itself, and any interactions with the operating system can be traced with strace. Before getting into details, first let me apologize in advance for the long strace output. This is a good example of a poor LD_LIBRARY_PATH, but unfortunately the output is very long.

```
ion 685% echo $LD_LIBRARY_PATH
/usr/lib:/home/wilding/sqllib/lib:/usr/java/lib:/usr/ucblib:/opt/
➥IBMcset/lib
```

With this LD_LIBRARY_PATH, the run time linker will have to search /usr/lib first, then /home/wilding/sqllib/lib, then /usr/java/lib, and so on. The strace tool will show just how much work is involved:

```
ion 206% strace telnet
execve("/usr/bin/telnet", ["telnet", "foo", "136"], [/* 64 vars */
➥]) = 0
uname({sys="Linux", node="ion", ...})   = 0
➥brk(0)                                 = 0x8066308
mmap2(NULL, 4096, PROT_READ|PROT_WRITE, MAP_PRIVATE|MAP_ANONYMOUS, -
1, 0) = 0x40013000
open("/etc/ld.so.preload", O_RDONLY)     = -1 ENOENT (No such file or
➥directory)
open("/usr/lib/i686/mmx/libncurses.so.5", O_RDONLY) = -1 ENOENT (No
```

```
➥such file or directory)
stat64("/usr/lib/i686/mmx", 0xbfffe59c) = -1 ENOENT (No such
➥file or directory)
open("/usr/lib/i686/libncurses.so.5", O_RDONLY) = -1 ENOENT
➥(No such file or directory)
stat64("/usr/lib/i686", 0xbfffe59c)      = -1 ENOENT (No such
➥file or directory)
open("/usr/lib/mmx/libncurses.so.5", O_RDONLY) = -1 ENOENT (No
➥such file or directory)
stat64("/usr/lib/mmx", 0xbfffe59c)       = -1 ENOENT (No such
➥file or directory)
open("/usr/lib/libncurses.so.5", O_RDONLY) = -1 ENOENT (No
➥such file or directory)
stat64("/usr/lib", {st_mode=S_IFDIR|0755, st_size=32768, ...})
= 0
open("/home/wilding/sqllib/lib/i686/mmx/libncurses.so.5",
➥O_RDONLY) = -1 ENOENT (No such file or directory)
stat64("/home/wilding/sqllib/lib/i686/mmx", 0xbfffe59c) = -1
➥ENOENT (No such file or directory)
open("/home/wilding/sqllib/lib/i686/libncurses.so.5",
➥O_RDONLY) = -1 ENOENT (No such file or directory)
stat64("/home/wilding/sqllib/lib/i686", 0xbfffe59c) = -1
➥ENOENT (No such file or directory)
open("/home/wilding/sqllib/lib/mmx/libncurses.so.5", O_RDONLY)
➥= -1 ENOENT (No such file or directory)
stat64("/home/wilding/sqllib/lib/mmx", 0xbfffe59c) = -1 ENOENT
➥(No such file or directory)
open("/home/wilding/sqllib/lib/libncurses.so.5", O_RDONLY) = -1
➥ENOENT (No such file or directory)
stat64("/home/wilding/sqllib/lib",
{st_mode=S_IFDIR|S_ISGID|0755, st_size=12288, ...}) = 0
open("/usr/java/lib/i686/mmx/libncurses.so.5", O_RDONLY) = -1
➥ENOENT (No such file or directory)
stat64("/usr/java/lib/i686/mmx", 0xbfffe59c) = -1 ENOENT (No
➥such file or directory)
open("/usr/java/lib/i686/libncurses.so.5", O_RDONLY) = -1
➥ENOENT (No such file or directory)
stat64("/usr/java/lib/i686", 0xbfffe59c) = -1 ENOENT (No such
➥file or directory)
open("/usr/java/lib/mmx/libncurses.so.5", O_RDONLY) = -1
➥ENOENT (No such file or directory)
stat64("/usr/java/lib/mmx", 0xbfffe59c) = -1 ENOENT (No such
➥file or directory)
open("/usr/java/lib/libncurses.so.5", O_RDONLY) = -1 ENOENT (No
➥such file or directory)
stat64("/usr/java/lib", 0xbfffe59c)      = -1 ENOENT (No such
➥file or directory)
open("/usr/ucblib/i686/mmx/libncurses.so.5", O_RDONLY) = -1
➥ENOENT No such file or directory)
stat64("/usr/ucblib/i686/mmx", 0xbfffe59c) = -1 ENOENT (No such
```

```
➥file or directory)
open("/usr/ucblib/i686/libncurses.so.5", O_RDONLY) = -1 ENOENT (No
➥such file or directory)
stat64("/usr/ucblib/i686", 0xbfffe59c)  = -1 ENOENT (No such file or
➥directory)
open("/usr/ucblib/mmx/libncurses.so.5", O_RDONLY) = -1 ENOENT(No
➥such file or directory)
stat64("/usr/ucblib/mmx", 0xbfffe59c)   = -1 ENOENT (No such file or
➥directory)
open("/usr/ucblib/libncurses.so.5", O_RDONLY) = -1 ENOENT (No such
➥file or directory)
stat64("/usr/ucblib", 0xbfffe59c)       = -1 ENOENT (No such file or
➥directory)
open("/opt/IBMcset/lib/i686/mmx/libncurses.so.5", O_RDONLY) = -1
➥ENOENT (No such file or directory)
stat64("/opt/IBMcset/lib/i686/mmx", 0xbfffe59c) = -1 ENOENT (No such
➥file or directory)
open("/opt/IBMcset/lib/i686/libncurses.so.5", O_RDONLY) = -1 ENOENT
➥ (No such file or directory)
stat64("/opt/IBMcset/lib/i686", 0xbfffe59c) = -1 ENOENT (No such
➥file or directory)
open("/opt/IBMcset/lib/mmx/libncurses.so.5", O_RDONLY) = -1 ENOENT
➥ (No such file or directory)
stat64("/opt/IBMcset/lib/mmx", 0xbfffe59c) = -1 ENOENT (No such
➥file or directory)
open("/opt/IBMcset/lib/libncurses.so.5", O_RDONLY) = -1 ENOENT (No
➥such file or directory)
stat64("/opt/IBMcset/lib", 0xbfffe59c)  = -1 ENOENT (No such file or
➥directory)
open("/etc/ld.so.cache", O_RDONLY)      = 3
fstat64(3, {st_mode=S_IFREG|0644, st_size=65169, ...}) = 0
mmap2(NULL, 65169, PROT_READ, MAP_PRIVATE, 3, 0) = 0x40014000
➥close(3)                              = 0
open("/lib/libncurses.so.5", O_RDONLY)  = 3 read(3,
"\177ELF\1\1\1\0\0\0\0\0\0\0\0\0\3\0\3\0\1\0\0\0P\357\0"..., 1024) =
➥1024
```

The strace output shows 20 failed attempts to find the libncurses.so.5 library. In fact, 40 of the 52 lines of this strace deal with the failed attempts to find the curses library. The LD_LIBRARY_PATH includes too many paths (starting from the beginning) that do not contain libncurses.so.5. A better LD_LIBRARY_PATH would contain /lib (where libncurses.so.5 was eventually found) near the beginning of the path list:

```
ion 689% echo $LD_LIBRARY_PATH
/lib:/usr/lib:/home/wilding/sqllib/lib:/usr/java/lib
```

The strace shows that this LD_LIBRARY_PATH is much more efficient:

```
ion 701% strace telnet | & head -15
execve("/usr/bin/telnet", ["telnet"], [/* 77 vars */]) = 0
```

```
uname({sys="Linux", node="ion", ...})   = 0
brk(0)                                   = 0x8066308
mmap2(NULL, 4096, PROT_READ|PROT_WRITE, MAP_PRIVATE|MAP_ANONYMOUS, -
1, 0) = 0x40013000
open("/etc/ld.so.preload", O_RDONLY)     = -1 ENOENT (No such file or
➡directory)
open("/lib/i686/29/libncurses.so.5", O_RDONLY) = -1 ENOENT (No such
➡file or directory)
stat64("/lib/i686/29", 0xbfffe41c)       = -1 ENOENT (No such file or
➡directory)
open("/lib/i686/libncurses.so.5", O_RDONLY) = -1 ENOENT (No such
➡file or directory)
stat64("/lib/i686", 0xbfffe41c)          = -1 ENOENT (No such file or
➡directory)
open("/lib/29/libncurses.so.5", O_RDONLY) = -1 ENOENT (No such file
➡or directory)
stat64("/lib/29", 0xbfffe41c)            = -1 ENOENT (No such file or
➡directory)
open("/lib/libncurses.so.5", O_RDONLY)   = 3
```

A bad LD_LIBRARY_PATH environment variable is not usually a problem for everyday human-driven command line activity; however, it can really affect the performance of scripts and Common Gateway Interface (CGI) programs. It is always worth testing CGI programs and scripts to ensure that the library path picks up the libraries quickly and with the least amount of failures.

2.5.2 The PATH Environment Variable

Tracing a shell can also reveal a bad PATH environment variable. From a different shell, run `strace -fp <shell pid>`, where `<shell pid>` is the process ID of the target shell. Next, run the program of your choice and look for `exec` in the strace output. In the following example, there are only two failed searches for the program called `main`.

```
[pid 27187] execve("main", ["main"], [/* 64 vars */]) = -1 ENOENT
➡(No such file or directory)
[pid 27187] execve("/usr/sbin/main", ["main"], [/* 64 vars */]) = -1
➡ENOENT (No such file or directory)
[pid 27187] execve("/home/wilding/bin/main", ["main"], [/* 64 vars
➡*/]) = 0
```

A bad PATH environment variable can cause many failed executions of a script or tool. This too can impact the startup costs of a new program.

2.5.3 stracing inetd or xinetd (the Super Server)

Most Linux systems are connected to a network and can accept remote connections via TCP. Some common examples include telnet and Web communications. For the most part, everything usually works as expected, although what if the software that is driven by a remote connection encounters a problem? For example, what if a remote user cannot connect to a system and log in using a telnet client? Is it a problem with the user's shell? Does the user's shell get hung up on a path mounted by a problematic NFS server?

Here is an example of how strace can be used to examine an incoming telnet connection. This example requires root access.

The first step is to find and strace the inetd daemon on the telnet server (as root):

```
ion 200# ps -fea | grep inetd | grep -v grep
root       986     1  0 Jan27 ?        00:00:00 /usr/sbin/inetd
ion 201# strace -o inetd.strace -f -p 986
```

Then, on a remote system use the telnet client to log in to the telnet server:

```
sunfish % telnet ion
```

After logging in to the telnet server, hit control-C to break out of the strace command and examine the strace output:

> **Note:** lines with ... represent strace output that was removed for simplicity.

```
ion 203# less inetd.strace
986   select(13, [4 5 6 7 8 9 10 11 12], NULL, NULL, NULL) = 1(in
➡[5])
986   accept(5, 0, NULL)                  = 3
986   getpeername(3, {sin_family=AF_INET, sin_port=htons(63117),
➡sin_addr=inet_addr("9.26.48.230")}}, [16]) = 0
...
986   fork()                              = 27202
...
986   close(3 <unfinished ...>
27202 socket(PF_UNIX, SOCK_STREAM, 0 <unfinished ...>
986   <... close resumed> )               = 0
27202 <... socket resumed> )              = 13
```

The select system call waits for a new connection to come in. The new connection comes in on the inetd's socket descriptor 5. The accept system call creates a new socket descriptor that is directly connected to the remote telnet client. Immediately after accepting the new connection, the inetd gathers information about the source of the connection, including the remote port and IP address. The inetd then forks and closes the socket description. The strace output is continued as follows:

```
27202 connect(13, {sin_family=AF_UNIX, path="/var/run/
↪.nscd_socket"}, 110) = 0
...
27202 dup2(3, 0)                        = 0
27202 close(3)                          = 0
27202 dup2(0, 1)                        = 1
27202 dup2(0, 2)                        = 2
27202 close(1022)                       = -1 EBADF (Bad file
↪descriptor)
27202 close(1021)                       = -1 EBADF (Bad file
↪descriptor)
...
27202 close(4)                          = 0
27202 close(3)                          = -1 EBADF (Bad file
↪descriptor)
27202 rt_sigaction(SIGPIPE, {SIG_DFL}, NULL, 8) = 0
27202 execve("/usr/sbin/tcpd", ["in.telnetd"], [/* 16 vars */])=0
```

The strace output here shows a connection to the name service cache daemon (see man page for nscd). Next, the file descriptors for stdin (0), stdout (1), and stderr (2) are created by duplicating the socket descriptor. The full list of socket descriptors are then closed (from 1022 to 3) to ensure that none of the file descriptors from the inetd are inherited by the eventual shell. Last, the forked inetd changes itself into the access control program.

```
...
27202 open("/etc/hosts.allow", O_RDONLY) = 3
...
27202 execve("/usr/sbin/in.telnetd", ["in.telnetd"], [/* 16 vars */
↪]) = 0
...
27202 open("/dev/ptmx", O_RDWR)         = 3
...
27202 ioctl(3, TIOCGPTN, [123])         = 0
27202 stat64("/dev/pts/123", {st_mode=S_IFCHR|0620,
↪st_rdev=makedev(136, 123), ...}) = 0
...
27202 open("/dev/pts/123", O_RDWR|O_NOCTTY) = 4
...
27203 execve("/bin/login", ["/bin/login", "-h",
↪"sunfish.torolab.ibm.com", "-p"], [/* 3 vars */] <unfinished ...>
```

The access control program checks the hosts.allow file to ensure the remote client is allowed to connect via telnet to this server. After confirming that the remote client is allowed to connect, the process turns itself into the actual telnet daemon, which establishes a new pseudo terminal (number 123). After opening the pseudo terminal, the process changes itself into the login process.

```
...
27202 open("/dev/tty", O_RDWR <unfinished ...
...
27203 readlink("/proc/self/fd/0", "/dev/pts/123", 4095) = 12
...
27203 open("/dev/pts/123", O_RDWR|O_NONBLOCK|O_LARGEFILE) = 3
...
27203 open("/etc/shadow", O_RDONLY)     = 3
...
27203 access("/var/log/wtmpx", F_OK)    = -1 ENOENT (No such file
➥or directory)
27203 open("/var/log/wtmp", O_WRONLY)   = 3
...
27203 open("/var/log/lastlog", O_RDWR|O_LARGEFILE) = 3
...
27204 chdir("/home/wilding" <unfinished ...>
...
27204 execve("/bin/tcsh", ["-tcsh"], [/* 9 vars */]) = 0
...
27202 select(4, [0 3], [], [0], NULL <unfinished ...>
```

Lastly, the login process goes through the login steps, confirms the user's password by checking the /etc/shadow file, records the user's login (lastlog, for example), and changes the directory to the user's home directory. The final step is the process changing itself into the shell (tcsh in this example) and the shell waiting for input from stdin. When the remote user types any character, the `select` call will wake up, and the shell will handle the character as appropriate.

> **Note:** When using strace to trace the startup of a daemon process, it will not return because the traced processes will still be alive. Instead, the user must hit control-C to break out of strace once the error has been reproduced.

2.5.4 Communication Errors

The following example shows how strace can be used to provide more detail about a telnet connection failure.

```
ion 203% strace -o strace.out telnet foo 136
Trying 9.26.78.114...
telnet: connect to address 9.26.78.114: Connection refused
ion 204% less strace.out
```

```
...
open("/etc/resolv.conf", O_RDONLY)        = 3
...
open("/etc/nsswitch.conf", O_RDONLY)      = 3
...
open("/etc/hosts", O_RDONLY)              = 3
...
open("/etc/services", O_RDONLY)           = 3
...
socket(PF_INET, SOCK_STREAM, IPPROTO_TCP) = 3
setsockopt(3, SOL_IP, IP_TOS, [16], 4)  = 0
connect(3, {sin_family=AF_INET, sin_port=htons(136),
➥sin_addr=inet_addr("9.26.78.114")}}, 16) = -1 ECONNREFUSED
Connection refused)
```

Most of the strace output is not included here for the sake of simplicity. The only interesting system call is the last one where the connect fails. The IP address and the port number are clearly shown in the strace output. This could be useful if the host name had several IP addresses or when the problem is more complex. The man page for the connect system call will have a clear description of ECONNREFUSED or any other error that may be returned for connect.

2.5.5 Investigating a Hang Using strace

If the problem is occurring now or can be reproduced, use the strace with the -ttt switch to get a system call trace with timestamps. If the hang is in user code, the last line of the strace will show a completed system call. If the hang is in a system call, the last line of the strace will show an incomplete system call (that is, one with no return value). Here is a simple problem to show the difference:

```c
#include <stdio.h>
#include <sys/types.h>
#include <unistd.h>
#include <string.h>


int main( int argc, char *argv[] )
{

   getpid( ) ; // a system call to show that we've entered this code

     if ( argc < 2 )
   {
     printf( "hang (user|system)" ) ;
     return 1 ;
   }
```

```
if ( !strcmp( argv[1], "user" ) )
{
    while ( 1 ) ;
}
else if ( !strcmp( argv[1], "system" ) )
{
    sleep( 5000 ) ;
}

return 0 ;
}
```

Here is an example of a "user hang" using the hang tool. The strace shows that the system call getpid() completed and no other system calls were executed.

```
ion 191% g++ hang.C -o hang
ion 192% strace -ttt hang user
...
1093627399.734539 munmap(0x400c7000, 65169) = 0
1093627399.735341 brk(0)                 = 0x8049660
1093627399.735678 brk(0x8049688)         = 0x8049688
1093627399.736061 brk(0x804a000)         = 0x804a000
1093627399.736571 getpid()               = 18406
```

Since the last system call has completed, the hang must be in the user code somewhere. Be careful about using a screen pager like "more" or "less" because the buffered I/O may not show the last system call. Let strace run until it hangs in your terminal.

If the strace tool traces an application that hangs in a system call, the last system call will be incomplete as in the following sample output:

```
ion 193% strace -ttt hang system
1093627447.115573 brk(0x8049688)         = 0x8049688
1093627447.115611 brk(0x804a000)         = 0x804a000
1093627447.115830 getpid()               = 18408
1093627447.115887 rt_sigprocmask(SIG_BLOCK, [CHLD], [], 8) = 0
1093627447.115970 rt_sigaction(SIGCHLD, NULL, {SIG_DFL}, 8) = 0
1093627447.116026 rt_sigprocmask(SIG_SETMASK, [], NULL, 8) = 0
1093627447.116072 nanosleep({5000, 0},
```

Notice that nanosleep() does not have a return code because it has not yet completed. A hang in a system call can tell you a lot about the type of hang. If the hang was in a system call such as read, it may have been waiting on a socket or reading from a file. The investigation from this point on will depend on what you find in the strace output and from gdb. A hang in a system call also can tell you a lot about the cause of the hang. If you are not familiar with the system call, read the man page for it and try to understand under what circumstances it can hang.

The arguments to the system call can give you additional hints about the hang. If the hang is on a `read` system call, the first argument will be the file description. With the file descriptor, you can use the lsof tool to understand which file or socket the `read` system call is hung on.

```
ion 1000% strace -p 23735
read(16,
```

The `read` system call in the preceding example has a file descriptor of 16. This could be a file or socket, and running lsof will tell you which file or socket it is. If the hang symptom is affecting a network client, try to break the problem down into a client side hang, network hang, or server side hang.

2.5.6 Reverse Engineering (How the strace Tool Itself Works)

The strace tool can also be used to understand how something works. Of course, this example of reverse engineering is illustrated here for educational purposes only. In this example, we'll use strace to see how it works.

First, let's strace the strace tool as it traces the /bin/ls program.

> **Note**: Uninteresting strace output has been replaced by a single line with ...

```
ion 226% strace -o strace.out strace /bin/ls
ion 227% less strace.out
execve("/usr/bin/strace", ["strace", "/bin/ls"], [/* 75 vars */])= 0
...
fork()                                           = 16474
...
wait4(-1, [WIFSTOPPED(s) && WSTOPSIG(s) == SIGTRAP], 0x40000000,
➥NULL) = 16474
rt_sigprocmask(SIG_BLOCK, [HUP INT QUIT PIPE TERM], NULL, 8) = 0
ptrace(PTRACE_SYSCALL, 16474, 0x1, SIG_0) = 0
    rt_sigprocmask(SIG_SETMASK, [], NULL, 8) = 0
wait4(-1, [WIFSTOPPED(s) && WSTOPSIG(s) == SIGTRAP], 0x40000000,
➥NULL) = 16474
— SIGCHLD (Child exited) —
rt_sigprocmask(SIG_BLOCK, [HUP INT QUIT PIPE TERM], NULL, 8) = 0
ptrace(PTRACE_PEEKUSER, 16474, 4*ORIG_EAX, [0x7a]) = 0
ptrace(PTRACE_PEEKUSER, 16474, 4*EAX, [0xffffffda]) = 0
ptrace(PTRACE_PEEKUSER, 16474, 4*EBX, [0xbfffed2c]) = 0
write(2, "uname(", 6)                    = 6
ptrace(PTRACE_SYSCALL, 16474, 0x1, SIG_0) = 0
```

The first system call of interest is the fork to create another process. This fork call is required to eventually spawn the /bin/ls program. The next interesting system call is the `wait4` call. This call waits for any child processes of the strace program to change state. The process that stops is the child process of the previous fork call (`pid: 16474`). Shortly after the `wait` call, there is a call to ptrace with the PTRACE_SYSCALL value for the first argument. The man page for ptrace states:

> *TRACE_SYSCALL, PTRACE_SINGLESTEP*
> *Restarts the stopped child as for PTRACE_CONT, but arranges for the child to be stopped at the next entry to or exit from a system call, or after execution of a single instruction, respectively. (The child will also, as usual, be stopped upon receipt of a signal.) From the parent's perspective, the child will appear to have been stopped by receipt of a SIGTRAP. So, for PTRACE_SYSCALL, for example, the idea is to inspect the arguments to the system call at the first stop, then do another PTRACE_SYSCALL and inspect the return value of the system call at the second stop. (addr is ignored.)*

So the strace tool is waiting for the child process to stop and then starts it in such a way that it will stop on the next entry or exit of a system call. After the second call to `wait4`, there are a number of calls to ptrace with PTRACE_PEEKUSER as the first argument. According to the ptrace man page, this argument does the following:

> *PTRACE_PEEKUSR*
> *Reads a word at offset addr in the child's USER area, which holds the registers and other information about the process (see <linux/user.h> and <sys/user.h>). The word is returned as the result of the ptrace call. Typically the offset must be word-aligned, though this might vary by architecture. (Data is ignored.)*

From this information, it appears that strace is reading information from the user area of the child process. In particular, it can be used to get the registers for the process. The registers are used for the arguments to system calls as per the calling conventions for system calls. Notice the second to last system call that writes the strace output to the terminal. The /bin/ls program just called the `uname` system call, and the strace output printed the information about that system call to the terminal.

The strace output continues:

```
rt_sigprocmask(SIG_SETMASK, [], NULL, 8) = 0
wait4(-1, [WIFSTOPPED(s) && WSTOPSIG(s) == SIGTRAP], 0x40000000,
➥NULL) = 16474
− SIGCHLD (Child exited) −
rt_sigprocmask(SIG_BLOCK, [HUP INT QUIT PIPE TERM], NULL, 8) = 0
ptrace(PTRACE_PEEKUSER, 16474, 4*ORIG_EAX, [0x5]) = 0
ptrace(PTRACE_PEEKUSER, 16474, 4*EAX, [0xfffffffda]) = 0
ptrace(PTRACE_PEEKUSER, 16474, 4*EBX, [0xbfffe3e8]) = 0
ptrace(PTRACE_PEEKUSER, 16474, 4*ECX, [0]) = 0
ptrace(PTRACE_PEEKUSER, 16474, 4*EDX, [0]) = 0
ptrace(PTRACE_PEEKDATA, 16474, 0xbfffe3e8, [0x7273752f]) = 0
ptrace(PTRACE_PEEKDATA, 16474, 0xbfffe3ec, [0x62696c2f]) = 0
ptrace(PTRACE_PEEKDATA, 16474, 0xbfffe3f0, [0x3836692f]) = 0
ptrace(PTRACE_PEEKDATA, 16474, 0xbfffe3f4, [0x39322f36]) = 0
ptrace(PTRACE_PEEKDATA, 16474, 0xbfffe3f8, [0x62696c2f]) = 0
ptrace(PTRACE_PEEKDATA, 16474, 0xbfffe3fc, [0x732e7472]) = 0
ptrace(PTRACE_PEEKDATA, 16474, 0xbfffe400, [0x312e6f]) = 0
write(2, "open(\"/usr/lib/i686/29/librt.so.".., 44) = 44
```

This strace output shows the processing of another system call. However, in this snippet of strace output, there are several calls to ptrace with the PTRACE_PEEKDATA value as the first argument. The ptrace man page has the following information on this value:

PTRACE_PEEKTEXT, PTRACE_PEEKDATA
Reads a word at the location addr in the child's memory, returning the word as the result of the ptrace call. Linux does not have separate text and data address spaces, so the two requests are currently equivalent. (The argument data is ignored.)

The strace utility was retrieving information from the process' address space. The last system call listed provides a clue as to why strace needed to read from the address space. According to what the strace utility was printing to the terminal, the system call that was being processed was open(). The calling convention for a system call uses the registers, but the argument to the open system call is an address in the process' address space … the file name that is to be opened. In other words, the register for the first argument of the open system call is the address for the file name, and strace had to read the file name from the process' address space.

Now there is still one missing piece of information about how strace works. Remember, we straced the strace utility without the -f switch, which means that we did not follow the forked strace process. For the sake of completeness, let's see what that reveals:

```
ion 220% strace -f strace /bin/ls | & less
...
fork()                                = 18918
[pid 18914] write(2, "execve(\"/bin/ls\", [\"/bin/ls\"],
["..., 52execve("/bin/ls", ["/bin/ls"], [/* 64 vars */]
) = 0
 <unfinished ...>
[pid 18918] ptrace(PTRACE_TRACEME, 0, 0x1, 0 <unfinished ...>
[pid 18914] <... write resumed> )       = 52
[pid 18918] <... ptrace resumed> )         = -1 EPERM (Operation not
➥permitted)
```

The EPERM error occurs because the kernel only allows one process (at a time) to trace a specific process. Since we traced with the -f switch, both strace commands were trying to strace the /bin/ls process, which caused the EPERM error (the one directly and the other because of the -f switch).

The strace utility forks off a process, which immediately tries to call the ptrace system call with PTRACE_TRACEME as the first argument. The man page for ptrace states the following:

> PTRACE_TRACEME
> *Indicates that this process is to be traced by its parent. Any signal (except SIGKILL) delivered to this process will cause it to stop and its parent to be notified via wait. Also, all subsequent calls to exec by this process will cause a SIGTRAP to be sent to it, giving the parent a chance to gain control before the new program begins execution. A process probably shouldn't make this request if its parent isn't expecting to trace it. (pid, addr, and data are ignored.)*

When tracing a process off of the command line, the strace output should contain all the system calls. Without this ptrace feature, the strace utility may or may not capture the initial system calls because the child process would be running unhampered calling system calls at will. With this feature, the child process (which will eventually be /bin/ls in this example) will stop on any system call and wait for the parent process (the strace process) to process the system call.

2.6 SYSTEM CALL TRACING EXAMPLE

Given what we've learned from reverse engineering strace, we now have enough information to build a simple strace-like utility from scratch. Building a tool like strace includes a lot of formatting work. Error numbers and system call numbers need to be formatted, as do the various system call arguments. This is the reason for the two large arrays in the following source code, one for error numbers and one for system call numbers.

> **Note:** Notice the check for -ENOSYS. In the kernel source, we saw that the kernel set EAX to -ENOSYS for system call entries.

2.6.1 Sample Code

```
#include <asm/unistd.h>
#include <stdio.h>
#include <stdlib.h>
#include <unistd.h>
#include <stdarg.h>
#include <errno.h>
#include <string.h>
#include <sys/types.h>
#include <sys/wait.h>
#include <sys/ptrace.h>
#include <asm/user.h>

const char *errors[] =
{
  "NULL:"
 ,"EPERM"                     //numeric value: 1
 ,"ENOENT"                    //numeric value: 2
 ,"ESRCH"                     //numeric value: 3
 ,"EINTR"                     //numeric value: 4
 ,"EIO"                       //numeric value: 5
 ,"ENXIO"                     //numeric value: 6
 ,"E2BIG"                     //numeric value: 7
 ,"ENOEXEC"                   //numeric value: 8
 ,"EBADF"                     //numeric value: 9
 ,"ECHILD"                    //numeric value: 10
 ,"EAGAIN"                    //numeric value: 11
 ,"ENOMEM"                    //numeric value: 12
 ,"EACCES"                    //numeric value: 13
 ,"EFAULT"                    //numeric value: 14
 ,"ENOTBLK"                   //numeric value: 15
 ,"EBUSY"                     //numeric value: 16
 ,"EEXIST"                    //numeric value: 17
 ,"EXDEV"                     //numeric value: 18
 ,"ENODEV"                    //numeric value: 19
 ,"ENOTDIR"                   //numeric value: 20
 ,"EISDIR"                    //numeric value: 21
 ,"EINVAL"                    //numeric value: 22
 ,"ENFILE"                    //numeric value: 23
 ,"EMFILE"                    //numeric value: 24
 ,"ENOTTY"                    //numeric value: 25
 ,"ETXTBSY"                   //numeric value: 26
 ,"EFBIG"                     //numeric value: 27
 ,"ENOSPC"                    //numeric value: 28
 ,"ESPIPE"                    //numeric value: 29
 ,"EROFS"                     //numeric value: 30
```

```
,"EMLINK"              //numeric value: 31
,"EPIPE"               //numeric value: 32
,"EDOM"                //numeric value: 33
,"ERANGE"              //numeric value: 34
,"EDEADLK"             //numeric value: 35
,"ENAMETOOLONG"        //numeric value: 36
,"ENOLCK"              //numeric value: 37
,"ENOSYS"              //numeric value: 38
,"ENOTEMPTY"           //numeric value: 39
,"ELOOP"               //numeric value: 40
,"NULL"                //numeric value: 41
,"ENOMSG"              //numeric value: 42
,"EIDRM"               //numeric value: 43
,"ECHRNG"              //numeric value: 44
,"EL2NSYNC"            //numeric value: 45
,"EL3HLT"              //numeric value: 46
,"EL3RST"              //numeric value: 47
,"ELNRNG"              //numeric value: 48
,"EUNATCH"             //numeric value: 49
,"ENOCSI"              //numeric value: 50
,"EL2HLT"              //numeric value: 51
,"EBADE"               //numeric value: 52
,"EBADR"               //numeric value: 53
,"EXFULL"              //numeric value: 54
,"ENOANO"              //numeric value: 55
,"EBADRQC"             //numeric value: 56
,"EBADSLT"             //numeric value: 57
,"NULL"                //numeric value: 58
,"EBFONT"              //numeric value: 59
,"ENOSTR"              //numeric value: 60
,"ENODATA"             //numeric value: 61
,"ETIME"               //numeric value: 62
,"ENOSR"               //numeric value: 63
,"ENONET"              //numeric value: 64
,"ENOPKG"              //numeric value: 65
,"EREMOTE"             //numeric value: 66
,"ENOLINK"             //numeric value: 67
,"EADV"                //numeric value: 68
,"ESRMNT"              //numeric value: 69
,"ECOMM"               //numeric value: 70
,"EPROTO"              //numeric value: 71
,"EMULTIHOP"           //numeric value: 72
,"EDOTDOT"             //numeric value: 73
,"EBADMSG"             //numeric value: 74
,"EOVERFLOW"           //numeric value: 75
,"ENOTUNIQ"            //numeric value: 76
,"EBADFD"              //numeric value: 77
,"EREMCHG"             //numeric value: 78
,"ELIBACC"             //numeric value: 79
,"ELIBBAD"             //numeric value: 80
,"ELIBSCN"             //numeric value: 81
,"ELIBMAX"             //numeric value: 82
```

```
 ,"ELIBEXEC"              //numeric value: 83
 ,"EILSEQ"                //numeric value: 84
 ,"ERESTART"              //numeric value: 85
 ,"ESTRPIPE"              //numeric value: 86
 ,"EUSERS"                //numeric value: 87
 ,"ENOTSOCK"              //numeric value: 88
 ,"EDESTADDRREQ"          //numeric value: 89
 ,"EMSGSIZE"              //numeric value: 90
 ,"EPROTOTYPE"            //numeric value: 91
 ,"ENOPROTOOPT"           //numeric value: 92
 ,"EPROTONOSUPPORT"       //numeric value: 93
 ,"ESOCKTNOSUPPORT"       //numeric value: 94
 ,"EOPNOTSUPP"            //numeric value: 95
 ,"EPFNOSUPPORT"          //numeric value: 96
 ,"EAFNOSUPPORT"          //numeric value: 97
 ,"EADDRINUSE"            //numeric value: 98
 ,"EADDRNOTAVAIL"         //numeric value: 99
 ,"ENETDOWN"              //numeric value: 100
 ,"ENETUNREACH"           //numeric value: 101
 ,"ENETRESET"             //numeric value: 102
 ,"ECONNABORTED"          //numeric value: 103
 ,"ECONNRESET"            //numeric value: 104
 ,"ENOBUFS"               //numeric value: 105
 ,"EISCONN"               //numeric value: 106
 ,"ENOTCONN"              //numeric value: 107
 ,"ESHUTDOWN"             //numeric value: 108
 ,"ETOOMANYREFS"          //numeric value: 109
 ,"ETIMEDOUT"             //numeric value: 110
 ,"ECONNREFUSED"          //numeric value: 111
 ,"EHOSTDOWN"             //numeric value: 112
 ,"EHOSTUNREACH"          //numeric value: 113
 ,"EALREADY"              //numeric value: 114
 ,"EINPROGRESS"           //numeric value: 115
 ,"ESTALE"                //numeric value: 116
 ,"EUCLEAN"               //numeric value: 117
 ,"ENOTNAM"               //numeric value: 118
 ,"ENAVAIL"               //numeric value: 119
 ,"EISNAM"                //numeric value: 120
 ,"EREMOTEIO"             //numeric value: 121
 ,"EDQUOT"                //numeric value: 122
 ,"ENOMEDIUM"             //numeric value: 123
 ,"EMEDIUMTYPE"           //numeric value: 124
 } ;

#define MAX_ERRORS (sizeof( errors )/sizeof( char * ) )

const char *syscalls[] =
{
 "NULL"
 ,"exit"                  // numeric value: 1
 ,"fork"                  // numeric value: 2
 ,"read"                  // numeric value: 3
```

```
,"write"                    // numeric value: 4
,"open"                     // numeric value: 5
,"close"                    // numeric value: 6
,"waitpid"                  // numeric value: 7
,"creat"                    // numeric value: 8
,"link"                     // numeric value: 9
,"unlink"                   // numeric value: 10
,"execve"                   // numeric value: 11
,"chdir"                    // numeric value: 12
,"time"                     // numeric value: 13
,"mknod"                    // numeric value: 14
,"chmod"                    // numeric value: 15
,"lchown"                   // numeric value: 16
,"break"                    // numeric value: 17
,"oldstat"                  // numeric value: 18
,"lseek"                    // numeric value: 19
,"getpid"                   // numeric value: 20
,"mount"                    // numeric value: 21
,"umount"                   // numeric value: 22
,"setuid"                   // numeric value: 23
,"getuid"                   // numeric value: 24
,"stime"                    // numeric value: 25
,"ptrace"                   // numeric value: 26
,"alarm"                    // numeric value: 27
,"oldfstat"                 // numeric value: 28
,"pause"                    // numeric value: 29
,"utime"                    // numeric value: 30
,"stty"                     // numeric value: 31
,"gtty"                     // numeric value: 32
,"access"                   // numeric value: 33
,"nice"                     // numeric value: 34
,"ftime"                    // numeric value: 35
,"sync"                     // numeric value: 36
,"kill"                     // numeric value: 37
,"rename"                   // numeric value: 38
,"mkdir"                    // numeric value: 39
,"rmdir"                    // numeric value: 40
,"dup"                      // numeric value: 41
,"pipe"                     // numeric value: 42
,"times"                    // numeric value: 43
,"prof"                     // numeric value: 44
,"brk"                      // numeric value: 45
,"setgid"                   // numeric value: 46
,"getgid"                   // numeric value: 47
,"signal"                   // numeric value: 48
,"geteuid"                  // numeric value: 49
,"getegid"                  // numeric value: 50
,"acct"                     // numeric value: 51
,"umount2"                  // numeric value: 52
,"lock"                     // numeric value: 53
,"ioctl"                    // numeric value: 54
,"fcntl"                    // numeric value: 55
```

```
,"mpx"                        // numeric value: 56
,"setpgid"                    // numeric value: 57
,"ulimit"                     // numeric value: 58
,"oldolduname"                // numeric value: 59
,"umask"                      // numeric value: 60
,"chroot"                     // numeric value: 61
,"ustat"                      // numeric value: 62
,"dup2"                       // numeric value: 63
,"getppid"                    // numeric value: 64
,"getpgrp"                    // numeric value: 65
,"setsid"                     // numeric value: 66
,"sigaction"                  // numeric value: 67
,"sgetmask"                   // numeric value: 68
,"ssetmask"                   // numeric value: 69
,"setreuid"                   // numeric value: 70
,"setregid"                   // numeric value: 71
,"sigsuspend"                 // numeric value: 72
,"sigpending"                 // numeric value: 73
,"sethostname"                // numeric value: 74
,"setrlimit"                  // numeric value: 75
,"getrlimit"                  // numeric value: 76
,"getrusage"                  // numeric value: 77
,"gettimeofday"               // numeric value: 78
,"settimeofday"               // numeric value: 79
,"getgroups"                  // numeric value: 80
,"setgroups"                  // numeric value: 81
,"select"                     // numeric value: 82
,"symlink"                    // numeric value: 83
,"oldlstat"                   // numeric value: 84
,"readlink"                   // numeric value: 85
,"uselib"                     // numeric value: 86
,"swapon"                     // numeric value: 87
,"reboot"                     // numeric value: 88
,"readdir"                    // numeric value: 89
,"mmap"                       // numeric value: 90
,"munmap"                     // numeric value: 91
,"truncate"                   // numeric value: 92
,"ftruncate"                  // numeric value: 93
,"fchmod"                     // numeric value: 94
,"fchown"                     // numeric value: 95
,"getpriority"                // numeric value: 96
,"setpriority"                // numeric value: 97
,"profil"                     // numeric value: 98
,"statfs"                     // numeric value: 99
,"fstatfs"                    // numeric value: 100
,"ioperm"                     // numeric value: 101
,"socketcall"                 // numeric value: 102
,"syslog"                     // numeric value: 103
,"setitimer"                  // numeric value: 104
,"getitimer"                  // numeric value: 105
,"stat"                       // numeric value: 106
,"lstat"                      // numeric value: 107
```

```
,"fstat"                    // numeric value: 108
,"olduname"                 // numeric value: 109
,"iopl"                     // numeric value: 110
,"vhangup"                  // numeric value: 111
,"idle"                     // numeric value: 112
,"vm86old"                  // numeric value: 113
,"wait4"                    // numeric value: 114
,"swapoff"                  // numeric value: 115
,"sysinfo"                  // numeric value: 116
,"ipc"                      // numeric value: 117
,"fsync"                    // numeric value: 118
,"sigreturn"                // numeric value: 119
,"clone"                    // numeric value: 120
,"setdomainname"            // numeric value: 121
,"uname"                    // numeric value: 122
,"modify_ldt"               // numeric value: 123
,"adjtimex"                 // numeric value: 124
,"mprotect"                 // numeric value: 125
,"sigprocmask"              // numeric value: 126
,"create_module"            // numeric value: 127
,"init_module"             // numeric value: 128
,"delete_module"            // numeric value: 129
,"get_kernel_syms"          // numeric value: 130
,"quotactl"                 // numeric value: 131
,"getpgid"                  // numeric value: 132
,"fchdir"                   // numeric value: 133
,"bdflush"                  // numeric value: 134
,"sysfs"                    // numeric value: 135
,"personality"             // numeric value: 136
,"afs_syscall"              // numeric value: 137
,"setfsuid"                 // numeric value: 138
,"setfsgid"                 // numeric value: 139
,"_llseek"                  // numeric value: 140
,"getdents"                 // numeric value: 141
,"_newselect"               // numeric value: 142
,"flock"                    // numeric value: 143
,"msync"                    // numeric value: 144
,"readv"                    // numeric value: 145
,"writev"                   // numeric value: 146
,"getsid"                   // numeric value: 147
,"fdatasync"                // numeric value: 148
,"_sysctl"                  // numeric value: 149
,"mlock"                    // numeric value: 150
,"munlock"                  // numeric value: 151
,"mlockall"                 // numeric value: 152
,"munlockall"               // numeric value: 153
,"sched_setparam"           // numeric value: 154
,"sched_getparam"           // numeric value: 155
,"sched_setscheduler"       // numeric value: 156
,"sched_getscheduler"       // numeric value: 157
,"sched_yield"              // numeric value: 158
,"sched_get_priority_max"   // numeric value: 159
```

```
,"sched_get_priority_min"  // numeric value: 160
,"sched_rr_get_interval"   // numeric value: 161
,"nanosleep"               // numeric value: 162
,"mremap"                  // numeric value: 163
,"setresuid"               // numeric value: 164
,"getresuid"               // numeric value: 165
,"vm86"                    // numeric value: 166
,"query_module"            // numeric value: 167
,"poll"                    // numeric value: 168
,"nfsservctl"              // numeric value: 169
,"setresgid"               // numeric value: 170
,"getresgid"               // numeric value: 171
,"prctl"                   // numeric value: 172
,"rt_sigreturn"            // numeric value: 173
,"rt_sigaction"            // numeric value: 174
,"rt_sigprocmask"          // numeric value: 175
,"rt_sigpending"           // numeric value: 176
,"rt_sigtimedwait"         // numeric value: 177
,"rt_sigqueueinfo"         // numeric value: 178
,"rt_sigsuspend"           // numeric value: 179
,"pread"                   // numeric value: 180
,"pwrite"                  // numeric value: 181
,"chown"                   // numeric value: 182
,"getcwd"                  // numeric value: 183
,"capget"                  // numeric value: 184
,"capset"                  // numeric value: 185
,"sigaltstack"             // numeric value: 186
,"sendfile"                // numeric value: 187
,"getpmsg"                 // numeric value: 188
,"putpmsg"                 // numeric value: 189
,"vfork"                   // numeric value: 190
,"ugetrlimit"              // numeric value: 191
,"mmap2"                   // numeric value: 192
,"truncate64"              // numeric value: 193
,"ftruncate64"             // numeric value: 194
,"stat64"                  // numeric value: 195
,"lstat64"                 // numeric value: 196
,"fstat64"                 // numeric value: 197
,"lchown32"                // numeric value: 198
,"getuid32"                // numeric value: 199
,"getgid32"                // numeric value: 200
,"geteuid32"               // numeric value: 201
,"getegid32"               // numeric value: 202
,"setreuid32"              // numeric value: 203
,"setregid32"              // numeric value: 204
,"getgroups32"             // numeric value: 205
,"setgroups32"             // numeric value: 206
,"fchown32"                // numeric value: 207
,"setresuid32"             // numeric value: 208
,"getresuid32"             // numeric value: 209
,"setresgid32"             // numeric value: 210
,"getresgid32"             // numeric value: 211
```

```
,"chown32"              // numeric value: 212
,"setuid32"             // numeric value: 213
,"setgid32"             // numeric value: 214
,"setfsuid32"           // numeric value: 215
,"setfsgid32"           // numeric value: 216
,"pivot_root"           // numeric value: 217
,"mincore"              // numeric value: 218
,"madvise"              // numeric value: 219
,"getdents64"           // numeric value: 220
,"fcntl64"              // numeric value: 221
,"<none>"               // numeric value: 222
,"security"             // numeric value: 223
,"gettid"               // numeric value: 224
,"readahead"            // numeric value: 225
,"setxattr"             // numeric value: 226
,"lsetxattr"            // numeric value: 227
,"fsetxattr"            // numeric value: 228
,"getxattr"             // numeric value: 229
,"lgetxattr"            // numeric value: 230
,"fgetxattr"            // numeric value: 231
,"listxattr"            // numeric value: 232
,"llistxattr"           // numeric value: 233
,"flistxattr"           // numeric value: 234
,"removexattr"          // numeric value: 235
,"lremovexattr"         // numeric value: 236
,"fremovexattr"         // numeric value: 237
,"tkill"                // numeric value: 238
,"sendfile64"           // numeric value: 239
,"futex"                // numeric value: 240
,"sched_setaffinity"    // numeric value: 241
,"sched_getaffinity"    // numeric value: 242
} ;

#define MAX_SYSCALLS (sizeof( syscalls )/sizeof( char * ) )

/*  *** eprintf ***
    * Description: general error printing function
*/

void eprintf( char const *fmt, ... )
{
  va_list ap;

  va_start(ap, fmt);

  vfprintf( stderr, fmt, ap ) ;

  va_end(ap);

}
```

```
int readString( pid_t pid, void *addr, char *string, size_t maxSize)
{
    int rc = 0 ;
    long peekWord ;
    char *peekAddr ;
    int i ;
    int stringIndex = 0 ;
    char *tmpString ;
    int stringFound = 0 ;

    string[0] = '\0' ;
    peekAddr = (char *) ((long)addr & ~(sizeof(long) - 1 ) ) ;

    // The PTRACE_PEEKDATA feature reads full words from the process'
    // address space.
    peekWord = ptrace( PTRACE_PEEKDATA, pid, peekAddr, NULL ) ;

    if ( -1 == peekWord )
    {
        perror( "ptrace( PTRACE_PEEKDATA..." ) ;
        rc = -1 ;
        goto exit ;
    }

    // Keep in mind that since peekAddr is aligned
    // it might contain a few characters at the beginning

    int charsToCopy = sizeof( long ) - ( (long)addr - long)peekAddr )
;

    tmpString = (char *)&peekWord ;
    tmpString += sizeof( long ) - charsToCopy ;

    for ( i = 0 ; i < charsToCopy ; i++ )
    {
        string[ stringIndex ] = tmpString[ i ] ;
        stringIndex++ ;
        if ( maxSize - 1 == stringIndex )
            {
                string[ stringIndex ] = '\0';
            goto exit ;
        }
    }

    tmpString = (char *)&peekWord ;
    peekAddr += sizeof( long) ;

    // Fall into a loop to find the end of the string
    do
    {
        peekWord = ptrace( PTRACE_PEEKDATA, pid, peekAddr, NULL ) ;
```

```
        if ( -1 == peekWord )
        {
            perror( "ptrace( PTRACE_PEEKDATA..." ) ;
            rc = -1 ;
            goto exit ;
        }

        for ( i = 0 ; i < sizeof(long) ; i++ )
        {
            string[ stringIndex ] = tmpString[ i ] ;

            if ( maxSize - 1 == stringIndex )
            {
                string[ stringIndex ] = '\0';
                goto exit ;
            }

            if ( string[ stringIndex ] == '\0' )
            {
                stringFound = 1 ;
                break ;
            }
            stringIndex++ ;
        }

        peekAddr += sizeof( long) ;

    } while ( !stringFound ) ;

exit:

    return rc ;
}

int spawnChildProcess( int argc, char *argv[] )
{
    int   mRC  = 0 ;      // Return code for this function
    int   sRC  = 0 ;      // Return code for system calls
    sRC = ptrace( PTRACE_TRACEME, 0, 0, 0 ) ;

    if ( -1 == sRC )
    {
        eprintf( "ptrace failed with request \"PTRACE_TRACEME\":
➡%s\n", strerror( errno ) ) ;
        sRC = errno ;
        goto exit ;
    }

    sRC = execv( argv[0], argv ) ;

    if ( -1 == sRC )
    {
```

```
          eprintf( "exec failed: %s\n", strerror( errno ) ) ;
          sRC = errno ;
          goto exit ;
      }

   exit :

   return mRC ;
}

int traceChildProcess( pid_t tracedPid )
{
   int    mRC       = 0 ;  // Return code for this function
   int    sRC       = 0 ;  // Return code for system calls
   int    status    = 0 ;  // Status of the stopped child process
   pid_t stoppedPid = 0 ;  // Process ID of stopped child process
   struct user_regs_struct registers;

   stoppedPid = waitpid( tracedPid, &status, 0 ) ;

   printf( "Child process stopped for exec\n" ) ;
   if ( -1 == stoppedPid )
   {
      eprintf( "waitpid failed: %s\n", strerror( errno ) ) ;
      mRC = 1 ;
      goto exit ;
   }

   // Tell the child to stop in a system call entry or exit
   ptrace( PTRACE_SYSCALL, stoppedPid, 0, 0 ) ;

   // This is the main tracing loop. When the child stops,
   // we examine the system call and its arguments
   while ( ( stoppedPid = waitpid( tracedPid, &status, 0 ) )
➥!= -1 )
   {
      sRC = ptrace( PTRACE_GETREGS, stoppedPid, 0, &registers ) ;
      if ( -1 == sRC )
      {
          eprintf( "ptrace failed with request PTRACE_GETREGS:
➥%s\n", strerror( errno ) ) ;
          mRC = 1 ;
          goto exit ;
      }

      if ( registers.eax == -ENOSYS )
      {
          fprintf( stderr, "%d: %s( ", stoppedPid,
➥syscalls[registers.orig_eax] ) ;
          switch( registers.orig_eax )
          {
             case __NR_open:
```

```
                {
                    // Get file name and print the "file name" argument
➥in a more fancy way
                    char fileName[1024] = "";
                    readString( stoppedPid, (void *)registers.ebx,
➥fileName, 1024 ) ;
                    fprintf( stderr, "\"%s\", %#08x, %#08x",
                        fileName, registers.ecx, registers.edx ) ;
                }
                break ;
                case __NR_exit:
                    // If the traced process is bailing, so should we
                    fprintf( stderr, "%#08x, %#08x, %#08x ) = ?\n",
                        registers.ebx, registers.ecx, registers.edx
➥) ;
                    goto exit ;
                break ;
                default:
                fprintf( stderr, "%#08x, %#08x, %#08x",
                    registers.ebx, registers.ecx, registers.edx
➥) ;
                break ;
            }
            fprintf( stderr, " ) = " ) ;
        }
        else
        {
            if ( registers.eax < 0 )
            {
                // error condition
                fprintf( stderr, "#Err: %s\n", errors[ abs(
➥registers.eax ) ] ) ;
            }
            else
            {
                // return code
                fprintf( stderr, "%#08x\n", registers.eax ) ;
            }
        }

        ptrace( PTRACE_SYSCALL, stoppedPid, 0, 0 ) ;
    }

exit :

    fclose( stdin ) ;
    fclose( stderr ) ;
    fclose( stdout ) ;

    exit( 1 ) ;

    return mRC ;
```

```
         }

         int main( int argc, char *argv[] )
         {
            int   mRC  = 0 ;       // Return code for this function
            pid_t cpid     ;       // Child process ID

            cpid = fork() ;

            if ( cpid > 0 )
            {
               // Parent
               traceChildProcess( -1 ) ;
            }
            else if ( 0 == cpid )
            {
               // Child
               spawnChildProcess( argc, &argv[1] ) ;
            }
            else
            {
               fprintf( stderr, "Could not fork child (%s)\n", strerror(
         ➥errno ) ) ;
               mRC = 1 ;
            }


            return  mRC ;
         }
```

2.6.2 The System Call Tracing Code Explained

The `spawnChildProcess()` function forks off a child process and runs ptrace with PTRACE_TRACEME to ensure that the child process will stop when entering or exiting a system call. The function then executes the process to be traced.

The `traceChildProcess()` function waits for the process to stop (presumably due to a system call entry or exit) and then gets information about the stopped process. It uses the ptrace call with PTRACE_GETREGS to get the registers for the process. In particular, it tests the EAX register to see whether the process is stopped on an entry or exit from a system call. When the traced process stops on a system call entry, the EAX register will contain -ENOSYS. The EAX normally contains the return code from the system call, and because the process stopped on a system call entry, ENOSYS is an impossible return for a system call to return (hence making it a good differentiator). For a system call exit, the EAX register will be some value that is not -ENOSYS.

When a system call is entered, the original EAX will contain the system call number. When a system call is identified, the system call calling convention provides information about the arguments to the system call as shown in the following code snippet:

```
char fileName[1024] = "";
readString( stoppedPid, (void *)registers.ebx, fileName, 1024 ) ;
fprintf( stderr, "\"%s\"", %#08x, %#08x",
         fileName, registers.ecx, registers.edx ) ;
```

The `readString` function reads in a single string at a particular address space in the stopped process. For the `open` system call, the code reads the first argument at the address stored in EBX. This is the file name for the `open` system call.

This is how strace prints symbolic information for a system call. For every system call, there is an opportunity to print the symbolic information that is more descriptive than the numeric values in the registers.

If the EAX contains a value that is not minus ENOSYS, then the process is presumed to be stopped at the exit of a system call. A positive value in EAX means a successful completion of the system call, and the return code would contain the successful return code of the system call. If the return code is negative, it is assumed to be an error, and an error is printed in the strace output.

The main loop in `traceChildProcess()` continues until the traced process exits for some reason:

```
while ( ( stoppedPid = waitpid( tracedPid, &status, 0 ) ) != -1 )
```

It continuously waits for the traced process to stop and then prints the information for the system call entry and exit. Most of the source code is used for formatting of the information.

2.7 CONCLUSION

As shown throughout this chapter, strace is one of the most useful problem determination tools for Linux. It can quickly diagnose many types of problems, and in many cases, it can help narrow down the scope of a problem with little effort. The next chapter covers the /proc file system, which is also very useful for problem determination.

CHAPTER **3**

The /proc Filesystem

3.1 INTRODUCTION

One of the big reasons why Linux is so popular today is the fact that it combines many of the best features from its UNIX ancestors. One of these features is the /proc filesystem, which it inherited from System V and is a standard part of all kernels included with all of the major distributions. Some distributions provide certain things in /proc that others don't, so there is no one standard /proc specification; therefore, it should be used with a degree of caution.

The /proc filesystem is one of the most important mechanisms that Linux provides for examining and configuring the inner workings of the operating system. It can be thought of as a window directly into the kernel's data structures and the kernel's view of the user processes running on the system. It appears to the user as a filesystem just like / or /home, so all the common file manipulation programs and system calls can be used with it such as cat(1), more(1), grep(1), open(2), read(2), and write(2)[1]. If permissions are sufficient, writing values to certain files is also easily performed by redirecting output to a file with the > shell character from a shell prompt or by calling the system call write(2) within an application.

The goal of this chapter is not to be an exhaustive reference of the /proc filesystem, as that would be an entire publication in itself. Instead the goal is to point out and examine some of the more advanced features and tricks primarily related to problem determination and system diagnosis. For more general reference, I recommend reading the proc(5) man page.

> **Note:** If you have the kernel sources installed on your system, I also recommend reading /usr/src/linux/Documentation/filesystems/procfs.txt.

[1] When Linux operation names are appended with a number in parentheses, the number directly refers to a man page section number. Section 1 is for executable programs or shell commands, and section 2 is for system calls (functions provided by the kernel). Typing man 2 read will view the read system call man page from section 2.

3.2 PROCESS INFORMATION

Along with viewing and manipulating system information, obtaining user process information is another way in which the /proc filesystem shines. When you look at the listing of files in /proc, you will immediately notice a large number of directories identified by a number. These numbers represent process IDs and contain more detailed information on that process ID within it. All Linux systems will have the /proc/1 directory. The process with ID 1 is always the "init" process and is the first user process to be started on the system during bootup. Even though this is a special program, it is a process just like any other, and the /proc/1 directory will contain the same information as any other process including the ls command you use to see the contents of this and any other directory! The following sections will go into more detail on the most useful information that can be found in the /proc/<pid>[2] directory such as viewing and understanding a process' address space, viewing CPU and memory configuration information, and understanding settings that can greatly enhance application and system troubleshooting.

3.2.1 /proc/self

As a quick introduction into how processes are represented in the /proc filesystem, let's first look at the special link "/proc/self." The kernel provides this as a link to the currently executing process. Typing "cd /proc/self" will take you directly into the directory containing the process information for your shell process. This is because cd is a function provided by the shell (the currently running process at the time of using the "self" link) and not an external program. If you perform an ls -l /proc/self, you will see a link to the process directory for the ls process, which goes away as soon as the directory listing completes and the shell prompt returns. The following sequence of commands and their associated output illustrate this.

Note: $$ is a special shell environment variable that stores the shell's process ID, and "/proc/<pid>/cwd" is a special link provided by the kernel that is an absolute link to the current working directory.

---

[2] A common way of generalizing a process' directory name under the /proc filesystem is to use /proc/<pid> considering a process' number is random with the exception of the init process.

```
penguin> echo $$
2602
penguin> ls -l /proc/self
lrwxrwxrwx  1 root    root    64 2003-10-13 08:04 /proc/self -> 2945
penguin> cd /proc/self
penguin> ls -l cwd
lrwxrwxrwx  1 dbehman  build   0 2003-10-13 13:00 cwd -> /proc/2602
penguin>
```

The main thing to understand in this example is that 2945 is the process ID of the ls command. The reason for this is that the /proc/self link, just as all files in /proc, is dynamic and will change to reflect the current state at any point in time. The cwd link matches the same process ID as our shell process because we first used "cd" to get into the /proc/self directory.

3.2.2 /proc/<pid> in More Detail

With the understanding that typing "cd /proc/self" will change the directory to the current shell's /proc directory, let's examine the contents of this directory further. The commands and output are as follows:

```
penguin> cd /proc/self
penguin> ls -l
total 0
-r--r--r--    1 dbehman  build  0 2003-10-13 13:34   cmdline
lrwxrwxrwx    1 dbehman  build  0 2003-10-13 13:34 cwd -> /proc/2602
-r--------    1 dbehman  build  0 2003-10-13 13:34 environ
lrwxrwxrwx    1 dbehman  build  0 2003-10-13 13:34 exe-> /bin/bash
dr-x------    2 dbehman  build  0 2003-10-13 13:34 fd
-rw-------    1 dbehman  build  0 2003-10-13 13:34 mapped_base
-r--r--r--    1 dbehman  build  0 2003-10-13 13:34 maps
-rw-------    1 dbehman  build  0 2003-10-13 13:34 mem
-r--r--r--    1 dbehman  build  0 2003-10-13 13:34 mounts
lrwxrwxrwx    1 dbehman  build  0 2003-10-13 13:34 root -> /
-r--r--r--    1 dbehman  build  0 2003-10-13 13:34 stat
-r--r--r--    1 dbehman  build  0 2003-10-13 13:34 statm
-r--r--r--    1 dbehman  build  0 2003-10-13 13:34 status
```

Notice how the sizes of all the files are 0, yet when we start examining some of them more closely it's clear that they do in fact contain information. The reason for the 0 size is because these files are basically a window directly into the kernel's data structures and therefore are not really files; rather they are very special types of files. When filesystem operations are performed on files within the /proc filesystem, the kernel recognizes what is being requested by the user and dynamically returns the data to the calling process just as if it were being read from the disk.

3.2.2.1 /proc/<pid>/maps The "maps" file provides a view of the process'
memory address space. Every process has its own address space that is handled
and provided by the Virtual Memory Manager. The name "maps" is derived
from the fact that each line represents a mapping of some part of the process
to a particular region of the address space. For this discussion, we'll focus on
the 32-bit x86 hardware. However, 64-bit hardware is becoming more and more
important, especially when using Linux, so we'll discuss the differences with
Linux running on x86_64 at the end of this section.

Figure 3.1 shows a sample maps file which we will analyze in subsequent
sections.

```
08048000-080b6000 r-xp 00000000 03:08 10667   /bin/bash
080b6000-080b9000 rw-p 0006e000 03:08 10667   /bin/bash
080b9000-08101000 rwxp 00000000 00:00 0
40000000-40018000 r-xp 00000000 03:08 6664    /lib/ld-2.3.2.so
40018000-40019000 rw-p 00017000 03:08 6664    /lib/ld-2.3.2.so
40019000-4001a000 rw-p 00000000 00:00 0
4001a000-4001b000 r--p 00000000 03:08 8598    /usr/lib/locale/
➥en_US/LC_IDENTIFICATION
4001b000-4001c000 r--p 00000000 03:08 9920    /usr/lib/locale/
➥en_US/LC_MEASUREMENT
4001c000-4001d000 r--p 00000000 03:08 9917    /usr/lib/locale/
➥en_US/LC_TELEPHONE
4001d000-4001e000 r--p 00000000 03:08 9921    /usr/lib/locale/
➥en_US/LC_ADDRESS
4001e000-4001f000 r--p 00000000 03:08 9918    /usr/lib/locale/
➥en_US/  LC_NAME
4001f000-40020000 r--p 00000000 03:08 9939    /usr/lib/locale/
➥en_US/LC_PAPER
40020000-40021000 r--p 00000000 03:08 9953       /usr/lib/
➥locale/en_US/LC_MESSAGES/SYS_LC_MESSAGES
40021000-40022000 r--p 00000000 03:08 9919    /usr/lib/locale/
➥en_US/LC_MONETARY
40022000-40028000 r--p 00000000 03:08 10057   /usr/lib/locale/
➥en_US/LC_COLLATE
40028000-40050000 r-xp 00000000 03:08 10434   /lib/
➥libreadline.so.4.3
40050000-40054000 rw-p 00028000 03:08 10434   /lib/
➥libreadline.so.4.3
40054000-40055000 rw-p 00000000 00:00 0
40055000-4005b000 r-xp 00000000 03:08 10432   /lib/
➥libhistory.so.4.3
4005b000-4005c000 rw-p 00005000 03:08 10432   /lib/
➥libhistory.so.4.3
4005c000-40096000 r-xp 00000000 03:08 6788    /lib/
➥libncurses.so.5.3
40096000-400a1000 rw-p 00039000 03:08 6788    /lib/
➥libncurses.so.5.3
```

```
400a1000-400a2000 rw-p 00000000 00:00 0
400a2000-400a4000 r-xp 00000000 03:08 6673      /lib/libdl.so.2
400a4000-400a5000 rw-p 00002000 03:08 6673      /lib/libdl.so.2
400a5000-401d1000 r-xp 00000000 03:08 6661      /lib/i686/
➥libc.so.6
401d1000-401d6000 rw-p 0012c000 03:08 6661      /lib/i686/
➥libc.so.6
401d6000-401d9000 rw-p 00000000 00:00 0
401d9000-401da000 r--p 00000000 03:08 8600      /usr/lib/locale/
➥en_US/LC_TIME
401da000-401db000 r--p 00000000 03:08 9952      /usr/lib/locale/
➥en_US/LC_NUMERIC
401db000-40207000 r--p 00000000 03:08 10056     /usr/lib/locale/
➥en_US/LC_CTYPE
40207000-4020d000 r--s 00000000 03:08 8051      /usr/lib/gconv/
➥gconv-modules.cache
4020d000-4020f000 r-xp 00000000 03:08 8002      /usr/lib/gconv/
➥ISO8859-1.so
4020f000-40210000 rw-p 00001000 03:08 8002      /usr/lib/gconv/
➥ISO8859-1.so
40210000-40212000 rw-p 00000000 00:00 0
bfffa000-c0000000 rwxp ffffb000 00:00 0
```

Fig. 3.1 A /proc/<pid>/ maps file.

The first thing that should stand out is the name of the executable /bin/bash. This makes sense because the commands used to obtain this maps file were "cd /proc/self ; cat maps." Try doing "less /proc/self/maps" and note how it differs.

Let's look at what each column means. Looking at the first line in the output just listed as an example we know from the proc(5) man page that 08048000-080b6000 is the address space in the process occupied by this entry; the r-xp indicates that this mapping is readable, executable, and private; the 00000000 is the offset into the file; 03:08 is the device (major:minor); 10667 is the inode; and /bin/bash is the pathname. But what does all this really mean?

It means that /bin/bash, which is inode 10667 ("stat /bin/bash" to confirm) on partition 8 of device 03 (examine /proc/devices and /proc/partitions for number to name mappings), had the readable and executable sections of itself mapped into the address range of 0x08048000 to 0x080b6000.

Now let's examine what each individual line means. Because the output is the address mappings of the /bin/bash executable, the first thing to point out is where the program itself lives in the address space. On 32-bit x86-based architectures, the first address to which any part of the executable gets mapped is 0x08048000. This address will become very familiar the more you look at maps files. It will appear in every maps file and will always be this address unless someone went to great lengths to change it. Because of Linux's open source nature, this is possible but very unlikely. The next thing that becomes obvious is that the first two lines are very similar, and the third line's address mapping follows immediately after the second line. This is because all three lines combined contain all the information associated with the executable / bin/bash.

Generally speaking, each of the three lines is considered a *segment* and can be named the *code segment*, *data segment*, and *heap segment* respectively. Let's dissect each segment along with its associated line in the maps file.

3.2.2.1.1 Code Segment The code segment is also very often referred to as the *text* segment. As will be discussed further in Chapter 9, "ELF: Executable and Linking Format," the *.text* section is contained within this segment and is the section that contains all the executable code.

> **Note:** If you've ever seen the error message *text file busy* (ETXTBSY) when trying to delete or write to an executable program that you know to be binary and not ASCII text, the meaning of the error message stems from the fact that executable code is stored in the *.text* section

---

Using /bin/bash as our example, the code segment taken from the maps file in Figure 3.1 is represented by this line:

```
08048000-080b6000 r-xp 00000000 03:08 10667    /bin/bash
```

This segment contains the program's executable instructions. This fact is confirmed by the r-xp in the permissions column. Linux does not support self modifying code, therefore there is no write permission, and since the code is actually executed, the execute permission is set. To give a hands-on practical example of demonstrating what this really means, consider the following code:

```
#include <stdio.h>

int main( void )
{
   printf( "Address of function main is 0x%x\n", &main );
   printf( "Sleeping infinitely; my pid is %d\n", getpid() );

   while( 1 )
   sleep( 5 );

   return 0;
}
```

Compiling and running this code will give this output:

```
Address of function main is 0x804839c
Sleeping infinitely; my pid is 4059
```

While the program is sleeping, examining /proc/4059/maps gives the following maps file:

```
08048000-08049000 r-xp 00000000 03:08 130198 /home/dbehman/testing/c
08049000-0804a000 rw-p 00000000 03:08 130198 /home/dbehman/testing/c
40000000-40018000 r-xp 00000000 03:08 6664   /lib/ld-2.3.2.so
40018000-40019000 rw-p 00017000 03:08 6664   /lib/ld-2.3.2.so
40019000-4001b000 rw-p 00000000 00:00 0
40028000-40154000 r-xp 00000000 03:08 6661   /lib/i686/libc.so.6
40154000-40159000 rw-p 0012c000 03:08 6661   /lib/i686/libc.so.6
40159000-4015b000 rw-p 00000000 00:00 0
bfffe000-c0000000 rwxp fffff000 00:00 0
```

Looking at the code segment's address mapping of 08048000 - 08049000 we see that main's address of 0x804839c does indeed fall within this range. This is an important observation to understand when debugging programs especially when using a debugger such as GDB. The reason for this is because when looking at various addresses in a debugging session, knowing roughly what they are can often help to put the puzzle pieces together much more quickly.

3.2.2.1.2 Data Segment For quick reference, the data segment of /bin/bash is represented by line two in Figure 3.1:

```
080b6000-080b9000 rw-p 0006e000 03:08 10667   /bin/bash
```

At first glance it appears to be very similar to the code segment line but in fact is quite different. The primary differences are the address mapping and the permissions setting of rw-p which means read-write, non-executable, and private. Logically speaking, a program consists mostly of instructions and variables. We now know that the instructions are in the code segment, which is read-only and executable. Because variables can certainly change throughout the execution of a program and are not considered to be executable, it makes perfect sense that they belong in the data segment. It is important to know that only certain kinds of variables exist in this segment, however. How and where they are declared in the program's source code will dictate what segment and section they appear in the process' address space. Variables that exist in the data segment are initialized global variables. The following program demonstrates this.

```
#include <stdio.h>

int global_var = 3;

int main( void )
{
   printf( "Address of global_var is 0x%x\n", &global_var );
   printf( "Sleeping infinitely; my pid is %d\n", getpid() );

           while( 1 )
           sleep( 5 );

   return 0;
}
```

Compiling and running this program produces the following output:

```
Address of global_var is 0x8049570
Sleeping infinitely; my pid is 4472
```

While this program sleeps, examining /proc/4472/maps shows the following:

```
08048000-08049000 r-xp 00000000 03:08 130200   /home/dbehman/
➥testing/d
08049000-0804a000 rw-p 00000000 03:08 130200   /home/dbehman/
➥testing/d
40000000-40018000 r-xp 00000000 03:08 6664     /lib/ld-2.3.2.so
40018000-40019000 rw-p 00017000 03:08 6664     /lib/ld-2.3.2.so
40019000-4001b000 rw-p 00000000 00:00 0
40028000-40154000 r-xp 00000000 03:08 6661     /lib/i686/libc.so.6
40154000-40159000 rw-p 0012c000 03:08 6661     /lib/i686/libc.so.6
40159000-4015b000 rw-p 00000000 00:00 0
bfffe000-c0000000 rwxp fffff000 00:00 0
```

We see that the address of the global variable does indeed fall within the data segment address mapping range of 0x08049000 - 080804a000. Two other very common types of variables are stack and heap variables. Stack variables will be discussed in the Stack Section further below, and heap variables will be discussed next.

3.2.2.1.3 Heap Segment As the name implies, this segment holds a program's heap variables. *Heap variables* are those that have their memory dynamically allocated via programming APIs such as malloc() and new(). Both of these APIs call the brk() system call to extend the end of the segment to accommodate the memory requested. This segment also contains the *bss section*, which is a special section that contains uninitialized global variables. The reason why a separate section to the *data section* is used for these types of variables is because space can be saved in the file's on-disk image because no value needs to be stored in association with the variable. This is also why the *bss segment* is located at the end of the executable's mappings — space is only allocated in memory when these variables get mapped. The following program demonstrates how variable declarations in source code correspond to the heap segment.

```
#include <stdio.h>

int g_bssVar;

int main( void )
{
   char *pHeapVar = NULL;
   char szSysCmd[128];

   sprintf( sysCmd, "cat /proc/%d/maps", getpid() );

   printf( "Address of bss_var is 0x%x\n", &bss_var );
   printf( "sbrk( 0 ) value before malloc is 0x%x\n", sbrk( 0 ));
   printf( "My maps file before the malloc call is:\n" );
   system( sysCmd );

   printf( "Calling malloc to get 1024 bytes for heap_var\n" );
         heap_var = (char*)malloc( 1024 );

   printf( "Address of heap_var after malloc is 0x%x\n",
         heap_var );

   printf( "sbrk( 0 ) value after malloc is 0x%x\n", sbrk( 0 ));
   printf( "My maps file after the malloc call is:\n" );
   system( sysCmd );

   return 0;
}
```

> **Note:** Notice the unusual variable naming convention used. This is taken from what's called "Hungarian Notation," which is used to embed indications of the type and scope of the variable in the name itself. For example, sz means NULL terminated string, p means pointer, and g_ means global in scope.

Compiling and running this program produces the following output:

```
penguin> ./heapseg
Address of g_bssVar is 0x8049944
sbrk( 0 ) value before malloc is 0x8049948
My maps file before the malloc call is:
08048000-08049000 r-xp 00000000 03:08 130260 /home/dbehman/book/src/
➥heapseg
```

```
08049000-0804a000 rw-p 00000000 03:08 130260 /home/dbehman/book/src/
➥heapseg
40000000-40018000 r-xp 00000000 03:08 6664    /lib/ld-2.3.2.so
40018000-40019000 rw-p 00017000 03:08 6664    /lib/ld-2.3.2.so
40019000-4001b000 rw-p 00000000 00:00 0
40028000-40154000 r-xp 00000000 03:08 6661    /lib/i686/libc.so.6
40154000-40159000 rw-p 0012c000 03:08 6661    /lib/i686/libc.so.6
40159000-4015b000 rw-p 00000000 00:00 0
bfffe000-c0000000 rwxp fffff000 00:00 0
Calling malloc to get 1024 bytes for pHeapVar
Address of pHeapVar after malloc is 0x8049998
sbrk( 0 ) value after malloc is 0x806b000
My maps file after the malloc call is:
08048000-08049000 r-xp 00000000 03:08 130260 /home/dbehman/book/src/
➥heapseg
08049000-0804a000 rw-p 00000000 03:08 130260 /home/dbehman/book/src/
➥heapseg
0804a000-0806b000 rwxp 00000000 00:00 0
40000000-40018000 r-xp 00000000 03:08 6664    /lib/ld-2.3.2.so
40018000-40019000 rw-p 00017000 03:08 6664    /lib/ld-2.3.2.so
40019000-4001b000 rw-p 00000000 00:00 0
40028000-40154000 r-xp 00000000 03:08 6661    /lib/i686/libc.so.6
40154000-40159000 rw-p 0012c000 03:08 6661    /lib/i686/libc.so.6
40159000-4015b000 rw-p 00000000 00:00 0
bfffe000-c0000000 rwxp fffff000 00:00 0
```

When examining this output, it may seem that a contradiction exists as to where the bss section actually exists. I've written that it exists in the heap segment, but the preceding output shows that the address of the bss variable lives in data segment (that is, 0x8049948 lies within the address range 0x08049000-0x0804a000). The reason for this is that there is unused space at the end of the data segment, due to the small size of the example and the small number of global variables declared, so the bss segment appears in the data segment to limit wasted space. This fact in no way changes its properties.

Note: As will be discussed in Chapter 9, the curious reader can verify that g_bssVar's address of 0x08049944 is in fact in the .bss section by examining readelf - e <exe_name> output and searching for where the .bss section begins. In our example, the .bss section header is at 0x08049940.

Also done to limit wasted space in this example, the brk pointer (determined by calling sbrk with a parameter of 0) appears in the data segment when we would expect to see it in the heap segment. The moral of this example is that the three separate entries in the maps files for the exe do not necessarily correspond to hard segment ranges; rather they are more of a soft guide.

The next important thing to note from this output is that before the `malloc` call, the `heapseg` executable only had two entries in the maps file. This meant that there was no heap at that particular point in time. After the `malloc` call, we now see the third line, which represents the heap segment. Next we see that after the `malloc` call, the brk pointer is now pointing to the end of the range reported in the maps file, `0x0806b000`. Now you may be a bit confused because the brk pointer moved from `0x08049948` to `0x0806b000` which is a total of 136888 bytes. This is an awful lot more than the 1024 that we requested, so what happened? `Malloc` is smart enough to know that it's quite likely that more heap memory will be required by the program in the future so rather than continuously calling the expensive `brk()` system call to move the pointer for every `malloc` call, it asks for a much larger chunk of memory than immediately needed. This way, when `malloc` is called again to get a relatively small chunk of memory, `brk()` need not be called again, and `malloc` can just return some of this extra memory. Doing this provides a huge performance boost, especially if the program requests many small chunks of memory via `malloc` calls.

3.2.2.1.4 Mapped Base / Shared Libraries Continuing our examination of the maps file, the next point of interest is what's commonly referred to as the *mapped base address*, which defines where the shared libraries for an executable get loaded. In standard kernel source code (as downloaded from `kernel.org`), the mapped base address is a hardcoded location defined as TASK_UNMAPPED_BASE in each architecture's processor.h header file. For example, in the 2.6.0 kernel source code, the file, include/asm-i386/processor.h, contains the definition:

```
/* This decides where the kernel will search for a free chunk of vm
 * space during mmap's.
 */
#define TASK_UNMAPPED_BASE    (PAGE_ALIGN(TASK_SIZE / 3))
```

Resolving the definitions of PAGE_ALIGN and TASK_SIZE, this equates to `0x40000000`. Note that some distributions such as SuSE include a patch that allows this value to be dynamically modified. See the discussion on the /proc/<pid>/mapped_base file in this chapter. Continuing our examination of the mapped base, let's look at the maps file for bash again:

```
08048000-080b6000 r-xp 00000000 03:08 10667    /bin/bash
080b6000-080b9000 rw-p 0006e000 03:08 10667    /bin/bash
080b9000-08101000 rwxp 00000000 00:00 0
40000000-40018000 r-xp 00000000 03:08 6664     /lib/ld-2.3.2.so
40018000-40019000 rw-p 00017000 03:08 6664     /lib/ld-2.3.2.so
40019000-4001a000 rw-p 00000000 00:00 0
```

```
4001a000-4001b000 r--p 00000000 03:08 8598    /usr/lib/locale/
➥en_US/LC_IDENTIFICATION
4001b000-4001c000 r--p 00000000 03:08 9920    /usr/lib/locale/
➥en_US/LC_MEASUREMENT
4001c000-4001d000 r--p 00000000 03:08 9917    /usr/lib/locale/
➥en_US/LC_TELEPHONE
4001d000-4001e000 r--p 00000000 03:08 9921    /usr/lib/locale/
➥en_US/LC_ADDRESS
4001e000-4001f000 r--p 00000000 03:08 9918    /usr/lib/locale/
➥en_US/LC_NAME
4001f000-40020000 r--p 00000000 03:08 9939    /usr/lib/locale/
➥en_US/LC_PAPER
40020000-40021000 r--p 00000000 03:08 9953     /usr/lib/
➥locale/en_US/LC_MESSAGES/SYS_LC_MESSAGES
40021000-40022000 r--p 00000000 03:08 9919    /usr/lib/locale/
➥en_US/LC_MONETARY
40022000-40028000 r--p 00000000 03:08 10057   /usr/lib/locale/
➥en_US/LC_COLLATE
40028000-40050000 r-xp 00000000 03:08 10434   /lib/
➥libreadline.so.4.3
40050000-40054000 rw-p 00028000 03:08 10434   /lib/
➥libreadline.so.4.3
40054000-40055000 rw-p 00000000 00:00 0
40055000-4005b000 r-xp 00000000 03:08 10432   /lib/
➥libhistory.so.4.3
4005b000-4005c000 rw-p 00005000 03:08 10432   /lib/
➥libhistory.so.4.3
4005c000-40096000 r-xp 00000000 03:08 6788    /lib/
➥libncurses.so.5.3
40096000-400a1000 rw-p 00039000 03:08 6788    /lib/
➥libncurses.so.5.3
400a1000-400a2000 rw-p 00000000 00:00 0
400a2000-400a4000 r-xp 00000000 03:08 6673    /lib/libdl.so.2
400a4000-400a5000 rw-p 00002000 03:08 6673    /lib/libdl.so.2
400a5000-401d1000 r-xp 00000000 03:08 6661    /lib/i686/
➥libc.so.6
401d1000-401d6000 rw-p 0012c000 03:08 6661    /lib/i686/
➥libc.so.6
401d6000-401d9000 rw-p 00000000 00:00 0
401d9000-401da000 r--p 00000000 03:08 8600    /usr/lib/locale/
➥en_US/LC_TIME
401da000-401db000 r--p 00000000 03:08 9952    /usr/lib/locale/
➥en_US/LC_NUMERIC
401db000-40207000 r--p 00000000 03:08 10056   /usr/lib/locale/
➥en_US/LC_CTYPE
40207000-4020d000 r--s 00000000 03:08 8051    /usr/lib/gconv/
➥gconv-modules.cache
4020d000-4020f000 r-xp 00000000 03:08 8002    /usr/lib/gconv/
➥ISO8859-1.so
4020f000-40210000 rw-p 00001000 03:08 8002    /usr/lib/gconv/
➥ISO8859-1.so
40210000-40212000 rw-p 00000000 00:00 0
bffffa000-c0000000 rwxp ffffb000 00:00 0
```

Note the line:

```
40000000-40018000 r-xp 00000000 03:08 6664    /lib/ld-2.3.2.so
```

This shows us that /lib/ld-2.3.2.so was the first shared library to be loaded when this process began. /lib/ld-2.3.2.so is the linker itself, so this makes perfect sense and in fact is the case in all executables that dynamically link in shared libraries. Basically what happens is that when creating an executable that will link in one or more shared libraries, the linker is implicitly linked into the executable as well. Because the linker is responsible for resolving all external symbols in the linked shared libraries, it must be mapped into memory first, which is why it will always be the first shared library to show up in the maps file.

After the linker, all shared libraries that an executable depends upon will appear in the maps file. You can check to see what an executable needs without running it and looking at the maps file by running the ldd command as shown here:

```
penguin> ldd /bin/bash
    libreadline.so.4 => /lib/libreadline.so.4 (0x40028000)
    libhistory.so.4 => /lib/libhistory.so.4 (0x40055000)
    libncurses.so.5 => /lib/libncurses.so.5 (0x4005c000)
    libdl.so.2 => /lib/libdl.so.2 (0x400a2000)
    libc.so.6 => /lib/i686/libc.so.6 (0x400a5000)
    /lib/ld-linux.so.2 => /lib/ld-linux.so.2 (0x40000000)
```

You can now correlate the list of libraries and their addresses to Figure 3.1 and see what they look like in the maps file.

Note: ldd is actually a script that does many things, but the main thing it does is it sets the LD_TRACE_LOADED_OBJECTS environment variable to non-NULL. Try the following sequence of commands and see what happens:

```
export LD_TRACE_LOADED_OBJECTS=1
less
```

Note: Be sure to do an unset LD_TRACE_LOADED_OBJECTS to return things to normal.

But what about all those extra LC_ lines in the maps file in Figure 3.1? As the full path indicates, they are all special mappings used by libc's locale functionality. The glibc library call, setlocale(3), prepares the executable for localization functionality based on the parameters passed to the call. Compiling and running the following source will demonstrate this.

```
#include <stdio.h>
#include <locale.h>

  int main( void )
{
  char szCommand[64];

  setlocale( LC_ALL, "en_US" );

  sprintf( szCommand, "cat /proc/%d/maps", getpid() );

  system( szCommand );

  return 0;
}
```

Running the program produces the following output:

```
08048000-08049000 r-xp 00000000 03:08 206928 /home/dbehman/book/src/
➥1
08049000-0804a000 rw-p 00000000 03:08 206928 /home/dbehman/book/src/
➥1
0804a000-0806b000 rwxp 00000000 00:00 0
40000000-40018000 r-xp 00000000 03:08 6664   /lib/ld-2.3.2.so
40018000-40019000 rw-p 00017000 03:08 6664   /lib/ld-2.3.2.so
40019000-4001a000 rw-p 00000000 00:00 0
4001a000-4001b000 r--p 00000000 03:08 8598   /usr/lib/locale/en_US/
➥LC_IDENTIFICATION
4001b000-4001c000 r--p 00000000 03:08 9920   /usr/lib/locale/en_US/
➥LC_MEASUREMENT
4001c000-4001d000 r--p 00000000 03:08 9917   /usr/lib/locale/en_US/
➥LC_TELEPHONE
4001d000-4001e000 r--p 00000000 03:08 9921   /usr/lib/locale/en_US/
➥LC_ADDRESS
4001e000-4001f000 r--p 00000000 03:08 9918   /usr/lib/locale/en_US/
➥LC_NAME
4001f000-40020000 r--p 00000000 03:08 9939   /usr/lib/locale/en_US/
➥LC_PAPER
40020000-40021000 r--p 00000000 03:08 9953   /usr/lib/locale/en_US/
➥LC_MESSAGES/SYS_LC_MESSAGES
40021000-40022000 r--p 00000000 03:08 9919   /usr/lib/locale/en_US/
➥LC_MONETARY
40022000-40028000 r--p 00000000 03:08 10057  /usr/lib/locale/en_US/
➥LC_COLLATE
```

```
40028000-40154000 r-xp 00000000 03:08 6661  /lib/i686/libc.so.6
40154000-40159000 rw-p 0012c000 03:08 6661  /lib/i686/libc.so.6
40159000-4015b000 rw-p 00000000 00:00 0
4015b000-4015c000 r--p 00000000 03:08 8600  /usr/lib/locale/en_US/
➥LC_TIME
4015c000-4015d000 r--p 00000000 03:08 9952  /usr/lib/locale/en_US/
➥LC_NUMERIC
4015d000-40189000 r--p 00000000 03:08 10056 /usr/lib/locale/en_US/
➥LC_CTYPE
bfffe000-c0000000 rwxp fffff000 00:00 0
```

The LC_* mappings here are identical to the mappings in Figure 3.1.

3.2.2.1.5 Stack Segment   The final segment in the maps output is the stack segment. The stack is where local variables for all functions are stored. Function parameters are also stored on the stack. The stack is very aptly named as data is "push"ed onto it and "pop"ed from it just as in the fundamental data structure. Understanding how the stack works is key to diagnosing and debugging many tricky problems, so it's recommended that Chapter 5, "The Stack," be referred to. In the context of the maps file, it is important to understand that the stack will grow toward the heap segment. It is commonly said that on x86 hardware, the stack grows "downward." This can be confusing when visualizing the maps file. All it really means is that as data is added to the stack, the locations (addresses) of the data become smaller. This fact is demonstrated with the following program:

```c
#include <stdio.h>

int main( void )
{
    int stackVar1 = 1;
    int stackVar2 = 2;
    char szCommand[64];

    printf( "Address of stackVar1 is 0x%x\n\n", &stackVar1 );
    printf( "Address of stackVar2 is 0x%x\n\n", &stackVar2 );

    sprintf( szCommand, "cat /proc/%d/maps", getpid() );

    system( szCommand );

    return 0;
}
```

Compiling and running this program produces the following output:

```
Address of stackVar1 is 0xbffff2ec

Address of stackVar2 is 0xbffff2e8

08048000-08049000 r-xp 00000000 03:08 206930   /home/dbehman/book/
➡src/stack
08049000-0804a000 rw-p 00000000 03:08 206930   /home/dbehman/book/
➡src/stack
40000000-40018000 r-xp 00000000 03:08 6664      /lib/ld-2.3.2.so
40018000-40019000 rw-p 00017000 03:08 6664      /lib/ld-2.3.2.so
40019000-4001b000 rw-p 00000000 00:00 0
40028000-40154000 r-xp 00000000 03:08 6661      /lib/i686/libc.so.6
40154000-40159000 rw-p 0012c000 03:08 6661      /lib/i686/libc.so.6
40159000-4015b000 rw-p 00000000 00:00 0
bfffe000-c0000000 rwxp fffff000 00:00 0
```

As you can see, the first stack variable's address is higher than the second one
by four bytes, which is the size of an int.

So if stackVar1 is the first stack variable and its address is 0xbffff2ec,
then what is in the address space above it (at higher addresses closer to
0xc0000000)? The answer is that the kernel stores information such as the
environment, the argument count, and the argument vector for the program.
As has been alluded to previously, the linker plays a very important role in the
execution of a program. It also runs through several routines, and some of its
information is stored at the beginning of the stack as well.

3.2.2.1.6 The Kernel Segment The only remaining segment in a process'
address space to discuss is the kernel segment. The kernel segment starts at
0xc0000000 and is inaccessible by user processes. Every process contains this
segment, which makes transferring data between the kernel and the process'
virtual memory quick and easy. The details of this segment's contents, however,
are beyond the scope of this book.

Note: You may have realized that this segment accounts for one
quarter of the entire address space for a process. This is called *3/1 split
address space*. Losing 1GB out of 4GB isn't a big deal for the average
user, but for high-end applications such as database managers or Web
servers, this can become an issue. The real solution is to move to a 64-bit
platform where the address space is not limited to 4GB, but due to the
large amount of existing 32-bit x86 hardware, it is advantageous to
address this issue. There is a patch known as the 4G/4G patch, which can
be found at ftp.kernel.org/pub/linux/kernel/people/akpm/patches/ or
http://people.redhat.com/mingo/4g-patches. This patch moves the 1GB
kernel segment out of each process' address space, thus providing the
entire 4GB address space to applications.

3.2.2.1.7 64-bit /proc/<pid>/maps Differences 32-bit systems are limited
to 2^{32}-1 = 4GB total addressable memory. In other words, `0xffffffff` is the
largest address that a process on a 32-bit system can handle. 64-bit computing
raises this limit to 2^{64}-1 = 16 EB (1 EB = 1,000,000 TB), which is currently only
a theoretical limit. Because of this, the typical locations for the various segments
in a 32-bit program do not make sense in a 64-bit address space. Following is
the maps file for /bin/bash on an AMD64 Opteron machine. Note that due to
the length of each line, word-wrapping is unavoidable. Using the 32-bit maps
file as a guide, it should be clear what the lines really look like.

```
0000000000400000-0000000000475000 r-xp 0000000000000000 08:07 10810
➥/bin/bash
0000000000575000-0000000000587000 rw-p 0000000000075000 08:07 10810
➥/bin/bash
0000000000587000-0000000000613000 rwxp 0000000000000000 00:00 0
0000002a95556000-0000002a9556b000 r-xp 0000000000000000 08:07 6820
➥/lib64/ld-2.3.2.so
0000002a9556b000-0000002a9556c000 rw-p 0000000000000000 00:00 0
0000002a9556c000-0000002a9556d000 r--p 0000000000000000 08:07 8050
➥/usr/lib/locale/en_US/
LC_IDENTIFICATION
0000002a9556d000-0000002a9556e000 r--p 0000000000000000 08:07 9564
➥/usr/lib/locale/en_US/
LC_MEASUREMENT
0000002a9556e000-0000002a9556f000 r--p 0000000000000000 08:07 9561
➥/usr/lib/locale/en_US/
LC_TELEPHONE
0000002a9556f000-0000002a95570000 r--p 0000000000000000 08:07 9565
➥/usr/lib/locale/en_US/
LC_ADDRESS
0000002a95570000-0000002a95571000 r--p 0000000000000000 08:07 9562
➥/usr/lib/locale/en_US/
LC_NAME
0000002a95571000-0000002a95572000 r--p 0000000000000000 08:07 9583
➥/usr/lib/locale/en_US/
LC_PAPER
0000002a95572000-0000002a95573000 r--p 0000000000000000 08:07 9597
➥/usr/lib/locale/en_US/
LC_MESSAGES/SYS_LC_MESSAGES
0000002a95573000-0000002a95574000 r--p 0000000000000000 08:07 9563
➥/usr/lib/locale/en_US/
LC_MONETARY
0000002a95574000-0000002a9557a000 r--p 0000000000000000 08:07 9701
➥/usr/lib/locale/en_US/
LC_COLLATE
0000002a9557a000-0000002a9557b000 r--p 0000000000000000 08:07 8052
➥/usr/lib/locale/en_US/
LC_TIME
0000002a9557b000-0000002a9557c000 r--p 0000000000000000 08:07 9596
➥/usr/lib/locale/en_US/
```

```
LC_NUMERIC
0000002a9557c000-0000002a9557d000 rw-p 0000000000000000 00:00 0
0000002a95581000-0000002a95583000 rw-p 0000000000000000 00:00 0
0000002a95583000-0000002a955af000 r--p 0000000000000000 08:07 9700
➥/usr/lib/locale/en_US/
LC_CTYPE
0000002a955af000-0000002a955b5000 r--s 0000000000000000 08:07 9438
➥/usr/lib64/gconv/gconv-modules.cache
0000002a9566b000-0000002a9566d000 rw-p 0000000000015000 08:07 6820
➥/lib64/ld-2.3.2.so
0000002a9566d000-0000002a9569b000 r-xp 0000000000000000 08:07 10781
➥/lib64/libreadline.so.4.3
0000002a9569b000-0000002a9576d000 ---p 000000000002e000 08:07 10781
➥/lib64/libreadline.so.4.3
0000002a9576d000-0000002a957a6000 rw-p 0000000000000000 08:07 10781
➥/lib64/libreadline.so.4.3
0000002a957a6000-0000002a957a7000 rw-p 0000000000000000 00:00 0
0000002a957a7000-0000002a957ad000 r-xp 0000000000000000 08:07 10779
➥/lib64/libhistory.so.4.3
0000002a957ad000-0000002a958a7000 ---p 0000000000006000 08:07 10779
➥/lib64/libhistory.so.4.3
0000002a958a7000-0000002a958ae000 rw-p 0000000000000000 08:07 10779
➥/lib64/libhistory.so.4.3
0000002a958ae000-0000002a958f8000 r-xp 0000000000000000 08:07 9799
➥/lib64/libncurses.so.5.3
0000002a958f8000-0000002a959ae000 ---p 000000000004a000 08:07 9799
➥/lib64/libncurses.so.5.3
0000002a959ae000-0000002a95a0f000 rw-p 0000000000000000 08:07 9799
➥/lib64/libncurses.so.5.3
0000002a95a0f000-0000002a95a12000 r-xp 0000000000000000 08:07 6828
➥/lib64/libdl.so.2
0000002a95a12000-0000002a95b0f000 ---p 0000000000003000 08:07 6828
➥/lib64/libdl.so.2
0000002a95b0f000-0000002a95b12000 rw-p 0000000000000000 08:07 6828
➥/lib64/libdl.so.2
0000002a95b12000-0000002a95c36000 r-xp 0000000000000000 08:07 6825
➥/lib64/libc.so.6
0000002a95c36000-0000002a95d12000 ---p 0000000000124000 08:07 6825
➥/lib64/libc.so.6
0000002a95d12000-0000002a95d50000 rw-p 0000000000100000 08:07 6825
➥/lib64/libc.so.6
0000002a95d50000-0000002a95d54000 rw-p 0000000000000000 00:00 0
0000002a95d54000-0000002a95d56000 r-xp 0000000000000000 08:07 9389
➥/usr/lib64/gconv/ISO8859-1.so
0000002a95d56000-0000002a95e54000 ---p 0000000000002000 08:07 9389
➥/usr/lib64/gconv/ISO8859-1.so
0000002a95e54000-0000002a95e56000 rw-p 0000000000000000 08:07 9389
➥/usr/lib64/gconv/ISO8859-1.so
0000007fbfffa000-0000007fc0000000 rwxp fffffffffffb000 00:00 0
```

Notice how each address in the address ranges is twice as big as those in the 32-bit maps file. Also notice the following differences:

	X86 (32 bit)	AMD64 (64 bit)
Start of code segment	0x08048000	0x0000000000400000
Start of shared libraries	0x40000000	0x0000002a95556000
Start of stack segment	0x7fffffff	0x0000007fbfffffff
Start of kernel segment	0xc0000000	0x0000007fc0000000

Table 3.1 Address Mapping Comparison.

3.2.3 /proc/<pid>/cmdline

The cmdline file contains the process' complete argv. This is very useful to quickly determine exactly how a process was executed including all command-line parameters passed to it. Using the bash process again as an example, we see the following:

```
penguin> cd /proc/self
penguin> cat cmdline
bash
```

3.2.4 /proc/<pid>/environ

The environ file provides a window directly into the process' current environment. It is basically a link directly to memory at the very bottom of the process' stack, which is where the kernel stores this information. Examining this file can be very useful when you need to know settings for environment variables during the program's execution. A common programming error is misuse of the `getenv` and `putenv` library functions; this file can help diagnose these problems.

3.2.5 /proc/<pid>/mem

By accessing this file with the `fseek` library function, one can directly access the process' pages. One possible application of this could be to write a customized debugger of sorts. For example, say your program has a rather large and complex control block that stores some important information that the rest of the program relies on. In the case of a program malfunction, it would be advantageous to dump out that information. You could do this by opening the mem file for the PID in question and seeking to the known location of a control block. You could then read the size of the control block into another structure, which the homemade debugger could display in a format that programmers and service analysts can understand.

3.2.6 /proc/<pid>/fd

The fd directory contains symbolic links pointing to each file for which the process currently has a file descriptor. The name of the link is the number of the file descriptor itself. File descriptor leaks are common programming errors that can be difficult problems to diagnose. If you suspect the program you are debugging has a leak, examine this directory carefully throughout the life of the program.

3.2.7 /proc/<pid>/mapped_base

As was mentioned previously, the starting point for where the shared library mappings begin in a process' address space is defined in the Linux kernel by TASK_UNMAPPED_BASE. In the current stable releases of the 2.4 and 2.6 kernels, this value is hardcoded and cannot be changed. In the case of i386, 0x40000000 is not the greatest location because it occurs about one-third into the process' addressable space. Some applications require and/or benefit from allocating very large contiguous chunks of memory, and in some cases the TASK_UNMAPPED_BASE gets in the way and hinders this.

To address this problem, some distributions such as SuSE Linux Enterprise Server 8 have included a patch that allows the system administrator to set the TASK_UNMAPPED_BASE value to whatever he or she chooses. The /proc/<pid>/mapped_base file is the interface you use to view and change this value.

To view the current value, simply cat the file:

```
penguin> cat /proc/self/mapped_base
1073741824penguin>
```

This shows the value in decimal form and is rather ugly. Viewing it as hex is much more meaningful:

```
penguin> printf "0x%x\n" `cat /proc/self/mapped_base`
0x40000000
penguin>
```

We know from our examination of the maps file that the executable's mapping begins at 0x08048000 in the process address space. We also now know that the in-memory mapping is likely to be larger than the on-disk size of the executable. This is because of variables that are in the BSS segment and because of dynamically allocating memory from the process heap. With mapped_base at the default value, the space allowed for all of this is 939229184 (0x40000000 - 0x08048000). This is just under 1GB and certainly overkill. A more reasonable value would be 0x10000000, which would give the executable room for 133922816 (0x10000000 - 0x08048000). This is just over 128MB and should be plenty of space for most applications. To make this change, root authority is required. It's also very important to note that the change is only picked up by children of the process in which the change was made, so it might be necessary to call execv() or a similar function for the change to be picked up. The following command will update the value:

```
penguin> echo 0x10000000 > /proc/<pid>/mapped_base
```

3.3 KERNEL INFORMATION AND MANIPULATION

At the same level in the /proc filesystem hierarchy that all the process ID directories are located are a number of very useful files and directories. These files and directories provide information and allow setting various items at the system and kernel level rather than per process. Some of the more useful and interesting entries are described in the following sections.

3.3.1 /proc/cmdline

This is a special version of the cmdline that appears in all /proc/<pid> directories. It shows all the parameters that were used to boot the currently running kernel. This can be hugely useful especially when debugging remotely without direct access to the computer.

3.3.2 /proc/config.gz or /proc/sys/config.gz

This file is not part of the mainline kernel source for 2.4.24 nor 2.6.0, but some distributions such as SuSE have included it in their distributions. It is very useful to quickly examine exactly what options the current kernel was compiled with. For example, if you wanted to quickly find out if your running kernel was compiled with Kernel Magic SysRq support, search /proc/config.gz for SYSRQ:

```
penguin> zcat config.gz | grep SYSRQ
CONFIG_MAGIC_SYSRQ=y
```

3.3.3 /proc/cpufreq

At the time of this writing, this file is not part of the mainline 2.4.24 kernel but is part of the 2.6.0 mainline source. Many distributions such as SuSE have back-ported it to their 2.4 kernels, however. This file provides an interface to manipulate the speed at which the processor(s) in your machine run, depending on various governing factors. There is excellent documentation included in the /usr/src/linux/Documentation/cpu-freq directory if your kernel contains support for this feature.

3.3.4 /proc/cpuinfo

This is one of the first files someone will look at when determining the characteristics of a particular computer. It contains detailed information on each of the CPUs in the computer such as speed, model name, and cache size.

> **Note:** To determine if the CPUs in your system have Intel HyperThreaded(TM) technology, view the cpuinfo file, but you need to know what to look for. If for example, your system has four HyperThreaded CPUs, cpuinfo will report on eight total CPUs with a processor number ranging from 0 to 7. However, examining the "physical id" field for each of the eight entries will yield only four unique values that directly represent each physical CPU.

3.3.5 /proc/devices

This file displays a list of all configured character and block devices. Note that the device entry in the maps file can be cross-referenced with the block devices of this section to translate a device number into a name. The following shows the /proc/devices listing for my computer.

```
Character devices:
  1 mem
  2 pty
  3 ttyp
  4 ttyS
  5 cua
  6 lp
  7 vcs
 10 misc
 13 input
 14 sound
 21 sg
 29 fb
 81 video_capture
116 alsa
119 vmnet
128 ptm
136 pts
162 raw
171 ieee1394
```

```
180 usb
188 ttyUSB
254 pcmcia

Block devices:
  1 ramdisk
  2 fd
  3 ide0
  7 loop
  9 md
 11 sr
 22 ide1
```

Figure 3.1 shows that /bin/bash is mapped from device 03 which, according to my devices file, is the "ide0" device. This makes perfect sense, as I have only one hard drive, which is IDE.

3.3.6 /proc/kcore

This file represents all physical memory in your computer. With an unstripped kernel binary, a debugger can be used to examine any parts of the kernel desired. This can be useful when the kernel is doing something unexpected or when developing kernel modules.

3.3.7 /proc/locks

This file shows all file locks that currently exist in the system. When you know that your program locks certain files, examining this file can be very useful in debugging a wide array of problems.

3.3.8 /proc/meminfo

This file is probably the second file after cpuinfo to be examined when determining the specs of a given system. It displays such things as total physical RAM, total used RAM, total free RAM, amount cached, and so on. Examining this file can be very useful when diagnosing memory-related issues.

3.3.9 /proc/mm

This file is part of Jeff Dike's User Mode Linux (UML) patch, which allows an instance of a kernel to be run within a booted kernel. This can be valuable in kernel development. One of the biggest advantages of UML is that a crash in a UML kernel will not bring down the entire computer; the UML instance simply needs to be restarted. UML is not part of the mainstream 2.4.24 nor 2.6.0

kernels, but some distributions have back-ported it. The basic purpose of the mm file is to create a new address space by opening it. You can then modify the new address space by writing directly to this file.

3.3.10 /proc/modules

This file contains a listing of all modules currently loaded by the system. Generally, the lsmod(8) command is a more common way of seeing this information. lsmod will print the information, but it doesn't add anything to what's in this file. Running lsmod is very useful after running modprobe(8) or insmod(8) to dynamically load a kernel module to see if the kernel has, in fact, loaded it. It's also very useful to view when it is desired to unload a module using the rmmod(8) command. Usually if a module is in use by at least one process, that is, its "Used by" count is greater than 0, it cannot be unloaded by the kernel.

3.3.11 /proc/net

This directory contains several files that represent many different facets of the networking layer. Directly accessing some can be useful in specific situations, but generally it's much easier and more meaningful to use the netstat(8) command.

3.3.12 /proc/partitions

This file holds a list of disk partitions that Linux is aware of. The partition file categorizes the system's disk partitions by "major" and "minor." The major number refers to the device number, which can be cross-referenced with the /proc/devices file. The minor refers to the unique partition number on the device. The partition number also appears in the maps file immediately next to the device number.

Looking at the maps output for /bin/bash in Figure 3.1, the device field is "03:08." We can look up the device and partition directly from the partitions file. Using the following output in conjunction with Figure 3.1, we can see that /bin/bash resides on partition 8 of block device 3, or /dev/hda8.

```
major minor  #blocks  name     rio rmerge rsect ruse wio wmerge
↪wsect wuse running use aveq
   3      0   46879560 hda 207372 1315792 7751026 396280 91815 388645
↪3871184 1676033 -3 402884 617934
   3      1   12269848 hda1 230 1573 1803 438 0 0 0 0 0 438 438
   3      2          1 hda2 0 0 0 0 0 0 0 0 0 0 0
```

```
     3       5    15119968 hda5 6441 625334 631775 911375 0 0 0 0 0
➡1324183 911375
     3       6     1028128 hda6 8 0 8 58 0 0 0 0 0 58 58
     3       7     1028128 hda7 66 275 2728 1004 445 4071 38408 27407 0
➡2916 28525
     3       8    17425768 hda8 200618 688575 7114640 3778237 91370
➡384574 3832776 1648626 0 1585895 1170787
```

3.3.13 /proc/pci

This file contains detailed information on each device connected to the PCI bus of your computer. Examining this file can be useful when diagnosing problems with a certain PCI device. The information contained within this file is very specific to each particular device.

3.3.14 /proc/slabinfo

This file contains statistics on certain kernel structures and caches. It can be useful to examine this file when debugging system memory-related problems. Refer to the slabinfo(5) man page for more detailed information.

3.4 SYSTEM INFORMATION AND MANIPULATION

A key subdirectory in the /proc filesystem is the sys directory. It contains many kernel configuration entries. These entries can be used to view or in some cases manipulate kernel settings. Some of the more useful and important entries will be discussed in the following sections.

3.4.1 /proc/sys/fs

This directory contains a number of pseudo-files representing a variety of file system information. There is good documentation in the proc(5) man page on the files within this directory, but it's worth noting some of the more important ones.

3.4.1.1 dir-notify-enable This file acts as a switch for the Directory Notification feature. This can be a useful feature in problem determination in that you can have a program watch a specific directory and be notified immediately of any change to it. See /usr/src/linux/Documentation/dnotify.txt for more information and for a sample program.

3.4.1.2 file-nr This read-only file contains statistics on the number of files presently opened and available on the system. The file shows three separate values. The first value is the number of allocated file handles, the second is the number of free file handles, and the third is the maximum number of file handles.

```
penguin> cat /proc/sys/fs/file-nr
2858     177      104800
```

On my system I have 2858 file handles allocated; 177 of these handles are available for use and have a maximum limit of 104800 total file handles. The kernel dynamically allocates file handles but does not free them when they're no longer used. Therefore the first number, 2858, is the high water mark for total file handles in use at one time on my system. The maximum limit of file handles is also reflected in the /proc/sys/fs/file-max file.

3.4.1.3 file-max This file represents the system wide limit for the number of files that can be open at the same time. If you're running a large workload on your system such as a database management system or a Web server, you may see errors in the system log about running out of file handles. Examine this file along with the file-nr file to determine if increasing the limit is a valid option. If so, simply do the following as root:

```
echo 104800 > /proc/sys/fs/file-max
```

This should only be done with a fair degree of caution, considering an overly excessive use of file descriptors could indicate a programming error commonly referred to as a file descriptor leak. Be sure to refer to your application's documentation to determine what the recommended value for file-max is.

3.4.1.4 aio-max-nr, aix-max-pinned, aix-max-size, aio-nr, and aio-pinned These files are not included as part of the 2.4.24 and 2.6.0 mainline kernels. They provide additional interfaces to the Asynchronous I/O feature, which is a part of the 2.6.0 mainline kernel but not 2.4.24.

3.4.1.5 overflowgid and overflowuid These files represent the group IDs and user IDs to use on remote systems that have filesystems that do not support 32-bit gids and uids as Linux does. It is important to make a mental note of this because NFS is very commonly used even though diagnosing NFS-related problems can be very tricky. On my system, these values are defined as follows:

```
penguin> cat overflowgid
65534
penguin> cat overflowuid
65534
```

3.4.2 /proc/sys/kernel

This directory contains several very important files related to kernel tuning and information. Much of the information here is low-level and will never need to be examined or changed by the average user, so I'll just highlight some of the more interesting entries, especially pertaining to problem determination.

3.4.2.1 core_pattern This file is new in the 2.6 kernel, but some distributions such as SuSE have back ported it to their 2.4 kernels. Its value is a template for the name of the file written when an application dumps its core. The advantage of using this is that with the use of % specifiers, the administrator has full control of where the core files get written and what their names will be. For example, it may be advantageous to create a directory called /core and set the core_pattern with a command something like the following:

```
penguin> echo "/core/%e.%p" > core_pattern
```

For example, if the program `foo` causes an exception and dumps its core, the file /core/foo.3135 will be created.

3.4.2.2 msgmax, msgmnb, and msgmni These three files are used to configure the kernel parameters for System V IPC messages. msgmax is used to set the limit for the maximum number of bytes that can be written on a single message queue. msgmnb stores the number of bytes used to initialize subsequently created message queues. msgmni defines the maximum number of message queue identifiers allowed on the system. These values are often very dependent on the workload that your system is running and may need to be updated. Many applications will automatically change these values but some might require the administrator to do it.

3.4.2.3 panic and panic_on_oops The panic file lets the user control what happens when the kernel enters a panic state. If the value of either file is 0, the kernel will loop and therefore the machine will remain in the panic state until manually rebooted. A non-zero value represents the number of seconds the kernel should remain in panic mode before rebooting. Having the kernel automatically reboot the system in the event of a panic could be a very useful feature if high availability is a primary concern.

The panic_on_oops file is new in the 2.6.0 mainline kernel and when set to 1, it informs the kernel to pause for a few seconds before panicking when encountering a BUG or an Oops. This gives the klogd an opportunity to write the Oops or BUG Report to the disk so that it can be easily examined when the system is returned to a normal state.

3.4.2.4 printk This file contains four values that determine how kernel error messages are logged. Generally, the default values suffice, although changing the values might be advantageous when debugging the kernel.

3.4.2.5 sem This file contains four numbers that define limits for System V IPC semaphores. These limits are SEMMSL, SEMMNS, SEMOPM, and SEMMNI respectively. SEMMSL represents the maximum number of semaphores per semaphore set; SEMMNS is the maximum number of semaphores in all semaphore sets for the whole system; SEMOPM is the maximum number of operations that can be used in a `semop(2)` call; and SEMMNI represents the maximum number of semaphore identifiers for the whole system. The values needed for these parameters will vary by workload and application, so it is always best to consult your application's documentation.

3.4.2.6 shmall, shmmax, and shmmni These three files define the limits for System V IPC shared memory. shmall is the limit for the total number of pages of shared memory for the system. shmmax defines the maximum shared memory segment size. shmmni defines the maximum number of shared memory segments allowed for the system. These values are very workload-dependent and may need to be changed when running a database management system or a Web server.

3.4.2.7 sysrq This file controls whether the "kernel magic sysrq key" is enabled or not. This feature may have to be explicitly turned on during compilation. If /proc/sys/kernel/sysrq exists, the feature is available; otherwise, you'll need to recompile your kernel before using it. It is recommended to have this feature enabled because it can help to diagnose some of the tricky system hangs and crashes.

The basic idea is that the kernel can be interrupted to display certain information by bypassing the rest of the operating system via the ALT-SysRq hotkey combination. In many cases where the machine seems to be hung, the ALT-SysRq key can still be used to gather kernel information for examination and/or forwarding to a distribution cause's support area or other experts.

To enable this feature, do the following as root:

```
penguin> echo 1 > /proc/sys/kernel/sysrq
```

To test the kernel magic, switch to your first virtual console. You need not log in because the key combination triggers the kernel directly. Hold down the right ALT key, then press and hold the PrtSc/SysRq key, then press the number 5. You should see something similar to the following:

```
SysRq : Changing Loglevel
Loglevel set to 5
```

If you do not see this message, it could be that the kernel is set to send messages to virtual console 10 by default. Press CTRL-ALT-F10 to switch to virtual console 10 and check to see if the messages appear there. If they do, then you know that the kernel magic is working properly. If you'd like to switch where the messages get sent by default, say, virtual console 1 by default instead of 10, then run this command as root:

```
/usr/sbin/klogmessage -r 1
```

This change will only be in effect until the next reboot, so to make the change permanent, grep through your system's startup scripts for "klogmessage" to determine where it gets set to virtual console 10 and change it to whichever virtual console you wish. For my SuSE Pro 9.0 system, this setting occurs in /etc/init.d/boot.klog.

Where the messages get sent is important to note because in the event your system hangs and kernel magic may be of use, you'll need to have your system already be on the virtual console where messages appear. This is because it is very likely that the kernel won't respond to the CTRL-ALT-Function keys to switch virtual consoles.

So what can you do with the kernel magic stuff then?

Press ALT-SysRq-h to see a Help screen. You should see the following:

```
SysRq : HELP : loglevel0-8 reBoot Crash Dumpregisters tErm kIll saK
showMem showPc unRaw Sync showTasks Unmount
```

If you're seeing these messages you can gather this information to determine the cause of the problem. Some of the commands such as showTasks will dump a large amount of data, so it is highly recommended that a serial console be set up to gather and save this information. See the "Setting up a Serial Console" section for more information. Note however, that depending on the state of the kernel, the information may be saved to the /var/log/messages file as well so you may be able to retrieve it after a reboot.

The most important pieces of information to gather would be showPc, showMem, showTasks. Output samples of these commands are shown here. Note that the output of the showTasks command had to be truncated given that quite a bit of data is dumped. Dumpregisters is also valuable to have, but it requires special configuration and is not enabled by default. After capturing this information, it is advisable to execute the sync and reBoot commands to properly restart the system if an Oops or other kernel error was encountered. Simply using kernel magic at any given time is usually harmless and does not require a sync and or reBoot command to be performed.

3.4.2.7.1 showPc Output:

```
SysRq : Show Regs

Pid: 0, comm:                 swapper
EIP: 0010:[default_idle+36/48] CPU: 0 EFLAGS: 00003246    Tainted:
➡PF
EIP: 0010:[<c0106f94>] CPU: 0 EFLAGS: 00003246    Tainted: PF
EAX: 00000000 EBX: c0106f70 ECX: 00000000 EDX: 00000019
ESI: c0326000 EDI: c0326000 EBP: ffffe000 DS: 0018 ES: 0018
CR0: 8005003b CR2: 4001a000 CR3: 05349000 CR4: 000006d0
Call Trace:    [cpu_idle+50/96] [rest_init+0/32]
Call Trace:    [<c0106ff2>] [<c0105000>]
```

3.4.2.7.2 showMem Output:

```
SysRq : Show Memory
Mem-info:     •
Free pages:        15316kB (  2044kB HighMem)
Zone:DMA freepages:  3780kB
Zone:Normal freepages:  9492kB
Zone:HighMem freepages:  2044kB
( Active: 128981, inactive: 102294, free: 3829 )
1*4kB 0*8kB 0*16kB 0*32kB 1*64kB 1*128kB 0*256kB 1*512kB 1*1024kB
1*2048kB 0*4096kB = 3780kB)
65*4kB 54*8kB 72*16kB 157*32kB 15*64kB 1*128kB 0*256kB 1*512kB
1*1024kB 0*2048kB 0*4096kB = 9492kB)
7*4kB 2*8kB 3*16kB 15*32kB 9*64kB 1*128kB 1*256kB 1*512kB 0*1024kB
0*2048kB 0*4096kB = 2044kB)
Swap cache: add 295, delete 32, find 0/0, race 0+0
Free swap:        1026940kB
262000 pages of RAM
32624 pages of HIGHMEM
3973 reserved pages
457950 pages shared
263 pages swap cached
33 pages in page table cache
Buffer memory:    74760kB
Cache memory:    778952kB
```

3.4.2.7.3 showTasks Output:

```
SysRq : Show Memory
SysRq : Show State

                           free                      sibling
    task            PC     stack   pid father child younger older
init              S CDFED120  236     1      0   4746
(NOTLB)
Call Trace:      [schedule_timeout+99/176] [process_timeout+0/16]
➡[do_select+481/560] [__pollwait+0/208] [sys_select+80
8/1232]
Call Trace:      [<c0125923>] [<c01258b0>] [<c0154471>] [<c01540d0>]
➡[<c0154818>]
  [system_call+51/64]
  [<c0108dd3>]
keventd           S C4925AC0    0     2      1            3
➡(L-TLB)
Call Trace:      [context_thread+259/448] [rest_init+0/32]
➡[rest_init+0/32] [arch_kernel_thread+35/48] [context_thread+
➡0/448]
Call Trace:      [<c0129d53>] [<c0105000>] [<c0105000>] [<c0107333>]
➡[<c0129c50>]
ksoftirqd_CPU S CDFED080      0     3      1            4     2
➡(L-TLB)
Call Trace:      [rest_init+0/32] [ksoftirqd+183/192]
[arch_kernel_thread+35/48] [ksoftirqd+0/192]
Call Trace:      [<c0105000>] [<c0121e57>] [<c0107333>] [<c0121da0>]
kswapd            S C764E680 1260     4      1            5     3
➡(L-TLB)
Call Trace:      [kswapd+171/176] [rest_init+0/32] [rest_init+0/32]
[arch_kernel_thread+35/48] [kswapd+0/176]
Call Trace:      [<c013c4ab>] [<c0105000>] [<c0105000>] [<c0107333>]
➡[<c013c400>]
bdflush           S C02DEEE0   60     5      1            6     4
➡ (L-TLB)
Call Trace:      [interruptible_sleep_on+61/96] [bdflush+195/208]
[rest_init+0/32] [arch_kernel_thread+35/48] [bdflush+
0/208]
Call Trace:      [<c011a24d>] [<c01490a3>] [<c0105000>] [<c0107333>]
➡[<c0148fe0>]
kupdated          S C4925AC0  820     6      1            7     5
➡(L-TLB)
Call Trace:      [schedule_timeout+99/176] [process_timeout+0/16]
[kupdate+205/384] [rest_init+0/32] [rest_init+0/32]
Call Trace:      [<c0125923>] [<c01258b0>] [<c014917d>] [<c0105000>]
➡[<c0105000>]
  [arch_kernel_thread+35/48] [kupdate+0/384]
  [<c0107333>] [<c01490b0>]

<<SNIP>>
```

3.4.2.8 tainted This file gives an indication of whether or not the kernel has loaded modules that are not under the GPL. If it has loaded proprietary modules, the tainted flag will be logically ORed with 1. If a module were loaded forcefully (that is, by running `insmod -F`), then the tainted flag will be logically ORed with 2. During a kernel Oops and panic, the value of the tainted flag is dumped to reflect the module loading history.

3.4.3 /proc/sys/vm

This directory holds several files that allow the user to tune the Virtual Memory subsystem of the kernel. The default values are normally fine for everyday use; therefore, these files needn't be modified too much. The Linux VM is arguably the most complex part of the Linux kernel, so discussion of it is beyond the scope of this book. There are many resources on the Internet that provide documentation for it such as Mel Gorman's "Understanding the Linux Virtual Memory Manager" Web site located at `http://www.csn.ul.ie/~mel/projects/vm/guide/html/understand`.

3.5 CONCLUSION

There is more to the /proc filesystem than was discussed in this chapter. However, the goal here was to highlight some of the more important and commonly used entries. The /proc filesystem will also vary by kernel version and by distribution as various features appear in some versions and not others. In any case, the /proc filesystem offers a wealth of knowledge into your system and all the processes that run on it.

Compiling

4.1 Introduction

Because the Linux kernel and all GNU software are fully open source, the act of compiling and working with compilers is a very important part of becoming a Linux expert. There will often be times when a particular software package or a particular feature in a software package isn't included in your distribution, so the only option is to obtain the source and compile it yourself. Another common task in Linux is recompiling your kernel. The reasons for doing this could be to disable or enable a particular feature of the current kernel, apply a patch to fix a problem to add a new feature, or to migrate the system to a completely different kernel source level. This chapter does not give complete instructions on how to carry out these tasks. Rather, it provides information on some of the lesser known details related to these actions. Furthermore, the intent is to help arm you with some of the skills to enable you to solve compilation difficulties on your own. First, a bit of background on the primary tool used to perform compilation—the compiler.

4.2 The GNU Compiler Collection

The GNU Compiler Collection, or GCC as it is commonly referred to, is currently the most widely used compiler for developing GNU/Linux, BSDs, Mac OS X, and BeOS systems. GCC is free (as in freedom) software and is freely available for anyone to use for any purpose. There are a large number of developers around the world that contribute to GCC, which is guided by the GCC Steering Committee.

4.2.1 A Brief History of GCC

GCC originally started out as the "GNU C Compiler" back when the GNU Project was first started in 1984 by the GNU Project founder Richard Stallman. With funding from the Free Software Foundation (FSF), the first release of GCC was in 1987. At that time it was the first portable, optimizing compiler freely available, which quickly paved the way for the open source movement and ultimately the GNU/Linux operating system.

Version 2.0 was released in 1992 and provided support for C++. In 1997, the Experimental/Enhanced GNU Compiler System (EGCS) project was spun off of GCC by a group of developers who wanted to focus more on expanding GCC, improving C++ support, and improving optimization. The success of EGCS resulted in it being named the official version of GCC in April of 1999. The release of GCC 3.0 in 2001 made the new compiler widely available.

The evolution of GCC has resulted in support for several different languages including Objective C, Java, Ada, and Fortran. This prompted the renaming of the GCC acronym to the more appropriate "GNU Compiler Collection."

Today, GCC has been ported to more hardware architectures than any other compiler and is a crucial part of the success of the GNU/Linux operation system. GCC continues to grow and stabilize. Current versions of SuSE Linux Enterprise Server 9 use GCC version 3.3.3, and Redhat Enterprise Linux 3 uses GCC version 3.2.3.

4.2.2 GCC Version Compatibility

When new versions of GCC are released, there is always the potential for library incompatibilities to be introduced, particularly with C++ code. For example, when compiling a C++ application with GCC version 3.3.1, the system library libstdc++.so.5 will be automatically linked in. When compiling the same C++ application with GCC 3.4.1, the system library libstdc++.so.6 is automatically linked in. This is because between GCC version 3.3.3 and version 3.4.1, the C++ *Application Binary Interface* (ABI) (see the "Calling Conventions" section for more information) was changed, resulting in the two versions of the compiler generating binaries that use differing C++ interfaces.

To resolve this issue, both versions of the libstdc++.so library must be available on any system that could potentially run an application compiled with differing versions of GCC.

4.3 OTHER COMPILERS

There are other compilers available for Linux, but none are nearly as portable as GCC and are generally only available on specific hardware platforms. GCC's main competition on the i386, IA64, and x86-64 architectures is the Intel C++ Compiler. This compiler is a commercial product and must be properly licensed. It claims to have better performance than GCC and offers differing support packages to the purchaser.

An alternative compiler to GCC on the PowerPC platform running Linux is the IBM xlC C++ Compiler. Just as with the Intel compiler, this one also claims greater performance and enhanced support but is, again, a commercial product requiring proper licensing.

4.4 COMPILING THE LINUX KERNEL

Thanks to Linux's open source policy, users are free to choose any kernel they wish to use and even make changes to it if they desire! Making changes to a kernel does not require that you are a kernel developer or even a programmer. There are a plethora of *patches* available on the Internet from those who are programmers and kernel developers.

> **Note:** A *patch* is a set of any number of source code changes commonly referred to as *diffs* because they are created by the `diff(1)` utility. A patch can be applied to a set of source files effectively acting as an automatic source code modification system to add features, fix bugs, and make other changes.

Caution does need to be exercised if you are not confident with this task, as the kernel is the brain of the operating system; if it is not working properly, bad things will happen, and your computer may not even boot.

It is important to know roughly how to compile a Linux kernel in case the need arises. Here's a perfect example—when the 2.6 kernel was officially released in December 2003, the new kernel did not appear in any distributions for several months. Even though a lot of features found in the mainline 2.6 kernel source have been back-ported to the major distributions' 2.4-based products, there are still many fundamental features of the 2.6 kernel that have not been back-ported, which makes running it very attractive. So the only option at that point in time was to obtain the 2.6 source code and compile the kernel manually. It is not the intention of this book to go into detail on how to do this because there is a great deal of information commonly available to do so. Rather, the intention of this book is to help you troubleshoot and solve problems that may arise through this process on your own and with the help of others if need be. Linux is a massive project, and there are an infinite number of different system configurations—so problems are a very real possibility.

4.4.1 Obtaining the Kernel Source

The Linux kernel source for all releases, including development/test releases, is found at `kernel.org`. Kernel source can be downloaded as one complete archive or as patches to a specific kernel level. The archives are available as compressed tar files. For example, the full 2.4.24 source tree is available on `kernel.org` in the pub/linux/kernel/v2.4 directory and is named linux-2.4.24.tar.gz and linux-2.4.24.tar.bz2.

> **Note:** bz2 is an alternate compression method to gzip that generally provides higher compression. Use the bunzip2 utility to uncompress the file. Alternatively, the archive can be untarred with a single command such as:
> ```
> bzcat linux-2.4.24.tar.bz2 | tar -xf -
> ```

The patch files are also available for every release and basically contain the difference between the release for which they're named and one release previous. The idea is that for those who want to always have the latest officially released kernel, they don't need to download the full source archive each time; rather they can download the patch file, apply it to their current kernel source tree, rename the directory to reflect the new version (though not required), and rebuild only what's changed with their existing configurations.

4.4.2 Architecture Specific Source

The kernel source trees contain a directory in the top level called "arch" under which is all the architecture-specific code. Usually all code required for a particular architecture is included, but there are occasions, especially when a particular architecture is relatively new, when the architecture specific code is incomplete and/or buggy. In this case, there is often a dedicated server on the Internet that holds patchkits to be applied to the mainline kernel source.

> **Note**: A *patchkit* is a term used to refer to a large set of patches provided in a single downloadable archive.

A prime example of the need for a patchkit is the x86-64 architecture and the early 2.6 kernel releases. The 2.6.0 kernel source on `kernel.org` does not contain all fixes needed to properly run on the x86-64 architecture, so a patchkit must be downloaded from x86-64.org in the pub/linux/v2.6 directory. The need for doing this will vary by architecture, so be sure to check for the architecture that you're interested in.

4.4.3 Working with Kernel Source Compile Errors

Even though the mainline kernel source is tested a great deal and compiled on many machines around the world before being declared an official release and posted to `kernel.org`, there is still no guarantee that it will compile flawlessly for you on your particular machine. Compile failures can occur for various reasons. Some of the more common reasons are:

1. Environment/setup errors or differences
2. Compiler version differences
3. Currently running kernel is incompatible with the kernel being compiled
4. User error
5. Code error

If you experience a compile error while compiling a fresh kernel, fear not; it may not be as difficult to fix it as it might seem. That's the beauty of Linux-there is always a wealth of help and information at your fingertips, and it's quite possible that someone else has already had and fixed the very same problem.

4.4.3.1 A Real Kernel Compile Error Example Let's work through a compile problem encountered when compiling the 2.4.20 kernel source downloaded directly from `kernel.org` as an example. The error message encountered was

```
gcc -D__KERNEL__  -I/usr/src/linux-2.4.20/include -Wall -Wstrict-
➥prototypes -Wno-trigraphs -O2 -fno-strict-aliasing -fno-common -
➥fomit-frame-pointer -pipe -mpreferred-stack-boundary=2 -
➥march=i686   -nostdinc -iwithprefix include -
➥DKBUILD_BASENAME=ide_probe
➥-DEXPORT_SYMTAB -c ide-probe.c
gcc -D__KERNEL__  -I/usr/src/linux-2.4.20/include -Wall -Wstrict-
➥prototypes -Wno-trigraphs -O2 -fno-strict-aliasing -fno-common
➥-fomit-frame-pointer -pipe -mpreferred-stack-boundary=2 -
➥march=i686   -nostdinc -iwithprefix include -
➥DKBUILD_BASENAME=ide_geometry  -c -o ide-geometry.o ide-geometry.c
➥ld -m elf_i386 -r -o ide-probe-mod.o ide-probe.o ide-geometry.o
gcc -D__KERNEL__  -I/usr/src/linux-2.4.20/include -Wall -Wstrict-
➥prototypes -Wno-trigraphs -O2 -fno-strict-aliasing -fno-common
➥-fomit-frame-pointer -pipe -mpreferred-stack-boundary=2 -
➥march=i686   -nostdinc -iwithprefix include -
➥DKBUILD_BASENAME=ide_disk  -c -o ide-disk.o ide-disk.c
gcc -D__KERNEL__  -I/usr/src/linux-2.4.20/include -Wall -Wstrict-
➥prototypes -Wno-trigraphs -O2 -fno-strict-aliasing -fno-common
➥-fomit-frame-pointer -pipe -mpreferred-stack-boundary=2 -
➥march=i686 -nostdinc -iwithprefix include -
➥DKBUILD_BASENAME=ide_cd  -c -o ide-cd.o ide-cd.c
In file included from ide-cd.c:318:
ide-cd.h:440: error: long, short, signed or unsigned used invalidly
➥for `slot_tablelen'
```

```
make[3]: *** [ide-cd.o] Error 1
make[3]: Leaving directory '/usr/src/linux-2.4.20/drivers/ide'
make[2]: *** [first_rule] Error 2
make[2]: Leaving directory '/usr/src/linux-2.4.20/drivers/ide'
make[1]: *** [_subdir_ide] Error 2
make[1]: Leaving directory '/usr/src/linux-2.4.20/drivers'
make: *** [_dir_drivers] Error 2
```

To the user unfamiliar with looking at compile and make errors, this can look quite daunting at first. The first thing to do when seeing error output like this is to identify its root cause. In the preceding output, it is important to see that some of the compilations shown are successful and only one failed. Each line that begins with `gcc` is a compilation, and if no error output follows the line, then the compilation was successful. So we can rule out the first three gcc compilation lines, as they were successful. The compilation that failed was

```
gc -D__KERNEL__  -I/usr/src/linux-2.4.20/include -Wall -Wstrict-
➥prototypes -Wno-trigraphs -O2 -fno-strict-aliasing -fno-common
➥-fomit-frame-pointer -pipe -mpreferred-stack-boundary=2 -march=i686
➥-nostdinc -iwithprefix include -DKBUILD_BASENAME=ide_cd  -c -o ide-
➥cd.o ide-cd.c
```

The next thing to do is to examine this compile line in more detail. The first objective is to determine the name of the source file being compiled. To do this, scan through the compile line and ignore all of the command line arguments that begin with a dash. The remaining command line arguments are `include` and `ide-cd.c`. The `include` is actually part of the `-iwithprefix` argument, so it too can be ignored, leaving us with the source file being compiled - ide-cd.c.

Next, we need to look at the error message dumped by gcc:

```
In file included from ide-cd.c:318:
ide-cd.h:440: error: long, short, signed or unsigned used invalidly
➥for 'slot_tablelen'
```

From this output, we can see that the code that failed to compile isn't actually in ide-cd.c; rather it's in ide-cd.h, which is #include'd by ide-cd.c at line 318. Line 440 of ide-cd.h is the line the compiler could not understand. The following is a snippet of code from ide-cd.h surrounding line 440, with line 440 highlighted.

```
        byte     curlba[3];
        byte     nslots;
        __u8 short slot_tablelen;
};


struct atapi_slot {
#if defined(__BIG_ENDIAN_BITFIELD)
```

By looking at the failing line, it might not be obvious right away what the problem could be without looking at the definition of __u8. Using cscope (see the section "Setting Up cscope to Index Kernel Sources" for more information), we see that __u8 is defined for each particular architecture. Because this was encountered on i386, the appropriate file to look at is /usr/src/linux-2.4.20/include/asm-i386/types.h. By selecting this file in cscope, the file is opened, and the cursor is placed directly on the line containing the definition:

```
typedef unsigned char __u8;
```

So now substituting this definition into the failing line to see exactly what the compiler sees, we get:

```
unsigned char short slot_tablelen;
```

This certainly doesn't look right given that a char and a short are two completely different primitive C data types. This appears to be a coding error or typo. The problem now is to try to figure out whether the code author actually wanted a char or a short. Just by considering the pathname of the failing code (drivers/ide/ide-cd.h) and the fact that this is a structure, I'm very hesitant to guess at the correct value since—if it is incorrect—that could be risking disk and filesystem corruption (IDE is a commonly used disk controller on x86-based computers).

With this kind of issue, it's very likely that others have had the same problem. Because of this, searching the Internet should be the next step. Plugging ide-cd.c slot_tablelen into a search engine instantly shows that this has in fact been reported by others.

It took a bit of time to read through the top five or so results to find the solution, but it turned out that it was in fact a typo, and the line should instead have read:

```
__u16 slot_tablelen;
```

When making this correction to ide-cd.h and re-running the compilation, ide-cd.c successfully compiled!

So what is the real cause of this particular compile failure? I did a little more investigative work and found that it could be categorized as a code error and as a compiler difference. The code itself really is incorrect; two primitive data types should never be used to declare a single variable as was done in this case. It seems however, that some compilers allow this particular case, and some don't. Moreover, in this particular case, older versions of gcc allowed this where newer versions did not.

This type of compilation error is very common when porting applications from one platform to another, for example from IBM AIX to Linux or Sun Solaris to HP-UX. This simply means that the developers of each respective compiler interprets the C/C++ Standards and implements them differently.

4.4.4 General Compilation Problems

When compiling your own code, compilation errors are often very easy to resolve. When downloading source from reputable locations on the Internet, resolving compilation errors can be very difficult. It can be especially difficult if the source that has been downloaded has been officially released and tested thoroughly. The instant thought is that it is a user error and you must be doing something wrong. This isn't always the case though, as I'll attempt to point out.

Reiterating what was just stated, compilation errors are generally due to one or a combination of the following reasons:

1. Environment/setup errors or differences
2. Compiler version differences or bugs
3. User error
4. Code error

4.4.4.1 Environment/Setup Errors or Differences
There are an infinite number of ways to configure Linux system environments, so the chances for a setup or environment error are fairly high. Further adding to the possibility for problems is a correctly set up environment—but one that differs from the environment in which the source code was written. This is a very real problem, especially with Linux, simply because things change so quickly and are constantly evolving.

Some examples of environment errors or differences that could easily lead to compilation problems are

☞ missing or outdated system include files

☞ outdated or differing glibc libraries

☞ insufficient disk space

Many modern software packages include scripts generated by the GNU autoconf package, which will automatically configure the Makefile(s) and source code based on the system's environment. The use of autoconf will immediately flag any differences or problems it finds with header files or libraries before compilation even begins, which greatly simplifies the problem determination process. Sample autoconf output for the gcc 3.3.2 source is shown here. The output can be quite lengthy, so a large chunk in the middle has been cut out (<<...>>) to show the beginning and end output.

```
linux> ./configure 2>&1 | tee conf.out
Configuring for a i686-pc-linux-gnu host.
Created "Makefile" in /home/dbehman/gcc-3.3.2 using "mt-frag"
Configuring libiberty...
creating cache ../config.cache
checking whether to enable maintainer-specific portions of
Makefiles... no
checking for makeinfo... no
checking for perl... perl
checking host system type... i686-pc-linux-gnu
checking build system type... i686-pc-linux-gnu
checking for ar... ar
checking for ranlib... ranlib
checking for gcc... gcc
checking whether we are using GNU C... yes
checking whether gcc accepts -g... yes
checking whether gcc and cc understand -c and -o together... yes

<<...>>

checking size of short... (cached) 2
checking size of int... (cached) 4
checking size of long... (cached) 4
checking size of long long... (cached) 8
checking byte ordering... (cached) little-endian
updating cache ../config.cache
creating ./config.status
creating Makefile
creating install-defs.sh
creating config.h
```

This isn't a foolproof method, though, and compilation problems could still occur even after a successful configuration. If running `configure` with or without a series of command line parameters is documented as one of the first steps for compiling and installing the software, then it's highly likely that autoconf is being used and your compilation experience has a greater chance of being problem-free.

4.4.4.2 Compiler Version Differences or Bugs A compilation failure due to a compiler version difference or a bug can be very tricky to diagnose. For version differences, the good news is that the GNU Compiler Collection (GCC) is the most commonly used set of compilers on Linux systems, so the scope of determining differences is much smaller than other systems. There are, however, a growing number of alternative compilers available for the various

architectures on which Linux runs, so using a compiler other than GCC
increases the chances of a compile failure. As GCC is almost always available
on a Linux system as well as additional compilers, a good first step in diagnosing
a compile failure with a different compiler is to re-attempt compilation with
GCC. If GCC compiles without error, you've identified a compiler difference. It
doesn't necessarily mean that either of the compilers is wrong or has a bug. It
could simply mean that the compilers interpret the programming standard
differently.

Version differences within GCC can easily result in compile failures. The
following example illustrates how the same code compiles clean, compiles with
a warning, and fails with a compile error when using different versions of
GCC. The source code is:

```
#include <stdio.h>

static const char msg[] = "This is a string
which spans a
couple of lines
to demonstrates differences
between gcc 2.96,
gcc 3.2,
and gcc 3.3";

int main( void )
{
   printf( "%s\n", msg );

   return 0;
}
```

Compiling and running this code with gcc 2.96 produces the following:

```
penguin> gcc -v
Reading specs from /usr/lib/gcc-lib/i386-suse-linux/2.95.3/specs
gcc version 2.95.3 20010315 (SuSE)
penguin> gcc multiline.c
penguin> ./a.out
This is a string
which spans a
couple of lines
to demonstrates differences
between gcc 2.96,
gcc 3.2,
and gcc 3.3
```

The compilation was successful with no warnings, and running the resulting
executable displays the desired message.

Compiling with gcc 3.2 produces the following:

```
penguin> gcc -v
Reading specs from /usr/lib64/gcc-lib/x86_64-suse-linux/3.2.2/specs
Configured with: ../configure —enable-threads=posix —prefix=/usr —
with-local-prefix=/usr/local —infodir=/usr/share/info —mandir=/usr/
share/man —libdir=/usr/lib64 —enable-
languages=c,c++,f77,objc,java,ada —enable-libgcj —with-gxx-include-
dir=/usr/include/g++ —with-slibdir=/lib —with-system-zlib —enable-
shared —enable-__cxa_atexit x86_64-suse-linux
Thread model: posix
gcc version 3.2.2 (SuSE Linux)
penguin> gcc multiline.c
multiline.c:3:27: warning: multi-line string literals are deprecated
penguin> ./a.out
This is a string
which spans a
couple of lines
to demonstrates differences
between gcc 2.96,
gcc 3.2,
and gcc 3.3
```

As the warning message states, multi-line string literals have been deprecated, but given this is just a warning, the compilation completes, and running the program produces our desired output.

Compiling the source with gcc 3.3 produces this:

```
penguin> /opt/gcc33/bin/gcc -v
Reading specs from /opt/gcc33/lib64/gcc-lib/x86_64-suse-linux/3.3/
➥specs
Configured with: ../configure —enable-threads=posix —prefix=/opt/
gcc33 —with-local-prefix=/usr/local —infodir=/opt/gcc33/share/
➥info —mandir=/opt/gcc33/share/man —libdir=/opt/gcc33/lib64 —enable-
➥languages=c,c++,f77,objc,java,ada —disable-checking —enable-libgcj
➥—with-gxx-include-dir=/opt/gcc33/include/g++ —with-slibdir=/lib64
➥—with-system-zlib —enable-shared —enable-__cxa_atexit x86_64-suse-
➥linux
Thread model: posix
gcc version 3.3 20030312 (prerelease) (SuSE Linux)
penguin> /opt/gcc33/bin/gcc multiline.c
multiline.c:3:27: missing terminating " character
multiline.c:4: error: parse error before "which"
multiline.c:9:11: missing terminating " character
```

Clearly, the error is due to the string spanning multiple lines. If gcc 3.3 is the compiler version to be used, the only solution is to fix the code as shown in this updated script:

```
#include <stdio.h>

static const char msg[] = "This is a string\n"
"which spans a\n"
"couple of lines\n"
"to demonstrates differences\n"
"between gcc 2.96,\n"
"gcc 3.2,\n"
"and gcc 3.3";

int main( void )
{
    printf( "%s\n", msg );

    return 0;
}
```

The point here is that code with strings spanning multiple lines certainly existed
when gcc 2.96 was the most current version. If that code doesn't get updated
by its author(s) and users attempt to compile it with a newer version of gcc,
they will get compile errors directly related to a compiler version difference.
Some C purists could argue that the first version of the sample code is incorrect
and should not have been used in the first place. However, the fact remains
that at one time the compiler allowed it without warning; therefore, it will be
used by many programmers. In fact, there were several instances in kernel
code, mostly drivers, which had multi-line strings that have since been fixed.

Compiler bugs are certainly another very real possibility for compilation
errors. A compiler is a piece of software written in a high-level language as
well, so it is by no means exempt from the same kinds of bugs that exist in
programs being compiled. As with all unexpected compilation errors and
compiler behavior, the best way to determine the cause of the problem is to
eliminate anything nonessential and set up a minimalist scenario; this generally
means making a standalone test program that is made up of a very small
number of source files and functions. The test program should do nothing but
clearly demonstrate the problem. When this is achieved, this test program can
be sent to the parties supporting the compiler. In the case of gcc, this would
generally be the distribution's support team, but it could be gcc developers at
gnu.org directly.

4.4.4.3 User Error Compilation failures due to user error are extremely
ccommon and could be the result of the user incorrectly doing almost anything.
Some examples include

☞ Incorrectly expanding the source archive
☞ Incorrectly applying a necessary patch

☞ Incorrectly setting required flags, options, or environment variables

☞ Executing `make` incorrectly

☞ Using insufficient permissions

☞ Downloading incorrect or insufficient packages

The list is endless...

Generally, software packages come with documents in the highest level directory of the archive with a name to catch your attention. INSTALL, README, or COMPILE are examples. These files usually contain excellent documentation and instructions for building the software package quickly and easily. If the instructions are followed along with a little care and common knowledge, building a software package should be an error free experience.

4.4.4.4 Code Error Compilation failures due to code errors or bugs are the simplest way for a compilation to fail. In general, a source package gets thoroughly tested before it is made available. Testing cannot occur without compilation, so a very high percentage of compilation bugs, if not all, are flushed out during the testing phase. However, because of a huge variety of environments and compilation needs, real compile-time bugs can slip through the cracks to the end user. When this happens, the user can attempt to fix the problem on his own, but often correspondence with the author is required. A word of caution, though: The reason for discussing this section last is to stress the importance of ensuring that a compilation failure isn't due to any of the causes just listed before assuming it is a code error. Reporting a problem as a bug to an author when it is actually user error, for example, is frustrating for everyone, so it is important to be sure of the diagnosis.

It's also very important to note that a compilation failure could very easily be due to a combination of code error and any of the other causes mentioned such as compiler version differences. Using the example of the string spanning multiple lines, even though gcc 2.96 happily compiled it without warning, this doesn't necessarily mean that it is 100% "correct" code.

4.5 ASSEMBLY LISTINGS

A key to debugging various software problems is the ability to generate an assembly listing of a particular source file. Assembly is one step above machine language and is therefore extremely terse and difficult to program in. Modern third-generation languages (3GL) such as C incorporate an "assembly phase" that converts the source code into assembly language. This assembly source is then passed to the assembler for conversion into machine language. Because assembly involves the direct management of low-level system hardware such as registers, machine instructions, and memory, examining the assembly listing produced by the compiler will illustrate exactly what will happen during execution. This is often invaluable in debugging large applications as the C code can get quite complex and difficult to read.

4.5.1 Purpose of Assembly Listings

Applications, especially large ones such as database management systems or Web servers, will often include problem determination features used to dump information to log files, which can be examined later to determine the location and cause of a particular problem. In smaller applications, a debugger can be used to gather necessary information for tracking down the cause of the problem (see Chapter 6, "The GNU Debugger (GDB)" for more information). For speed and binary size reasons, application's binaries are as close to machine language as possible and contain very little human readable information. When a problem arises somewhere in the execution of the binaries, techniques are needed to convert the machine language into something somewhat human readable to be able to determine the cause of the problem. This could mean compiling the application with the -g flag, which will add extra debugging symbols to the resulting machine code binaries. These debug symbols are read by debuggers that will combine them with the assembly language interpretation of the machine language to make the binaries as humanly readable as possible. This adds a great deal of size overhead to the resulting binaries and is often not practical for everyday production use. What this means is that extra knowledge and skill is required by whoever is examining the problem because the highest level of readability that can be achieved is usually the assembly level.

The ultimate objective whenever a problem such as a segmentation fault or bus error occurs is to convert the machine language location of the trap into a high-level source line of code. When the source line of code is obtained, the developer can examine the area of code to see why the particular trap may have occurred. Sometimes the problem will be instantly obvious, and other times more diagnostics will be needed.

So how then does one even determine the machine language or assembly location of the trap? One way is to dump diagnostic information to a log file from an application's problem determination facilities. Generally, the diagnostic information will include a stack traceback (see Chapter 5 for more information) as well as an offset into each function in the stack traceback that represents where the execution currently is or will return to in that function. This stack traceback information is usually very similar to the information that is obtainable using a debugger. The following output shows a stack traceback obtained after attaching gdb to an xterm process:

```
(gdb) where
#0  0x40398f6e in select () from /lib/i686/libc.so.6
#1  0x08053a47 in in_put ()
#2  0x080535d5 in VTparse ()
#3  0x080563d5 in VTRun ()
#4  0x080718f4 in main ()
(gdb) print &select
$1 = (<text variable, no debug info> *) 0x40398f50 <select>
(gdb) print /x 0x40398f6e - 0x40398f50
$2 = 0x1e
```

The important thing to understand is that from this simple output we know
that the offset into the function `select()` at which execution is currently at is
`0x1e`. With the source code used to compile the /lib/i686/libc.so.6 library, we
could then easily determine the exact line of source code by creating an assembly
listing.

We will focus more on stack tracebacks, problem determination facilities,
and using a debugger in other chapters. For now, we will concentrate on the
steps needed to create an assembly listing and how to correlate an offset with
a line of code.

4.5.2 Generating Assembly Listings

For most high-level language programmers, looking at raw assembly isn't very
easy and could take a great deal of time. Fortunately, mixing the high-level
source code with the assembly is an option.

There are two methods to achieving this. One is with the `objdump(1)` utility.
Another way to do this is by telling the compiler to stop at the assembly phase
and write the listing to a file. This raw assembly listing can then be run through
the system assembler with certain command line parameters to produce an
output file that intermixes assembly and high-level source code. An example
of this is done with the source code in the code saved in file `as_listing.c` and
listed here:

```c
#include <stdio.h>

int main( void )
{
    int a = 5;
    int b = 3;
    int c = 0;
    char s[] = "The result is";

    c = a + b;

    printf( "%s %d\n", s, c );
```

```
    return 0;
}
```

A typical compilation of this source code would consist of running:

```
gcc -o as_listing as_listing.c
```

This produces the executable file `as_listing`. For gcc, specifying the `-s` flag causes the compilation to stop before the assembling phase and dump out the generated assembly code. By default, if `-o` is not used to specify an output filename, gcc converts the input source filename extension (such as .c) to .s. To be able to properly intermix the assembly and high-level source code, it is also required to use the `-g` flag to produce debug symbols and line number information. For the code in `as_listing.c`, to produce an assembly output, run the following command:

```
gcc as_listing.c -S -g
```

The resulting as_listing.s text file can be examined, but unless you know assembly very well, it likely won't make much sense. This is where the importance of mixing in the high-level language comes to play. To do this, run the system assembler, `as`, with the command line arguments, which turn on listings to include assembly and high-level source:

```
as -alh as_listing.s > as_listing.s_c
```

> **Note:** Certain compilations done using make files will compile a source file from a different directory rather than the current one. In this case, it may be necessary to run `objdump` or `as -alh` from the same directory in which the make process compiled the file.

4.5.3 Reading and Understanding an Assembly Listing

For the most part, the reason for examining an assembly listing is to determine how the compiler interpreted the high-level language and what assembly language resulted. When first looking at an assembly listing, it can be quite intimidating. It's important to understand that there is a lot of information in this file that is only of use to a system's assembler. Generally, much of this data can be ignored as often only a very specific area of the code will be desired and referred to by a function name and an offset in a stack dump or stack traceback for example. With this information and the assembly listing in hand, the first thing to do is to search for the function name in the assembly listing. The assembly listing from the code in `as_listing.c` is shown below:

```
16                              .globl main
17                                  .type   main, @function
18                              main:
19                              .LFB3:
20                                  .file 1 "as_listing.c"
 1:as_listing.c  ****  #include <stdio.h>
 2:as_listing.c  ****
 3:as_listing.c  ****  int main( void )
 4:as_listing.c  ****  {
21                                  .loc 1 4 0
22 0000 55                         pushl   %ebp
23                              .LCFI0:
24 0001 89E5                       movl    %esp, %ebp
25                              .LCFI1:
26 0003 83EC28                     subl    $40, %esp
27                              .LCFI2:
28 0006 83E4F0                     andl    $-16, %esp
29 0009 B8000000                   movl    $0, %eax
29      00
30 000e 29C4                       subl    %eax, %esp
 5:as_listing.c  ****      int a = 5;
31                                  .loc 1 5 0
32                              .LBB2:
33 0010 C745F405                   movl    $5, -12(%ebp)
33      000000
 6:as_listing.c  ****      int b = 3;
34                                  .loc 1 6 0
35 0017 C745F003                   movl    $3, -16(%ebp)
35      000000
 7:as_listing.c  ****      int c = 0;
36                                  .loc 1 7 0
37 001e C745EC00                   movl    $0, -20(%ebp)
37      000000
 8:as_listing.c  ****      char s[] = "The result is";
^LGAS LISTING as_listing.s                      page 2


38                                  .loc 1 8 0
39 0025 A1000000                   movl    .LC0, %eax
39      00
40 002a 8945D8                     movl    %eax, -40(%ebp)
41 002d A1040000                   movl    .LC0+4, %eax
41      00
42 0032 8945DC                     movl    %eax, -36(%ebp)
43 0035 A1080000                   movl    .LC0+8, %eax
43      00
44 003a 8945E0                     movl    %eax, -32(%ebp)
45 003d 66A10C00                   movw    .LC0+12, %ax
```

```
45      0000
46 0043 668945E4                    movw    %ax, -28(%ebp)
 9:as_listing.c  ****
10:as_listing.c  ****   c = a + b;
```

As you can see, assembly is quite terse and much more lengthy than C! The numbers at the far left that start at 16 and go up to 46 are the assembly listing line numbers. If you open up `as_listing.s` and look at line 16 for example, you will see:

```
.globl main
```

Some of the assembly listing lines will have four digit hexadecimal numbers to the right of them. This is the offset number and is a very important number. In the preceding assembly listing we can see that the start of the `main()` function has an offset of 0:

```
22 0000 55                          pushl   %ebp
```

It's also important to understand that the first assembly instruction in any function on x86 based hardware is `pushl %ebp`, which pushes the calling function's frame pointer onto the stack.

> **Note**: Some architectures such as x86-64 support the `-fomit-frame-pointer` optimization flag, which is turned on by default with the `-O2` optimization level (see the section, "Compiler Optimization," for more information). When an object is compiled with this flag, there will not be any instructions at the beginning of a function to save and set up the frame registers. Doing this is advantageous for performance reasons because an extra register is freed up for other uses along with a few less instructions being run. Compiling with this option can make debugging a little more difficult, so caution may be warranted depending on your application's need. The SuSE distributions on x86-64 are compiled with this flag, so manual stack analysis using the frame registers is not possible. The x86 architecture does not support the `-fomit-frame-pointer` flag because debugging is impossible with it.

Note also that the start of a function is not necessarily always at offset 0; it could potentially be any value. If it isn't 0 and you have an offset into the function to look for, simply subtract the offset at the beginning of the function from the offset you are looking for. This is a rule of thumb to always follow. In the example of `main()`, just shown, we would be subtracting 0 from the offset, which simply gives us the offset itself.

Now, looking at the line immediately above assembly line 22, we see this:

```
21                  .loc 1 4 0
```

The `.loc` is an assembly directive that stands for "line of code." The numbers that follow it each have their own significance. The first number, 1 in this example, indicates which source file this line of code comes from. To determine which file 1 represents, you need to look through the assembly listing for the .file directives. Looking again at the assembly listing, we see the following line:

```
20                    .file 1 "as_listing.c"
```

The 1 after `.file` indicates which file number this is, and of course the following string is the filename itself. The code in `as_listing.c` is very simple, so there is only one file. In more complex programs, though, especially when inline functions and macros defined in #include'd files are used, there could be several .file directives, so it's important to understand this.

The next number after the 1 in the `.loc` directive, in this example, "4," is the actual line of code in the file referred to by 1. For our example, line 4 of `as_listing.c` is in fact

```
    {
```

which indicates the start of the `main()` function.

The final number in the `.loc` directive, `0`, is meant to be the column number; however, for GCC compiled objects, this value is always 0.

As an aside, during this writing, I did not yet know what the final number in the `.loc` directive meant. Searching through documentation did not uncover any information other than indicating it was a "column" number. I then decided to harness the power of open source and look at the source code itself to see where that number came from. I found that the `.loc` directive is indeed emitted by GCC. I downloaded the gcc-3.3.2.tar.gz source tar-ball from `ftp.gnu.org` and untarred it. I then searched through the source for anything to do with `.loc`. The function `dwarf2out_source_line`, as the name implies, writes out information related to the source code line and is found in the file `gcc/dwarf2out.c`. The lines of interest from that function are

```
        /* Emit the .loc directive understood by GNU as.  */
        fprintf (asm_out_file, "\t.loc %d %d 0\n", file_num, line);
```

As you can see, the "0" is constant; therefore I can only assume that it's not used for anything important. In any case, the point of discussing this is to show just how powerful open source can be. With a little knowledge and motivation, learning what makes things tick for any purpose is easily within everyone's reach.

4.6 COMPILER OPTIMIZATIONS

High-level source compilers have the complex task of converting human readable source code into machine-specific assembly language. This task is complicated even more by various optimization options and levels that are applied during compilation. The intent here is not to give an exhaustive reference of what each optimization option and level does, but rather to make you aware of what effects compiler optimizations can have on your resulting binaries and the ability to debug them. For simplicity, only GCC will be discussed.

There are several optimization levels that perform varying degrees of optimization. For GCC, these levels are specified with the -o parameter immediately followed by zero or one level specifiers. -o implies -o1, which is the first optimization level. Refer to the gcc(1) man page for more information and to see exactly which specific options that are controlled with a flag are enabled at each level. It's important to understand that the -o2 and -o3 levels perform additional optimizations that consume more resources during compile time but will likely result in faster binaries.

A crucial aspect of compiler optimizations to understand is that debugging abilities are inhibited as more optimizations are performed. This is because for optimizations to work, the compiler must be free to rearrange and manipulate the resulting assembly code in any way it wishes, while of course not changing the desired programming logic. Because of this, correlating a line of C code, for example, directly to a small set of assembly instructions becomes more difficult. This results in a trade-off that the developer must deal with. Having the application run as fast as it possibly can is of course an important goal, but if the resulting application cannot be easily debugged and serviced, huge customer satisfaction issues could result. A good compromise is to use the -o2 optimization level. Excellent optimizations are performed while the ability to debug is still within reach. It's also important to understand that if a real coding bug exists, it will exist at any optimization level. Therefore when a bug is found when the binaries are compiled with -o2 for example, simply re-compile with -o0 and the same bug should occur. The application can then be debugged with a debugger, which will easily allow the developer to examine all variables and step through individual lines of source.

Everything good has its cost and usually with optimizations, one of the costs is increased code size. Again, reading the GCC man page and manual will detail exactly what each of the options and levels do and how they affect size, but in general code size will increase proportionally with the optimization levels 1, 2, and 3. There also exists -os, which will optimize the code for size. This is good consideration for the AMD Opteron-based architecture, for example, as the cache size is relatively small at 1MB.

To illustrate how much the compiler optimization can affect binaries, let's use the following very simple code and call it `simple.c`:

```
#include <stdio.h>

int add_them_up( int a, int b, int c )
{
    return a + b + c;
}

int main( void )
{
    int a = 1;
    int b = 2;
    int c = 3;
    int z = 0;

    z = add_them_up( 1, 2, 3 );

    printf( "Answer is: %d\n", z );

    return 0;
}
```

Next, produce two separate assembly listings—one compiled with -oo and one with -o3 by doing the following:

```
penguin$ gcc -O0 -S -g simple.c
penguin$ as -alh simple.s > simple.out.no-opt
penguin$ gcc -O3 -S -g simple.c
penguin$ as -alh simple.s > simple.out.opt
```

The output of `as -alh` will produce a lot of additional symbol information that we're generally not interested in. Omitting the uninteresting parts of `simple.out.no-opt`, here's the produced output:

```
10        .globl add_them_up
11              .type   add_them_up, @function
12        add_them_up:
13        .LFB3:
14              .file 1 "simple.c"
```

```
 1:simple.c       **** #include <stdio.h>
 2:simple.c       ****
 3:simple.c       **** int add_them_up( int a, int b, int c )
 4:simple.c       **** {
15               .loc 1 4 0
16 0000 55              pushl   %ebp
17      .LCFI0:
18 0001 89E5            movl    %esp, %ebp
19      .LCFI1:
 5:simple.c       ****     return a + b + c;
20               .loc 1 5 0
21 0003 8B450C          movl    12(%ebp), %eax
22 0006 034508          addl    8(%ebp), %eax
23 0009 034510          addl    16(%ebp), %eax
 6:simple.c       **** }
24               .loc 1 6 0
25 000c 5D              popl    %ebp
26 000d C3              ret
27      .LFE3:
28               .size   add_them_up, .-add_them_up
29               .section        .rodata
30      .LC0:
31 0000 416E7377                .string "Answer is: %d\n"
31      65722069
31      733A2025
31      640A00
32               .text
33      .globl main
34               .type   main, @function
35      main:
36      .LFB5:
 7:simple.c       ****
 8:simple.c       **** int main( void )
 9:simple.c       **** {
37               .loc 1 9 0
38 000e 55              pushl   %ebp
39      .LCFI2:
40 000f 89E5            movl    %esp, %ebp
41      .LCFI3:
```

GAS LISTING simple.s   page 2

```
42 0011 83EC18          subl    $24, %esp
43      .LCFI4:
44 0014 83E4F0          andl    $-16, %esp
45 0017 B8000000                movl    $0, %eax
45      00
46 001c 29C4            subl    %eax, %esp
10:simple.c       ****     int a = 1;
47               .loc 1 10 0
48      .LBB2:
49 001e C745FC01                movl    $1, -4(%ebp)
```

```
49        000000
11:simple.c      ****    int b = 2;
50                .loc 1 11 0
51 0025 C745F802                movl    $2, -8(%ebp)
51        000000
12:simple.c      ****    int c = 3;
52                .loc 1 12 0
53 002c C745F403                movl    $3, -12(%ebp)
53        000000
13:simple.c      ****    int z = 0;
54                .loc 1 13 0
55 0033 C745F000                movl    $0, -16(%ebp)
55        000000
14:simple.c      ****
15:simple.c      ****    z = add_them_up( 1, 2, 3);
56                .loc 1 15 0
57 003a 83EC04          subl    $4, %esp
58 003d 6A03            pushl   $3
59 003f 6A02            pushl   $2
60 0041 6A01            pushl   $1
61        .LCFI5:
62 0043 E8FCFFFF                call    add_them_up
62        FF
63 0048 83C410          addl    $16, %esp
64 004b 8945F0          movl    %eax, -16(%ebp)
16:simple.c      ****
17:simple.c      ****    printf( "Answer is: %d\n", z );
65                .loc 1 17 0
66 004e 83EC08          subl    $8, %esp
67 0051 FF75F0          pushl   -16(%ebp)
68 0054 68000000                pushl   $.LC0
68        00
69 0059 E8FCFFFF                call    printf
69        FF
70 005e 83C410          addl    $16, %esp
18:simple.c      ****
19:simple.c      ****    return 0;
71                .loc 1 19 0
72 0061 B8000000                movl    $0, %eax
72        00
20:simple.c      **** }
73                .loc 1 20 0
74 0066 C9              leave
75 0067 C3              ret
76        .LBE2:
77        .LFE5:
78                .size  main, .-main
    GAS LISTING simple.s                    page 3
```

Next, let's cut the uninteresting parts of simple.out.opt and examine it more closely:

```
15        .globl main
16                .type    main, @function
17        main:
18        .LFB14:
19                .file 1 "simple.c"
 1:simple.c       **** #include <stdio.h>
 2:simple.c       ****
 3:simple.c       **** int add_them_up( int a, int b, int c )
 4:simple.c       **** {
 5:simple.c       ****    return a + b + c;
 6:simple.c       **** }
 7:simple.c       ****
 8:simple.c       **** int main( void )
 9:simple.c       **** {
20                .loc 1 9 0
21 0000 55            pushl   %ebp
22        .LCFI0:
23 0001 89E5          movl    %esp, %ebp
24        .LCFI1:
25 0003 52            pushl   %edx
26 0004 52            pushl   %edx
27 0005 83E4F0        andl    $-16, %esp
10:simple.c       ****    int a = 1;
11:simple.c       ****    int b = 2;
12:simple.c       ****    int c = 3;
13:simple.c       ****    int z = 0;
14:simple.c       ****
15:simple.c       ****    z = add_them_up( 1, 2, 3);
16:simple.c       ****
17:simple.c       ****    printf( "Answer is: %d\n", z );
28                .loc 1 17 0
29        .LBB2:
30 0008 50            pushl   %eax
31 0009 50            pushl   %eax
32 000a 6A06          pushl   $6
33 000c 68000000          pushl   $.LC0
GAS LISTING simple.s                          page 2


33        00
34        .LCFI2:
35 0011 E8FCFFFF          call    printf
35        FF
18:simple.c       ****
19:simple.c       ****    return 0;
20:simple.c       **** }
36                .loc 1 20 0
37        .LBE2:
38 0016 31C0          xorl    %eax, %eax
39 0018 C9            leave
40 0019 C3            ret
41        .LFE14:
```

```
42                .size   main, .-main
43 001a 8DB60000              .p2align 4,,15
43      0000
44      .globl add_them_up
45              .type   add_them_up, @function
46      add_them_up:
47      .LFB25:
48              .loc 1 4 0
49 0020 55            pushl   %ebp
50      .LCFI3:
51 0021 89E5          movl    %esp, %ebp
52      .LCFI4:
53 0023 8B450C        movl    12(%ebp), %eax
54              .loc 1 5 0
55 0026 8B4D08        movl    8(%ebp), %ecx
56 0029 8B5510        movl    16(%ebp), %edx
57 002c 01C8          addl    %ecx, %eax
58 002e 01D0          addl    %edx, %eax
59              .loc 1 6 0
60 0030 5D            popl    %ebp
61 0031 C3            ret
62      .LFE25:
63              .size   add_them_up, .-add_them_up
```

Comparing these two assembly listings, we can quickly see that the interesting parts in the optimized version are smaller than the interesting parts in the non-optimized version. For a small and simple program such as `simple.c`, this is expected because the compiler optimizations will strip out unnecessary instructions and make other changes in favor of performance. Remember that every single assembly instruction in a program represents a finite amount of time running on a processor, so less assembly instruction leads to greater performance. Of course, optimization techniques go well above and beyond that statement and could easily comprise a specialized book.

A very interesting observation regarding the difference in size between the two assembly listings is that the file size of the optimized version is almost exactly twice as large as the non-optimized version.

```
penguin> ls -l simple.out.opt simple.out.no-opt
-rw-r—r— 1 dbehman  users    17482 2004-08-30 21:46 simple.out.
➥no-opt
-rw-r—r— 1 dbehman  users    35528 2004-08-30 21:46 simple.out.opt
```

So even though the assembly instructions are streamlined, there is a lot of extra data generated in the optimized listing over the non-optimized one. A significant portion of this extra data is the additionally inserted debug info. Often, when the compiler implements various optimization tricks and techniques, as mentioned, debugging capability is sacrificed. In an effort to alleviate this, more debugging info is added to the assembly, thus the larger file size.

Examining the assembly instructions more closely for the two assembly listings will show that `simple.out.opt` will look quite a bit more compressed and advanced than the non-optimized assembly. You should also notice right away that something strange has happened with the `add_them_up()` function in `simple.out.opt`. The function's location was placed after `main` instead of before `main` as it is in the non-optimized version. This confuses the `as -alh` command; therefore the C source code is not properly intermixed. The C source is nicely intermixed with `add_them_up()` in the non-optimized assembly listing, which is very easy to read and associate assembly instructions with C source lines of code.

Let's look a little closer at the generated assembly in each listing around this line of C source code:

```
z = add_them_up( 1, 2, 3 );
```

In the associated assembly we would expect to see a `call add_them_up` instruction. In fact, we do see this in `simple.out.no-opt`, but we do not see it in simple.out.opt! What happened? Let's look closer at the area in the optimized assembly listing where we expect the call to `add_them_up()`:

```
15:simple.c     ****      z = add_them_up( 1, 2, 3 );
16:simple.c     ****
17:simple.c     ****      printf( "Answer is: %d\n", z );
28                .loc 1 17 0
29        .LBB2:
30 0008 50               pushl   %eax
31 0009 50               pushl   %eax
32 000a 6A06             pushl   $6
33 000c 68000000         pushl   $.LC0
GAS LISTING simple.s                      page 2


33        00
34        .LCFI2:
35 0011 E8FCFFFF         call    printf
```

We can see that there is no assembly associated with C source code on line 15, which is where we call `add_them_up()` with the constant values 1, 2, and 3. Note the two `pushl` instructions which immediately precede the `call printf` instruction. These instructions are part of the procedure calling conventions-see the section on calling conventions for more details. The basic idea, however, is that on the i386 architecture, procedure arguments get pushed onto the stack in reverse order. Our call to `printf` takes two arguments - the string "`Answer is: %d\n`" and the variable `z`. So we know that the first push is for the variable `z`:

```
32 000a 6A06          pushl   $6
```

> **Note:** GCC for Linux uses the AT&T assembly syntax instead of the Intel syntax. The primary differences between the two syntaxes are as follows in Table 4.1.

	AT&T	Intel
Operand order	source, destination	destination, source
Register naming	Prefix of %	No prefix
Constant values	Prefix of $	No prefix
Example: move the constant value 1 into the eax register	mov $1, %eax	mov eax, 1

Table 4.1 Assembly Syntax Comparison.

So the compiler's optimizer was smart enough to understand that the `add_them_up()` function was simply adding constant values and returning the result. Function calls are expensive in terms of performance, so any time a function call can be avoided is a huge bonus. This is why the compiler completely avoids calling `add_them_up()` and simply calls `printf` with the computed value of 6.

To take our examination a step further, let's create an assembly listing for simple.c at the `-O2` optimization level to see how it affects our call to `add_them_up()` and `printf()`. The section of interest is:

```
15:simple.c      ****      z = add_them_up( 1, 2, 3);
49                              .loc 1 15 0
50                          .LBB2:
51 0028 50                      pushl   %eax
52 0029 6A03                    pushl   $3
53 002b 6A02                    pushl   $2
54 002d 6A01                    pushl   $1
55                          .LCFI4:
56 002f E8FCFFFF                call    add_them_up
56      FF
57 0034 5A                      popl    %edx
58 0035 59                      popl    %ecx
16:simple.c      ****
```

```
17:simple.c      ****      printf( "Answer is: %d\n", z );
59                          .loc 1 17 0
60 0036 50                  pushl   %eax
61 0037 68000000            pushl   $.LC0
61      00
62 003c E8FCFFFF            call    printf
```

The setup prior to the `printf` call looks very similar to the non-optimized assembly listing, but there is one significant difference. At the -02 level, the `%eax` register is pushed onto the stack for our variable z. Recall from the section on calling conventions that `%eax` always holds a procedure's return value. The GCC optimizer at -02 is smart enough to know that we can simply leave the return value from the call to `add_them_up()` in the `%eax` register and push that directly onto the stack for the call to `printf`. The non-optimized assembly takes the return value in the `%eax` register from the call to `add_them_up()` and copies it to the stack which is where the variable z is stored. This then results in pushing the value from where it's stored on the stack in preparation for the call to `printf`. This is much more expensive than register accesses.

Another major difference between the assembly at the -02 and -03 levels is that -02 still makes a call to `add_them_up()` just as the non-optimized assembly does. This tells us that there is some optimization done specific to the -03 level that results in saving an unnecessary function call. Looking at the GCC(1) man page, we see the following:

```
-O3 Optimize yet more.   -O3 turns on all optimizations specified by
-O2 and also turns on the -finline-functions,
   -fweb,
   -funit-at-a-time, -ftracer, -funswitch-loops and
   -frename-registers options.
```

Looking at the options enabled at -03, `-finline-functions` looks very interesting. The man page documents the following:

```
-finline-functions
   Integrate all simple functions into their callers.  The compiler
   heuristically decides which functions are simple enough to be
   worth integrating in this way.

   If all calls to a given function are integrated, and the function
   is declared "static," then the function is normally not output as
   assembler code in its own right.

   Enabled at level -O3.
```

This explains exactly what we've observed with the call to `add_them_up()` at the -03 level. To confirm, we can produce another assembly listing with the following commands:

```
penguin$ gcc -O2 -finline-functions -S -g simple.c
penguin$ as -alh simple.s > simple.out.opt-O2-finline_functions
```

The interesting parts from `simple.out.opt-O2-finline-functions` shows:

```
15:simple.c       ****      z = add_them_up( 1, 2, 3);
16:simple.c       ****
17:simple.c       ****      printf( "Answer is: %d\n", z );
28                          .loc 1 17 0
29                 .LBB2:
30 0008 50                  pushl   %eax
31 0009 50                  pushl   %eax
32 000a 6A06                pushl   $6
33 000c 68000000            pushl   $.LC0
^LGAS LISTING simple.s.opt-O2-inline-functions             page 2


33     00
34                 .LCFI2:
35 0011 E8FCFFFF             call    printf
```

Bingo! We have identified a specific assembly change made by using an additional compiler optimization switch.

4.7 CONCLUSION

With the information presented in this chapter, you should now be much better armed to defend against many compilation-related problems that may come your way. With more knowledge of problem determination at runtime, you're well on your way to becoming a completely self-sufficient Linux user.

## CHAPTER 5

The Stack

5.1 INTRODUCTION

The stack is one of the most important and fundamental parts of a computer's architecture. It is something that many computer users may have heard of but likely don't know much about what it is used for or how it works. Many software problems can involve the stack, so it is important to have a working knowledge to troubleshoot effectively. Let's start out by defining the term *stack*. The definition taken directly from `Dictionary.com` is

stack(stak)

n.

1. A large, usually conical pile of straw or fodder arranged for outdoor storage.
2. An orderly pile, especially one arranged in layers. See Synonyms at <u>heap</u>.
3. *Computer Science.* A section of memory and its associated registers used for temporary storage of information in which the item most recently stored is the first to be retrieved.
4. A group of three rifles supporting each other, butt downward and forming a cone.
   a. A chimney or flue.
   b. A group of chimneys arranged together.
5. A vertical exhaust pipe, as on a ship or locomotive.
6. An extensive arrangement of bookshelves. Often used in the plural.
7. stacks The area of a library in which most of the books are shelved.
8. A stackup.
9. An English measure of coal or cut wood, equal to 108 cubic feet (3.06 cubic meters).
10. *Informal.* A large quantity: *a stack of work to do.*

Of course, 3) is the definition that we're looking for in the context of this book. That definition is very accurate and should lay out a great starting point for readers who aren't familiar with what a stack is or what it is used for. Stacks exist and are integral for program execution on most major architectures, but the layout and exact functionality of them vary on certain architectures. The basic idea, though, is the same: As a program calls functions and uses storage local to those functions, data gets *pushed* or placed onto the stack. As the program returns from the functions, the data is *popped* or removed from the stack. In the sense of data storage, the *heap* can be thought of as opposite to the stack. Data storage in the heap does not need to be local to any particular function. This is an important difference to understand. Heaps are discussed in more detail in the "Heap Segment" section of Chapter 3, "The /proc Filesystem."

5.2 A REAL-WORLD ANALOGY

To help understand the purpose and functionality of a program stack, a real-world analogy is useful. Consider Joe who likes to explore new places, but once he gets to his destination he is always afraid that he'll forget how to get back home. To prevent this, Joe devises a plan that he calls his "travel stack." The only supplies he needs are several pieces of paper, a pencil, and a box to hold the paper. When he leaves his apartment, he writes down "My apartment" on a piece of paper and places it in the empty box. As he walks and sees landmarks or things of interest, he writes them down on another piece of paper and places that piece of paper onto the forming pile in the box. So for example, the first landmark he passed was a hot dog stand on the sidewalk, so he wrote down "Bob's Hot Dog Stand" on a piece of paper and placed it in the box. He did the same thing for several more landmarks:

☞ Tim's Coffee Shop
☞ Large statue of Linus Torvalds
☞ George's Auto Body Shop
☞ Penguin Park

He finally made it to his destination—the bookstore where he could purchase a good Linux book such as this one! So now that he's at the bookstore, he wants to make sure he makes it home safely with his new purchase. To do this, he simply pulls the first piece of paper out of the box and reads it. "Penguin Park" is written on the top piece of paper, so he walks toward it. When he reaches it, he discards the piece of paper and gets the next piece from the box. It reads "George's Auto Body Shop," so Joe walks toward it next. He continues this process until he reaches his apartment where he can begin learning fabulous things about Linux!

This example is exactly how a computer uses a stack to execute a program. In a computer, Joe would be the CPU, the box would be the program stack, the pieces of paper would be the stack frames, and the landmarks written on the paper would be the function return addresses.

The stack is a crucial part of program execution. Each stack frame, which will be discussed in more detail later, corresponds to a single instance of a function and stores variables and data local to that instance of the function. This concept allows function recursion to work because each time the function is executed, a stack frame for it is created and placed onto the stack with its own copy of the variables, which could be very different from the previous execution instance of the very same function. If a recursive function was executed 10 times, there would be 10 stack frames, and as execution finishes, the associated stack frame is removed and execution moves on to the next frame.

5.3 STACKS IN X86 AND X86-64 ARCHITECTURES

Considering the most popular Linux architecture is x86 (also referred to as i386) and because x86-64 is very similar and quickly gaining in popularity, this section focuses on them. Stacks on these architectures are said to grow "down" because they start at a high memory address and grow toward low memory addresses. See section "/proc/<pid>/maps" in Chapter 3 for more information on the process address space. Figure 5.1 shows a diagram of the process address space with the stack starting at the top and growing down toward lower memory addresses.

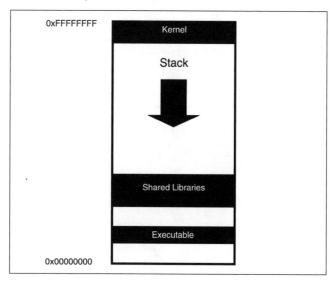

Fig. 5.1 Example of Stack Growing Down.

So now that we know conceptually where the stack resides and how it works, let's find out where it *really* is and how it *really* works. The exact location will vary by architecture, but it will also vary by distribution. This is because some distributions include various patches and changes to the kernel source that modify the process address space. On SUSE 9.0 Professional and SLES 8 distributions running on x86 hardware, the stack segment starts at 0xc0000000 as shown in this very simple /proc/<pid>/maps file.

```
08048000-08049000 r-xp 00000000 03:08 293559   /u/dbehman/book/working/
➡foo
08049000-0804a000 rw-p 00000000 03:08 293559    /u/dbehman/book/working/
➡foo
40000000-40018000 r-xp 00000000 03:08 6664       /lib/ld-2.3.2.so
40018000-40019000 rw-p 00017000 03:08 6664       /lib/ld-2.3.2.so
40019000-4001b000 rw-p 00000000 00:00 0
40028000-40154000 r-xp 00000000 03:08 6661       /lib/i686/libc.so.6
40154000-40159000 rw-p 0012c000 03:08 6661       /lib/i686/libc.so.6
40159000-4015b000 rw-p 00000000 00:00 0
bfffe000-c0000000 rwxp fffff000 00:00 0
```

Remember, the stack grows down toward smaller addresses, thus the reason why 0xc0000000 is the end value in the stack address range of 0xbfffe000 - 0xc0000000.

Now to prove to ourselves that this range is in fact the stack segment, let's write a small program that simply declares a local variable and then prints out that variable's address.

Note: Local variables are also referred to as stack variables given that the storage for them is obtained from the stack segment.

The source code for the program is as follows:

```
#include <stdio.h>

int main( void )
{
    int stackVar = 3;
    char szCommand[64];

    printf( "Address of stackVar is 0x%x\n\n", &stackVar );

    sprintf( szCommand, "cat /proc/%d/maps", getpid() );
    system( szCommand );

    return 0;
}
```

Compiling and running this program gives this output:

```
penguin> ./stack
Address of stackVar is 0xbffff2dc

08048000-08049000 r-xp 00000000 03:08 293568 /u/dbehman/book/code/
➥stack
08049000-0804a000 rw-p 00000000 03:08 293568 /u/dbehman/book/code/
➥stack
40000000-40018000 r-xp 00000000 03:08 6664    /lib/ld-2.3.2.so
40018000-40019000 rw-p 00017000 03:08 6664    /lib/ld-2.3.2.so
40019000-4001b000 rw-p 00000000 00:00 0
40028000-40154000 r-xp 00000000 03:08 6661    /lib/i686/libc.so.6
40154000-40159000 rw-p 0012c000 03:08 6661    /lib/i686/libc.so.6
40159000-4015b000 rw-p 00000000 00:00 0
bfffe000-c0000000 rwxp fffff000 00:00 0
```

As we can see, `0xbffff2dc` does indeed fall within `0xbfffe000` and `0xc0000000`. Examining this further, since there was only one stack variable in our very simple program example, what is on the stack in between `0xc0000000` and `0xbffff2dc`?

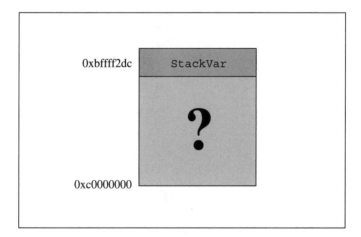

Fig. 5.2 Stack space.

The answer to this question is in the standard ELF specification, which is implemented in the kernel source file fs/elf_binfmt.c. Basically, what happens is that beginning with the terminating NULL byte at `0xbffffffb` and working down toward lower addresses, the kernel copies the following information into this area:

☞ the pathname specified to `exec()`

☞ the full process environment

☞ all argv strings

☞ argc

☞ the auxiliary vector

We could verify this by enhancing our simple program, which displays the address of a stack variable, to also dump the locations of some of the information just listed. The enhanced code is as follows:

```
#include <stdio.h>
extern char **environ;

int main( int argc, char *argv[] )
{
   int stackVar = 3;
   char szCommand[64];

   printf( "Address of stackVar is 0x%x\n", &stackVar );
   printf( "Address of argc is    0x%x\n", &argc );
   printf( "Address of argv is    0x%x\n", argv );
   printf( "Address of environ is 0x%x\n", environ );
   printf( "Address of argv[0] is 0x%x\n", argv[0] );
   printf( "Address of *environ is 0x%x\n\n", *environ );

   sprintf( szCommand, "cat /proc/%d/maps", getpid() );
   system( szCommand );

   return 0;
}
```

Compiling and running this enhanced program gives the following output:

```
penguin> ./stack2
Address of stackVar is 0xbffff2dc
Address of argc is    0xbffff2f0
Address of argv is    0xbffff334
Address of environ is 0xbffff33c
Address of argv[0] is 0xbffff4d5
Address of *environ is 0xbffff4de

08048000-08049000 r-xp 00000000 03:08 188004   /u/dbehman/book/code/
➥stack2
08049000-0804a000 rw-p 00000000 03:08 188004   /u/dbehman/book/code/
➥stack2
40000000-40018000 r-xp 00000000 03:08 6664     /lib/ld-2.3.2.so
40018000-40019000 rw-p 00017000 03:08 6664     /lib/ld-2.3.2.so
40019000-4001b000 rw-p 00000000 00:00 0
```

```
40028000-40154000 r-xp 00000000 03:08 6661    /lib/i686/libc.so.6
40154000-40159000 rw-p 0012c000 03:08 6661    /lib/i686/libc.so.6
40159000-4015b000 rw-p 00000000 00:00 0
bfffe000-c0000000 rwxp fffff000 00:00 0
```

From the first few lines of output, we can now see some of the things that lie
between the top of the stack and the program's first stack frame.

It's also important to note that with C applications, `main()` isn't really the
first function to be executed. Functions that get executed before `main()` include
`__libc_start_main()`, `_start()`, and `__libc_csu_init()`.

5.4 WHAT IS A STACK FRAME?

A single stack frame can be thought of as a contiguous address range, usually
relatively small, in the stack segment that contains everything local to a
particular function. Every function (except special cases such as inline or static
functions) has a stack frame. More specifically, every individual execution of a
function has an associated stack frame. The stack frame holds all local variables
for that function as well as parameters that are passed to other functions that
are called during execution. Consider the source code from stack3.c:

```c
#include <stdio.h>

void function3( int *passedByReference )
{
    int dummy = '\0';

    printf( "My pid is %d;  Press <ENTER> to continue", getpid() );
    dummy = fgetc( stdin );
    *passedByReference = 9;
}

void function2( char *paramString )
{
    int localInt = 1;

    function3( &localInt );
    printf( "Value of localInt = %d\n", localInt );
}

void function1( int paramInt )
{
    char localString[] = "This is a string.";

    function2( localString );
}
```

```
int main( void )
{
    int stackVar = 3;

    function1( stackVar );

    return 0;
}
```

There's a lot going on in the example, but for now we're most interested in the fact that running this program will cause main() to call function1(), which calls function2(), which then calls function3(). function3() then displays its PID and waits for the user to hit ENTER to continue. Also pay attention to the local variables that are declared in each function. When we run this program and let it pause in function3(), we can visualize the stack frames by what is shown in Figure 5.3:

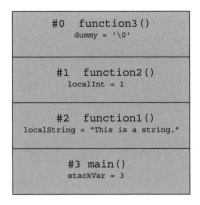

Fig. 5.3 Functions and stack frames.

This conceptual view can be viewed practically in gdb by compiling and running stack.c and then running the stack program under gdb with a breakpoint set in function3(). Once the breakpoint is hit, enter the command backtrace (synonymous with bt and where) to display the stack frames. The output will look like the following:

```
penguin> gdb stack3
GNU gdb 5.3.92
Copyright 2003 Free Software Foundation, Inc.
GDB is free software, covered by the GNU General Public License, and
you are welcome to change it and/or distribute copies of it under
certain conditions.
Type "show copying" to see the conditions.
There is absolutely no warranty for GDB.  Type "show warranty" for
```

```
details.
This GDB was configured as "i586-suse-linux"...
(gdb) break function3
Breakpoint 1 at 0x80483d2: file stack3.c, line 5.
(gdb) run
Starting program: /home/dbehman/book/code/stack3

Breakpoint 1, function3 (passedByReference=0xbffff284) at stack3.c:5
5            int dummy = '\0';
(gdb) backtrace
#0  function3 (passedByReference=0xbffff284) at stack3.c:5
#1  0x0804842d in function2 (paramString=0xbffff2a0 "This is a
string.")
     at stack3.c:16
#2  0x08048481 in function1 (paramInt=3) at stack3.c:24
#3  0x080484a8 in main () at stack3.c:31
(gdb)
```

For more information on the various GDB commands used to view and manipulate stacks, see Chapter 6, "The GNU Debugger (GDB)."

5.5 How Does the Stack Work?

The stack's functionality is implemented at many different levels of a computer including low-level processor instructions. On x86 for example, the pop and push instructions are specifically for placing data on and removing data from the stack respectively. Most architectures also supply dedicated registers to use for manipulating and managing the stack. On x86 and x86-64, the bp and sp registers (for "base pointer" and "stack pointer"—see following sections) are used. They are named slightly differently for each architecture in that a prefix is used to indicate the size of the register. For x86, the prefix letter "e" is used to indicate a size of 32-bit, and for x86-64 the prefix letter of "r" is used to indicate a size of 64-bit.

5.5.1 The BP and SP Registers

The bp, or base pointer (also referred to as frame pointer) register is used to hold the address of the beginning or base of the current frame. The purpose of this is so that a common reference point for all local stack variables can be used. In other words, stack variables are referenced by the bp register plus an offset. When working in a particular stack frame, the value of this register will never change. Each stack frame has its own unique bp value.

The sp, or stack pointer register is used to hold the address of the end of the stack. A program's assembly instructions will modify its value when new space is needed in the current stack frame for local variables. Because the sp is always the end of the stack, when a new frame is created, its value is used to set the new frame's bp value. The best way to understand exactly how these two registers work is to examine the assembly instructions involved in starting a new function and allocating stack variables within it. Consider the following source code:

```
#include <stdio.h>

void function1( int param )
{
    int localVar = 99;
}

int main( void )
{
    int stackVar = 3;

    function1( stackVar );

    return 0;
}
```

Compiling this code with the -s switch will produce the following assembly listing:

```
            .file   "stack4.c"
            .text
.globl function1
            .type   function1, @function
function1:
            pushl   %ebp
            movl    %esp, %ebp
            subl    $4, %esp
            movl    $99, -4(%ebp)
            leave
            ret
            .size   function1, .-function1
.globl main
            .type   main, @function
main:
            pushl   %ebp
            movl    %esp, %ebp
            subl    $8, %esp
            andl    $-16, %esp
            movl    $0, %eax
            subl    %eax, %esp
            movl    $3, -4(%ebp)
            subl    $12, %esp
            pushl   -4(%ebp)
            call    function1
```

```
addl    $16, %esp
movl    $0, %eax
leave
ret
.size   main, .-main
.ident  "GCC: (GNU) 3.3.1 (SuSE Linux)"
```

> **Note**: Because the source program was very simple, this assembly listing is also quite simple. Without any prior knowledge of or experience with assembly listings, you should be able to easily look at this listing and pick out the beginning of the two functions, function1 and main.

In function1, the first instruction pushl %ebp saves the value of the base pointer from the previous frame on the stack. The next instruction movl %esp, %ebp copies the value of the stack pointer into the base pointer register. Recall that the stack pointer, esp in this example, always points to the top of the stack. The next instruction subl $4, %esp subtracts 4 from the current value stored in the stack pointer register. This effectively opens up storage in the newly created stack frame for 4 bytes. This is the space needed for the local variable localVar, which is indeed 4 bytes in size (an int). These three instructions combined form what's commonly referred to as the *function prologue*. The function prologue is code added to the beginning of every function that is compiled by gcc and most, if not all, compilers. It is responsible for defining and preparing a new stack frame for upcoming function execution.

Along with a function prologue is an associated *function epilogue*. In the assembly code shown for the preceding function1(), the epilogue consists of the leave and ret instructions. The epilogue is effectively the reverse of the prologue. It is hard to tell this because those unfamiliar with the x86 instruction set will not know that the leave instruction is actually a high-level instruction equivalent to these instructions:

```
movl %ebp, %esp
popl %ebp
```

Comparing these two instructions to the first two instructions in the prologue, we can see that they are in fact the mirror image of each other. The function epilogue code is completed by the ret instruction, which transfers program control to the address located at the end of the stack.

The function prologue and epilogue are extremely important contributors to the proper execution and isolation of individual function calls. They make up what's commonly referred to as the *function* or *procedure calling conventions*. We will discuss the remaining details of the calling conventions, but first a special note is required regarding the prologue and epilogue.

5.5.1.1 Special Case: gcc's -fomit-frame-pointer Compile Option

Some architectures support gcc's `-fomit-frame-pointer` compile option, which is used to avoid the need for the function prologue and epilogue, thus freeing up the frame pointer register to be used for other purposes. This optimization is done at the cost of the ability to debug the application because certain debugging tools and techniques rely on the frame pointer being present. SUSE 9.0 Professional and SLES 8 on the x86-64 architecture have been compiled with the `-fomit-frame-pointer` option enabled, which could improve performance in certain areas of the operating system. GDB is able to handle this properly, but other debugging techniques might have difficulties such as using a home-grown stack traceback function. It is also important to note that when using gcc 3.3.x with the `-O1` or greater optimization level, the `-fomit-frame-pointer` flag is automatically turned on for the x86-64 architecture. If omitting the frame pointer is not desired but optimization is, be sure to compile your program with something like the following:

```
gcc -o myexe myexe.c -O1 -fno-omit-frame-pointer
```

5.5.2 Function Calling Conventions

When you strip away all the peripherals, storage, sound, and video devices, computers are relatively simple machines. The "guts" of a computer basically consist of two main things: the CPU and RAM. RAM stores the instructions that run on the CPU, but given that the CPU is really just a huge maze of logic gates, there is a need for intermediate storage areas that are very close to the CPU and still fast enough to feed it as quickly as it can process the instructions. These intermediate storage areas are the system's *registers* and are integral parts of a computer system.

Most systems have only a very small number of registers, and some of these registers have a dedicated purpose and so cannot simply be used at will. Because every function that executes has access to and can manipulate the exact same registers, there must be a set of rules that govern how registers are used between function calls. The function caller and function callee must know exactly what to expect from the registers and how to properly use them without clobbering one another. This set of rules is called the *function* or *procedure calling conventions*. They are architecture-specific and very important to know and understand for all software developers.

The purpose of this section is to give an overview of the basics of the calling conventions and should not be considered an exhaustive reference. The calling conventions are quite a bit more detailed than what is presented here—for example, what to do when structures contain various data classification types, how to properly align data, and so on. For more detailed information, it is recommended to download and read the calling convention sections from the architecture's Application Binary Interface (ABI) specification document. The ABI is basically a blueprint for how software interacts with an architecture, so there is great value in reading these documents. The links are:

```
x86 ABI - http://www.caldera.com/developers/devspecs/abi386-4.pdf
x86-64 ABI - http://www.x86-64.org/documentation/abi.pdf
```

Again, the following sections will give an overview of the calling conventions on x86 and x86-64, which will provide a great base understanding.

5.5.2.1 x86 Architecture

We have already discussed what a function must do at the very beginning of its execution (prologue) and at the very end (epilogue), which are important parts of the calling conventions. Now we must learn the rules for calling a function. For example, if `function1` calls `function2` with five parameters, how does `function2` know where to find these parameters and what to do with them?

The answer to this is actually quite simple. The calling function simply *push*es the function arguments onto the stack starting with the right-most parameter and working toward the left. This is illustrated in the following diagram.

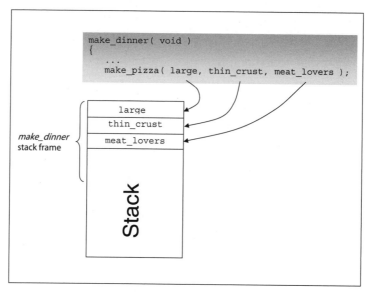

Fig. 5.4 Illustration of calling conventions on x86.

Also as shown, the arguments are all pushed onto the stack in the calling function's stack frame.

Let's consider the following program, `pizza.c`, to illustrate how this really works.

```c
#define pizza 1
#define large 2
#define thin_crust 6
#define meat_lovers 9

int make_pizza( int size, int crust_type, int specialty )
{
    int return_value = 0;

    /* Do stuff */

    return return_value;
}

int make_dinner( int meal_type )
{
    int return_value = 0;

    return_value = make_pizza( large, thin_crust, meat_lovers );

    return return_value;
}

int main( void )
{
    int return_value = 0;

    return_value = make_dinner( pizza );

    return return_value;
}
```

To really see the calling conventions in action, we need to look at the assembly listing for this program. Recall that creating an assembly listing can be done with the following command assuming our program is called `pizza.c`:

```
gcc -S pizza.c
```

This will produce `pizza.s`, which is shown here:

```
        .file   "pizza.c"
        .text
.globl make_pizza
        .type   make_pizza, @function
```

```
make_pizza:
        pushl   %ebp
        movl    %esp, %ebp
        subl    $4, %esp
        movl    $0, -4(%ebp)
        movl    -4(%ebp), %eax
        leave
        ret
        .size   make_pizza, .-make_pizza
.globl make_dinner
        .type   make_dinner, @function
make_dinner:
        pushl   %ebp
        movl    %esp, %ebp
        subl    $8, %esp
        movl    $0, -4(%ebp)
        subl    $4, %esp
        pushl   $9
        pushl   $6
        pushl   $2
        call    make_pizza
        addl    $16, %esp
        movl    %eax, -4(%ebp)
        movl    -4(%ebp), %eax
        leave
        ret
        .size   make_dinner, .-make_dinner
.globl main
        .type   main, @function
main:
        pushl   %ebp
        movl    %esp, %ebp
        subl    $8, %esp
        andl    $-16, %esp
        movl    $0, %eax
        subl    %eax, %esp
        movl    $0, -4(%ebp)
        subl    $12, %esp
        pushl   $1
        call    make_dinner
        addl    $16, %esp
        movl    %eax, -4(%ebp)
        movl    -4(%ebp), %eax
        leave
        ret
        .size   main, .-main
        .ident  "GCC: (GNU) 3.3.1 (SuSE Linux)"
```

Recall that a C function name, such as make_dinner in our example, will always appear in the assembly listing as a *label*,—or as make_dinner: in the previous listing, for example. This function contains the instructions of interest that clearly illustrate the x86 calling conventions. In particular, note these instructions:

```
pushl   $9
pushl   $6
pushl   $2
call    make_pizza
```

> **Note:** In Linux assembly, any instruction argument prefixed with
> "$" is a constant, which means that the value prefixed is the actual value
> used.

Looking back at `pizza.c`, we see the following macro definitions:

```
#define large 2
#define thin_crust 6
#define meat_lovers 9
```

So we can now clearly see that the calling conventions have been followed, and
our function parameters were *push*ed onto the stack starting with meat_lovers
and followed by thin_crust and then large.

5.5.2.1.1 Return Value Another important aspect of calling conventions to
know and understand is how a function's return value is passed back to the
calling function. In `pizza.c` just shown, the call to `make_pizza` is

```
return_value = make_pizza( large, thin_crust, meat_lovers );
```

This means that we want the return value of the function call to be stored in
the return_value variable, which is local to the calling function. The x86 calling
conventions state that the `%eax` register is used to store the function return
value between function calls. This is illustrated in the previous assembly listing.
At the very end of the `make_pizza` function, we see the following instructions:

```
movl    -4(%ebp), %eax
leave
ret
```

We now know that `leave` and `ret` make up the function epilogue and notice
immediately before that, a `move` instruction is done to move the value stored at
the address `%ebp` contains offset by 4 bytes into the `%eax` register. If we look
back through the assembly for the `make_pizza` function, we will see that `-4`
`(%ebp)` does in fact represent the `return_value` stack variable.

So now at this point, the `%eax` register contains the return value just
before the function returns to its caller, so let's now look at what happens back
in the calling function. In our example, that function is `make_dinner`:

```
call    make_pizza
addl    $16, %esp
movl    %eax, -4(%ebp)
```

Immediately after the call to `make_pizza` we can see that the stack is shrunk by 16 bytes by adding 16 to the `%esp` register. We then see that the value from the `%eax` register is moved to a stack variable specified by `-4 (%ebp)`, which turns out to be the `return_value` variable.

5.5.2.2 x86-64 Architecture

The calling conventions for x86-64 are a bit more complex than for x86. The primary difference is that rather than all the functions' arguments being *push*ed on the stack before a function call as is done on x86, x86-64 makes use of some of the general purpose registers first. The reason for this is that the x86-64 architecture provides a few more general purpose registers than x86, and using them rather than *push*ing the arguments onto the stack that resides on much slower RAM is a very large performance gain.

Function parameters are also handled differently depending on their data type classification. The main classification, referred to as INTEGER, is any integral data type that can fit into one of the general purpose registers (GPR). Because the GPRs on x86-64 are all 64-bit, this covers the majority of data types passed as function arguments. The calling convention that is used for this data classification is (arguments—from left to right—are assigned to the following GPRs)

```
%rdi
%rsi
%rdx
%rcx
%r8
%r9
```

Remaining arguments are *push*ed onto the stack as on x86.

To illustrate this, consider a modified `pizza.c` program:

```
#define pizza        50
#define large        51
#define thin_crust   52
#define cheese       1
#define pepperoni    2
#define onions       3
#define peppers      4
#define mushrooms    5
#define sausage      6
#define pineapple    7
```

```
#define bacon     8
#define ham       9

int make_pizza( int size, int crust_type, int topping1, int
➡topping2,int topping3, int topping4, int topping5,int topping6,
➡int topping7, int topping8,int topping9 )
{
   int return_value = 0;

   /* Do stuff */

   return return_value;
}

int make_dinner( int meal_type )
{
   int return_value = 0;

   return_value = make_pizza( large, thin_crust, cheese,
➡pepperoni,onions, peppers, mushrooms, sausage,pineapple, bacon,
➡ham );

   return return_value;
}

int main( void )
{
   int return_value = 0;

   return_value = make_dinner( pizza );

   return return_value;
}
```

Again, we produce the assembly listing for this program with the command:

```
gcc -S pizza.c
```

The assembly listing produced is:

```
        .file   "pizza.c"
        .text
.globl make_pizza
        .type   make_pizza,@function
make_pizza:
.LFB1:
        pushq   %rbp
.LCFI0:
        movq    %rsp, %rbp
.LCFI1:
        movl    %edi, -4(%rbp)
```

```
               movl      %esi, -8(%rbp)
               movl      %edx, -12(%rbp)
               movl      %ecx, -16(%rbp)
               movl      %r8d, -20(%rbp)
               movl      %r9d, -24(%rbp)
               movl      $0, -28(%rbp)
               movl      -28(%rbp), %eax
               leave
               ret
.LFE1:
.Lfe1:
               .size     make_pizza,.Lfe1-make_pizza
.globl make_dinner
               .type     make_dinner,@function
make_dinner:
.LFB2:
               pushq     %rbp
.LCFI2:
               movq      %rsp, %rbp
.LCFI3:
               subq      $48, %rsp
.LCFI4:
               movl      %edi, -4(%rbp)
               movl      $0, -8(%rbp)
               movl      $9, 32(%rsp)
               movl      $8, 24(%rsp)
               movl      $7, 16(%rsp)
               movl      $6, 8(%rsp)
               movl      $5, (%rsp)
               movl      $4, %r9d
               movl      $3, %r8d
               movl      $2, %ecx
               movl      $1, %edx
               movl      $52, %esi
               movl      $51, %edi
               call      make_pizza
               movl      %eax, -8(%rbp)
               movl      -8(%rbp), %eax
               leave
               ret
.LFE2:
.Lfe2:
               .size     make_dinner,.Lfe2-make_dinner
.globl main
               .type     main,@function
main:
.LFB3:
               pushq     %rbp
.LCFI5:
               movq      %rsp, %rbp
.LCFI6:
               subq      $16, %rsp
```

```
    .LCFI7:
            movl    $0, -4(%rbp)
            movl    $50, %edi
            call    make_dinner
            movl    %eax, -4(%rbp)
            movl    -4(%rbp), %eax
            leave
            ret
    .LFE3:
    .Lfe3:
            .size   main,.Lfe3-main
            .section    .eh_frame,"aw",@progbits
    —8<— SNIPPED UNIMPORTANT INFO —8<—
```

The instructions we're most interested in are the ones that come before the call to make_pizza in the make_dinner function. Specifically, they are

```
    movl    $9, 32(%rsp)
    movl    $8, 24(%rsp)
    movl    $7, 16(%rsp)
    movl    $6, 8(%rsp)
    movl    $5, (%rsp)
    movl    $4, %r9d
    movl    $3, %r8d
    movl    $2, %ecx
    movl    $1, %edx
    movl    $52, %esi
    movl    $51, %edi
    call    make_pizza
```

We can look at this graphically in Figure 5.5.

As you can see, the six general purpose registers are used up with six left-most function arguments. The remaining five function arguments are pushed onto the stack. Note, however, that the last five arguments are not *push*ed onto the stack as they are on x86; rather they are *mov*ed directly to the addresses in memory referenced by %rsp.

5.5.2.2.1 Return Value The convention used to handle the function return value is very similar to x86. The data is first classified to determine the method used to handle the return. For the INTEGER data classification, the %rax register is first used. If it is unavailable at the time of return, the %rdx register can be used instead. There are other possibilities for different return scenarios, but the general idea remains the same. For all the details, it is recommended to refer to the x86-64 ABI.

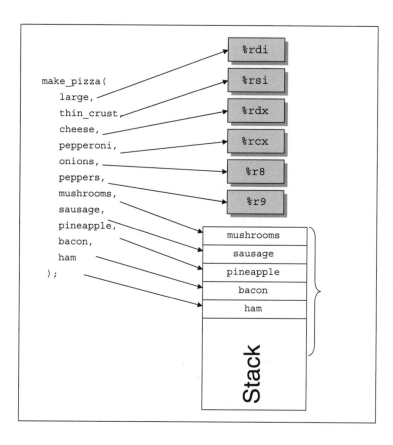

Fig. 5.5 Illustration of calling conventions on x86-64.

5.6 REFERENCING AND MODIFYING DATA ON THE STACK

We've seen by now that the stack is crucial for proper and flexible program execution. We've also seen that the stack really isn't as complex as it first may seem to be. This section will explain how data is stored on the stack and how it is manipulated.

Recall our simple C program from the earlier section, "The BP and SP Registers," where we declare a simple stack variable like this:

```
int localVar = 99;
```

Recall further that the assembly produced for this area of the program consisted of these three instructions, which make up the function prolog:

```
pushl    %ebp
movl     %esp, %ebp
subl     $4, %esp
```

The subl instruction effectively increases the size of the stack by 4 bytes–keep in mind that the stack grows down toward lower addresses on x86. Because we know that the function in question only declares one local variable, int localVar, we know that this space is created for it. Therefore, at this point we could define the memory location holding localVar's value as whatever the register esp holds. This method does not work very well, however, because the value of esp will change as more local variables are declared. The correct method is to reference ebp (the base or frame pointer) instead. We can see that this is done, in fact, by looking at the next instruction in the assembly listing from our small program:

```
movl     $99, -4(%ebp)
```

This instruction is taking care of assigning the value 99 to localVar, or as it's referred to in assembly, -4 (%ebp) which essentially means "the value stored in ebp offset by -4 bytes." Note that some assembly outputs, for example objdump -d <object>, might show the values as hex instead, which would look like:

```
movl     $0x63,0xfffffffc(%ebp)
```

When it is known in which offset relative to the frame pointer a particular variable is stored, you can see other places that variable is referenced through an assembly listing of the same function.

Let us quickly look at how this reflects on the term "pass by reference." To summarize, when passing a parameter to a C function where it is desired to change the value of a parameter within the called function, the programmer must be sure to pass the address of the parameter rather than the value of it. Understanding how the stack works can solidify this rule in one's mind. Recall function3 from the stack.c source code, which is declared as:

```
void function3( int *passedByReference )
```

Also bear in mind that a call to this function is made in function2, which passes the address of the local variable localInt to it:

```
function3( &localInt );
```

The assembly just prior to and including the call to function3 looks like this:

```
leal    -4(%ebp), %eax
pushl   %eax
call    function3
```

The key instruction in this sequence is the leal, or load effective address of the frame pointer offset by 4 bytes and store that address into the eax register. The address stored in the eax register is then pushed onto the stack in preparation for the call to function3. Now when function3 executes, it will know exactly where the storage for localInt is on the stack and will be able to modify it directly as it does in this example.

5.7 VIEWING THE RAW STACK IN A DEBUGGER

When debugging real problems in a production environment, the compiled binaries will likely not contain debugging information, and recompiling the source code with the -g debug flag is not an option. In these cases, finding the cause of the problem will require some skill and some knowledge of the program at the machine language level. One of the most important things to watch in these cases is the raw stack. Examining the stack while following through assembly instructions can be crucial to finding the nastiest of software bugs. The easiest way to watch the raw stack is to use DDD (see section "Data Display Debugger" in Chapter 6, "The GNU Debugger (GDB)" for more information). The nice thing about DDD is that the Data Display window will highlight changes made to anything being displayed in it after each instruction. With this, you can see exactly how each instruction does or does not affect the stack. Figure 5.6 shows a DDD session of the program created from the stack.c source code used earlier in this chapter. For quick reference, the source code is as follows:

```
#include <stdio.h>

void function3( int *passedByReference )
{
    int dummy = '\0';

    printf( "My pid is %d;  Press <ENTER> to continue", getpid() );
    dummy = fgetc( stdin );
    *passedByReference = 9;
}

void function2( char *paramString )
{
    int localInt = 1;
```

```
        function3( &localInt );
        printf( "Value of localInt = %d\n", localInt );
    }

    void function1( int paramInt )
    {
        char localString[] = "This is a string.";

        function2( localString );
    }

    int main( void )
    {
        int stackVar = 3;

        function1( stackVar );

        return 0;
    }
```

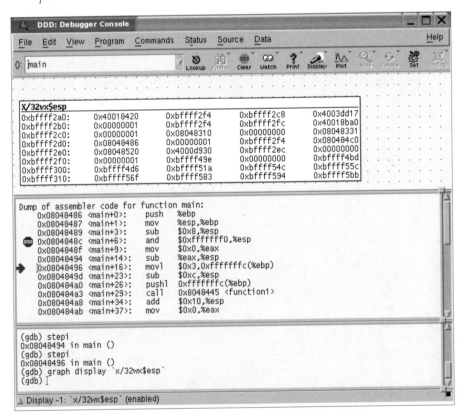

Fig. 5.6 stack.c in a DDD session, part 1.

A breakpoint was set in main before running. Notice how the "stop sign" is on the instruction line:

```
0x0804848c <main+6>:    and    $0xfffffff0,%esp
```

rather than the very first instruction line in `main()`. This is because the three instructions before `main+6` are the standard function prologue instructions, and GDB executes them automatically.

Also notice that three `stepi` commands were issued along with the command `graph display 'x/32wx$esp'`, which produces a data display showing the top 32 words in hex on the stack. Recall that the esp register always points to the top (lowest address for x86 based architecture) of the stack.

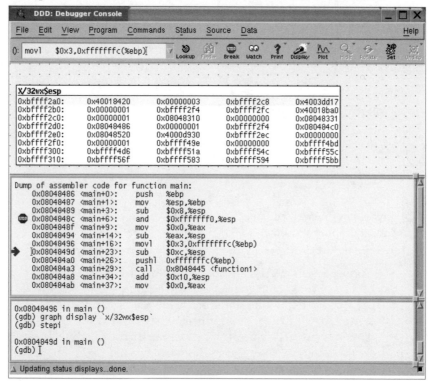

Fig. 5.7 stack.c in a DDD session, part 2.

Notice that the arrow points to the next instruction to be executed, which is `movl $0x3,0xfffffffc(%ebp)`. As was discussed in the "Referencing and Modifying Data on the Stack" section, we know that the destination address is on the stack given that it is an offset of the base pointer. Figure 5.7 shows the

DDD session after the next "`stepi`" instruction is issued. Notice how the first line in the data display of the stack is highlighted showing us that a value in there has changed. We can also see that our value of 3 has been copied onto the stack at address `0xbffff2a4`.

5.8 EXAMINING THE RAW STACK IN DETAIL

Now that we know all the registers and instructions involved with the stack and how to display it in a debugger, let's examine the raw stack in detail. For this section, let's again use `stack.c` from prior sections as our example. To get some interesting data on the stack, let's compile and run `stack3.c` and set a breakpoint in `function3`. When we're stopped in `function3`, let's display our stack using the command `graph display 'x/48wx$esp'`.

Tip: When you find that you're typing similar lengthy commands over and over, it may be time to create a GDB user-defined function. To do this and to ensure it is usable when you restart GDB/DDD, add the following lines to your $HOME/.gdbinit file:

```
define rawstack
    graph display 'x/48wx$esp'
end
document rawstack
    Display the top 48 hex words on the stack (requires
DDD).
    end
```

Now whenever you type `rawstack`, the raw stack will be displayed in the data display window of DDD.

Figure 5.8 shows our initial DDD session after executing the instruction that sets the value of our stack variable `dummy` to `'\0'`. We can see that the line in DDD's data display of the stack that holds the value of `dummy` has been highlighted to show that something changed after running the last instruction.

This tells us just from quickly looking at the display of our stack that the address of `dummy` is `0xbffff224`. But why doesn't `esp` point to the address of `dummy`, which is the only thing on our stack thus far? Looking at `function3`'s prolog, we see the instruction:

```
0x080483cf <function3+3>:        sub     $0x8,%esp
```

which opens eight bytes of space on the stack. The only stack variable in `function3` is "dummy", which is only four bytes wide. So why the extra four bytes of garbage? The answer lies in the fact that an unaligned stack on the x86 architecture can negatively affect performance. GCC is taking this into account at the cost of wasted space on the stack. Notice that there is a call to `printf()` and a call to `fgetc()` in `function3`. If you remove these calls from `stack3.c`, recompile, and examine `function3`'s prologue again, you'll see that the sub instruction moves the `esp` register by 4 instead of 8. This is because GCC knows about the entire program's memory usage and therefore doesn't have to worry about external function calls. When there are external function calls, GCC assumes the worst and takes precautions to properly align the stack.

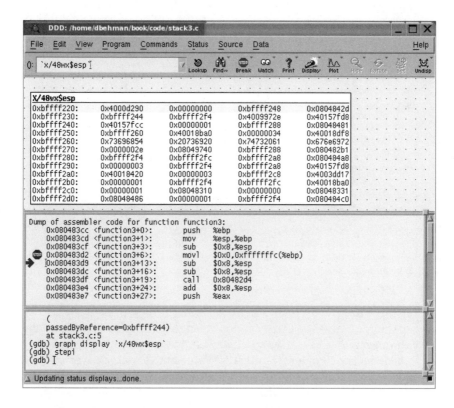

Fig. 5.8 DDD showing the raw stack.

> **Tip**: GCC's default stack aligning behavior can be overridden with the -mpreferred-stack-boundary=NUM parameter, where NUM will be the power that 2 is raised to for calculating the boundary value. NUM's default value is 4, which means the default boundary is 16 bytes.

So now that we know what the top two values on our stack are, let's look at the third word, which is address 0xbffff228 and contains the value 0xbffff248. The value should also set off red lights. We've learned in previous sections that an executable gets mapped to 0x08048000 in the process address space, so it's a pretty good guess that this address is pointing to an instruction in the executable. We can use the debugger to help our investigation. Since we think it's an instruction, let's try to disassemble the function that contains this address.

```
(gdb) disas 0x0804842d
Dump of assembler code for function function2:
0x08048414 <function2+0>:      push    %ebp
0x08048415 <function2+1>:      mov     %esp,%ebp
0x08048417 <function2+3>:      sub     $0x8,%esp
0x0804841a <function2+6>:      movl    $0x1,0xfffffffc(%ebp)
0x08048421 <function2+13>:     sub     $0xc,%esp
0x08048424 <function2+16>:     lea     0xfffffffc(%ebp),%eax
0x08048427 <function2+19>:     push    %eax
0x08048428 <function2+20>:     call    0x80483cc <function3>
0x0804842d <function2+25>:     add     $0x10,%esp
0x08048430 <function2+28>:     sub     $0x8,%esp
0x08048433 <function2+31>:     pushl   0xfffffffc(%ebp)
0x08048436 <function2+34>:     push    $0x8048629
0x0804843b <function2+39>:     call    0x80482f4
0x08048440 <function2+44>:     add     $0x10,%esp
0x08048443 <function2+47>:     leave
0x08048444 <function2+48>:     ret
End of assembler dump.
(gdb)
```

Looking at the instruction that immediately precedes the instruction at 0x0804842d, we see the instruction used to call function3. So now we know that value 0x0804842d is the *return instruction pointer*. The call assembly instruction itself is responsible for pushing this value onto the stack. At the end of a function, the ret instruction is used to send execution back to the instruction immediately following the call instruction.

Looking further in the stack, at the address 0xbffff230, we see the value 0xbffff244. The value certainly looks like a stack address; looking at that address, we see 0x00000001. This is certainly curious and looks like it could be function2's localInt stack variable. Using the debugger to help us, we see:

```
(gdb) frame 1
#1  0x0804842d in function2 (paramString=0xbffff260 "This is a string.")
    at stack3.c:16
```

```
(gdb) print &localInt
$1 = (int *) 0xbffff244
(gdb)
```

So the value stored at 0xbffff230 seems to be a pointer to a stack variable. Looking at function2's source code, we see that we call function3 with the address of localInt! This makes perfect sense because function parameters are pushed onto the stack immediately before a call to a function, and we can see this in function2's assembly:

```
leal    -4(%ebp), %eax
pushl   %eax
call    function3
```

This assembly sequence loads the effective address (the lea instruction) of our stack variable localInt (referenced by -4(%ebp) in assembly) into the eax register. This address then gets *pushed* onto the stack, and function3 is then *called*.

The values stored at addresses 0xbffff234, 0xbffff238, 0xbffff23c, and 0xbffff40 are all garbage because of stack alignment. We know this by looking at the two subl instructions used to move the stack pointer in function2.

We already know that localInt is stored at 0xbffff244, so let's now look at 0xbffff248. The value stored here is 0xbffff288, which again looks like a stack address. It's very likely a base pointer. We now know that a return instruction address follows a base pointer on the stack, so let's first look at the next word in the stack at address 0xbffff24c. Here we see the value 0x08048481, which definitely does look like an executable instruction address. Using the debugger, we see:

```
(gdb) disas 0x08048481
Dump of assembler code for function function1:
0x08048445 <function1+0>:     push    %ebp
0x08048446 <function1+1>:     mov     %esp,%ebp
0x08048448 <function1+3>:     sub     $0x28,%esp
0x0804844b <function1+6>:     mov     0x8048641,%eax
0x08048450 <function1+11>:    mov     %eax,0xffffffd8(%ebp)
0x08048453 <function1+14>:    mov     0x8048645,%eax
0x08048458 <function1+19>:    mov     %eax,0xffffffdc(%ebp)
0x0804845b <function1+22>:    mov     0x8048649,%eax
0x08048460 <function1+27>:    mov     %eax,0xffffffe0(%ebp)
0x08048463 <function1+30>:    mov     0x804864d,%eax
0x08048468 <function1+35>:    mov     %eax,0xffffffe4(%ebp)
0x0804846b <function1+38>:    mov     0x8048651,%ax
0x08048471 <function1+44>:    mov     %ax,0xffffffe8(%ebp)
0x08048475 <function1+48>:    sub     $0xc,%esp
0x08048478 <function1+51>:    lea     0xffffffd8(%ebp),%eax
```

```
0x0804847b <function1+54>:    push    %eax
0x0804847c <function1+55>:    call    0x8048414 <function2>
0x08048481 <function1+60>:    add     $0x10,%esp
0x08048484 <function1+63>:    leave
0x08048485 <function1+64>:    ret
End of assembler dump.
(gdb)
```

Indeed, the instruction preceding 0x08048481 is a call to function2, so we can confirm that the stack address 0xbffff248 does indeed hold a base pointer.

The analysis of a raw stack can continue in this fashion all the way through to the beginning of a function. Armed with the assembly and the source code, any stack analysis can be done fairly easily. Even without the source code, stack analysis is possible. The next section will build on the patterns observed here to create a homegrown stack traceback very similar to what GDB's "backtrace" shows.

5.8.1 Homegrown Stack Traceback Function

One of the most important pieces of information to know when debugging a problem is the path of execution taken to get to the current point. A big part of this is examining the stack traceback output from GDB using the backtrace command. Very often, however, running the program under GDB or attaching to it is not possible because access to the machine is not available. This is where a homegrown stack traceback function is extremely useful to problem determination. The function can be called at any point throughout the program's execution life; it can be called when a recoverable error is detected, when a non-recoverable error such as a segv is detected, or when code and execution analysis is needed. For GNU/Linux, two ways of accomplishing this will be discussed as certain environments may be limited in what can be used.

5.8.1.1 Using GLIBC's backtrace() GLIBC includes several functions that can be used to display a stack from within a running program. The main function is called backtrace() and has this prototype:

```
int backtrace (void **BUFFER, int SIZE)
```

SIZE determines the maximum number of frames backtrace will "walk" through, and BUFFER is an array of void pointers wherein backtrace will store the return instruction pointer. To convert the return instruction address pointers into more meaningful information, the function backtrace_symbols() is provided. Its prototype is:

```
char ** backtrace_symbols (void *const *BUFFER, int SIZE)
```

The parameters are the same as those of the `backtrace()` function. An array of strings will be returned. The number of strings will be SIZE, and the memory for the strings is allocated within `backtrace_symbols()`. It is up to the caller to free the memory used by the array of strings. The following is a sample program that makes use of these APIs.

```c
#include <stdio.h>
#include <execinfo.h>

void print_gnu_backtrace( void )
{
   void *frame_addrs[16];
   char **frame_strings;
   size_t backtrace_size;
   int i;

   backtrace_size = backtrace( frame_addrs, 16 );
   frame_strings = backtrace_symbols( frame_addrs, backtrace_size );

   for ( i = 0; i < backtrace_size; i++ )
   {
     printf( "%d: [0x%x] %s\n", i, frame_addrs[i], frame_strings[i]);
   }

   free( frame_strings );
}

int foo( void )
{
   print_gnu_backtrace();
   return 0;
}

int bar( void )
{
   foo();
   return 0;
}

int boo( void )
{
   bar();
   return 0;
}

int baz( void )
{
   boo();
   return 0;
   }

int main( void )
```

```
{
    baz();
    return 0;
}
```

Compiling and running this program produces the following:

```
penguin> gcc -o bt_gnu backtrace_gnu.c
penguin> ./bt_gnu
0: [0x8048410] ./bt_gnu(backtrace_symbols+0xe4) [0x8048410]
1: [0x8048485] ./bt_gnu(backtrace_symbols+0x159) [0x8048485]
2: [0x8048497] ./bt_gnu(backtrace_symbols+0x16b) [0x8048497]
3: [0x80484a9] ./bt_gnu(backtrace_symbols+0x17d) [0x80484a9]
4: [0x80484bb] ./bt_gnu(backtrace_symbols+0x18f) [0x80484bb]
5: [0x80484d7] ./bt_gnu(backtrace_symbols+0x1ab) [0x80484d7]
6: [0x4003dd17] /lib/i686/libc.so.6(__libc_start_main+0xc7) [0x4003dd17]
7: [0x8048361] ./bt_gnu(backtrace_symbols+0x35) [0x8048361]
```

Wait a second! Why do all the function names appear to be backtrace_symbols except for __libc_start_main? The answer lies in the fact that symbol names in a shared library are exported; whereas, the static symbols in the executable are not. So in this case, the shared library libc contains the exported function __libc_start_main, but all other symbols are static to the executable and do not appear in the dynamic symbol table. A workaround exists for this problem, which tells the linker to export all symbols to the dynamic symbol table. To use this workaround, recompile the program with the -rdynamic parameter (see the end of this section for more information).

```
penguin> gcc -o bt_gnu backtrace_gnu.c -rdynamic
penguin> ./bt_gnu
0: [0x8048730] ./bt_gnu(print_gnu_backtrace+0x14) [0x8048730]
1: [0x80487a5] ./bt_gnu(foo+0xb) [0x80487a5]
2: [0x80487b7] ./bt_gnu(bar+0xb) [0x80487b7]
3: [0x80487c9] ./bt_gnu(boo+0xb) [0x80487c9]
4: [0x80487db] ./bt_gnu(baz+0xb) [0x80487db]
5: [0x80487f7] ./bt_gnu(main+0x15) [0x80487f7]
6: [0x4003dd17] /lib/i686/libc.so.6(libc_start_main+0xc7)
➡ [0x4003dd17]
7: [0x8048681] ./bt_gnu(backtrace_symbols+0x31) [0x8048681]
```

As you can see, this works much better. However, frame 7 doesn't appear to be correct. If we look at this executable under a debugger, we will find that the return instruction pointer 0x8048681 is in the _start function. This function is fundamental to the execution of programs on Linux and cannot be made dynamic, so this explains why the backtrace function still displays the incorrect name for this symbol. To avoid confusion, the for loop in our print_gnu_backtrace function could be modified to never display the frame containing __libc_start_main nor the following frame, which would be the frame for _start.

5.8.1.1.1 The -rdynamic Switch
If you search through GCC and LD's documentation for -rdynamic, you likely won't find anything. GCC converts the -rdynamic switch into -export-dynamic, which gets passed to the linker. With this in mind, an alternative compile line for backtrace_gnu.c would be:

```
gcc -o bt_gnu backtrace_gnu.c -Wl,—export-dynamic
```

or simpler yet

```
gcc -o bt_gnu backtrace_gnu.c -Wl,-E
```

5.8.1.2 Manually "Walking the Stack"
Another method for implementing a stack backtrace function on the x86 architecture is to apply our knowledge of the raw layout of the stack to manually "walk" it frame by frame. As we find each frame and return instruction pointer, we can use the undocumented function dladdr found in the /usr/include/dlfcn.h header file to determine symbol names. Note that the same concepts discussed here can be applied on the x86_64 architecture. For this reason, the discussion will be focused on x86, followed by a discussion on getting this function working on x86_64.

The source code for a program, which demonstrates the manual stack walking, is as follows:

```
#define _GNU_SOURCE
#include <stdio.h>
#include <dlfcn.h>

void **getEBP( int dummy )
{
   void **ebp = (void **)&dummy - 2;
   return( ebp );
}

void print_walk_backtrace( void )
{
   int dummy;
   int frame = 0;
   Dl_info dlip;
   void **ebp = getEBP( dummy );
   void **ret = NULL;                 /* return instruction pointer */

   printf( "Stack backtrace:\n" );
   while( *ebp )
   {
```

```
            ret = ebp + 1;
            dladdr( *ret, &dlip );
            printf( "    Frame %d: [ebp=0x%08x] [ret=0x%08x] %s\n",
                    frame++, *ebp, *ret, dlip.dli_sname );
            ebp = (void**)(*ebp);           /* get the next frame pointer */
    }
}

int foo( void )
{
    print_walk_backtrace();
    return 0;
}

int bar( void )
{
    foo();
    return 0;
}

int boo( void )
{
    bar();
    return 0;
}

int baz( void )
{
    boo();
    return 0;
}

int main( void )
{
    baz();
    return 0;
}
```

The first point of interest in this code is the `#define _GNU_SOURCE`. This is needed to enable GNU extensions, in particular, the use of the `dladdr()` function. Note this line must come before any `#include` lines.

The next line worth mentioning is the `#include <dlfcn.h>`, which is required for the definitions of `dladdr()` and the `Dl_info` typed structure.

Next we see the function `getEBP`. This function, as the name says, is used to set a pointer directly to what the EBP register is pointing to in `getEBP`'s frame. When this is found, "walking the stack" is very easy. The term "walking the stack" refers to the iterative act of examining the frame pointer and dereferencing it to find the next frame pointer. This continues until dereferencing results in 0 or NULL. Figure 5.9 shows a data display of the raw stack for our `stack3.c` program. The base pointers are highlighted, and as you can see, dereferencing each one refers to the next one until `0x00000000`.

X/48wx$esp				
0xbffff210:	0x4000d290	0x0000037f	0xbffff238	0x08048870
0xbffff220:	0xbffff234	0xbffff2e4	0x4009c72e	0x4015afd8
0xbffff230:	0x4015afcc	0x00000001	0xbffff278	0x080488c4
0xbffff240:	0xbffff250	0x40018ba0	0x00000069	0x40018df8
0xbffff250:	0x73696854	0x20736920	0x74732061	0x676e6972
0xbffff260:	0x0000002e	0x08049be8	0xbffff278	0x08048641
0xbffff270:	0xbffff2e4	0xbffff2ec	0xbffff298	0x080488eb
0xbffff280:	0x00000003	0xbffff2e4	0xbffff298	0x4015afd8
0xbffff290:	0x40018420	0x00000003	0xbffff2b8	0x40040d17
0xbffff2a0:	0x00000001	0xbffff2e4	0xbffff2ec	0x40018ba0
0xbffff2b0:	0x00000001	0x080486b0	0x00000000	0x080486d1
0xbffff2c0:	0x080488c9	0x00000001	0xbffff2e4	0x08048900

Fig. 5.9 Walking the raw stack.

This concept of dereferencing pointers might set off alarms for the seasoned C programmer. We can easily use pointers in C to programmatically accomplish this for us. The key to walking the stack is being able to first reliably find the EBP on the stack. We can determine this by observing what happens during a function call on the x86 architecture:

☞ Function parameters are pushed onto the stack.

☞ The `call` instruction pushes the return instruction pointer onto the stack.

☞ Execution is passed to the start of the callee function.

☞ The function prologue pushes the value in the `ebp` register onto the stack.

☞ The body of the function is executed.

The trick is to take the address of the passed-in parameter and use pointer arithmetic to subtract 2 from it. The 2 is used to move the pointer over the return instruction pointer and then to the start of the base pointer.

Now we know it is pretty easy to get to get all the frame pointer values. However, displaying these to the user is not very informative; displaying the function names would be much better. This is where the use of the `dladdr` function becomes apparent. The trick now is to make use of the fact that the return instruction pointer is always next to the base pointer on the stack. Again using C pointer arithmetic, we can easily obtain the return instruction pointer and pass this into the `dladdr` function, which will fill a structure containing symbol information for that address. The structure definition and prototype for `dladdr` (taken from /usr/include/dlfcn.h on a SuSE 9.0 Professional system) is:

```
#ifdef __USE_GNU
/* Structure containing information about object searched using
   'dladdr'. */
typedef struct
{
    __const char *dli_fname;       /* File name of defining object. */
    void *dli_fbase;               /* Load address of that object. */
    __const char *dli_sname;       /* Name of nearest symbol. */
    void *dli_saddr;               /* Exact value of nearest symbol. */
} Dl_info;

/* Fill in *INFO with the following information about ADDRESS.
   Returns 0 iff no shared object's segments contain that address. */
extern int dladdr (__const void *__address, Dl_info *__info) __THROW;
```

Looking at `print_walk_backtrace`, after getting the base pointer, the return
instruction pointer is easily found using the following:

```
ret = ebp + 1;
```

After this is obtained, we can simply dereference `ret` and pass that into `dladdr`
to have it determine the symbol name containing this address. After displaying
the relevant information to the user, the next key in this function is to find the
next frame pointer. This is done with this code:

```
ebp = (void**)(*ebp);
```

If the new value of `ebp` is not NULL, we perform the same steps again. If it is
NULL, we know that we've hit the end of the stack, so we terminate the loop.
    Note that the same issue that prevented the proper symbol names from
being displayed when using GLIBC's `backtrace` function will affect this program.
We must be sure to compile with the `-rdynamic` flag here as well. Compiling
and running our manual stack walking program produces:

```
penguin> gcc -o bt_walk backtrace_walk.c -rdynamic -g
/tmp/ccEiAjgE.o(.text+0x65): In function 'print_walk_backtrace':
/home/dbehman/book/code/backtrace_walk.c:23: undefined reference to
'dladdr'
collect2: ld returned 1 exit status
```

What happened? Note that this error is being produced by the linker and not
GCC, so we compiled successfully but did not link properly. The linker was
unable to find `dladdr`, which is a somewhat unusual function that isn't used all
the time. `dladdr` is in the family of functions used to manipulate dynamic
libraries. The seasoned Unix programmer will know that these functions are
provided in the libdl.so shared system library.

> **Note:** If you're not a seasoned Unix programmer, how could you find out what library `dladdr` was defined in? Use the `nm(1)` utility to dump the symbols from all system libraries and `grep` the output for the symbol we want - in this case, `dladdr`.
>
> ```
> penguin> nm -A /lib/*.so* | grep dladdr
> /lib/libdl.so.2:00001680 T dladdr
> /lib/libdl.so.2:000016b0 T dladdr1
> ```

Recompiling and running now produces:

```
penguin> ./bt_walk
Stack backtrace:
   Frame 0: [ebp=0xbffff2c8]  [ret=0x08048755]  print_walk_backtrace
   Frame 1: [ebp=0xbffff2d8]  [ret=0x08048795]  foo
   Frame 2: [ebp=0xbffff2e8]  [ret=0x080487a7]  bar
   Frame 3: [ebp=0xbffff2f8]  [ret=0x080487b9]  boo
   Frame 4: [ebp=0xbffff308]  [ret=0x080487cb]  baz
   Frame 5: [ebp=0xbffff318]  [ret=0x080487e7]  main
   Frame 6: [ebp=0xbffff338]  [ret=0x40040d17]  __libc_start_main
```

This is exactly the output we want! An advantage of using this method over GLIBC's `backtrace()` is that the output is 100% configurable.

5.8.1.2.1 Modifying for x86-64

Because the x86-64 architecture is so similar to the x86 architecture, many of the same concepts apply there as well. The big difference however, is that the function calling conventions for x86-64 work differently than on x86. Rather than all function parameters being pushed on the stack as they are on x86, parameters are passed in a specified set of registers. What this means for our manual stack walking program is that our `getEBP` function must be modified accordingly. After examining the assembly instructions used in a function call such as `getEBP`, we can see that the function parameter gets copied from the register used to pass it onto the stack immediately after the frame pointer. We can then simply take the address of this parameter and add 1 to it to get the address of the previous frame pointer. The following code shows the modified `getEBP`, which has been renamed to `getRBP` considering all register names on x86-64 begin with R instead of E on x86. This is to distinguish them as 64-bit instead of 32-bit registers.

```
void **getRBP( long dummy )
{
    void **rbp = (void **)&dummy + 1;
    return( rbp );
}
```

```
void print_walk_backtrace( void )
{
   long dummy;
   int frame = 0;
   Dl_info dlip;
   void **rbp = getRBP( dummy );
   void *ret = *(rbp + 1);
   void *save_rbp = *rbp;

   printf( "Stack backtrace:\n" );
   while( save_rbp )
   {
      dladdr( ret, &dlip );
      printf( "   Frame %d: [rbp=0x%016lx] [ret=0x%016lx] %s\n",
            frame++, save_rbp, ret, dlip.dli_sname );
      rbp = (void**)save_rbp;
      save_rbp = *rbp;
      ret = *(rbp + 1);
   }
}
```

This code also shows the modified `print_walk` function. The main difference is that the RBP obtained from `getRBP` needed to be saved along with the return instruction pointer. The reason for this is because the function calls to `printf` and `dladdr` overwrite the top of the stack, thus rendering the initial values of the RBP, and return instruction pointer incorrect. Subsequent values remain untouched so the rest of the logic could remain pretty much intact. Other 64-bit specific changes were also made. Compiling and running the manual stack walking program with the functions modified for x86-64 yields:

```
penguin> gcc -o bt_walk backtrace_walk_x86-64.c -ldl -rdynamic
penguin> ./bt_walk
Stack backtrace:
    Frame  0: [rbp=0x0000007fbfffed20] [ret=0x000000004000080a]
➧print_walk_backtrace
   Frame 1: [rbp=0x0000007fbfffed30] [ret=0x00000000400008ae] foo
   Frame 2: [rbp=0x0000007fbfffed40] [ret=0x00000000400008be] bar
   Frame 3: [rbp=0x0000007fbfffed50] [ret=0x00000000400008ce] boo
   Frame 4: [rbp=0x0000007fbfffed60] [ret=0x00000000400008de] baz
   Frame 5: [rbp=0x0000007fbfffed70] [ret=0x00000000400008ee] main
    Frame  6: [rbp=0x0000002a95669d50] [ret=0x0000002a95790017]
_➧libc_start_main
```

Take note with respect to compiling on x86-64—if we add the `-O2` switch to tell GCC to optimize the code and run the program, we will see:

```
penguin> gcc -o bt_walk backtrace_walk_x86-64.c -ldl -rdynamic -O2
penguin> ./bt_walk
Stack backtrace:
Memory fault
```

The reason for this is because on x86-64, GCC includes the `-fomit-frame-pointer` optimization option at the `-o2` level. This instantly invalidates all of the assumptions we make based on the base pointer in our program. To correct this, we need to tell GCC not to omit the frame pointer:

```
penguin> gcc -o bt_walk backtrace_walk_x86-64.c -ldl -rdynamic -O2 -
fno-omit-frame-pointer
penguin> ./bt_walk
Stack backtrace:
    Frame  0: [rbp=0x0000007fbfffed20]  [ret=0x0000000040000857]
print_walk_backtrace
   Frame 1: [rbp=0x0000007fbfffed30] [ret=0x00000000400008c9] foo
   Frame 2: [rbp=0x0000007fbfffed40] [ret=0x00000000400008d9] bar
   Frame 3: [rbp=0x0000007fbfffed50] [ret=0x00000000400008e9] boo
   Frame 4: [rbp=0x0000007fbfffed60] [ret=0x00000000400008f9] baz
   Frame 5: [rbp=0x0000007fbfffed70] [ret=0x0000000040000909] main
    Frame  6: [rbp=0x0000002a95669d50]  [ret=0x0000002a95790017]
__libc_start_main
```

5.8.1.3 Stack Corruption A very common cause of abnormal program termination or other unexpected behavior is stack corruption. Often stack corruption bugs are caused by the now infamous buffer overrun problem, which many well-published computer viruses have used to hack computers on the Internet. Great care must be used by the programmer when working with buffers. The tips and techniques to use are important, but it is not the intention of this section to discuss them; rather, the intention is to illustrate what stack corruptions can do and how to debug them. Consider the following source code, which is a very simple illustration of a horrible buffer overrun coding flaw:

```
#include <stdio.h>

int main ( int argc, char *argv[] )
{
    int foo = 3;
    int bar = 9;
    char string[8];

    strcpy( string, argv[1] );

    printf( "foo = %d\n", foo );
    printf( "bar = %d\n", bar );

    return 0;
}
```

In fact, it hurt to write this code because it is so bad! To the inexperienced developer, however, this code could look very normal and legitimate—we want the user to specify a command-line argument of, say, one or two characters and store that value in our string for later use. However, when a user disregards our expectations and passes in a larger command-line parameter than we expect, all heck breaks loose. Let's try this out:

```
penguin> ./stack_corruption aaaaaaaaaaaa
foo = 0
bar = 1633771873
```

Ouch! How did foo and bar change from their assigned values of 3 and 9 respectively? The answer is: a buffer-overrun! To verify, using gdb to convert 1633771873 into hex reveals:

```
(gdb) p /x 1633771873
$1 = 0x61616161
(gdb)
```

Of course, 0x61 is the ASCII representation of our evil letter a. But why is foo 0? This is because the strcpy() function copies the entire source string to the destination string (without any bounds checking) and adds a NULL terminating character with an ASCII hex value of 0x00.

As you can see, the values we expected our foo and bar variables to be and the values they ended up to be after a simple (but very poorly used) strcpy call are very different, which can easily lead to very bad things happening in a program. Buffer overruns also often cause segmentation violation traps. Some of the memory in the stack that gets overwritten could be pointers, which after corruption, will very likely point to an unreadable area of memory. It's also possible for the overrun to overwrite the function's return address with a bad value—thus causing execution to jump to an invalid area of memory and trap. This is how hackers exploit buffer overruns.

5.8.1.4 SIGILL Signals   Stack corruption can often lead to an illegal instruction signal, or SIGILL, being raised in your program. If the return address for a frame is overwritten by buffer overrun, execution will attempt to jump to that return instruction and continue executing instructions. This is where the SIGILL can occur. A SIGILL can also occur when the stack overflows or when the system encounters a problem executing a signal handler.

5.8.1.4.1 Signals and the Stack   Signals are an important resource provided by Unix-based operating systems, and Linux provides a full feature implementation of them. It is important to understand how a signal manipulates the user-land stack, but knowing the gory details is not necessary.

> **Note:** For this particular discussion, "stack" needs to be qualified as either "user" or "kernel" considering both modes have their own stack and are very different.

A Linux application has the ability to define what to do when a particular signal is received either from the kernel or from another application. When the application is configured to execute a signal handler for a particular signal, the kernel must perform some intricate trickery to ensure that this functionality works properly.

Basically, when a process receives the signal sent to it, the following happens:

☞ The kernel copies its internal view of the process' hardware context directly onto the user-land process' stack.

☞ The kernel modifies the user-land process' stack to force a call to `sigreturn` after the execution of the signal handler in user-mode completes.

☞ The kernel forces the address of the signal handler that was defined by the application into the user-land process' program counter register.

☞ The kernel passes execution over to the user process.

☞ The user process executes the signal handler.

☞ The signal handler completes, and `sigreturn` is called as setup by the kernel.

☞ `sigreturn` copies the hardware context that was saved on the user-land process' stack back onto the kernel stack.

☞ The user process' stack is restored back to normal by removing the extra information copied to it by the kernel.

☞ Execution continues at the point at which the signal was received.

The main point to understand here is that when executing in a signal handler, the user-land process' stack is modified by the kernel.

5.9 CONCLUSION

The stack really is nothing more than a big chunk of memory that grows and shrinks as a program runs. Without a stack, programs would be extremely limited and probably a lot more complex. Understanding how the stack works is a huge step toward successfully troubleshooting some of the most difficult problems that an application on Linux can present you with.

The GNU Debugger (GDB)

6.1 INTRODUCTION

A good debugger is perhaps the single most important and comprehensive tool for troubleshooting any problem, developing applications, using reverse engineering, or just self-educating. There are many different kinds of debuggers across all different platforms—some are commercial products that may or may not be included with an associated commercial compiler. The GNU Debugger, or more commonly called GDB, is one of the few that is available across a myriad of hardware platforms running Linux including i386, x86-64, SPARC, PA-RISC, RS/6000, IA64, s390 as well as various flavors of Unix operating systems including AIX, HP-UX, and Solaris. There is a great deal of documentation currently available for GDB and the various Graphical User Interfaces (GUIs) that act as front-ends for it, so the goal of this chapter is to explain some of the key aspects of the debugger in more detail as well as present some of the lesser known tips and tricks of the trade.

A full-featured debugger should be considered a necessity on any operating system, but unfortunately most operating systems do not come with one. A debugger gives you the ability to peek "under the hood" to see exactly what a process is doing. Using a debugger, you can examine values in memory, look at the stack trace, and control the process. Some operating systems include a very basic debugger (for example, adb), while others include no debugger at all. Fortunately, Linux ships with one of the best debuggers available: GDB. The GDB debugger is full-featured, stable, and available for free, which means that Linux has an advantage over most other operating systems. GDB is also the most portable debugger currently available on all major architectures.

Learning how to use GDB on Linux is important for two reasons. The first is that in an open source environment, many of the applications have the source code freely available. This makes a debugger a very useful tool for self-service given that the application can often be rebuilt with debug information (see Chapter 4, "Compiling," for more information on compiling in debug). The other reason it is important to learn GDB is that it is a freely available tool that can help to solve many types of problems on Linux. For example, a memory corruption or code logic error is extremely challenging to debug without a debugger (these can be difficult enough with a debugger!).

A good deal of documentation already exists for GDB, but most of this documentation is similar to a command reference. This chapter is different and focuses on how and when to use GDB and will also reveal many of the hard-to-find tips used to tackle difficult problems.

Last, this chapter can be used to translate existing knowledge about other debuggers to the corresponding GDB commands. As users migrate to Linux from Windows and Unix-based operating systems, they need to translate their existing knowledge into the corresponding Linux equivalent. Many of these people already have the skills necessary to be an expert on Linux, and a book like this one will help to translate their knowledge to the Linux environment.

6.2 When To Use a Debugger

A debugger is usually used for a problem in a tool or application that cannot be solved through the application's inherent problem determination facilities (error log files, error messages, and so on) or through the system-level problem determination tools. A debugger is especially useful when source code is readily available (as is often the case on Linux).

Having the source code usually means being able to rebuild a tool or application with debug information such as variable names, information that links the machine instructions to a line of code, type information, and so on. Having the source code also means being able to step through the source code to debug a problem instead of having to step through machine instructions.

Source code certainly makes using a debugger much easier, but in general debuggers are fantastic tools for:

☞ **Point-in-time debugging**. This is when all of the evidence you need is available right now. In other words, you won't need any history of what led up to the problem.
☞ **When a problem can be easily reproduced**.
☞ **When the problem behavior can be predicted**. If you know the behavior of a problem, you can set a breakpoint in a function or on a condition and wait for the predicted behavior to occur.
☞ **When a problem can be localized to a small period of time**. This means that the problem will occur shortly after a predictable point in time.

Debuggers become less useful when the cause(s) of a problem span a long history or for a problem that is difficult to predict in nature. In both cases, you might want to consider adding trace points in the application or use the existing trace facility to understand the problem better.

6.3 COMMAND LINE EDITING

Before getting into details of GDB functionality, here is a quick overview of GDB command line editing. Command line editing will give you the ability to modify the command line and usually includes the ability to use previous commands again (with or without modification).

> **Note**: By default, GDB uses the Emacs command line editing style, although users who really prefer vi style command line editing can switch by adding the following to their inputrc file:
>
> ```
> $if gdb
>    set editing-mode vi
> $endif
> ```
>
> The inputrc file is used to configure the readline library (readline is a special library that handles command line editing), which certain tools (such as bash) use to read lines from the command line. /etc/inputrc controls system-wide settings for readLine while a user's individual ~/.inputrc can be used to override some of these settings. Note also that the INPUTRC environment variable setting will override the local and system-wide inpurtrc files.

Here are some basic Emacs editing commands for quick reference (consult the Emacs or vi documentation for more information).

Incantation	Result
Control-a	Move to beginning of the line
Control-e	Move to the end of the line
Control-d	Delete the character to the right and shift the line to the left
Backspace	Delete the character to the left and shift the line to the left
Control-u	Undo editing changes
Control-w	Erase the entire line to the left
Control-k	Erase the entire line to the right

> **Note**: When in Emacs editing mode, the up and down cursor keys will work to move between previously executed commands. The left and right keys will move within the current line.

6.4 Controlling a Process with GDB

GDB is designed to take control of a live process or to load a process image (a "core" file) into memory. In either case, GDB provides the ability to look at the contents of the memory for either a live process or the process image. When GDB is in control of a live process, it can also control the environment of the live process, change the memory used by the live process, or control how and when the live process is run. There are two ways to control a process and one way to get a process image into GDB:

1. **Run a program directly through the debugger.** Using this method, GDB actually creates and runs a new process off the command line.

2. **Attach to a running process.** Using this method, GDB attaches to an existing process.

3. **Use a core file for post-mortem analysis.** When using a core file, there is no live process, but there is a process image. A process image, or core file, contains the contents of memory for a process that was once running.

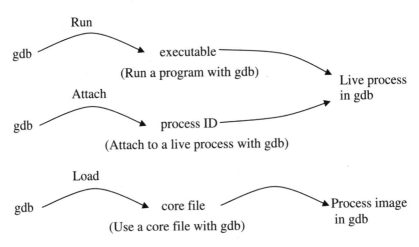

Fig. 6.1 Methods to get a process into GDB.

Regardless of how GDB gains control of a process (running a program directly off the command line or attaching to a live process), the resulting state is the same. GDB will have full control over the live process.

All three methods of using GDB will be explained in more detail.

6.4.1 Running a Program Off the Command Line with GDB

You should run a program through GDB if you want to be in control of the program from the beginning of its execution. For example, you might need to set a breakpoint (explained further down) in a function that gets run immediately after the program starts up. This could be for a C/C++ program where a function is simply called soon after the start up of a program or for a C++ program where some global constructors are triggered even before the `main()` function is called.

To run a program from within GDB, simply use GDB with the program as the only argument. When you first run GDB in this way, the program isn't actually started until you run it with the `run` command inside GDB. If you call run without setting a breakpoint, the program will run normally until it exits or hits a trap. Here is a quick example:

```
penguin> g++ hang.C -g -o hang
penguin> gdb hang
GNU gdb 5.2.1
Copyright 2002 Free Software Foundation, Inc.
gdb is free software, covered by the GNU General Public License, and
you are welcome to change it and/or distribute copies of it under
certain conditions.
Type "show copying" to see the conditions.
There is absolutely no warranty for gdb.  Type "show warranty" for
details.
This gdb was configured as "i586-suse-linux"...
(gdb) break main
Breakpoint 1 at 0x804843c: file hang.C, line 10.
(gdb) run user
Starting program: /home/wilding/src/Linuxbook/hang

Breakpoint 1, main (argc=1, argv=0xbffff104) at hang.C:10
10      getpid( ) ; // a system call to show that we've entered this code
(gdb) list
5
6
7       int main( int argc, char *argv[] )
8       {
9
10      getpid( ) ; // a system call to show that we've entered this code
11
12      if ( argc < 2 )
13      {
14      printf( "hang (user|system)" ) ;
```

In this example, the program was run inside of GDB with the command `run user`. The command `run` was used to run the program, and the `user` argument is passed as the first and only argument to the program. From the program's point of view, it is identical to being run from the shell as `hang user` (`hang` is the name of the program).

The command `break main` was used to set a breakpoint on the function `main()`. This is the first user-code function called in normal C programs and for C++ programs that do not have global objects to initialize. The term "user-code" is used to describe the code that would be compiled for the application and does not include the operating system functions that may be called in addition, such as the Run Time Linker functions (refer to the ELF chapter for more details on the Run Time Linker). Because the program was compiled with `-g`, it contains debug information that allows the debugger to identify the lines of code in the main function. Unless you're debugging the constructors of global C++ objects, the `main` function is a good way to stop the debugger at the beginning of the program execution.

You can also use the `args` GDB variable to set the command line arguments instead of including them behind the `run` command. This is particularly useful if the command line arguments are long and difficult to type in. With the args variable, you can set the command line arguments once and then use `run` on its own from then on. Here is short example to show how this works:

```
(gdb) show args
Argument list to give program being debugged when it is started is "".
(gdb) set args 6 7
(gdb) show args
Argument list to give program being debugged when it is started is "6
➥7".
(gdb) run
```

In the preceding example, the program is executed as if from a shell prompt with arguments 6 and 7 as the first and second arguments, respectively.

Environment variables are another way in which the user can affect the execution of a program. Because GDB provides a controlled environment for a program in which to run, the environment variables can be manipulated as well. The command `show environment` will display the current environment just as the `env` command would in a bash shell. To set an environment variable, use the `set environment` command with a `variable=value` pair. To unset a variable use the `unset environment` command. This is shown in the following example:

```
(gdb) set environment FOO=BAR
(gdb) show environment FOO
FOO = BAR
(gdb) unset environment FOO
(gdb) show environment FOO
Environment variable "FOO" not defined.
(gdb)
```

> **Note**: When using Emacs editing mode, to save some typing, use TAB command completion. Typing "env<TAB>" will complete `environment` for you. GDB also accepts short forms for all commands. If you don't know the short form, start with the first letter and work up from that:
>
> ```
> (gdb) show e FOO
> Ambiguous show command "e FOO": editing, endian, environment,
> eventdebug, exec-done-display.
> (gdb) show en FOO
> Ambiguous show command "en FOO": endian, environment.
> (gdb) show env FOO
> Environment variable "FOO" not defined.
> (gdb)
> ```

6.4.2 Attaching to a Running Process

Attaching to a running process with GDB is usually done when it is difficult to get a process in the debugger at a key point in its execution. For example, there are situations where the startup procedure for an application is complex in that it forks or execs other processes, and you want to attach to one of the forked or exec'ed processes only. You might also need to attach to a process that is only started in a client-server modeled application. In other words, a remote client might start a local process you cannot start manually from a command line. Another example of when it is useful to attach to a process is when a problem has already occurred and you need to attach to the process to debug it.

To demonstrate attaching GDB to a running process, let's use the little hanging program, `hang`, again:

```
penguin> hang system
```

This simply causes the hang process to hang in a system call so that we can attach to the process with GDB:

```
penguin> gdb - 3051
GNU gdb 5.2.1
Copyright 2002 Free Software Foundation, Inc.
gdb is free software, covered by the GNU General Public License, and
you are welcome to change it and/or distribute copies of it under
certain conditions.
Type "show copying" to see the conditions.
There is absolutely no warranty for gdb. Type "show warranty" for
details.
This gdb was configured as "i586-suse-linux"...-: No such file or
directory.
```

```
Attaching to process 3051
Reading symbols from /home/wilding/src/Linuxbook/hang...done.
Reading symbols from /usr/lib/libstdc++.so.5...done.
Loaded symbols for /usr/lib/libstdc++.so.5
Reading symbols from /lib/libm.so.6...done.
Loaded symbols for /lib/libm.so.6
Reading symbols from /lib/libgcc_s.so.1...done.
Loaded symbols for /lib/libgcc_s.so.1
Reading symbols from /lib/libc.so.6...done.
Loaded symbols for /lib/libc.so.6
Reading symbols from /lib/ld-linux.so.2...done.
Loaded symbols for /lib/ld-linux.so.2
0x4019fd01 in nanosleep () from /lib/libc.so.6
(gdb) bt
#0  0x4019fd01 in nanosleep () from /lib/libc.so.6
#1  0x4019fbd9 in sleep () from /lib/libc.so.6
#2  0x080484a7 in main (argc=2, argv=0xbffff134) at hang.C:24
#3  0x4011a4a2 in __libc_start_main () from /lib/libc.so.6
(gdb) up
#1  0x4019fbd9 in sleep () from /lib/libc.so.6
(gdb) up
#2  0x080484a7 in main (argc=2, argv=0xbffff134) at hang.C:24
24          sleep( 5000 ) ;
(gdb) list
19          {
20              while ( 1 ) ;
21          }
22          else if ( !strcmp( argv[1], "system" ) )
23          {
24              sleep( 5000 ) ;
25          }
26
27          return 0 ;
28      }
```

The process is stopped, as expected, at the point where the process was hung. There is no need to set a breakpoint because the program will simply stop where it was when GDB attached to it. In this case, of course, the process was already stopped.

Notice that there is no line number displayed for nanosleep(). This is because this function is in libc.so.6, which was not compiled with -g. Running bt to get the stack trace shows the line of code in function main() is 24. The up command was used twice to walk up the stack until the debugger was looking at the stack frame where source code was available.

6.4.3 Use a Core File

Core files are often used to debug programs and applications on Linux and Unix-based operating systems. Core files are useful for debugging because they contain the memory image of the process at the time when the core file was created. A core file contains the process heap, the stack, and any writable memory segments that were in a process' address space. A core file can be used long after a problem occurs to debug a problem in a debugger such as GDB.

Core files can also be useful for situations where a problem has to be debugged remotely and cannot be reproduced on any system but the original. In such a case, core files can be transferred to another system for analysis as long as the libraries' versions used by the process are the same on the other system.

The kernel will automatically create a core file if a process traps with a signal such as SIGSEGV and if the resource limits allow it. To demonstrate the generation of core files, let's use a very simple program that dereferences a NULL pointer. The source code for this program is:

```
int main( void )
{
    int *trap = 0;

    *trap = 1;

    return 0;
}
```

When running this program, we get the following output:

```
penguin> simple_trap
Segmentation fault
penguin> ls -l core
/bin/ls: core: No such file or directory
```

So why was no core file generated? The answer lies in the shell's default resource settings. For a bash shell, we can view and manipulate these settings with the ulimit command. To see a listing of all current settings, use the -a parameter:

```
penguin> ulimit -a
core file size        (blocks, -c) 0
data seg size         (kbytes, -d) unlimited
file size             (blocks, -f) unlimited
max locked memory     (kbytes, -l) unlimited
max memory size       (kbytes, -m) unlimited
open files                   (-n) 1024
pipe size        (512 bytes, -p) 8
stack size            (kbytes, -s) unlimited
cpu time            (seconds, -t) unlimited
max user processes           (-u) 7168
virtual memory        (kbytes, -v) unlimited
```

> **Note**: The command `ulimit` is built into the bash shell. For different shells, the command and its output may differ.

According to the output, the core file size is limited to 0 blocks, meaning that no core files will be generated for traps. To generate a core file, we need to increase this limit. Bash's ulimit output is nice because it displays the command line parameter to use for each setting in parentheses after the units of size. Setting the core file size to unlimited and rerunning our program gives us this output:

```
penguin> ulimit -c unlimited
penguin> simple_trap
Segmentation fault (core dumped)
penguin> ls -l core
-rw——    1 dbehman   users        53248 2004-09-12 10:36 core
```

> **Note**: If you always want core files to be generated for programs that produce traps, add the `ulimit - unlimited` command to your $HOME/.profile bash startup script. This is assuming you use bash; the command and startup script will differ for other shells.

If you want to know what is in a core file, you can quickly peek into the core file by running `readelf -all core`. For more information about the contents of the core file, refer to the ELF chapter (Chapter 9).

When you have a core file, you just need to get it into GDB along with the application for which the core was generated. Here are the simple steps using the core file just generated:

```
penguin> gdb simple_trap core
GNU gdb 5.3.92
Copyright 2003 Free Software Foundation, Inc.
gdb is free software, covered by the GNU General Public License, and
you are welcome to change it and/or distribute copies of it under
certain conditions.
Type "show copying" to see the conditions.
There is absolutely no warranty for gdb.  Type "show warranty" for
details.
This gdb was configured as "i586-suse-linux"...
Core was generated by 'simple_trap'.
Program terminated with signal 11, Segmentation fault.
Reading symbols from /lib/i686/libc.so.6...done.
Loaded symbols for /lib/i686/libc.so.6
Reading symbols from /lib/ld-linux.so.2...done.
Loaded symbols for /lib/ld-linux.so.2
```

```
#0  0x08048326 in main () at simple_trap.c:5
5               *trap = 1;
(gdb)
```

After GDB has fully read the core file, the process will look exactly the same as if we had run the simple_trap program inside of GDB on the command line. The core file gives us the advantage of easily seeing the trapped state of the process at any time on any machine without the need to run the program again.

Because a core file is not a running process, you can't use any of the execution commands in GDB given the program is not actually running. There is no live process to control. The rest of the commands, including all of the ones that examine or print memory, will work as if there were a live process being controlled by GDB.

6.4.3.1 Changing Core File Name and Location
In some cases, you want to set the location where the core files on the system get saved to. One reason for doing this is to prevent core files from being scattered throughout the file system. Another reason is that more complex applications that manipulate the user permissions and directory locations internally while running may not have proper access to generate a core file in their respective default locations.

To control the naming of core files generated, the /proc/sys/kernel/core_pattern control file is used. Note that this is a 2.6 kernel feature, though it is very likely that your distribution has back-ported it to its 2.4 based kernels. SuSE Linux Professional 9.0 and SuSE Linux Enterprise Server 8, for example, both have this control file. As an example, let's say we want all core files to be generated in /core_files and have their names made up of the process name, the user ID running the process, and the process ID. First, as root, ensure that the /core_files directory exists and is fully writeable by any user. Then execute the following:

```
echo "/core_files/%u.%e.%p.core" > /proc/sys/kernel/core_pattern
```

Now when rerunning our simple_trap program, we will see the following:

```
penguin> ls -l /core_files
total 52
-rw----    1 dbehman    users          53248  2004-09-12  11:22
↪500.simple_trap.12589.core
```

Refer to the proc(5) man page for a detailed explanation of what core-pattern can be set to.

6.4.3.2 Saving the State of a GDB Session If you had attached GDB to a running process or run the program through GDB from the command line, you may have had the desire to save the current state of the debugging session to a file. Reasons for doing this would be to resume the debugging session at a later time or to transfer the debugging session to a co-worker on another system. In any case, GDB has a useful command that creates a core file from within a GDB session:

```
(gdb) help generate-core-file
Save a core file with the current state of the debugged process.
Argument is optional filename.  Default filename is 'core.<process_id>'.
(gdb) generate-core-file
Saved corefile core.13112
(gdb)
```

This core file is in the same format as if the kernel produced it directly and can be loaded using the technique explained previously.

6.5 EXAMINING DATA, MEMORY, AND REGISTERS

At this point, we've covered all of the ways to get a process (or a memory image of a process) into GDB. In this section, we discuss how to examine data, memory, and registers. This section introduces important GDB commands that work regardless of whether the process is debugging a live process or whether you're performing post-mortem with a core file. When there is a difference, there will be a note to indicate it.

6.5.1 Memory Map

Strictly speaking, viewing the memory map for a process is not part of GDB but is still very important to understand, which is why it is covered briefly here in the context of GDB and in more detail in Chapter 3, "The /proc Filesystem." There must be a live process for there to be a corresponding "maps" file under /proc. You cannot get a memory map using /proc for a process image that is loaded in GDB as a core file.

The memory map is the list of memory segments (aka regions) that a process has in its address space. There is a memory segment for every type of memory that a process is using, including the process heap, the process stack, memory that stores the contents of an executable, memory for the shared libraries, and so on. Memory segments also have different attributes such as read, write, and execute. These attributes will depend on the purpose of the memory segment. Shared libraries, for example, will have a large read/execute segment that cannot be written to. This is for the machine code (the actual code that gets run) in the shared library.

The memory map is important for a few reasons:

☞   It tells you which shared libraries are loaded and at which addresses.

☞   It tells you where each memory segment is. Memory accessed outside of the valid memory segments will cause a segmentation violation.

☞   The memory map will tell you a bit more about an address. If the address is in the memory map for a shared library, it is probably a global variable or function in that shared library.

☞   You can tell if the heap or stack collided with another memory segment (for example, there is no space between the heap or stack and the next segment).

The best way to look at the memory map for a *live* process in GDB is to use a shell escape, making use of GDB's `info program` and `shell` commands (the latter is to make direct calls to programs outside of GDB):

```
(gdb) info program
    Using the running image of attached process 11702.
Program stopped at 0x4019fd01.
It stopped with signal SIGSTOP, Stopped (signal).
(gdb) shell cat /proc/11702/maps
08048000-08049000  r-xp 00000000  08:13 3647282    /home/wilding/src/
➥Linuxbook/hang2
08049000-0804a000  rw-p 00000000  08:13 3647282    /home/wilding/src/
➥Linuxbook/hang2
40000000-40012000  r-xp 00000000  08:13 1144740  /lib/ld-2.2.5.so
40012000-40013000  rw-p 00011000  08:13 1144740  /lib/ld-2.2.5.so
40013000-40014000  rw-p 00000000  00:00 0
40014000-400ad000  r-xp 00000000  08:13 1847971  /usr/lib/libstdc++.so.5.0.0
400ad000-400c2000  rw-p 00098000  08:13 1847971  /usr/lib/libstdc++.so.5.0.0
400c2000-400c7000  rw-p 00000000  00:00 0
400d7000-400f9000  r-xp 00000000  08:13 1144751  /lib/libm.so.6
400f9000-400fa000  rw-p 00021000  08:13 1144751  /lib/libm.so.6
400fa000-40101000  r-xp 00000000  08:13 1144783  /lib/libgcc_s.so.1
40101000-40102000  rw-p 00007000  08:13 1144783  /lib/libgcc_s.so.1
40102000-40216000  r-xp 00000000  08:13 1144746  /lib/libc.so.6
40216000-4021c000  rw-p 00113000  08:13 1144746  /lib/libc.so.6
4021c000-40221000  rw-p 00000000  00:00 0
bfffe000-c0000000  rwxp fffff000  00:00 0
```

For more information on a process' address space and the various mappings, refer to the /proc/<pid>/maps section in Chapter 3.

6.5.2 Stack

The stack is important because it contains information about "where" in the code a process is running. The stack contains one stack "frame" for each unfinished function that called another function. This leads to a hierarchical chain or *stack* of function callers and callees. The functions on the stack have not finished—in other words, each function will continue if the function they called finishes. A "stack trace" or "back trace" is the list of functions in the stack. In GDB, the backtrace or bt command will dump the stack trace for the process currently being debugged:

```
(gdb) backtrace
#0 0x400d6f0b in pause () from /lib/i686/libc.so.6
#1 0x080483d0 in function4 (a=97 'a') at gdb_stack.c:9
#2 0x080483e9 in function3 (string=0xbffff340 "This is a local string")at
➥gdb_stack.c:16
#3 0x0804843a in function2 (param=3) at gdb_stack.c:23
#4 0x08048456 in function1 (param=3) at gdb_stack.c:31
#5 0x0804847d in main () at gdb_stack.c:38
```

From this stack trace (a.k.a. back trace), we know that the main() function called function1(), and that function1() called function2(), and so forth. The last function on the stack is pause(). If pause finishes (that is, exits), function4 will continue. If function4 finishes, function3 will continue, and so on.

Note that in this output the arguments, filename, and line number for all functions except pause() are shown. This is because gdb_stack.c (a little program specifically for this example) was compiled with -g to include debug symbols, but the source used to create libc.so.6, where pause is contained, was not. If the program was built without -g, we would only know the address of the program counter for each stack frame and not the line of code.

Note: Some distributions strip their shared libraries, removing the main symbol table and other information. However, there is usually a non-stripped shared library (such as libc6-dbg.so) that contains the main symbol table and additional information useful for debugging.

The function names themselves aren't stored in each stack frame. The function names are too long, and the reality is that function names aren't much use to the computer. Instead each stack frame contains the saved instruction pointer or program counter. The saved program counter can be translated into the function name by looking at the address of the program counter and the instruction of the library or executable that is loaded in that region of memory.

The full set of steps to translate a program counter address into a line of code can be found in Chapter 4, which contains detailed information about compiling programs. More information on stack traces can be found in Chapter 5.

Let's go back to the stack trace output to explain the format. The numbers on the left indicate the frame number for each stack frame. These numbers can be used with various GDB frame-related commands to reference a specific frame. The next column in the stack trace output is a hexadecimal address of the program counter stored for each stack frame. On x86-based hardware, shared libraries usually get loaded around address 0x40000000, and the executable gets mapped in at 0x08048000. See the /proc/<pid>/maps section in the /proc filesystem chapter (Chapter 3) for more information on address space mappings. It is good enough for this discussion to know that the program counter address of 0x400d6f0b for the function *pause* makes sense because it is found in a shared library and is near the starting address for shared libraries of 0x40000000. The program counter addresses starting with 0x08048 for the other functions also makes sense because it is part of the executable created from the gdb_stack.c source code.

Use the bt full command to see more information in the stack trace including a dumping of local variables for each frame:

```
(gdb) bt full
#0  0x400d6f0b in pause () from /lib/i686/libc.so.6
No symbol table info available.
#1  0x080483d0 in function4 (a=97 'a') at gdb_stack.c:9
        b = 1
#2  0x080483e9 in function3 (string=0xbffff340 "This is a local string")
    at gdb_stack.c:16
        a = 97 'a'
#3  0x0804843a in function2 (param=3) at gdb_stack.c:23
        string = "This is a local string"
#4  0x08048456 in function1 (param=3) at gdb_stack.c:31
        localVar = 99
#5  0x0804847d in main () at gdb_stack.c:38
        stackVar = 3
(gdb)
```

This will include the local variables for each stack frame that has debug information. Usually, though, you'll want to see specific local variables and just print them as needed. See the following section on printing values and variables.

6.5.2.1 Navigating Stack Frames

GDB can only see local variables that belong to the current frame (that is, in the "scope" of the current function). If you want to view a local variable that is part of another function in the stack, you must tell GDB to switch its focus to that frame. You may also want to

change the current stack frame (that is, function) to perform other operations
in that scope. For example, you can tell GDB to "finish" a function, and GDB
will run the process until the current function (at the current stack frame)
finishes and returns control to the function that called it.

Unless any previous frame navigation has been performed, you will always be
in frame #0 to start. This is always the "top" frame on the stack. The quickest
way to switch stack frames is to use the `frame` command with the specific
frame number.

```
(gdb) frame 3
#3  0x0804843a in function2 (param=3) at gdb_stack.c:23
23          function3( string );
(gdb)
```

You can also use the `up` and `down` commands to walk up and down frames in the
stack:

```
(gdb) up
#1 0x080483d0 in function4 (a=97 'a') at gdb_stack.c:9
9      pause();
(gdb) down
#0 0x400d6f0b in pause () from /lib/i686/libc.so.6
(gdb) down
Bottom (i.e., innermost) frame selected; you cannot go down.
(gdb) up
#1 0x080483d0 in function4 (a=97 'a') at gdb_stack.c:9
9      pause();
(gdb) up
#2 0x080483e9 in function3 (string=0xbffff340 "This is a local string")
   at gdb_stack.c:16
16     function4( a );
(gdb) up
#3 0x0804843a in function2 (param=3) at gdb_stack.c:23
23     function3( string );
(gdb)
```

GDB won't let you go past the beginning or the end of the stack, so you can use
up and down without concern.

> **Note**: Stacks grow downward toward smaller addresses on x86-
> based hardware, so the "bottom" of the stack will have the highest stack
> frame address. The top of the stack is the stack frame in GDB that has a
> frame number of 0 (zero) and will have the lowest numbered address in
> memory. Please also note that there is a diagram of stack traces in Chapter
> 5.

6.5.2.2 Obtaining and Understanding Frame Information Sometimes you'll want/need to get more information about a stack frame. For example, a stack frame contains information about function arguments, local variables, and some interesting registers. This can be particularly useful if you don't have the source code for the application. To get more information on a particular stack frame, use the `info frame` command:

```
(gdb) info frame 2
Stack frame at 0xbffff330:
 eip = 0x80483e9 in function3 (gdb_stack.c:16); saved eip 0x804843a
 called by frame at 0xbffff370, caller of frame at 0xbffff310
 source language c.
 Arglist at 0xbffff328, args: string=0xbffff340 "This is a local string"
 Locals at 0xbffff328, Previous frame's sp is 0xbffff330
 Saved registers:
 ebp at 0xbffff328, eip at 0xbffff32c
(gdb)
```

There's a lot of information here, so let's break it down a little.

```
Stack frame at 0xbffff330:
```

This is simply the address of the stack frame.

```
eip = 0x80483e9 in function3 (gdb_stack.c:16); saved eip 0x804843a
```

The `eip` (Extended Instruction Pointer) address points to the next instruction to be executed in this frame. We can then see that this frame is associated with `function3()`. Because this source code was compiled with debug symbols, the source file name and line number is also displayed. The *saved eip* is the address that points to the next instruction to be executed in the *previous* frame in the stack. So for example, if we look at the information for the previous frame in the stack, its `eip` will be this stack's *saved eip*.

```
called by frame at 0xbffff370, caller of frame at 0xbffff310
```

`called by frame` indicates the address of the frame that called this frame. `caller of frame` indicates which frame the current frame calls. So the `called by` and `caller of` basically display the addresses of the two frames that surround the current frame.

```
source language c.
```

This line tells us the language in which the program was written.

```
Arglist at 0xbffff328, args: string=0xbffff340 "This is a local string"
```

Arglist indicates the address in which the local function variables start. args: displays the arguments passed to this frame. Because this code was compiled with debug symbols, we can see the symbolic name of the argument, string. The address of this variable is also displayed. Note that since this particular variable is itself a local variable, the address appears in the stack frame that called the current frame.

```
Locals at 0xbffff328, Previous frame's sp is 0xbffff330
```

Locals displays the address in which the local variables start. Previous frame's sp displays stack pointer of the previous frame.

```
Saved registers:
ebp at 0xbffff328, eip at 0xbffff32c
```

This line displays the values of the ebp and eip registers in the current frame. The eip register is the instruction pointer, and the ebp pointer is the stack base pointer. For more information on these registers and the stack layout, refer to Chapter 5.

6.5.3 Examining Memory and Variables

Besides looking at the stack, looking at the contents of memory and variables is probably the next most useful feature of a debugger. In fact, you will spend most of your time in a debugger looking at variables and/or the contents of memory trying to understand what is going wrong with a process.

6.5.3.1 Variables and Scope and Type   Variables in a C/C++ program have different scope depending on how they were declared. A global variable is a variable that is defined to be externally visible all of the time. A static variable can be declared in the scope of a file or in a function. Static variables are not visible externally and are treated in a special way. An automatic variable is one that is declared inside a function and is only available on the stack while the corresponding function is running and has not finished. Here is a quick overview of how to declare the variables with the three scopes (this is important to understand how to handle each type in GDB).

```
Global variable:
int foo = 6 ;
```

> **Note**: You must declare the variable at the highest scope and outside of any function.

```
Static variable:
static int foo = 6 ;

Automatic variable:
int function1()
{
   int foo = 6 ;

}
```

Global symbols are always available to view in a debugger, although you might not always know the type. Static variables are also always available, but a stripped executable or library may not include the names of the static functions. Function local variables (also known as automatic variables) are only available for printing if the source code is compiled with -g. Building in debug mode provides two things necessary for printing automatic variables. The first is the type information. The second is the debug information for automatic variables, which includes linking them to the type information.

Consider a global variable defined as follows:

```
const char *constString = "This is a constant string!";
```

Printing this from inside GDB for a program that was not compiled with -g will produce the following:

```
(gdb) print constString
$2 = 134513832
```

GDB can find the global variable, but it does not know its type. As long as this is a base type (that is, not a structure, class, or union), we can still print this properly using the print formatting capabilities:

```
(gdb) printf "%s\n", constString
This is a constant string!
(gdb)
```

We were able to print constString as a string because it is a base type and is a global symbol. A local symbol would not be stored in the symbol table and would not reference it without building in debug.

Next, let's take a look at how to print a static variable. This is similar to a global variable except that there may be more than one static variable with the same name.

Consider the static function declared at the file level (that is, declared static but outside the scope of a function) as:

```
static int staticInt = 5 ;
```

Next, let's find out how many static functions there are:

```
(gdb) info variable staticInt
All variables matching regular expression "staticInt":

Non-debugging symbols:
0x08049544 staticInt
```

Because only one is listed, there is only one. Next, let's print its value:

```
(gdb) print /x staticInt
$3 = 0x5
(gdb)
```

Automatic variables are not stored in the process symbol table, meaning that without compiling in -g, automatic variables have no name in the compiled code. Consider the following simple function that defines an integer b:

```
int foo( int a )
{
  int b = 0 ;

...
}
```

If we compile this without debug (that is, without -g), GDB will have no information about this variable name or type.

```
g++ foo.C -o foo
```

And now in GDB (skipping the first part of the session for clarity)

```
(gdb) break foo
Breakpoint 1 at 0x8048422
(gdb) run
Starting program: /home/wilding/src/Linuxbook/foo

Breakpoint 1, 0x08048422 in foo(int) ()
(gdb) print b
No symbol "b" in current context.
```

Notice how GDB cannot find any information about the variable at all. This is one of the reasons it is much easier to use GDB when the program is compiled with -g. If the program was built with -g, GDB would be able to find the variable and print its value:

```
(gdb) break foo
Breakpoint 1 at 0x8048422: file foo.C, line 30.
(gdb) run
Starting program: /home/wilding/src/Linuxbook/foo

Breakpoint 1, foo(int) (a=6) at foo.C:30
30        int b = 0 ;
(gdb) print b
$1 = 1075948688
```

Examining memory and values of variables is another very important aspect of debugging. Most programs allocate memory using malloc or new (the latter for C++) to store variables. Variables that are stored in a heap (such as the one used by malloc or heap), do not have a symbol table, and the compiler does not create any link or any type information for such variables. Such variables do not really have a "scope" and need to be handled specially, as outlined in the section, "Viewing Data in Memory."

6.5.3.2 Print Formatting Print formatting allows users to change how variables and memory are displayed. For example, sometimes it is more useful to print an integer in hexadecimal format, and other times it helps to see it in decimal format. The most basic way (that is, without formatting) to see the value of a variable is with the print <variable_name> command.

```
(gdb) print stackVar
$1 = 10
```

You can specify what format you want print to display in. For example, to see it in hex, use the /x argument:

```
(gdb) print /x stackVar
$2 = 0xa
```

Notice how the value of the variable is always preceded by a dollar sign with a number followed by an equal sign. This is because GDB is automatically assigning and storing the value printed to an internal variable of that name. GDB calls these *convenience variables*. So for example, you can later reuse the newly created $1 variable in other calculations in this debugging session:

```
(gdb) print $1 + 5
$3 = 15
```

A more powerful alternative to the `print` command is the `printf` command. The `printf` command works much the same as the standard C library function works:

```
(gdb) printf "The value of stackVar in hex is 0x%x\n", stackVar
The value of stackVar in hex is 0xa
```

Printing an array is just as easy. Consider the following array:

```
int list[10] = { 0, 1, 2, 3, 4, 5, 6, 7, 8, 9 } ;
```

You can print this array in its entirety or just one element:

```
(gdb) print list
$2 = {0, 1, 2, 3, 4, 5, 6, 7, 8, 9}
 (gdb) print list[3]
$1 = 3
 (gdb)
```

Notice, though, that the array indexing is C-style with 0 (zero) being the first index value. Thus, the element whose index is 3 is actually the fourth element of the array.

In some cases, you may want to simulate an array with the @ character. Consider the following integer:

```
int globInt = 5 ;
```

We can treat this integer as an array that is three elements in length:

```
(gdb) print globInt@3
$16 = {5, 5, 134514112}
```

This is usually useful when dealing with memory that has been allocated in a heap and does not have any specific type according to GDB.

6.5.3.3 Determining the Type of Variable Occasionally, you'll want to figure out what kind of variable you're about to look at. This is mostly useful when looking at global and static variables. When needed, use the `whatis` command:

```
(gdb) whatis a
type = int
```

6.5.3.4 Viewing Data in Memory As mentioned earlier, if a problem is not compiled with `-g`, it won't have any of the debug information such as variable type information. In this case, you'll probably need to look at memory directly using the examine or x command. This command accepts a number of arguments —/FMT ADDRESS. FMT is a repeat count followed by a format letter and a size letter. ADDRESS specifies the address at which to start the display of data. The following example will dump eight 4-byte hex values starting at 0x08048000:

```
(gdb) x /8xw 0x08048000
0x8048000:     0x464c457f    0x00010101    0x00000000    0x00000000
0x8048010:     0x00030002    0x00000001    0x08048320    0x00000034
```

The GDB help output for constructing an x command is very useful, but for convenience, the most commonly used format codes are shown in the following table.

Format Description	Format Code
1-byte ASCII character	cb
2-byte decimal integer	dh
4-byte decimal integer	dw
1-byte hexadecimal number	xb
2-byte hexadecimal number	xh
4-byte hexadecimal number	xw
8-byte hexadecimal number	xg
String	s

Table 6.1 GDB Format Codes.

6.5.3.5 Formatting Values in Memory
If you have a variable in memory and you know the address, you can use casting to print with the correct formatting. Consider the string defined in the preceding example constString. Here are four different methods to print this variable correctly as a string.

```
(gdb) print constString
$5 = 0x80485c0 "This is a constant string!"
(gdb)  x /s 0x080485c0
0x80485c0 <_IO_stdin_used+28>:   "This is a constant string!"
  (gdb) printf "%s\n",0x080485c0
This is a constant string!
(gdb) print (char *) 0x080485c0
$6 = 0x80485c0 "This is a constant string!"
```

The first requires the shared library or executable that contains this variable to be built with debug information (compiled with -g). Without this debug information, the debugger will not have type information for the symbol constString. The second method uses the GDB examine command (x) with a string format (/s). The third method uses the GDB printf command with a string token (%s). The last method uses a casting feature in GDB to print an address as a specific type. The last three methods do not require any type information (that is, they will work on a program that is not compiled with -g).

The last method is interesting because it uses a C-style cast to tell GDB how to print it. This will work with any type, which makes this very useful when debugging values that are in memory but do not have any direct type information. For example, an application may use malloc or other memory allocation function to get memory to store a variable with a specific type. The compiler will include type information for the variable but will not link it with the memory that was allocated via malloc.

The cast formatting method is probably the most powerful method of formatting complex types in GDB. We could even use the address of the constant string constString and cast it to a C++ class type in order to print that region of memory as a C++ object.

```
class myClass
{
  public:

  int myVar ;

  myClass() {
   myVar = 5 ;
  }

};
```

See the section later in this chapter titled "Finding the Address of Variables and Functions" for information on how to find the address of variables like constString. Now we can print the region of memory for the constant string as this class (note that 0x080485c0 is the address of constString):

```
(gdb) print (myClass) *0x080485c0
$26 = {myVar = 1936287828}
```

Of course, this was a completely invalid address, but it shows just how flexible this cast formatting is! Just to prove the point further, though, the value of the member variable myVar is 1936287828 in decimal format and 0x73696854 in hex format which, when translated to a string is sihT or This in reverse (see the man page for ascii for the ascii table). Why is this in reverse? The answer is that 32-bit x86 platforms are "little endian," as explained later in this chapter.

6.5.3.6 Changing Variables GDB also allows you to make any changes you wish to variables and registers. To set the value of a variable, use the set variable command, or simply set:

```
(gdb) set variable a=5
```

or

```
(gdb) set a=5
(gdb) print a
$1 = 5
```

You can set the value of a register by referencing it the same way you reference it when printing its value:

```
(gdb) set $eax=1
(gdb) print $eax
$1 = 1
```

> **Warning**: Changing the value of a register without understanding what it is for will cause unpredictable behavior.

6.5.4 Register Dump

Examining the contents of the registers in a live debugging session may be necessary to diagnose complex problems, especially when you don't have the source code. Looking at a raw register dump can be like looking at a wall of hieroglyphics if you don't have experience with assembly language on the platform you are using. The contents of the registers make sense only when you examine and understand the assembly instructions (the human readable format of machine instructions) that are using the registers. Assembly instructions directly manipulate the memory and registers of a computer. When debugging a program that has been compiled with debug symbols enabled (-g), looking at register contents is usually not necessary. However, when debugging a program that has no debug symbols, you are forced to work at the assembly level.

The command used to see a register dump in GDB is "info registers" as shown here:

```
(gdb) info registers
eax       0x6    6
ecx       0x1    1
edx       0x4015c490      1075168400
```

```
ebx        0x4015afd8    1075163096
esp        0xbffff3a0    0xbffff3a0
ebp        0xbffff3a8    0xbffff3a8
esi        0x40018420    1073841184
edi        0xbffff3f4    -1073744908
eip        0x8048340     0x8048340
eflags       0x200386 2098054
cs         0x23    35
ss         0x2b    43
ds         0x2b    43
es         0x2b    43
fs         0x0    0
gs         0x0    0
(gdb)
```

We know from the procedure calling conventions on x86 (see the "Procedure Calling Conventions" section in Chapter 5 for more information) that `eax` is used to store the return value from a function call. We don't know for sure, but a possibility here is that a function will return the value of 6. However, without seeing the previously executed assembly instructions, we really don't know what has been executed to bring the registers to the state we see above. However, there is some interesting information that we can pick out of this dump.

The `eip` register is the instruction pointer (a.k.a program counter) and always contains the address of the current instruction in memory that will be executed. Memory addresses that are close to the `eip` above of `0x8048340` will become familiar the more debugging and problem determination you do on Linux for 32-bit x86 hardware. Executables always get mapped into a process' address space at `0x08048000` on this hardware, and so instructions in this range are very common. Refer to the /proc/<pid>/maps section in Chapter 3 for more information on a process' address space.

One final observation we can make from the register dump has to do with the values stored in the `ebp` and `esp` registers. Addresses near `0xbffff3a0` and `0xbffff3a8` for the registers `ebp` and `esp` will also become familiar as you become more accustomed to the address space layout. The `ebp` and `esp` registers are used to control the stack and the stack segment on 32-bit x86 hardware and are usually located around the `0xbfffffff` address range.

> **Note**: The meaning of each register is well beyond the scope of this chapter and will not be covered here (`http://linuxassembly.org/` may be a good reference for the interested reader).

If you do end up looking at a register dump, it will probably be for a trap that occurred for a process that was not built with `-g`. In this case, you'll probably look at the instruction that trapped and try to understand why an address that is stored in a register used by that instruction is invalid. If your program is getting a segmentation violation (SIGSEGV), it is very likely that the trapped instruction is dereferencing a bad pointer. For example, an address of 0x6 or 0x0 is outside the range of any memory segment and will result in a segmentation violation.

64-bit computing is becoming more and more mainstream, and it is worth covering some of the differences between 32-bit and 64-bit as far as registers are concerned. The following dump was performed on the x86-64 architecture and was done at the exact same point in a test program as the preceding dump:

```
(gdb) info registers
rax        0x6     6
rbx        0x7fbfffea48    548682066504
rcx        0x40000300      1073742592
rdx        0x7fbfffea58    548682066520
rsi        0x4     4
rdi        0x2     2
rbp        0x7fbfffe9e0    0x7fbfffe9e0
rsp        0x7fbfffe9d0    0x7fbfffe9d0
r8         0x40000488      1073742984
r9         0x2a955604d0    182894068944
r10        0x0     0
r11        0x2a956a2d40    182895390016
r12        0x40000300      1073742592
r13        0x1     1
r14        0x2a95879308    182897316616
r15        0x4000041a      1073742874
rip        0x4000043b      0x4000043b <main+33>
eflags     0x306   774
ds         0x33    51
es         0x2b    43
fs         0x0     0
gs         0x0     0
fctrl      0x0     0
fstat      0x0     0
ftag       0x0     0
fiseg      0x0     0
fioff      0x0     0
foseg      0x0     0
fooff      0x0     0
fop        0x0     0
xmm0       {f = {0x0, 0x0, 0x0, 0x0}}     {f = {0, 0, 0, 0}}
xmm1       {f = {0x0, 0x0, 0x0, 0x0}}     {f = {0, 0, 0, 0}}
xmm2       {f = {0x0, 0x0, 0x0, 0x0}}     {f = {0, 0, 0, 0}}
xmm3       {f = {0x0, 0x0, 0x0, 0x0}}     {f = {0, 0, 0, 0}}
xmm4       {f = {0x0, 0x0, 0x0, 0x0}}     {f = {0, 0, 0, 0}}
xmm5       {f = {0x0, 0x0, 0x0, 0x0}}     {f = {0, 0, 0, 0}}
xmm6       {f = {0x0, 0x0, 0x0, 0x0}}     {f = {0, 0, 0, 0}}
xmm7       {f = {0x0, 0x0, 0x0, 0x0}}     {f = {0, 0, 0, 0}}
xmm8       {f = {0x0, 0x0, 0x0, 0x0}}     {f = {0, 0, 0, 0}}
```

```
xmm9      {f = {0x0, 0x0, 0x0, 0x0}}    {f = {0, 0, 0, 0}}
xmm10     {f = {0x0, 0x0, 0x0, 0x0}}    {f = {0, 0, 0, 0}}
xmm11     {f = {0x0, 0x0, 0x0, 0x0}}    {f = {0, 0, 0, 0}}
xmm12     {f = {0x0, 0x0, 0x0, 0x0}}    {f = {0, 0, 0, 0}}
xmm13     {f = {0x0, 0x0, 0x0, 0x0}}    {f = {0, 0, 0, 0}}
xmm14     {f = {0x0, 0x0, 0x0, 0x0}}    {f = {0, 0, 0, 0}}
xmm15     {f = {0x0, 0x0, 0x0, 0x0}}    {f = {0, 0, 0, 0}}
mxcsr     0x1f80   8064
(gdb)
```

Note the number of registers and their different names. On different architectures the available registers and their naming will be different. Notice also that many of the values contained in the registers are much larger than the maximum 32-bit value of 0xffffffff.

To see the complete listing of registers including all floating point and extended registers, use the info all-registers GDB command.

Last, you can display the value of individual registers by referring to them by name with a $ prepended:

```
(gdb) print $eax
$1 = 0
```

Most of the time, you'll just need to know the value of a particular register as it is used by the assembly language. For more information on the register conventions for each hardware platform, refer to the corresponding vendor documentation. Each hardware platform will have different registers and assembly language.

> **Note**: Okay, so far in this chapter we've covered a lot of basics such as attaching to a process, looking at data, displaying register values, and so on. As we get further into this chapter, the focus will shift more and more from usage to examples. The next section is where the transition starts.

6.6 EXECUTION

The GDB execution commands give you full control over a process. Of course, these commands do not work when using a core file because there is no live process to control. This section of the chapter will introduce some of the most commonly used commands for controlling a live program. It will also present some of the more advanced and lesser known tips and tricks that can make your debugging session more efficient.

6.6.1 The Basic Commands

The following table summarizes the most common and most useful execution control commands:

Action	Command	Notes
Execute the next source code line and do not go into functions	`next <N>`	Requires debug symbols and source code. The optional argument sets the number of lines of source code to step through. Functions will be skipped over (but called under the covers).
Execute the next source code line and do go into functions	`step <N>`	Requires debug symbols and source code. The optional argument sets the number of lines of source code to step through.
Execute the next assembly instruction and do not go into functions	`nexti <N>`	The optional argument sets the number of instructions to step through. Functions will be skipped over (but called under the covers).
Execute the next assembly instruction and do go into functions	`stepi <N>`	The optional argument sets the number of instructions to step through.
Continue full execution	`continue`	
Continue execution until the current stack frame returns	`finish`	
Continue execution at a specific address	`jump <address>`	Use with caution. Jumping directly to an address can cause unexpected behavior given that the registers may not have been set properly to run the target instruction.
Continue execution until a source line or location greater than the current location or the location specified	`until`	
Call a function in the program	`call <function>`	
Manually stop execution of the program	`CTRL-C`	

Table 6.2 Basic GDB Execution Commands.

> **Note**: `<N>` represents a number. The number instructs GDB to run the
> command a certain number of times. For example, `next 5` will perform the
> `next` command 5 times.

The commands in Table 6.2 are pretty self-explanatory, but there are some
settings you can use in GDB that affect the way some of these commands work.
The next sections describe some of these in more detail.

6.6.1.1 Notes on stepi The `stepi` command allows you to execute a single
assembly instruction. You can also execute any number of instructions by
specifying that number as an argument to `stepi`. Stepping through each and
every assembly instruction can often reveal very low-level actions that normally
take place unnoticed in a program. Again using the dyn program as an example
(what dyn itself actually does is not important for this demonstration), let's
use the `stepi` command to step into the call to `printf`:

```
(gdb) break main
Breakpoint 1 at 0x804841c: file dyn_main.c, line 6.
(gdb) run
Starting program: /home/dbehman/book/code/dyn

Breakpoint 1, main () at dyn_main.c:6
6          void *dlhandle = NULL;
(gdb) next
9          printf( "Dynamically opening libdyn.so ...\n" );
(gdb) stepi
0x08048426     9          printf( "Dynamically opening libdyn.so ...\n"
);
(gdb) stepi
0x0804842b     9          printf( "Dynamically opening libdyn.so ...\n"
);
(gdb) stepi
0x08048330 in ?? ()
(gdb) stepi
0x08048336 in ?? ()
(gdb) stepi
0x0804833b in ?? ()
(gdb) stepi
0x08048300 in ?? ()
(gdb) stepi
0x08048306 in ?? ()
(gdb) stepi
0x4000d280 in _dl_runtime_resolve () from /lib/ld-linux.so.2
(gdb) stepi
0x4000d281 in _dl_runtime_resolve () from /lib/ld-linux.so.2
(gdb) stepi
0x4000d282 in _dl_runtime_resolve () from /lib/ld-linux.so.2
(gdb) stepi
```

```
0x4000d283 in _dl_runtime_resolve () from /lib/ld-linux.so.2
(gdb) stepi
0x4000d287 in _dl_runtime_resolve () from /lib/ld-linux.so.2
(gdb) stepi
0x4000d28b in _dl_runtime_resolve () from /lib/ld-linux.so.2
(gdb) stepi
0x4000cf90 in fixup () from /lib/ld-linux.so.2
(gdb) stepi
0x4000cf91 in fixup () from /lib/ld-linux.so.2
(gdb) stepi
0x4000cf93 in fixup () from /lib/ld-linux.so.2
(gdb) stepi
0x4000cf94 in fixup () from /lib/ld-linux.so.2
(gdb)
```

As you can see, several other things happen before we even enter the printf function. The functions we see here, _dl_runtime_resolve and fixup, are found in /lib/ld-2.3.2.so, which is the dynamic linker library. The "??" marked functions are GDB's way of saying that it couldn't find the function name for the corresponding stack frame. This often happens with special cases, such as when the dynamic linker is involved.

6.6.2 Settings for Execution Control Commands

6.6.2.1 Step-mode The step-mode allows you to control how the `step` command works with functions that do not have any debug symbols. Let's use an example program called dyn. It is compiled with debug symbols; however, it calls the standard C library function `printf()`, which by default has no debug symbols. Using `step` in the default manner, the following will occur:

```
(gdb) break main
Breakpoint 1 at 0x804841c: file dyn_main.c, line 6.
(gdb) run
Starting program: /home/dbehman/book/code/dyn

Breakpoint 1, main () at dyn_main.c:6
6           void *dlhandle = NULL;
(gdb) next
9           printf( "Dynamically opening libdyn.so ...\n" );
(gdb) step
Dynamically opening libdyn.so ...
11          dlhandle = dlopen( "./libdyn.so", RTLD_NOW );
(gdb)
```

As you can see, the `step` command did not go into the `printf` function because it does not have debug symbols. To override this behavior, we can use the "step-mode" setting in GDB:

```
(gdb) break main
Breakpoint 1 at 0x804841c: file dyn_main.c, line 6.
(gdb) run
Starting program: /home/dbehman/book/code/dyn

Breakpoint 1, main () at dyn_main.c:6
6               void *dlhandle = NULL;
(gdb) show step-mode
Mode of the step operation is off.
(gdb) set step-mode on
(gdb) show step-mode
Mode of the step operation is on.
(gdb) next
9               printf( "Dynamically opening libdyn.so ...\n" );
(gdb) step
0x4007eab0 in printf () from /lib/i686/libc.so.6
(gdb)
```

As shown in this example, the `step` command did enter the `printf` function even though `printf` was not built with `-g` (that is, it has no debug information). This special step-mode can be useful if you want to step through the assembly language of a call function regardless of whether it was built in debug (that is, built with `-g`) or not.

6.6.2.2 Following fork Calls If the controlled program uses `fork` or `vfork` system calls, you can tell GDB that you want to handle the `fork` calls in a few different ways. By default, GDB will follow the parent process (the one you are controlling now) and will let the child process (the newly created process) run free. The term `follow` here means that GDB will continue to control a process, and the term `run free` means that GDB will detach from the process, letting it run unimpeded and unaffected by GDB. If you want GDB to follow the child process, use the command `set follow-fork-mode child` before the fork occurs. An alternative is to have GDB ask you what you want to do when a fork is encountered. This can be done with the command `set follow-fork-mode ask`. You can view the current setting with the command `show follow-fork-mode`.

Let's assume that you are controlling a process that forks two children, and you want to eventually be in control of a "grandchild" process as shown in Figure 6.2.

You cannot get control of process 4 (as in the diagram) using the default GDB mode for following forks. In the default mode, GDB would simply keep control of process 1, and the other processes would run freely. You can't use `set follow-fork-mode child` because GDB would follow the first forked process (process 2), and the parent process (process 1) would run freely. When process 1 forked off its second child process, it would no longer be under the control of GDB. The only way to follow the forks properly to get process 4 under the control of GDB is to use `set follow-fork-mode ask`. In this mode, you would tell GDB to follow the parent after the first fork call and to follow the child process for the next two forks.

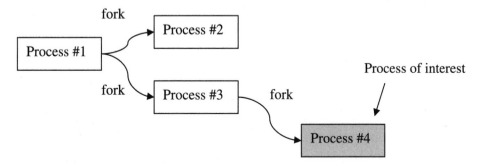

Fig. 6.2 Children and granchildren of a process.

6.6.2.3 Handling Signals Linux applications often receive various types of signals. Signals are a software convention similar to a very trivial message (the message being the signal number itself). Each signal has a different purpose, and GDB can be set to handle each in a different way. Consider the following simple program that sends itself a SIGALRM:

```
penguin> cat alarm.C
#include <stdio.h>
#include <unistd.h>
#include <sys/utsname.h>

int main()
{
  alarm(3) ;

  sleep(5) ;

  return 0 ;
}
```

This simple program calls the alarm system call with an argument of 3 (for three seconds). This will cause a SIGALRM to be sent to the program in three seconds. The second call is to sleep with an argument of 5 and causes the program to sleep for five seconds, two seconds longer than it will take to receive the SIGALRM. Running this program in GDB has the following effect:

```
(gdb) run
Starting program: /home/wilding/src/Linuxbook/alarm
```

```
Program terminated with signal SIGALRM, Alarm clock.
The program no longer exists.
```

The program was killed off because it did not have a handler installed for
SIGALRM. Signal handling is beyond the scope of this chapter, but we can
change how signals such as SIGALRM are handled through GDB. First, let's
take a look at how SIGALRM is handled in GDB by default:

```
(gdb) info signals SIGALRM
Signal    Stop    Print  Pass to program Description
SIGALRM    No     No     Yes             Alarm clock
```

The first column is the signal (in this case SIGALRM). The second column
indicates whether GDB will stop the program and hand control over to the
user of GDB when the signal is encountered. The third column indicates whether
GDB will print a message to the screen when a signal is encountered. The
fourth column indicates whether GDB will pass the signal to the controlled
program (in the preceding example, the program is the alarm program that
was run under the control of GDB). The last column is the description of the
signal.

    According to the output, GDB will not stop when the controlled program
encounters a SIGALRM, it will not print a message, and it will pass the signal
to the program. We can tell GDB to not pass the signal to the process by using
handle SIGALRM nopass:

```
(gdb) handle SIGALRM nopass
Signal    Stop    Print  Pass to program Description
SIGALRM    No     No     No              Alarm clock
(gdb) run
Starting program: /home/wilding/src/Linuxbook/alarm

Program exited normally.
(gdb)
```

In the preceding example, the program slept for the full five seconds and did
not receive the SIGALRM. Next, let's tell GDB to stop when the controlled
process receives SIGALRM:

```
(gdb) handle SIGALRM stop
Signal    Stop    Print  Pass to program Description
SIGALRM    Yes    Yes    Yes             Alarm clock
(gdb) run
Starting program: /home/wilding/src/Linuxbook/alarm

Program received signal SIGALRM, Alarm clock.
0x4019fd01 in nanosleep () from /lib/libc.so.6
```

```
(gdb) bt
#0 0x4019fd01 in nanosleep () from /lib/libc.so.6
#1 0x4019fbd9 in sleep () from /lib/libc.so.6
#2 0x080483e3 in main ()
#3 0x4011a4a2 in __libc_start_main () from /lib/libc.so.6
```

In this case, GDB stopped when the controlled program received a signal and handed control back to the GDB user (that is, gave us a prompt). The command bt was run in the example here to display the stack trace and to show that the signal was received while in sleep (specifically in nanosleep) as expected.

If the process receives a lot of signals and you just want to keep track of when it receives a signal (and not take any actions), we can tell GDB to print a message every time the controlled process receives a signal:

```
(gdb) run
The program being debugged has been started already.
Start it from the beginning? (y or n) y
Starting program: /home/wilding/src/Linuxbook/alarm

Program received signal SIGALRM, Alarm clock.
```

The program will continue to handle the signal as it was designed to, and GDB will simply report a message each time a SIGALRM is received. Sometimes this mode can be useful to see how often a process times out or when setting a breakpoint in a function that occurs after a signal is received by the process.

To see the full list of signals and how GDB is configured to handle them, use the info signals command:

```
(gdb) info signals
Signal     Stop    Print   Pass to program Description

SIGHUP             Yes     Yes     Yes         Hangup
SIGINT             Yes     Yes     No          Interrupt
SIGQUIT            Yes     Yes     Yes         Quit
SIGILL             Yes     Yes     Yes         Illegal instruction
SIGTRAP            Yes     Yes     No          Trace/breakpoint trap
SIGABRT            Yes     Yes     Yes         Aborted
SIGEMT             Yes     Yes     Yes         Emulation trap
SIGFPE             Yes     Yes     Yes         Arithmetic exception
SIGKILL            Yes     Yes     Yes         Killed
SIGBUS             Yes     Yes     Yes         Bus error
SIGSEGV            Yes     Yes     Yes         Segmentation fault
SIGSYS             Yes     Yes     Yes         Bad system call
SIGPIPE            Yes     Yes     Yes         Broken pipe
SIGALRM            No      No      Yes         Alarm clock
  . . .
```

> **Note**: "..." in this output is not part of the output but is used to show that the output is longer than what is printed here.

You can tell GDB to handle each signal differently to match the desired functionality for the problem you are investigating.

6.6.3 Breakpoints

Breakpoints are a method to stop the execution of a program in a function at a particular point in the code or on a particular condition. We've been using breakpoints throughout this chapter, which goes to show how common they are. To see the current list of breakpoints set, use the "info breakpoints" command.

```
(gdb) break main
Breakpoint 1 at 0x80483c2
(gdb) info break
Num Type        Disp Enb Address  What
1  breakpoint   keep y  0x080483c2 <main+6>
```

The breakpoint in the preceding example is set to stop the controlled program in the function main. This is the most common usage of breakpoints—that is, to stop in a particular function. The incantation for this is:

```
break <function name>
```

It can also be useful to set a breakpoint in a function only when one of the function parameters is a specific value. Say you had a function in your application that got called hundreds of times, but you're only interested in examining this function when one of the parameters is a specific value. Say the function is called common_func and takes one integer parameter called num. To set up a conditional breakpoint on this function when num equals 345 for example, you would first set the breakpoint:

```
(gdb) break common_func
Breakpoint 2 at 0x8048312: file common.c, line 3.
```

Now that the breakpoint is set, use the condition command to define a condition for this newly set breakpoint. We reference the breakpoint by number, in this case, 2.

```
(gdb) condition 2 num == 345
```

Notice the double equal signs—this is the same notation you would use for an expression in C programming.

Verify the correct setting of the breakpoint with the `info breakpoint` command:

```
(gdb) info breakpoint
Num Type           Disp Enb Address    What
1   breakpoint     keep y   0x0804832a in main at common.c:10
2   breakpoint     keep y   0x08048312 in common_func at common.c:3
        stop only if num == 345
```

When continuing program execution, breakpoint number 2 will only be triggered when the value of num is 345:

```
(gdb) cont
Continuing.

Breakpoint 2, common_func (num=345) at common.c:3
3            int foo = num;
```

If the program was compiled with -g, you can set a breakpoint on a particular line of code as in the next example:

```
(gdb) break hang2.C:20
Breakpoint 1 at 0x8048467: file hang2.C, line 20.
(gdb) run user
Starting program: /home/wilding/src/Linuxbook/hang2 user

Breakpoint 1, main (argc=2, argv=0xbfffefc4) at hang2.C:20
20     if ( !strcmp( argv[1], "user" ) )
(gdb)
```

If you don't have the source code, you can also still set a breakpoint at a specific address as follows:

```
(gdb) break * 0x804843c
Breakpoint 2 at 0x804843c
(gdb) cont
Continuing.

Breakpoint 2, 0x0804843c in main ()
(gdb)
```

Notice the * in front of the address; this is used when the argument to the break command is an address.

To delete a breakpoint, use the `delete` command with the breakpoint number as the argument.

6.6.4 Watchpoints

Watchpoints, as the name implies, are for watching data in your program, especially for alerting you when data at a specific address changes value. If you have a variable in your program that is getting changed for some bizarre and unknown reason, this could be a symptom of memory corruption. Memory corruption problems can be extremely difficult to track down given that it can happen long before the symptom (for example, trap or unexpected behavior). With a watchpoint, you can tell GDB to watch the specified variable and let you know immediately when it changes. For memory corruption, GDB will tell you exactly where and when the corruption occurs so you can easily fix the problem.

There are two kinds of watchpoints—hardware and software. The x86 hardware, for example, provides built-in support specifically for watchpoints, and GDB will make use of this support. If the support does not exist or if the conditions for the use of the hardware are not met, GDB will revert to using software watchpoints. A software watchpoint is much slower than a hardware watchpoint. The reason for this is because GDB must stop the program execution after each assembly instruction and examine every watchpoint for changes. Conversely, hardware watchpoints allow GDB to run normally but will instantly notify GDB of a change when/if it occurs.

To demonstrate watchpoints, let's use a simple program that simulates an employee record system. The source code is:

```
#include <stdio.h>

struct employee
{
   char name[8];
   int  serial_num;
};

void print_employee_rec( struct employee rec )
{
   printf( "Name: %s\n", rec.name );
   printf( "Number: %d\n", rec.serial_num );

   return;
}

void update_employee_name( struct employee *rec, char *name )
{
   strcpy( rec->name, name );

   return;
}
```

```
void add_employee( struct employee *rec, char *name, int num )
{
    strcpy( rec->name, name );
    rec->serial_num = num;

    return;
}

int main( void )
{
    struct employee rec;

    add_employee( &rec, "Fred", 25 );

    print_employee_rec( rec );

    printf( "\nUpdating employee's name ...\n\n" );

    update_employee_name( &rec, "Fred Smith" );

    print_employee_rec( rec );

    return 0;
}
```

The basic flow of the program is to create an employee record with the name "Fred" and serial number 25. Next, the program updates the employee's name to "Fred Smith" but does not touch the serial number. Running the program produces this output:

```
penguin> employee
Name: Fred
Number: 25

Updating employee's name ...

Name: Fred Smith
Number: 26740
```

If the program isn't supposed to update the serial number when the name is changed, then why did it change to 26740? This kind of error is indicative of memory corruption. If you've examined the source code, you might already know what the problem is, but let's use GDB and watchpoints to tell us what the problem is. We know that something bad happens after printing out the employee record the first time, so let's set a watchpoint on the `serial_num` member of the structure at that point:

```
(gdb) break main
Breakpoint 1 at 0x80483e6: file employee.c, line 36.
(gdb) run
Starting program: /home/dbehman/book/code/employee

Breakpoint 1, main () at employee.c:36
36          add_employee( &rec, "Fred", 25 );
(gdb) next
38          print_employee_rec( rec );
(gdb) next
Name: Fred
Number: 25
40          printf( "\nUpdating employee's name ...\n\n" );
(gdb) watch rec.serial_num
Hardware watchpoint 2: rec.serial_num
```

It is important to note that GDB was able to successfully engage the assistance of the hardware for this watchpoint. GDB indicates this with the message, "Hardware watchpoint 2...". If the keyword "Hardware" does not appear, then GDB was unable to use the hardware and defaulted to using a software watchpoint (which is much, much slower). Let's now continue our program execution and see what happens:

```
(gdb) cont
Continuing.

Updating employee's name ...

Hardware watchpoint 2: rec.serial_num

Old value = 25
New value = 116
0x400a3af9 in strcpy () from /lib/i686/libc.so.6
(gdb) backtrace
#0  0x400a3af9 in strcpy () from /lib/i686/libc.so.6
#1  0x080483af in update_employee_name (rec=0xbffff390, name=0x80485c0
"Fred Smith")
    at employee.c:19
#2  0x08048431 in main () at employee.c:42
```

Bingo! We can see that this program has the infamous buffer overrun bug. The strcpy function does not do any bounds checking or limiting and happily writes past our allotted buffer of eight bytes, which corrupts the next piece of memory occupied by the `serial_num` structure member.

If you have a reproducible problem and you can find the address that gets corrupted, a watchpoint can reduce the investigating time from days (of setting breakpoints or using print statements) to minutes.

Well, this is great, but what if you don't have the source code, and/or the program was not built with `-g`? You can still set hardware watchpoints, but you need to set them directly on an address as in the following example.

The program is simple and changes the value of a global symbol. We're using a global symbol because we can easily find the address of that regardless of whether or not the program is built with `-g`.

```
int a = 5 ;

int main()
{

  a = 6 ;

  return 0 ;
}
```

Now, inside of GDB we can find the address of the variable `a` and set a watchpoint on that address:

```
(gdb) print &a
$1 = (<data variable, no debug info> *) 0x80493e0
 (gdb) watch (int) *0x80493e0
Hardware watchpoint 1: (int) *134517728
```

The notation here told GDB to watch the contents of the address `0x80493e0` for any changes and to treat the address as an integer. Be sure to dereference the address with a "*," or GDB will not set the watchpoint correctly. We can now run the program and see the hardware watchpoint in action:

```
 (gdb) run
Starting program: /home/wilding/src/Linuxbook/watch
Hardware watchpoint 1: (int) *134517728
Hardware watchpoint 1: (int) *134517728
Hardware watchpoint 1: (int) *134517728
Hardware watchpoint 1: (int) *134517728
Hardware watchpoint 1: (int) *134517728
Hardware watchpoint 1: (int) *134517728

Old value = 5
New value = 6
0x08048376 in main ()
(gdb)
```

The watchpoint was triggered several times, but in each case the value of the address was not changed, so GDB did not stop the process. Only in the last occurrence did GDB stop the process because the value changed from 5 to 6.

There are three different types of watchpoints:

☞ watch   - Cause a break in execution for any write to an address
☞ rwatch   - Cause a break in execution for any read to an address
☞ awatch   - Cause a break in execution for a read or write to an address

Besides the different memory access attributes, the three types of watchpoints can be used in the same way. There are some situations where a read watchpoint can be useful. One example is called a "late read." A late read is a situation where a code path reads memory after it has been freed. If you know which block of memory is referenced after it has been freed, a read watchpoint can catch the culprit code path that references the memory.

> **Note**: To delete a watchpoint, use the `delete` command with the watchpoint number as the argument.

6.6.5 Display Expression on Stop

Throughout a debugging session, you will find that you will be checking the value of certain variables again and again. GDB provides a handy feature called displays. Displays allow you to tell GDB to display whatever expression you've set as a display after each execution stop. To set a display, use the `display` command. Here is an example:

```
(gdb) display a
(gdb) break main
Breakpoint 1 at 0x8048362
(gdb) run
Starting program: /home/wilding/src/Linuxbook/watch

Breakpoint 1, 0x08048362 in main ()
1: {<data variable, no debug info>} 134517792 = 5
```

The last line is the display line, and the display item has a number of 1. To delete this display, we use the `delete display` command:

```
(gdb) display
1: {<data variable, no debug info>} 134517792 = 5
(gdb) delete display 1
```

To enable or disable a preset display, use the `enable display` and `disable display` commands.

> **Note**: GDB's GUI brother, DDD (Data Display Debugger), is perfectly suited for using the concepts of displays. Please refer to the section on DDD for more information on displays.

6.6.6 Working with Shared Libraries

GDB has a command that will show the shared libraries that a program links in and to see where those libraries have been mapped into the process' address space. If you get an instruction address, you can use this information to find out which library the instruction is in (and eventually the line of code if you wish). It is also useful to confirm that the program is loading the correct libraries.

Use the `info sharedlibrary` command to see this information:

```
(gdb) info sharedlibrary
From       To        Syms Read  Shared Object Library
0x40040b40 0x4013b7b4 Yes       /lib/i686/libc.so.6
0x40000c00 0x400139ef Yes       /lib/ld-linux.so.2
(gdb)
```

Shared libraries are like common program extensions. They contain executable code and variables just like an executable, though the libraries can be shared by multiple executables at the same time.

6.6.6.1 Debugging Functions in Shared Libraries GDB normally does a great job of handling shared libraries that an executable links in. For example, GDB will happily set a breakpoint in a function that exists in a shared library, just as in an executable. There are times, however, when shared libraries get dynamically loaded in an application, which makes it almost impossible for GDB to know what functions could be run before the library is loaded. To illustrate this problem, consider the following two source files:

dyn.c:

```
#include <stdio.h>

void func2( void )
{
printf( "This function is not referenced in dyn_main.c\n" );
return;
}

void func1( void )
{
printf( "This function is in libdyn.so\n" );
```

```
  func2();

  return;
}
```

dyn_main.c:

```c
#include <stdio.h>
#include <dlfcn.h>

int main( void )
{
  void *dlhandle = NULL;
  void (*func1_ref)( void );

  printf( "Dynamically opening libdyn.so ...\n" );

  dlhandle = dlopen( "./libdyn.so", RTLD_NOW );

  func1_ref = dlsym( dlhandle, "func1" );

  func1_ref();

exit:

  return 0;
}
```

Now compile these modules with the following commands:

```
penguin> gcc -shared -o libdyn.so dyn.c -g
penguin> gcc -o dyn dyn_main.c -g -ldl
```

Now, in a debugging session let's say we only wanted to set a breakpoint in func2(). Attempting this after starting GDB with GDB dyn produces this error:

```
(gdb) break func2
Function "func2" not defined.
```

Using the command that follows, we list the shared libraries that are associated with this executable:

```
(gdb) info sharedlibrary
No shared libraries loaded at this time.
(gdb) break main
Note: breakpoint 1 also set at pc 0x804841c.
Breakpoint 2 at 0x804841c: file dyn_main.c, line 6.
```

```
(gdb) run
Starting program: /home/dbehman/book/code/dyn

Breakpoint 1, main () at dyn_main.c:6
6              void *dlhandle = NULL;
(gdb) info sharedlibrary
From        To          Syms Read    Shared Object Library
0x4002beb0  0x4002cde4  Yes          /lib/libdl.so.2
0x40043b40  0x4013e7b4  Yes          /lib/i686/libc.so.6
0x40000c00  0x400139ef  Yes          /lib/ld-linux.so.2
(gdb) break func2
Function "func2" not defined.
(gdb)
```

In the first part of the output, we see that no shared libraries are loaded. This is because the program has not actually started. To get the program running, we set a breakpoint in the main function and run the program using the GDB command, run. When the program is running, we can then see the information about the shared libraries, and as you can see, libdyn.so is not listed. This is why the break func2 attempt failed once again.

From the preceding source code, we know that libdyn.so will be dynamically loaded as the program runs (using dlopen). This is important because to set a breakpoint in a library that has not been loaded, we need to tell GDB to stop execution when the controlled program loads a new shared library. We can tell GDB to do this with the command set stop-on-solib-events 1. The current state of this flag can be shown with the show stop-on-solib-events command:

```
(gdb) show stop-on-solib-events
Stopping for shared library events is 0.
(gdb) set stop-on-solib-events 1
(gdb) show stop-on-solib-events
Stopping for shared library events is 1.
(gdb)
```

Now let's tell GDB to let the program continue:

```
(gdb) cont
Continuing.
Dynamically opening libdyn.so ...
Stopped due to shared library event
(gdb) backtrace
#0  0x4000dd60 in _dl_debug_state_internal () from /lib/ld-linux.so.2
#1  0x4000d7fa in _dl_init_internal () from /lib/ld-linux.so.2
#2  0x4013a558 in dl_open_worker () from /lib/i686/libc.so.6
#3  0x4000d5b6 in _dl_catch_error_internal () from /lib/ld-linux.so.2
#4  0x4013a8ff in _dl_open () from /lib/i686/libc.so.6
#5  0x4002bfdb in dlopen_doit () from /lib/libdl.so.2
```

```
#6   0x4000d5b6 in _dl_catch_error_internal () from /lib/ld-linux.so.2
#7   0x4002c48a in _dlerror_run () from /lib/libdl.so.2
#8   0x4002c022 in dlopen@@GLIBC_2.1 () from /lib/libdl.so.2
#9   0x08048442 in main () at dyn_main.c:11
(gdb) break func2
Breakpoint 3 at 0x4001b73e: file dyn.c, line 5.
(gdb)
```

As you can see by the stack trace output, GDB stopped deep inside the `dlopen()` system call. By that point in time, the symbol table was loaded, and we were able to set a breakpoint in the desired function. We can now choose to continue by issuing the `cont` command, but we will encounter more stops due to shared library events. Because we've accomplished our goal of being able to set a breakpoint in `func2()`, let's turn off the `stop-on-solib-event` flag and then continue:

```
(gdb) set stop-on-solib-events 0
(gdb) cont
Continuing.
This function is in libdyn.so

Breakpoint 3, func2 () at dyn.c:5
5            printf( "This function is not referenced in dyn_main.c\n" );
(gdb)
```

Mission accomplished!

6.7 SOURCE CODE

When a program is compiled with the `-g` compile switch, GDB will automatically recognize that there are debug symbols and will display all the debug information it can. This includes the source code for the program you are debugging. You can use the `list` command to display relevant lines of source code. You can change which lines of source code and how many of them are printed with various arguments passed to the `list` command.

One trick to be aware of is when the source code for the program being debugged is not in a directory that GDB expects it to be. This can happen for any number of reasons, so it is important to understand how to tell GDB where to find the source code. For example, using the gdb_stack.c program we used in the Stack section, assume the source file was moved into a directory called "new_source." Running GDB will produce the following:

```
(gdb) break main
Breakpoint 1 at 0x80484ab: file gdb_stack.c, line 36.
(gdb) run
```

```
Starting program: /home/dbehman/book/code/gdb_stack

Breakpoint 1, main () at gdb_stack.c:36
36          gdb_stack.c: No such file or directory.
            in gdb_stack.c
(gdb) list
31          in gdb_stack.c
(gdb)
```

> **Note**: GDB still knows the exact line numbers, even though
> the source code cannot be found. That's because when compiling
> with -g, line numbers and source file names get inserted into the
> assembly and ultimately linked into the resulting object/execut-
> able code.

To alleviate this problem, use the `show directories` and `directory` commands:

```
(gdb) show directories
Source directories searched: $cdir:$cwd
(gdb) directory ./new_source
Source  directories  searched:  /home/dbehman/book/code/./
new_source:$cdir:$cwd
(gdb) show directories
Source directories searched: /home/dbehman/code/./new_source:$cdir:$cwd
(gdb) list
31          function2( 3 );
32      }
33
34      int main( void )
35      {
36          int stackVar = 3;
37
38          function1( stackVar );
39
40          return 0;
(gdb)
```

You still need to know how to read source code, but it is much easier than
reading direct assembly language.

Note that there are two handy commands to search through source code:

☞ `forw <regular expression>`

☞ `rev <regular expression>`

The `forw` command will search forward from the current point in the source
code looking for a pattern that matches the regular expression. Similarly, the

`rev` command will search from the current point backward looking for a pattern that matches the regular expression.

6.8 ASSEMBLY LANGUAGE

Unfortunately, some situations may require you to examine the execution of the assembly instructions. To view assembly instructions in GDB, use the `disassemble` command with or without arguments. Arguments can be specified to indicate which range of addresses to disassemble (that is, which addresses to translate from machine instructions to human readable assembly language). The following shows an arbitrarily selected disassemble output:

```
(gdb) disass 0x804848b 0x80484bb
Dump of assembler code from 0x804848b to 0x80484bb:
0x804848b <main+95>:   sub  $0x8,%esp
0x804848e <main+98>:   push $0x804852c
0x8048493 <main+103>:  pushl (%eax)
0x8048495 <main+105>:  call 0x8048328 <strcmp>
0x804849a <main+110>:  add  $0x10,%esp
0x804849d <main+113>:  test %eax,%eax
0x804849f <main+115>:  jne  0x80484b1 <main+133>
0x80484a1 <main+117>:  sub  $0xc,%esp
0x80484a4 <main+120>:  push $0x1388
0x80484a9 <main+125>:  call 0x8048338 <sleep>
0x80484ae <main+130>:  add  $0x10,%esp
0x80484b1 <main+133>:  movl $0x0,0xfffffff8(%ebp)
0x80484b8 <main+140>:  mov  0xfffffff8(%ebp),%eax
End of assembler dump.
```

The first column shows the address of the instruction. The second address shows the function that contains the instructions and the offset from the beginning of the function for the instruction. The rest of the line is the actually disassembled machine instruction in assembly language format.

There may be times when you need to compare the assembly you see within GDB to the assembly generated by the compiler. For example, in the rare event of a compiler bug, the compiler may generate incorrect machine instructions. You may also want to view the assembly language to understand how a program works, even if you don't have the source code. In either case, you need to understand assembly language on the particular hardware platform you're using.

Refer to Chapter 4 for information on how to generate an assembly listing using the GCC compiler.

6.9 TIPS AND TRICKS

This next section covers some useful tips and tricks for more advanced debugging. The tips include more advanced ways to attach to a process at a particular point in time, methods to find the address of variables and functions, and a useful technique for viewing data structures fully formatted for an executable and/or library that was not built in debug mode (that is, with `-g`).

6.9.1 Attaching to a Process—Revisited

6.9.1.1 The pause() method Sometimes you run into a situation where you need to get a process into GDB under very specific conditions. For example, you might be investigating a problem that disappears when you compile the program with `-g`. In this case, you won't be able to set a breakpoint at a file name and line of code. Because there is no debug information, you might need/want to add some special code into the program to set a manual type of breakpoint.

There are three good ways to stop a program at a specific point and attach a debugger:

1. Use the `pause` function.
2. Use a `for` or `while` loop.
3. Use the `system()` function to spawn an xterm.

The `pause()` function will cause the process to wait until it receives a signal (see the pause(2) man page for more information). Unfortunately, GDB occasionally has difficulty in properly handling situations like this, so a simple trick may be needed to ensure it works properly. Consider the following code:

```
#include <stdio.h>
#include <unistd.h>

int main( void )
{
    int foo = 1;

    printf( "my pid = %d\n", getpid() );

    pause();

    printf( "got signal, resuming!\n" );

    return( 0 );
}
```

Compiling and running this program causes it to display its `pid` then wait for a signal. If we attach GDB to this process and look at the stack, we will see the following:

```
(gdb) where
#0  0x400d6f0b in pause () from /lib/i686/libc.so.6
#1  0x080483d4 in main () at mypause.c:11
(gdb)
```

With debuggers on other platforms such as dbx, you could simply type "next" to go to the next instruction, and the debugger would automatically jump to the next instruction for which debug symbols existed, which in this case is in the function `main()`. We can tell that `main()` has been compiled with debug symbols because the file and line number are displayed. If we give the `next` command to GDB, we will see the following:

```
(gdb) next
Single stepping until exit from function pause,
which has no line number information.
```

At this point, the GDB session will appear to be hung. In actuality, it is sitting in the `pause()` system call waiting for a symbol. If we use another shell to send the original process a SIGCONT, `pause()` will terminate, and the process will continue. Unless a breakpoint has been set at some point after the `pause()` call, the program will continue execution, possibly to completion.

That requires an additional shell and `kill -CONT <pid>` command, which is a little tedious. An easier way is to have GDB itself send the SIGCONT. Note that a breakpoint is also set at line 13 to stop execution after `pause()` terminates:

```
(gdb) where
#0  0x400d6f0b in pause () from /lib/i686/libc.so.6
#1  0x080483d4 in main () at mypause.c:11
(gdb) break 13
Breakpoint 1 at 0x80483d4: file mypause.c, line 13.
(gdb) signal SIGCONT
Continuing with signal SIGCONT.

Breakpoint 1, main () at mypause.c:13
13          printf( "got signal, resuming!\n" );
(gdb)
```

The debugging session can now continue exactly at the location desired.

6.9.1.2 The "for" or "while" Loop Method

The "for" or "while" loop method is similar but does not require sending a signal.

```
#include <stdio.h>
#include <unistd.h>

int main( void )
{
  int foo = 1;

  printf( "my pid = %d\n", getpid() );

  while ( foo == 1 ) ;

  return( 0 );
}

penguin> g++ pause.C -o pause -g
penguin> gdb pause
```

In this case, the program will loop indefinitely unless the variable foo is changed to a different value than 1. You can use the "top" program to find this process, given it will consume a lot of CPU time and will be near the top of the display (see Appendix A for more information on top). Attaching to the process in another window, we will see that the process is stopped on this loop.

```
penguin> gdb - 15205
... (unimportant output deleted) ...
10      while ( foo == 1 ) ;
(gdb) set foo=2
(gdb) step
12      printf( "got signal, resuming!\n" );
(gdb)
```

As soon as we set the value of foo to 2, the program can pop out of the loop and continue. We used step to move forward by one line to show that the program is indeed free of this loop.

6.9.1.3 The xterm method This method and the pause method work well if the program uses the terminal (the command line display), but what if the program is a daemon (that is, it runs in the background and has no terminal) or has graphical user interface? In this case, you can still get the process ID of the stopped process by spawning an xterm as in the following example:

```
#include <stdio.h>
#include <unistd.h>
#include <stdlib.h>

int main( void )
{
  char buf[1024] ;
```

```
    sprintf( buf, "/usr/bin/xterm -e \"/bin/echo $$ ; error\"\n", getpid()
➡ );

    system( buf ) ;

    return( 0 );
}
```

The command being run will actually cause an error on purpose to ensure that
the xterm doesn't exit after printing the process ID. The error message in the
newly created xterm will be xterm: Can't execvp /bin/echo 15634 ; error: No
such file or directory, where 15634 is the process ID (and will be different if
you try this method). You can also use the -title switch to xterm to change the
title of the xterm to match the process ID of the program that spawned the
process.

   Once you attach to the process ID with GDB, simply exit the xterm to
regain control of the process. It will continue as normal from that point on.

6.9.2 Finding the Address of Variables and Functions

Processes can have dozens of libraries loaded at any given time with hundreds
or thousands of global and static variables each. With this many global variables
in the address space at the same time, there is a chance that two or more
variables will have the same name. Worse, there is a chance that the wrong
variable will be used (the ELF chapter includes more detail on this) or that
you will look at the wrong variable using GDB. Fortunately, GDB provides a
quick and easy method to find all variables that match a pattern (a regular
expression). The following example finds all variables that have the string
"environ" in their name:

```
(gdb) info variables environ
All variables matching regular expression ".*environ.*":

File sh.func.c:
Char **STR_environ;
char **environ;

File tw.init.c:
Char **STR_environ;

File tw.parse.c:
Char **STR_environ;

File sh.c:
Char **STR_environ;
char **environ;
```

```
Non-debugging symbols:
0x08096184  __environ@@GLIBC_2.0
0x08096184  environ@@GLIBC_2.0
0x401acb38  __environ
0x401acb38  _environ
0x401b1c34  last_environ
0x400129d8  __environ
0x400129d8  _environ
```

There are several variables that have this string ("environ") and a few that have exactly the same name ("_environ"). The address of each variable is listed on the left for the variables that do not have debug information.

There can also be thousands of functions in the address space, including more than one function with the same name. Using a similar method to that just shown for variables, you can get GDB to display all of the functions that match a certain pattern. Here is an example where we find all of the functions that have the string "main" in them:

```
(gdb) info functions main
All functions matching regular expression ".*main.*":

File sh.c:
int main(int, char **);

Non-debugging symbols:
0x08049ca0  __libc_start_main
0x400b0400  __libc_start_main
0x400b05c0  __libc_main
0x400bce30  __bindtextdomain
0x400bce30  bindtextdomain
0x400bce60  __bind_textdomain_codeset
0x400bce60  bind_textdomain_codeset
0x400bdf10  _nl_find_domain
0x400be1e0  _nl_init_domain_conv
0x400be490  _nl_free_domain_conv
0x400be4e0  _nl_load_domain
0x400be900  _nl_unload_domain
0x400bf090  __textdomain
0x400bf090  textdomain
0x400fa4a0  _IO_switch_to_main_wget_area
0x40102410  _IO_switch_to_main_get_area
0x40107820  main_trim
0x4015de60  getdomainname
0x4015ded0  setdomainname
0x40170560  arg_trimdomain_list
0x401710a0  _res_hconf_trim_domain
0x40171130  _res_hconf_trim_domains
0x4017b4c0  nrl_domainname
0x40001990  dl_main
```

```
0x401c5dc0 xdr_domainname
0x401c6fd0 yp_get_default_domain
0x401cf670 nis_domain_of
0x401cf6b0 nis_domain_of_r
```

If you want to find a function or variable with a specific name, you can use the following regular expression `^<function or variable name>$`. The carrot `^` means the beginning of the string, and the dollar sign `$` means the end of the string. Here is an example of where we find all functions that have the exact name of `main` (Note: There is only one function with this name.):

```
(gdb) info functions ^main$
All functions matching regular expression "^main$":

File sh.c:
int main(int, char **);
```

6.9.3 Viewing Structures in Executables without Debug Symbols

When debugging, particularly commercial applications, it's very likely that the binaries have not been compiled with debug symbols (using the `-g` compile switch). When this happens, a knowledge of assembly, the machine's calling conventions, and a rough idea of the data structures involved is required to fully understand what the program is doing when viewing it in a debugger. In the case of open source software, the code is readily available, so even if the executables were compiled without debug symbols, one can examine the source along with the assembly to see what is happening. In a commercial software situation where the software is having a problem on the customer's computer, sending the source code to the customer is simply not an option for a support analyst.

For cases like these and many others, analyzing structures in raw memory as hex is certainly possible but can be very painstaking and tedious. This section introduces a trick one can use on ELF-based systems to dump data as structures from within a debugger where no debugging symbols are readily available. To demonstrate this, a very small and simple example will be used. The source code for this example is made up of one header file and one source module. The header file's name is employee.h and contains the following code:

```
struct employee_rec
{
    int employee_no;
    int is_ceo;
    char first_name[20];
    char last_name[20];
    int manager_emp_no;
```

```
    int department_no;
};
```

The source module's name is employee.c and contains this code:

```
#include "employee.h"

int foo( struct employee_rec *pEmp )
{
   pEmp->manager_emp_no = 10;
   return 0;
}

int main( void )
{
   struct employee_rec *pEmployee;

   pEmployee = (struct employee_rec*)malloc( sizeof( struct employee_rec
) ) );

   /* Set the record up */
   pEmployee->employee_no = 4416;
   pEmployee->is_ceo = 0;
   strcpy( pEmployee->first_name, "Dan" );
   strcpy( pEmployee->last_name, "Behman" );
   pEmployee->manager_emp_no = 3278;
   pEmployee->department_no = 321;

   foo( pEmployee );

   return c;
}
```

Let's compile this source to create an executable called emp:

```
gcc -o emp employee.c
```

Now let's assume that our newly created emp executable is a massive complex commercial application. Let's also assume that there is a functional problem somewhere in this massive program, and we've determined that a key to determining the cause is something that is being done in the function, foo. Also assume that we don't have access to all of the source code, but we do know the structure of each employee record. If we run emp under GDB, we're limited to working with addresses in memory, translating sizes, and converting hex to more meaningful values because the program was not compiled with debug symbols (the -g compile switch) and the source code is not readily available.

Instead of struggling through assembly and raw memory, we can make use of the LD_PRELOAD environment variable, which Linux's dynamic loader recognizes. When this environment variable is set to a valid library, the loader will load it before any other libraries get loaded. This gives us the opportunity to make our GDB session aware of any structure types we wish. To begin, create structure.c with the following code:

```
#include "employee.h"

struct employee_rec *floating_rec;
```

Compile this source file with the following command (`-shared` is used to create a shared library, and employee.c contains the simple source code from the preceding script):

```
gcc -shared -o libstructure.so -g employee.c
```

This will create a shared library called libstructure.so containing debug symbols. Next, we set the LD_PRELOAD environment variable to point to this file:

```
export LD_PRELOAD=/home/dbehman/structure.so
```

Now when we re-run `emp` under a debugger, our employee_rec structure will be known, and we can point our floating_rec pointer to any point in memory where this structure begins and print it out. To demonstrate, first launch `emp` under GDB and set a breakpoint in the function `foo`:

```
penguin> gdb emp
GNU gdb 5.3.92
Copyright 2003 Free Software Foundation, Inc.
gdb is free software, covered by the GNU General Public License, and
you are welcome to change it and/or distribute copies of it under
certain conditions.  Type "show copying" to see the conditions.
There is absolutely no warranty for gdb.  Type "show warranty" for
details.
This gdb was configured as "i586-suse-linux"...
(gdb) break foo
Breakpoint 1 at 0x804836f
(gdb)
```

Run `emp`, and when the breakpoint is hit, dump the assembly:

```
(gdb) run
Starting program: /home/dbehman/testing/emp

Breakpoint 1, 0x0804836f in foo ()
(gdb) disas
Dump of assembler code for function foo:
0x0804836c <foo+0>:     push   %ebp
```

```
0x0804836d <foo+1>:      mov     %esp,%ebp
0x0804836f <foo+3>:      mov     0x8(%ebp),%eax
0x08048372 <foo+6>:      movl    $0x1,0x4(%eax)
0x08048379 <foo+13>:     mov     $0x0,%eax
0x0804837e <foo+18>:     pop     %ebp
0x0804837f <foo+19>:     ret
End of assembler dump.
(gdb)
```

The first two instructions are standard, used to set up the stack for this function and comprise what is referred to as the function prologue (see Chapter 5 for more information). The third instruction copies an 8-byte value from the stack into the eax register. This is the address of the structure in memory that we want to look at. We can see by the message "Breakpoint 1, 0x0804836f in foo ()" from GDB above that the next instruction to be executed is the copying of our address into eax at 0x0804836f. Have the debugger execute this instruction and then examine the contents of eax.

```
(gdb) stepi
0x08048372 in foo ()
(gdb) print /x $eax
$1 = 0x8049690
(gdb)
```

Now that we know the address of our structure, we can examine the raw memory contents. By examining the structure in employee.h, we know that the size of our structure is 56 bytes. When examining memory, a count is specified, and because we want to see words of size four bytes each, we use a count of 14 (56 divided by 4).

```
(gdb) x /14wx $eax
0x8049690:    0x00001140    0x00000000    0x006e6144    0x00000000
0x80496a0:    0x00000000    0x00000000    0x00000000    0x6d686542
0x80496b0:    0x00006e61    0x00000000    0x00000000    0x00000000
0x80496c0:    0x00000cce    0x00000141
(gdb)
```

There's our structure in raw memory form! It is possible to get the information we're looking for out of this representation, but a lot of conversion is required to get the correct values. *Endian-ness* must also be considered on x86-based platforms (which this is), so another layer of conversion is required. See the section, "Understanding and Dealing with Endian-ness," that follows for more information. All of the conversion involved introduces many chances for human error and being off by one digit can put an analyst down the wrong path and potentially cause a loss of hours in debugging time.

Fortunately, we've preloaded a library that contains debug symbols for the structure we want. All we have to do now is point our dummy structure pointer at this memory, and then we can print it out normally!

```
(gdb) set variable floating_rec = $eax
(gdb) print *floating_rec
$2 = {employee_no = 4416, is_ceo = 0,
  first_name = "Dan", '\0' <repeats 16 times>,
  last_name = "Behman", '\0' <repeats 13 times>,
  manager_emp_no = 3278, department_no = 321}
(gdb)
```

As you can see, this way it is much easier to see what the values are and what they refer to. Let's now execute the next machine instruction and dump our structure again.

```
(gdb) stepi
0x08048379 in foo ()
(gdb) print *floating_rec
$3 = {employee_no = 4416, is_ceo = 1,
  first_name = "Dan", '\0' <repeats 16 times>,
  last_name = "Behman", '\0' <repeats 13 times>,
  manager_emp_no = 3278, department_no = 321}
(gdb)
```

We can easily see that the is_ceo field was changed from 0 to 1. We now know that the function foo() performs a very significant promotion of a regular employee to a Chief Executive Officer!

This example is scaled down, but it should show how valuable this technique can be, especially when working with large and complex data structures.

6.9.4 Understanding and Dealing with Endian-ness

The term *endian* refers to how a particular architecture stores data in memory. Specifically, the order in which the bytes are stored is dictated by the endianness of a particular architecture.

When viewing raw memory in a debugger or a hex dump of some kind, it is very important to know whether the system is big or little endian. If the system is big endian, no conversion is needed, but if the system is little endian, you will have to convert the raw data into the human-preferred form (big endian) when reading it.

Consider the following simple program:

```
int main()
{
  unsigned long long i64 = 0x0123456789abcdef ;
  char  *tmpPtr ;

  return 0 ;
}
```

This simple program sets the value of a 64-bit variable i64 to 0x0123456789abcdef. The program also includes a character pointer, tmpPtr, that will be used from within GDB to determine the order of the bytes for the 64-bit value as it is stored in memory. Let's see the byte order for this 64-bit value from within GDB:

```
penguin> g++ endian.c -o endian -g
penguin> gdb endian
GNU gdb 5.2.1
Copyright 2002 Free Software Foundation, Inc.
GDB is free software, covered by the GNU General Public License, and
you are welcome to change it and/or distribute copies of it under
certain conditions.
Type "show copying" to see the conditions.
There is absolutely no warranty for GDB. Type "show warranty" for
details.
This GDB was configured as "i586-suse-linux"...
(gdb) break main
Breakpoint 1 at 0x804836c: file endian.c, line 4.
(gdb) run
Starting program: /home/wilding/src/Linuxbook/endian

Breakpoint 1, main () at endian.c:4
4     unsigned long long i64 = 0x0123456789abcdef ;
Current language: auto; currently c++
(gdb) next
7     return 0 ;
(gdb) set tmpPtr = &i64
(gdb) printf "%x\n", (unsigned char)tmpPtr[0]
ef
(gdb) printf "%x\n", (unsigned char)tmpPtr[1]
cd
(gdb) printf "%x\n", (unsigned char)tmpPtr[2]
ab
(gdb) printf "%x\n", (unsigned char)tmpPtr[3]
89
(gdb) printf "%x\n", (unsigned char)tmpPtr[4]
67
(gdb) printf "%x\n", (unsigned char)tmpPtr[5]
45
(gdb) printf "%x\n", (unsigned char)tmpPtr[6]
23
(gdb) printf "%x\n", (unsigned char)tmpPtr[7]
1
```

In the GDB session, we set the character pointer to the address of the 64-bit variable with `set tmpPtr = &i64`. Because the pointer is a character pointer, we can use it as a character array to find each byte of the 64-bit value, i64. Each index into the character array (for example, tmpPtr[3]) shows another byte, in order, of the 64-bit value as it is stored in memory. From the GDB output here, the 64-bit value of `0x0123456789abcdef` is actually stored as `0xefcdab8967452301` in memory. In other words, the byte order is completely reversed.

> **Note**: Byte reversing only need be done when viewing data that is in words two or more bytes in size. Individual bytes are always displayed as expected.

6.10 WORKING WITH C++

C++ is a superset of C and includes some new concepts such as classes with constructors and destructors, inline functions, and exceptions. While the full list is beyond the scope of this chapter, we will outline a few of the differences and how to deal with them in GDB.

6.10.1 Global Constructors and Destructors

There are a few ways to handle global constructors and destructors. Constructors are run as part of an object initialization. This can occur even before the `main()` function is called. Destructors are run when an object is destroyed, which can occur after the `main()` function exits. If you know the constructor or destructor name, you can set a breakpoint in it. But what if you don't know which constructors or destructors an executable or library has?

There is a relatively simple set of steps that you can use to find the global constructors and destructors. The following example shows these steps to find a constructor.

Consider a simple program that has a class and defines a global object from that class. For example, here is a code snippet that includes a simple class, myClass, and global object, myObj2, created with the class as its type.

```
#include <stdio.h>

class myClass
{
  public:

  int myVar ;
```

```
myClass() {
  myVar = 5 ;
}

};

myClass myObj2 ;
```

When the object, `myObj2`, is instantiated, the constructor will be run to perform any initialization for the object. For now, we'll assume that we don't know about this global object and will try to find it using GDB.

The first step is to disassemble the `_init` function. This function is run when a library is loaded or when a program is first executed.

```
(gdb) disass _init
Dump of assembler code for function _init:
0x8048300 <_init>:      push    %ebp
0x8048301 <_init+1>:    mov     %esp,%ebp
0x8048303 <_init+3>:    sub     $0x8,%esp
0x8048306 <_init+6>:    call    0x8048384 <call_gmon_start>
0x804830b <_init+11>:   nop
0x804830c <_init+12>:   call    0x80483f0 <frame_dummy>
0x8048311 <_init+17>:   call    0x8048550 <__do_global_ctors_aux>
0x8048316 <_init+22>:   leave
0x8048317 <_init+23>:   ret
End of assembler dump.
(gdb)
```

In the disassembly listing, we can clearly see a call to `__do_global_ctors_aux`. Now let's disassemble that function:

```
(gdb) disass __do_global_ctors_aux
Dump of assembler code for function __do_global_ctors_aux:
0x8048550 <__do_global_ctors_aux>:      push    %ebp
0x8048551 <__do_global_ctors_aux+1>:    mov     %esp,%ebp
0x8048553 <__do_global_ctors_aux+3>:    push    %ebx
0x8048554 <__do_global_ctors_aux+4>:    push    %edx
0x8048555 <__do_global_ctors_aux+5>:    mov     0x80497fc,%eax
0x804855a <__do_global_ctors_aux+10>:   cmp     $0xffffffff,%eax
0x804855d <__do_global_ctors_aux+13>:   mov     $0x80497fc,%ebx
0x8048562 <__do_global_ctors_aux+18>:   je      0x804857c
<__do_global_ctors_aux+44>
0x8048564 <__do_global_ctors_aux+20>:   lea     0x0(%esi),%esi
0x804856a <__do_global_ctors_aux+26>:   lea     0x0(%edi),%edi
0x8048570 <__do_global_ctors_aux+32>:   sub     $0x4,%ebx
0x8048573 <__do_global_ctors_aux+35>:   call    *%eax
0x8048575 <__do_global_ctors_aux+37>:   mov     (%ebx),%eax
0x8048577 <__do_global_ctors_aux+39>:   cmp     $0xffffffff,%eax
0x804857a <__do_global_ctors_aux+42>:   jne     0x8048570
```

```
<__do_global_ctors_aux+32>
0x804857c <__do_global_ctors_aux+44>:   pop   %eax
0x804857d <__do_global_ctors_aux+45>:   pop   %ebx
0x804857e <__do_global_ctors_aux+46>:   pop   %ebp
0x804857f <__do_global_ctors_aux+47>:   ret
End of assembler dump.
(gdb)
```

The previous assembly listing shows the following `call *%eax` call. This takes the value of the EAX register, treats it as an address, dereferences the address, and the calls function stored at the dereferenced address. From code above this call, we can see EAX being set with `mov 0x80497fc,%eax`. Let's take a look at what is at that address:

```
(gdb) x/40x 0x80497fc
0x80497fc <__CTOR_LIST__+4>:   0x0804851e    0x00000000    0xffffffff
➥0x00000000
0x804980c <__JCR_LIST__>:      0x00000000    0x08049718    0x00000000
➥0x00000000
0x804981c <_GLOBAL_OFFSET_TABLE_+12>:     0x0804832e    0x0804833e
➥0x0804834e    0x00000000
0x804982c <completed.1>:       0x00000000    0x00000000    0x00000000
➥0x00000000
0x804983c:   Cannot access memory at address 0x804983c
```

That address is four bytes past the start of a variable called __CTOR_LIST__ (we know this from the text, <__CTOR_LIST__+4>). There is a value `0x0804851e` at this address, which according to the preceding assembly language, is the value that is called after dereferencing EAX. Let's see what's at that address:

```
(gdb) disass 0x0804851e
Dump of assembler code for function _GLOBAL__I_myObj2:
0x804851e <_GLOBAL__I_myObj2>: push   %ebp
0x804851f <_GLOBAL__I_myObj2+1>:   mov   %esp,%ebp
0x8048521 <_GLOBAL__I_myObj2+3>:   sub   $0x8,%esp
0x8048524 <_GLOBAL__I_myObj2+6>:   sub   $0x8,%esp
0x8048527 <_GLOBAL__I_myObj2+9>:   push  $0xffff
0x804852c <_GLOBAL__I_myObj2+14>:   push  $0x1
0x804852e <_GLOBAL__I_myObj2+16>:          call    0x80484d8
<__static_initialization_and_destruction_0>
0x8048533 <_GLOBAL__I_myObj2+21>:   add   $0x10,%esp
0x8048536 <_GLOBAL__I_myObj2+24>:   leave
0x8048537 <_GLOBAL__I_myObj2+25>:   ret
End of assembler dump.
(gdb)
```

This is the global constructor of the myObj2 object that we saw in the preceding source code. The __CTOR_LIST__ variable stores the list of global constructors for an executable or shared library. We find all the global constructor lists by using the `info variables` command in GDB:

```
(gdb) info variables __CTOR_LIST__
All variables matching regular expression "__CTOR_LIST__":

Non-debugging symbols:
0x0804966c  __CTOR_LIST__
0x400c0554  __CTOR_LIST__
0x400f95a8  __CTOR_LIST__
0x40101d4c  __CTOR_LIST__
0x4021ac7c  __CTOR_LIST__
```

We can also find out which libraries these constructor lists belong to (the constructor list at 0x0804966c is the one for the process itself). The list of libraries is as follows:

```
(gdb) info proc
process 18953
cmdline = '/home/wilding/src/Linuxbook/cpp'
cwd = '/home/wilding/src/Linuxbook'
exe = '/home/wilding/src/Linuxbook/cpp'
 (gdb) shell cat /proc/18953/maps
08048000-08049000 r-xp 00000000 08:13 3649928   /home/wilding/src/
➡Linuxbook/cpp
08049000-0804a000 rw-p 00000000 08:13 3649928   /home/wilding/src/
➡Linuxbook/cpp
40000000-40012000 r-xp 00000000 08:13 1144740  /lib/ld-2.2.5.so
40012000-40013000 rw-p 00011000 08:13 1144740  /lib/ld-2.2.5.so
40013000-40014000 rw-p 00000000 00:00 0
40014000-400ad000 r-xp 00000000 08:13 1847971  /usr/lib/libstdc++.so.5.0.0
400ad000-400c2000 rw-p 00098000 08:13 1847971  /usr/lib/libstdc++.so.5.0.0
400c2000-400c7000 rw-p 00000000 00:00 0
400d7000-400f9000 r-xp 00000000 08:13 1144751  /lib/libm.so.6
400f9000-400fa000 rw-p 00021000 08:13 1144751  /lib/libm.so.6
400fa000-40101000 r-xp 00000000 08:13 1144783  /lib/libgcc_s.so.1
40101000-40102000 rw-p 00007000 08:13 1144783  /lib/libgcc_s.so.1
40102000-40216000 r-xp 00000000 08:13 1144746  /lib/libc.so.6
40216000-4021c000 rw-p 00113000 08:13 1144746  /lib/libc.so.6
4021c000-40221000 rw-p 00000000 00:00 0
bfffe000-c0000000 rwxp fffff000 00:00 0
```

From the output of the /proc file "maps," we can see all of the address ranges for each shared library. Comparing the addresses of the various __CTOR_LIST__ variables and the address of the libraries, we can find which library contains which constructor list. For example, the constructor list at 0x400c0554 is contained in the second memory segment for the library /usr/lib/ libstdc++.so.5.0.0.

Of course, we can do something similar for global destructors, except we need to use the __DTOR_LIST__ variable. Now that we know the symbol names for the constructor and destructor lists, we can reference them directly and do not have to go through _init (or the corresponding _fini) to find the lists.

6.10.2 Inline Functions

Inline functions are special functions whose instructions can actually be embedded in the function that called the inline function. The keyword "inline" is a suggestion to the compiler, not an instruction, so a function may or may not be "inlined." A compiler may also choose to inline functions that were not declared as inline (for example, a small static function).

An inline function is harder to debug because it will not have a symbol or address (since the code is part of the function that called the inline function). You can't set a breakpoint by asking GDB to break when entering the inline function (break function1) because an inline function doesn't really exist as a function. There are also no variables that you can print out—and thus no type information, and so on.

If you compile without optimization, the functions will probably not be inlined. Keep in mind that the inline key word is only a suggestion to the compiler. Consider the following simple inline function:

```
inline int foo( int a )
{
  int b = 0 ;

  for ( b = a ; b < 100 ; b ++ ) ;

  noValueGlobInt = a ;
  return b + a ;
}
```

Compiling a program that contains this function without optimization will show that there is a symbol for this function (foo) which means that it has not been inlined by the compiler.

```
penguin> g++ cpp.C -g -o cpp
penguin> nm cpp | egrep foo
08048514 W _Z3fooi
```

Compiling with optimization (-o3), we'll see that the function foo no longer has a symbol, which means that the compiler inlined the actual machine code into the calling function.

```
penguin> g++ cpp.C -g -o cpp -O3
penguin> nm cpp | egrep foo
penguin>

(gdb) info functions foo
All functions matching regular expression "foo":
(gdb) quit
```

If you need to debug an inline function (and assuming you have the source code), rebuild the program with -g and without optimization so that you get a static function instead of the inlined function. This works in most cases except when the problem disappears when the program is rebuilt.

6.10.3 Exceptions

C++ exceptions are a special way of handling unexpected conditions. The reasons and methods of using exceptions won't be covered here, but we will cover how they relate to GDB. GDB has commands to handle exceptions, but they may not be well supported. For example:

```
(gdb) catch throw
warning: Unsupported with this platform/compiler combination.
warning: Perhaps you can achieve the effect you want by setting
warning: a breakpoint on __raise_exception().
```

Okay, let's try that:

```
(gdb) break __raise_exception
Function "__raise_exception" not defined.
```

We can't set a breakpoint in __raise_exception because it doesn't exist. So we're on our own and have to find another method to catch exceptions in GDB. Let's take a closer look at what happens when an exception is thrown using the following simple program:

```
#include <unistd.h>

#include <iostream>
#include <typeinfo>
using namespace std;

int main()
{
  getpid( ) ; // to mark where we entered the main function

  try
  {
    throw ( 5 ) ;
```

```
    }
    catch( int )
    {
      cout << "Exception raised.";
    }

    try
    {
      throw ( 5 ) ;
    }
    catch( int )
    {
      cout << "Second exception raised.";
    }

    return 0;
}
```

This simple program throws two identical exceptions. The sole purpose of the
first exception is to flush out the dynamic linking required to find the functions
used by the exception handling. The curious reader can try the exercise that
follows on the first exception to see how much is involved in finding the function
symbols behind the scenes (for more information on this, see Chapter 9, "ELF:
Executable and Linking Format").

The next step is to compile this program with -g and create an executable:

```
penguin> g++ excp.C -o excp -g
```

Then we need to start GDB and run the program, excp, from within GDB (steps
are not included here). Next, we set a breakpoint in main and run the program
as follows:

```
(gdb) break main
Breakpoint 1 at 0x804877d: file excp.C, line 9.
(gdb) run
Starting program: /home/wilding/src/Linuxbook/excp

Breakpoint 1, main () at excp.C:9
9       getpid( ) ; // to mark where we entered the main function
```

As just discussed, we'll go past the first exception using the GDB command
next until we're on the second exception.

```
(gdb) next
13        throw ( 5 ) ;
(gdb) next
15      catch( int )
(gdb) next
```

```
17       cout << "Exception raised.";
(gdb) next
22       throw ( 5 ) ;
```

So, according to GDB, we're about to throw the second exception. We need to switch to using `stepi` to see what happens under the covers:

```
(gdb) stepi
0x08048807   22       throw ( 5 ) ;
(gdb) stepi
0x08048809   22       throw ( 5 ) ;
(gdb) stepi
0x080485e4 in __cxa_allocate_exception ()
```

So according to GDB, the function `__cxa_allocate_exception` is called when an exception is thrown (at least on this Linux system—other systems might be slightly different). We could set a breakpoint on this function to catch exceptions in GDB. Before we do that, let's see what else is involved in an exception being thrown (a few `stepi` calls are omitted for simplicity):

```
(gdb) stepi
0x4009e478 in operator delete[] (void*, std::nothrow_t const&) () from
➥/usr/lib/libstdc++.so.5
(gdb) stepi
0x4009e47b in operator delete[] (void*, std::nothrow_t const&) () from
➥/usr/lib/libstdc++.so.5
(gdb) stepi
0x4009e494 in __cxa_allocate_exception () from /usr/lib/libstdc++.so.5
(gdb) stepi
0x4009e49a in __cxa_allocate_exception () from /usr/lib/libstdc++.so.5
(gdb) stepi
0x4009e49d in __cxa_allocate_exception () from /usr/lib/libstdc++.so.5
(gdb) stepi
0x4009e4a0 in __cxa_allocate_exception () from /usr/lib/libstdc++.so.5
(gdb) stepi
0x4009e4a3 in __cxa_allocate_exception () from /usr/lib/libstdc++.so.5
(gdb) stepi
0x4004cea0 in _init () from /usr/lib/libstdc++.so.5
(gdb) stepi
0x4016fd70 in malloc () from /lib/libc.so.6
```

There are two things worth noting from this output:

1. Exception handling apparently calls the delete operator.
2. Exception handling apparently calls `malloc`.

This is important to know because it means that exceptions should not be used for out of memory conditions or for memory corruptions in the process heap.

For lack of memory, throwing an exception could fail because `malloc` would fail to allocate memory. For memory corruption, there is a chance that `malloc` or `delete` would trap because memory corruption in the process heap often affects the data structures used by functions like `malloc`. When `malloc` attempts to read its data structures, the memory corruption could force it to use an incorrect pointer causing the trap. In any case, the key point here is to be careful when using exceptions that are due to a trap or for out of memory conditions.

Going back to the function `__cxa_allocate_exception`, we can indeed use this to catch an exception in GDB:

```
(gdb) break __cxa_allocate_exception
Breakpoint 1 at 0x80485e4
(gdb) run
Starting program: /home/wilding/src/Linuxbook/excp
Breakpoint 1 at 0x4009e486

Breakpoint 1, 0x4009e486 in __cxa_allocate_exception () from /usr/lib/
libstdc++.so.5
(gdb) where
#0 0x4009e486 in __cxa_allocate_exception () from /usr/lib/libstdc++.so.5
#1 0x0804878c in main () at excp.C:13
#2 0x4011a4a2 in __libc_start_main () from /lib/libc.so.6
```

From the output here, the program caused the breakpoint on the call to `__cxa_allocate_exception`, which is called from line 13 of the source file excp.C. By moving up one stack frame, we can see the original line of code that triggered the exception:

```
(gdb) up
#1 0x0804878c in main () at excp.C:13
13          throw ( 5 ) ;
```

6.11 THREADS

Threads are light weight processes that run in the same address space. They share the process heap, the shared libraries and the executable code. The only thing that threads do not share is their individual stacks. Technically, each thread has read/write access to the other thread stacks but never purposefully reads or writes to any stack but its own.

Problems in threaded applications can be very challenging to diagnose. When using threads (or processes that use shared memory), there is the potential for race conditions, also known as timing conditions. A race condition is a problem that may or may not occur depending on the order and/or duration of events between threads. For example, thread #1 could read the size of a list from memory and then start to use the list based on the size. While thread #1 is reading through the list, thread #2 could change the list or the size of the list, leading to inconsistent information for thread #1. If thread #1 reads through the list before thread #2 changes it, there would be no problem. Likewise, if thread #1 reads quickly (before thread #2 gets a chance to actually make changes), there would be no problem. Race conditions are often difficult to reproduce because changes that affect timing (such as attaching with GDB) can change the order or duration of events, effectively masking the problem.

Another challenging problem type when using threads is a multi-threaded memory corruption. In this case, one thread corrupts a range of memory, and another thread reads the memory (and the corrupted data) at some point in the future. This is a challenging type of problem since the symptom of the problem can be very disconnected from the original cause (and it can be difficult to tie the two together).

Watchpoints can really help out with multi-threaded memory corruptions, but unfortunately, watchpoints are generally not well supported with threads in GDB (at least not on Linux). The main problem is that GDB can only watch an address in a single thread. In other words, if you set a watchpoint for *writes* to an address from thread #1, it will not be triggered if thread #2 writes to the watched address. This really limits the usefulness of watchpoints for threaded applications!

If the program or application has some type of trace facility, it may be worth while to check or dump the address range that gets corrupted (if you know it) regularly or for every trace point. This way, you can narrow down the area of code that is corrupting the memory to the functions that were captured in the trace around the time that the corruption occurred. Unfortunately, because of the lack of watchpoint support for multi-threaded processes, GDB might not be the best tool for debugging a multi-threaded corruption. In any case, let's explore what GDB can do with multi-threaded processes.

The following program is used to illustrate the basic thread support in GDB. The program creates one thread that uses up stack space up to a certain amount or until the thread runs out of stack space:

```
#include <unistd.h>
#include <stdio.h>
#include <pthread.h>
#include <stdlib.h>
#include <sys/types.h>

void burnStackSpace( int *depth )
{
  char foo[8192] ;

  (*depth)- ;
```

```
    if ( *depth > 0 )
    {
     burnStackSpace( depth ) ;
    }
    else
    {
     sprintf( foo, "Hit final depth!\n" ) ; // actually use "foo" to
                        // ensure the compiler keeps it
     puts( foo ) ;
     sleep( 30 ) ;
    }

}

extern "C" void *useStackSpace( void *arg )
{
   int stackSpace = *(int *)arg ;

   int depth = ( stackSpace/8192 ) / 2 ;

   burnStackSpace( &depth ) ;

   return NULL ;
}


int main(int argc, char *argv[], char *envp[] )
{

   int sRC = 0 ;
   pthread_t newThread ;
   int stackSpace = 1008*1024;
   pthread_attr_t attr;

   pthread_attr_init(&attr);
   pthread_attr_setstacksize( &attr, 1024*1024 ) ;

    sRC = pthread_create( &newThread, &attr, useStackSpace, (void
➥*)&stackSpace ) ;

   pthread_join( newThread, NULL ) ;


}
```

The function, burnStackSpace, is a recursive function designed to consume stack space to illustrate what out of stack space conditions look like in GDB. The function, useStackSpace, is the first function that the newly created function calls. The main function simple creates a thread and waits for it to complete.

Here is the compile line we'll use to compile the program:

```
penguin> g++ threads.C -o threads -lpthread
```

Notice that we need to include -lpthread for the posix thread library. This is required for multi-threaded applications on Linux.

Before we examine this multi-threaded program, it is worth while to mention that the thread support in Linux depends on the version of your Linux kernel. If we run this program on an older Linux kernel (pre-version 2.6), there will be three new "processes" according to a ps listing (one original process and two new threads):

```
penguin> ps -fu wilding | egrep threads | egrep -v grep
wilding 19151 19400 0 08:46 pts/72   00:00:00 threads
wilding 19152 19151 0 08:46 pts/72   00:00:00 threads
wilding 19153 19152 0 08:46 pts/72   00:00:00 threads
```

This is due to the original implementation of threads (known as "Linux Threads"), which made each thread look very much like an individual process. It is also worth nothing that there are three threads when we would expect only two—the main thread and the thread created by the main thread. The extra thread may or many not be created, again depending on the implementation of threads on your system.

In a more recent Linux kernel (version 2.6+), you'll see only one process because the threads will not show up as processes as in earlier Linux kernels:

```
penguin2> ps -fu wilding |egrep threads
wilding 22959 22534 0 13:05 pts/10   00:00:00 threads
wilding 22964 22865 0 13:05 pts/16   00:00:00 /bin/grep -E threads
```

This newer thread implementation is called Native POSIX Threading Library (NPTL) and is included in recent versions of the Linux kernel. Despite the differences, the two implementations can be treated pretty much the same way from within GDB. In any case, let's see what these threads look like from within GDB, using the info threads command:

```
(gdb) info threads
 2 Thread 1074788704 (LWP 22996) 0x0000002a95c6d2af in __write_nocancel
() from /lib64/tls/libc.so.6
* 1 Thread 182902990144 (LWP 22979) 0x0000002a95673f9f in pthread_join
() from /lib64/tls/libpthread.so.0
```

From the preceding output, we can see two threads: the main thread and the one we created with pthread_create(). The * character beside thread #1 in the output indicates that the current thread in GDB is thread #1.

Let's display the stack trace for thread #1 to see which thread it is and what it is doing. We can use the `bt` (back trace) command in GDB to get the stack trace of the current thread (which is thread #1).

```
(gdb) bt
#0  0x0000002a95673f9f in pthread_join () from /lib64/tls/libpthread.so.0
#1  0x00000000004008ec  in  main  (argc=1,  argv=0x7fbfffedf8,
envp=0x7fbfffee08) at threads.C:53
```

From the stack trace output, thread #1 is the main thread for the process given that it has the `main` function on the stack. This would have been the only thread used by the process if we hadn't created any additional threads.

> **Note**: The key word `main` in used in both `main thread` and `main function` is actually a coincidence. The `main` function is historically the first user function called in a C program and existed long before threads.

Now, let's switch to the second thread using the `thread` command in GDB with `2` as the argument:

```
(gdb) thread 2
[Switching  to  thread  2  (Thread  1074788704  (LWP  22996))]#0
0x0000002a95c6d2af in __write_nocancel ()
   from /lib64/tls/libc.so.6
```

This changed the current thread context used by GDB to that of thread #2. All commands that used to act on thread #1 now act on thread #2. For example, the `bt` command will now display the stack trace for thread #2:

```
(gdb) bt 10
#0  0x0000002a95c6d2af in __write_nocancel () from /lib64/tls/libc.so.6
#1  0x0000002a95c25423 in _IO_new_file_write () from /lib64/tls/libc.so.6
#2  0x0000002a95c25170 in new_do_write () from /lib64/tls/libc.so.6
#3  0x0000002a95c253d5 in _IO_new_do_write () from /lib64/tls/libc.so.6
#4  0x0000002a95c25c64 in  _IO_new_file_overflow () from /lib64/tls/
➥libc.so.6
#5  0x0000002a95c275cc in _IO_default_xsputn_internal () from /lib64/
➥tls/libc.so.6
#6  0x0000002a95c25393 in _IO_new_file_xsputn () from /lib64/tls/libc.so.6
#7  0x0000002a95c0045d in vfprintf () from /lib64/tls/libc.so.6
#8  0x0000002a95c08aba in printf () from /lib64/tls/libc.so.6
#9  0x000000000040083e  in burnStackSpace (depth=0x400ff7e0)  at
➥threads.C:20
(More stack frames follow...)
(gdb)
```

From the stack output, thread #2 is the additional thread we created (it eventually calls burStackSpace()).

6.11.1 Running Out of Stack Space

One of the most common types of problems for multi-threaded processes is running out of stack space. This is because the amount of stack space for a typical thread is less than that for the main thread. With a small change to the threaded program source code, we can force the spawned thread to exceed its stack space and trap. Then we'll use GDB to show the typical symptoms of this somewhat common problem.

The small change is to switch the divide sign / to a multiply sign * for the following line of code:

```
int depth = ( stackSpace/8192 ) / 2 ;
```

After the change:

```
int depth = ( stackSpace/8192 ) * 2 ;
```

This will cause the recursive function burnStackSpace to continue past the depth at which the stack space runs out. Here is what the program does now after this small change:

```
penguin> g++ threads.C -o threads -lpthread -g
penguin> threads
Segmentation fault
```

The first thing to notice is that the common symptom for this type of problem is a segmentation fault (with a signal SIGSEGV). There are additional symptoms from within GDB:

```
(gdb) run
Starting program: /home/wilding/threads
[Thread debugging using libthread_db enabled]
[New Thread 182902990144 (LWP 23102)]
gdb threads
[New Thread 1074788704 (LWP 23123)]

Program received signal SIGSEGV, Segmentation fault.
[Switching to Thread 1074788704 (LWP 23123)]
0x000000000040080a in burnStackSpace (depth=0x400ff7e0) at threads.C:15
15        burnStackSpace( depth ) ;
```

According to the output in GDB, the trap occurred on the call to burnStackSpace(), a call to a function. This is a pretty good hint that we've run out of stack space considering the segmentation fault did not occur while trying to access a bad pointer or some other typical reason.

Further, from the assembly listing of the trapped instruction, we see the following:

```
gdb) disass 0x000000000040080a 0x000000000040081a
Dump of assembler code from 0x40080a to 0x40081a:
0x000000000040080a <_Z14burnStackSpacePi+34>:  callq 0x4007e8
➥<_Z14burnStackSpacePi>
0x000000000040080f <_Z14burnStackSpacePi+39>:  jmp  0x400848
➥<_Z14burnStackSpacePi+96>
0x0000000000400811 <_Z14burnStackSpacePi+41>:  mov
➥0xfffffffffffffff8(%rbp),%rax
0x0000000000400815 <_Z14burnStackSpacePi+45>:  lea
➥0xffffffffffffdff0(%rbp),%rdi
End of assembler dump.
```

The trapped instruction was a *callq* (a 64-bit call instruction for the x86-64 platform). This is even more conclusive that we've run out of stack space. The instruction that caused the segmentation fault is trying to call a function, which in turn is trapping because there is no more space on the stack for the called function.

There is actually quite a lot to know about using and debugging threads that is unrelated to GDB. If you are planning to do a great deal of multi-threaded programming, it would be worthwhile to buy a book specifically on this subject.

6.12 DATA DISPLAY DEBUGGER (DDD)

GDB is a very powerful debugger, but many shy away from it because it is command line-based and has no graphical interface. The Data Display Debugger (DDD) is an X11-based GUI front-end to GDB. It offers many powerful features that can greatly enhance any debugging session. It is available with most distributions—SUSE 9.0 Professional includes it in the package ddd-3.3.7.15; however, SUSE Linux Enterprise Server (SLES) 8 does not. SLES 8 is compatible with SUSE Professional 8.1, so the package ddd-3.3.1-340.x86_64.rpm can be used from SUSE Pro 8.1. Alternatively, you can download the source tarball and build DDD yourself.

The following section includes a high-level overview for those who might prefer DDD over GDB.

A great characteristic of DDD is that it only builds on GDB's functionality; in fact, the DDD GUI includes a GDB console window in which you can type commands directly to GDB just as if you were using it by itself. Figure 6.3 shows a freshly launched DDD window by executing "ddd hello" with the four main windows highlighted and labeled.

The figure shows four main areas of the graphical interface:

1. Data Display
2. Source Code
3. Machine Language
4. GDB Console

The first three areas of the graphical interface cover the three types of information that a problem investigator will need to see the most. The last area is the actual GDB console and can be used to send a direct command to GDB.

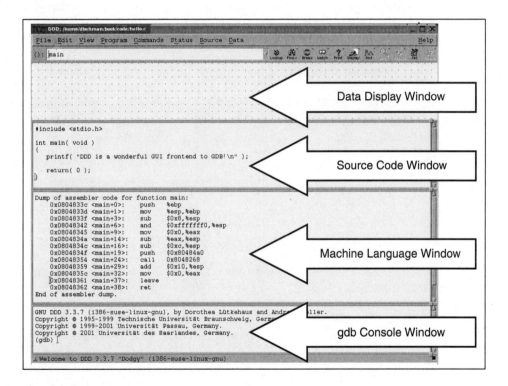

Fig. 6.3 Basics of DDD.

Each of these viewing areas or windows is explained in more detail in the following sections.

6.12.1 The Data Display Window

This window acts as a free-form style workspace where any kind of data that can be printed in a GDB console can be "graphed." The term "graphed" simply refers to the graphical and dynamic displaying of the selected data. The best feature of the data display window is that after each time the debugger stops, all graphed data in the display window is updated, and each individual change within each graph is highlighted. This makes seeing exactly what changed after each instruction or set of instructions extremely easy. For example, when debugging at the machine language level, it's very valuable to monitor the machine's registers to see what changes after each machine instruction. Figure 6.4 shows how this works after executing a single machine language instruction. There are two ways to display the set of registers in the data display window. One way is to execute this command in the GDB console window:

```
graph display `info registers`
```

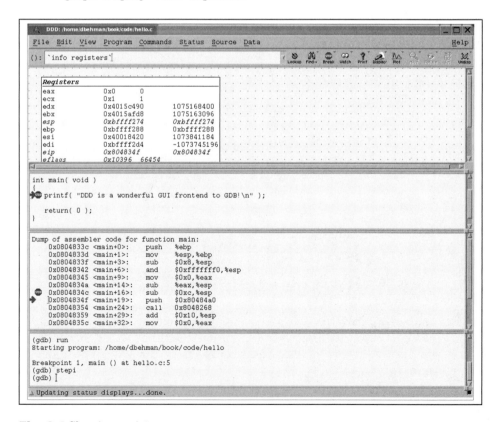

Fig. 6.4 Showing registers.

The second way is to click "Data" then "Status Displays." In the window that pops up, select "List of integer registers and their contents." Also note that for anything to be displayed in the registers, the program needs to be running, so using the simple "hello" example in Figure 6.3, I set a breakpoint in main and then started the program.

As we can see in Figure 6.4, after executing the instruction `sub $0xc, %esp` (which we can see by `stepi` in the GDB console window), the "Registers" graph in the data display window has the `esp`, `eip`, and `eflags` highlighted, showing that those registers were modified during this instruction's execution.

6.12.1.1 Viewing the Raw Stack

Examining the raw stack can be very useful for diagnosing problems, especially when debugging applications not compiled with debug symbols. DDD does not provide a simple menu option to do this, however. Using the data display window and with a little knowledge of stacks in general (see Chapter 5 for more information), we can get the information we need. We know that the esp register on the 32bit x86 architecture (rsp on the 64-bit x86-64 architecture) always points to the top of the stack (smallest memory address), so we can graph a display of the top 16 words on the stack at any given time by entering this command into the GDB console window:

```
graph display 'x /16wx $esp'
```

> **Note**: Using this command will work fine, but the graph that gets created in the display window will only have a title of "X". This is because DDD simply uses the first word of the expression for the title. Remove the spaces in the expression to make the graphs unique and a little more meaningful, especially when dealing with many graphs. For example, for figure 6.5 this command was used:
>
> ```
> graph display 'x/16wx$esp'
> ```

Figure 6.5 shows a DDD session of a hello.c program, which has code to assign a value to a local variable. The source code is shown in the source window. The green arrow points to the line of source code that will be executed next, so we can see that we have just executed the code that stores the value 5 into our stack_int variable. The graph highlights the line that changed, thus showing us our stack_int variable getting updated directly in memory (note the `0x00000005` value).

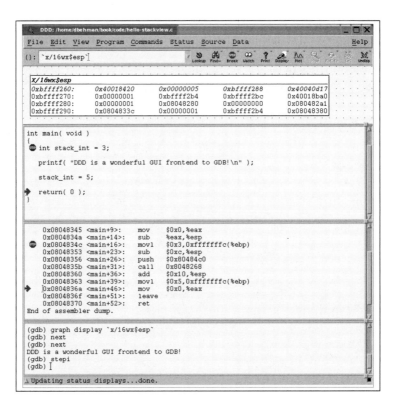

Fig. 6.5 Raw stack trace.

6.12.1.2 View Complex Data Structures The data display window is
also very powerful for displaying and organizing complex data structures.
Linked lists are a fundamental computer science data structure, but when a
particular implementation gets quite involved, debugging them can be difficult.
Figure 6.6 shows a DDD session using a very simplified linked list
implementation added into our `hello.c` source. The source code is as follows:

```
#include <stdio.h>

struct linked_list_struct
{
    int list_no;
    int data;
    struct linked_list_struct *pNext;
};

int main( void )
{
```

```
int stack_int = 3;
char stack_string[16];
struct linked_list_struct *node1 = (struct
    linked_list_struct*)malloc( sizeof(
        struct linked_list_struct ) );
struct linked_list_struct *node2 = (struct
    linked_list_struct*)malloc( sizeof(
        struct linked_list_struct ) );
struct linked_list_struct *node3 = (struct
    linked_list_struct*)malloc( sizeof(
        struct linked_list_struct ) );

node1->list_no = 1;
node1->data = 9234;
node1->pNext = node2;

node2->list_no = 2;
node2->data = 2342;
node2->pNext = node3;

node3->list_no = 3;
node3->data = 7987;
node3->pNext = node1;

printf( "DDD is a wonderful GUI frontend to GDB!\n" );

stack_int = 5;

return( 0 );
}
```

Typically, this isn't how linked lists would be implemented, but it serves the purpose at hand, which is to demonstrate the capabilities of the data display window. The steps followed to get the DDD session to the stage shown in Figure 6.6 were:

1. Set a breakpoint after the three nodes get fully set up:
   a. Set the breakpoint by double-clicking in the margin just to the left of the source code line containing the call to `printf`.
   b. A stop sign icon should appear indicating a breakpoint has been set
2. Run the program.
3. Right-click any occurrence of the node1 variable in the source window and choose "Display *node1" (scroll the source window if needed).
4. Right-click pNext in the newly created node1 data display graph and choose "Display *()."
5. Right-click pNext in the newly created node2 data display graph and choose "Display *()" (note that it is not labeled as node2).
6. Right-click pNext in the newly created node3 data display graph and choose "Display *()" (note that it is not labeled as node3).

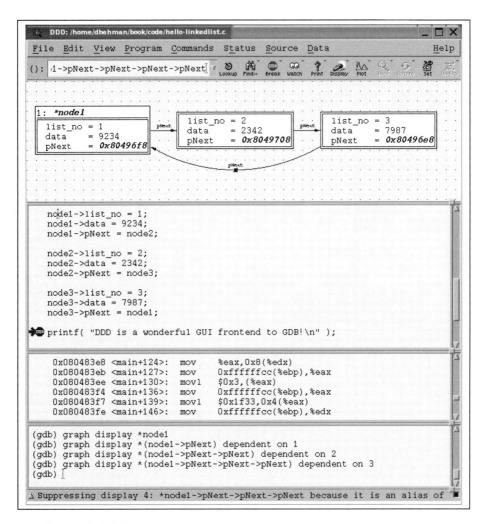

Fig. 6.6 Linked list.

As you can see, DDD gives a graphical representation of our simple circular linked list.

6.12.2 Source Code Window

As has been shown in the figures from the Data Display Windows section, the source code window can be very critical in a debugging session. It is important to understand however, that it is only available and usable when the program being debugged has been compiled with debug symbols (using the -g compile switch). It's also important to understand how compiling with optimization (GCC's -o1, -o2, -o3, -os options) affects the source code window (see the "Compiling with Optimization" section for more information).

Because compiler optimization often reorganizes the machine level instructions, the order in which the source code level instructions are executed changes. If the program being debugged has been compiled with debug symbols and some level of optimization, stepping through machine level instructions with the stepi or nexti GDB commands will cause the current source line of code marker to appear to jump around wildly from line of code to line of code. This is completely normal and in fact is very useful to debugging compiler optimization problems. It's quite interesting to see how much work a compiler's optimizer does in converting what the author might think is optimized code into optimized assembly.

The source code window is also interactive in that breakpoints can be set by double-clicking to the left of any source code line. You can also hover the mouse pointer over any variable to see a pop-up showing its value. Right-clicking the variable presents a menu you can use to print variable values to the GDB console window or display them to the data display window. This is especially useful for structures.

6.12.3 Machine Language Window

The machine language window basically displays the output of GDB's disassemble command with a specified range within the current function.

> **Note**: Machine language dumps of functions can be quite lengthy. By default DDD will only disassemble a maximum of 256 bytes at a time in the machine language window. Once execution goes beyond what's currently disassembled, DDD will disassemble and display another 256 bytes. This can be inconvenient in some cases, so to change this behavior, add the following to your $HOME/.ddd/init file:
>
> ```
> Ddd*maxDisassemble: 512
> ```

Try substituting 512 with whatever value you want; 0 means disassemble the entire function. Be sure to add this line to the top of the init file only, as DDD overwrites some settings with defaults when DDD is terminated.

The machine language window is also interactive in the same ways that the source code window is. You can set breakpoints on specific instructions as well as print or display memory addresses or symbols. The machine language window is extremely useful even for the simple fact that the next instruction to be executed is pointed to by an arrow. GDB's text-based interface does not do this, and disassembling the machine language instructions around the current area of execution can be very cumbersome.

6.12.4 GDB Console Window

The GDB console window is essentially what you get when executing GDB by itself. The difference is that it is being managed by DDD, so commands will be caught by DDD and integrated into its GUI. The beauty of the GDB console is that for people used to just using GDB by itself and for those die-hard command-line users, it still has everything that they're used to. DDD, however, enhances the GDB console and makes the debugging experience much easier and more efficient.

6.13 CONCLUSION

In an open source environment such as Linux, having a freely available debugger like GDB is part of the normal process of investigating. This is not necessarily the case on commercial operating systems because a) the debugger is often not free and b) the source code for the operating system and its tools is not available to the public. Hopefully after reading this chapter, you have a good understanding of what GDB can do to help with your problem determination needs on Linux.

Linux System Crashes and Hangs

7.1 INTRODUCTION

One of Linux's claims to fame is stability and infrequency of system crashes and hangs. Development versions of the kernel are less stable, but unfortunately, mainstream kernel versions will also sometimes crash or hang. The beauty of Linux is that when this happens, users have the ability to track the problem down to a failing line of source code and even fix it themselves if they're so inclined! With proprietary operating systems, your only course of action is to contact the company or author(s) of the operating system and hope that they can help you. Anyone that has had this happen to them in the past knows that this can be the start of a very lengthy battle full of frustration, which is still never guaranteed to end happily with a solution to the problem. At least with Linux, with a full set of debugging and diagnostic tools and some knowledge about where to look, one is much better armed and ready to seek and find a solution. The goal of this section is to discuss the many tools that Linux provides to get you well on your way to analyzing some of the most crucial operating system problems. We will discuss how to set up, configure, and use a serial console; how to read and understand a kernel Oops report; and how to determine the failing line of source code from it.

7.2 GATHERING INFORMATION

Gathering information for analysis either by you or by a support group of kernel developers on the Internet is the first step on the road to troubleshooting a serious system problem. There are really two main types of serious system problems—a crash and a hang. A crash occurs when the kernel is aware of the problem it has just encountered and is able to do something about it before putting itself to sleep or rebooting. A hang occurs when there is a serious deadlock within the kernel that happens without warning and does not give the kernel the ability to do anything about it. Much of the tools for tracking the cause of each type of problem are the same; however, with a hang some of the diagnostic information may not be available, as the kernel didn't have a chance to write it to disk or the screen.

7.2.1 Syslog Explained

The syslog is usually /var/log/messages but can be anywhere by modifying
values in /etc/syslog.conf. The syslog file is a text log of messages written by
the syslog daemon, which reads the messages directly from kernel buffers.
Monitoring this file regularly can often provide crucial hints about the general
health of your system such as disk space running out, memory being exhausted,
I/O errors, device failures, and so on. When restarting the system after a crash
or hang, this file should be examined first to see if anything was logged that
could give a hint as to what might have caused the problem.
When doing this, the recommended procedure is the following:

1. Wait for the system to fully restart.
2. Log in or `su` (switch user) to root.
3. Examine /etc/syslog.conf to determine the system log filename.
    For example, look for something like the following:

    ```
    #
    # save the rest in one file
    #
    *.*;mail.none;news.none    -/var/log/messages
    ```

4. Open /var/log/messages (or similar from Step 3) in `vi`, `less`, or your
    favorite editor.
5. Navigate to the end of the file.
6. Search backward for "restart." You should see a line like this:

    ```
    Mar 14 19:45:21 linux syslogd 1.4.1: restart.
    ```

7. The messages immediately prior to the line found in Step 5 are the last
    messages logged before the system restarted. Examine them for anything
    suspicious.

Generally, individual messages are composed of the following sequence of
tokens:

```
<timestamp> <hostname> <message origin> <message text>
```

An example showing a message coming from a kernel driver:

```
Mar 10 22:49:05 linux kernel: usb.c: deregistering driver serial

<timestamp> = Mar 10 22:49:05
<hostname> = linux
```

```
<message origin> = kernel: usb.c
<message text> = deregistering driver serial
```

We know from the message origin that the message came from the kernel, and we are also given the exact source file containing the message. We can now easily examine usb.c and search for the message text to see exactly where kernel execution was. The code in question looks like this:

```
/**
 *      usb_deregister - unregister a USB driver
 *      @driver: USB operations of the driver to unregister
 *
 *      Unlinks the specified driver from the internal USB driver list.
 */
void usb_deregister(struct usb_driver *driver)
{
        struct list_head *tmp;

        info("deregistering driver %s", driver->name);
        if (driver->fops != NULL)
                usb_minors[driver->minor/16] = NULL;
```

Knowing exactly what this code does is not important—it is important at this time only to know that by a simple log message we can determine exactly what was being executed, which can be invaluable in problem determination. One thing to note, though, is that info is a macro defined as:

```
#define info(format, arg...) printk(KERN_INFO __FILE__ ": " format
➥"\n" , ## arg)
```

As you can see, printk is the key function that performs the act of writing the message to the kernel message buffer. We can also see that the standard C macro __FILE__ is used to dump the source filename.

There is, however, no guarantee that anything will appear in the syslog. Often, even in the case of a crash, the klogd system logger is unable to write the information to disk. This is where a serial console becomes important. When properly configured, the kernel will send important log messages to the serial console as well as to the buffers where the syslog daemon picks them up. After the messages are sent over the serial line, the remote console will receive the messages and preserve them there.

7.2.2 Setting up a Serial Console

Possibly one of the most important tools in diagnosing and determining the cause of system crashes or hangs is the use of a serial console to gather diagnostic information. A serial console is not something that every system requires, although it doesn't hurt to have. But if your system inexplicably crashes or hangs more than a few times in a very short period of time, it is highly recommended.

Note: In the kernel source package included with most distributions, the file Documentation/serial-console.txt is an excellent guide on setting up and configuring a serial console.

In conjunction with using the serial console is to enable the kernel magic SysRq key; refer to the sysrq section of Chapter 3, "The /proc Filesystem," for more information. A serial console helps because often when a system enters a panic state, for example in the case of a kernel oops, the kernel will dump information to the kernel log daemon. This normally means that the information gets written to /var/log/messages; however, there are cases where the system is unable to perform the writes to disk, so this is where the serial console proves most useful. When properly set up, the information is dumped over the serial port as well so the remote system, which is in a healthy state, will receive and save this information. This information can then be analyzed using the techniques discussed in this section or forwarded to the appropriate support group.

7.2.3 Connecting the Serial Null-Modem Cable

The first thing to do is obtain a serial null-modem cable. These can commonly be found at any computer store and generally sell for a minimal amount. You should also check the external serial ports on both computers to determine whether you require 9 or 25 pin connectors. Newer null-modem cables are sold with both 9 and 25 pin connectors on each end, so it may be desirable to purchase this kind.

Once the cable is in place, it should be tested to ensure that data can be sent from one machine to the other. Do this by first starting a communications program on the serial console of a separate system. If the machine is running Linux, minicom is a good choice, and if Windows is running, HyperTerminal is also fine.

Note: minicom may not be installed on your Linux system by default. The executable is usually /usr/bin/minicom. If you do not have it installed, most distributions include it as an optionally installed package that can be installed at any time.

Generally, the default communications settings will suffice. Next, on the source machine run the following as root assuming the null-modem cable is connected to the first serial port on the computer (/dev/ttyS0):

```
"stty speed 38400 < /dev/ttyS0 ; echo 'This should appear on the remote
machine' >/dev/ttyS0"
```

The message, "This should appear on the remote machine," should appear in the communications program on the serial console. If it does not, some things to check for are

1. The cable is in fact a null-modem cable.
2. The cable is connected to the first serial port on the server; if it isn't, change /dev/ttyS0 to /dev/ttyS1 and try again.
3. The serial console communication program is listening on the correct serial port.
4. The speed is set to 38400 on the serial console in the communications program.

7.2.4 Enabling the Serial Console at Startup

When you've verified that the serial console works, the next step is to configure Linux to send important messages over the serial connection. This is generally done by booting with an additional kernel boot parameter. The boot parameter can be typed in manually at boot time with most boot loaders, or it can be added permanently to the boot loader's configuration file. The additional parameter should look like this:

```
console=ttyS0,38400
```

Note that this shouldn't replace any existing `console=` parameter but should be inserted before them instead. It is important to maintain any existing `console=tty` parameters so as not to render the virtual consoles unusable. For my system, I use GRUB, and here's my menu.lst entry to enable the serial console:

```
title Linux
kernel (hd0,7)/boot/vmlinuz-2.4.21-99-default root=/dev/hda8 vga=0x314
splash=silent desktop hdc=ide-scsi hdclun=0 showopts console=/dev/ttyS0
console=/dev/tty0
initrd (hd0,7)/boot/initrd-2.4.21-99-default
```

After rebooting with this entry, the serial console should be set up, and some of the boot messages should appear. Note that not all boot messages appear on the serial console. When the server is booted up, be sure to enable the logging or capture feature in the communications program on the serial console to save all messages sent to it. For your reference, here's an example of the kind of log captured in a serial console that would be sent to a distribution's support team or a kernel developer (in this particular case, VMWare Inc. may also need to be contacted because the process name is vmware-vmx, but note that this does not in any way mean that there is a problem with this program):

```
Unable to handle kernel NULL pointer dereference at virtual address
➥000005e8
 printing eip: c429aa52
*pde = 00000000
Oops: 0002 2.4.21-99-default #1 Wed Sep 24 13:30:51 UTC 2003
CPU:    0
EIP:     0010:[usb-uhci:uhci_device_operations+31708122/24331932]
Tainted: PF
EIP:     0010:[<c429aa52>]    Tainted: PF
EFLAGS: 00213246
eax: 00000000   ebx: 00000001   ecx: c36a4720   edx: 00000001
esi: 00000000   edi: 00000000   ebp: c7f7fe68   esp: c7f7fe50
ds: 0018   es: 0018   ss: 0018
Process vmware-vmx (pid: 2808, stackpage=c7f7f000)
Stack: 00000000 c7f7fec8 42826000 c0ed8860 c8dc7520 fffffffea c7f7ff88
➥c429886c
       cdf9ce00 00000000 00000000 00000000 c036a2e0 c0121ce2 c0121bc9
➥00000000
       00000001 c0121992 00003046 00003046 00000001 00000000 c02e0054
➥c7f7fec8
Call  Trace:     [usb-uhci:uhci_device_operations+31699444/24340610]
➥[bh_action+66
/80] [tasklet_hi_action+57/112] [do_softirq+98/224] [do_IRQ+156/176]
Call  Trace:     [<c429886c>] [<c0121ce2>] [<c0121bc9>] [<c0121992>]
➥[<c010a1dc>]
  [call_do_IRQ+5/13] [__do_mmap_pgoff+1361/1632] [__do_mmap_pgoff+1419/
➥1632] [__
do_mmap2+88/176] [__do_mmap2+119/176] [sys_ioctl+470/618]
   [<c010c4d8>] [<c0131ab1>] [<c0131aeb>] [<c010e8d8>] [<c010e8f7>]
➥[<c0153526>]
  [sys_mmap2+35/48] [system_call+51/64]
  [<c010e993>] [<c0108dd3>]
Modules: [(vmmon:<c4298060>:<c429defc>)]
Code: 89 9e e8 05 00 00 50 50 8b 45 0c 50 57 e8 ea 0c 00 00 83 c4
<3>sr0: CDROM (ioctl) reports ILLEGAL REQUEST.
➥spurious 8259A interrupt: IRQ7.
```

7.2.5 Using SysRq Kernel Magic

The SysRq Kernel Magic hotkey provides the ability to possibly communicate with a panicked kernel to dump information such as stack tracebacks of running tasks, the current program counter (PC) location, memory status, and so on. Refer to the /proc/sys/kernel/sysrq section in Chapter 3 for a detailed discussion of how to make use of this feature.

7.2.6 Oops Reports

An Oops Report is basically just a dumping of information by the kernel when it encounters a serious problem. The problem can be a code related bug such as dereferencing a NULL pointer, accessing out of bounds memory, and so on. The Oops Report is generated by the kernel to help the end user debug, locate, and fix the problem. Sometimes when an oops occurs, the system may seem to continue running normally, but is likely to be in an unstable state. It is a good idea to save all your work and reboot as soon as possible.

To demonstrate a real live kernel oops, we modified the kernel source to allow a user to trap the kernel at will. We discuss how we did this in the section, "Adding a Manual Kernel Trap," which may be skipped if you are not interested in the somewhat simple modifications we made to the kernel. In the sections that follow it, "Examining an Oops Report" and "Determining the Failing Line of Code," we will discuss the Oops Report generated by the manual kernel trap in detail. We will also illustrate how to find the exact line of source code that caused the kernel oops solely from the Oops Report, so you may wish to read the "Adding a Manual Kernel Trap" section after reading the other two sections.

7.2.7 Adding a Manual Kernel Trap

For the purposes of easily demonstrating a kernel oops and how to examine the resulting information, we modified the kernel source code to add an interface in the /proc filesystem, which root could manipulate to force a trap in the kernel. We used the 2.6.2 kernel source downloaded directly from ftp.kernel.org on an AMD64 machine. Describing kernel source code in detail is beyond the scope of this book, but we're including details on what we did for the curious reader who may be able to use this example as a very basic primer on how to get started with the kernel source.

First, we decided on the interface we wanted to use. We decided to create a new file in the /proc filesystem called "trap_kernel." The most logical place for it is in /proc/sys/kernel, as entries in this directory are very kernel-specific. Next, we needed to find where in the kernel source the addition of this new file would happen. Using the /proc/sys/kernel/sysrq file as an example, we located the source in kernel/sysctl.c [1]. When editing this file, we first needed to add a global variable that would be the storage for the value, which /proc/sys/kernel/trap_kernel represents. This was simply a matter of adding the following with the default value of 0 to the global declaration scope of the file:

```
int trap_kernel_value = 0;
```

Next we needed a new structure that contained information for our new file. The code that we added to the kern_table array of structures is shown in bold as follows:

```
            {
                        .ctl_name       = KERN_PRINTK_RATELIMIT_BURST,
                        .procname       = "printk_ratelimit_burst",
                        .data           = &printk_ratelimit_burst,
                        .maxlen         = sizeof(int),
                        .mode           = 0644,
                        .proc_handler   = &proc_dointvec,
            },
            {
                        .ctl_name       = KERN_TRAP_KERNEL,
                        .procname       = "trap_kernel",
                        .data           = &trap_kernel_value,
                        .maxlen         = sizeof (int),
                        .mode           = 0644,
                        .proc_handler   = &proc_dointvec_trap_kernel,
            },
            { .ctl_name = 0 }
    };
```

As is shown, we set the proc_handler to proc_dointvec_trap_kernel, which is basically a customized version of the real proc_dointvec. Without going into too much detail, proc_dointvec is used to handle user manipulation of an integer-based /proc file entry. /proc/sys/kernel/sysrq and /proc/sys/kernel/shmmni are examples of interfaces that work with integers. proc_dointvec is a "wrapper" function, which simply calls do_proc_dointvec with customized parameters:

```
int proc_dointvec(ctl_table *table, int write, struct file *filp,
                  void __user *buffer, size_t *lenp)
{
    return do_proc_dointvec(table,write,filp,buffer,lenp,
                            NULL,NULL);
}
```

---

[1] When referring to kernel source files, it's common to have the pathname start at the /usr/src/linux directory. For example /usr/src/linux/kernel/sysctl.c would be commonly referred to as kernel/sysctl.c.

The next step was to add the code for our proc_dointvec_trap_kernel customized handler, as follows:

```
int proc_dointvec_trap_kernel( ctl_table *table, int write,
                               struct file *filp,
                               void __user *buffer, size_t *lenp )
{
    char c;

    if ( write )
    {
        if ( ( get_user( c, (char *)buffer ) ) == 0 )
        {
            if ( c == '9' )
            {
             printk( KERN_ERR "trap_kernel: got '9'; trapping the kernel
now\n" );
                char *trap = NULL;
                *trap = 1;
            }
            else
            {
                printk( KERN_ERR "trap_kernel: ignoring '%c'\n", c );
            }
        }
        else
        {
            printk( KERN_ERR "trap_kernel: problem getting value\n" );
        }
    }

    return do_proc_dointvec(table,write,filp,buffer,lenp,NULL,NULL);
}
```

The idea is that before calling do_proc_dointvec, we added some logic to determine if the user really is requesting a kernel trap. The logic is first to check the write flag, which is set to 1 if a write is being performed by the user, with, for example, the following command:

```
linux> echo 1 > /proc/sys/kernel/trap_kernel
```

The write flag is set to 0 if a command such as this is being run:

```
linux> cat /proc/sys/kernel/trap_kernel
```

If a write is not being performed, nothing extra is done, and the real do_proc_dointvec function is called. The kernel carries on normally and returns the value of the trap_kernel_value global variable to the user. If a write is being performed, the buffer, which is a void pointer, is converted to the char c so that it can be examined. If converting this value is successful (that is, `get_user` returns 0), we check to see if the character is the number 9, which we chose as the trigger for trapping the kernel. If the char is a 9, we log a message indicating that the kernel will be trapped and then perform a simple NULL pointer dereference.

If the char is not 9, we log the fact that we're ignoring that value in terms of trapping the system and allow the kernel to perform the write and carry on normally.

So if the user performs the following:

```
linux> echo 3 > /proc/sys/kernel/trap_kernel
```

the action will be performed without a problem, and an entry in /var/log/ messages such as the following should appear:

```
Feb 12 11:27:40 linux kernel: trap_kernel: ignoring '3'
```

If the user executes this command:

```
linux> echo 9 > /proc/sys/kernel/trap_kernel
```

an Oops should immediately happen, which we will discuss in the next section.

7.2.8 Examining an Oops Report

Examining an Oops Report is not an exact science and requires a bit of ingenuity and experience. To know the basic steps to take and to understand how things generally work is a great start and is the goal of this section. The oops dumps are a little different between 2.4.x and 2.6.x kernels.

7.2.8.1 2.6.x Kernel Oops Dumps Oops dumps in a 2.6.x kernel can usually be examined as is without the need to process them through ksymoops, as is needed for 2.4.x oops. The /proc/sys/kernel/trap_kernel "feature" we added to manually force a kernel oops results in the oops dump shown as follows:

```
Oops: 0002 [1]
CPU 0
Pid: 2680, comm: bash Not tainted
RIP:                              0010:[<ffffffff8013ae64>]
<ffffffff8013ae64>{proc_dointvec_trap_kernel+84}
RSP: 0018:00000100111c9ea8  EFLAGS: 00010216
RAX: 0000000000000031 RBX: 00000100111c8000 RCX: ffffffff80413210
RDX: 0000010011cd9280 RSI: ffffffff80413970 RDI: 0000000000000000
```

```
RBP: 0000002a95e59000 R08: 0000000000000033 R09: 000001001f57dbc0
R10: 0000000000000000 R11: 0000000000000175 R12: 0000000000000001
R13: 00000100111c9ee8 R14: 000001001115b980 R15: ffffffff803a1390
FS:      00000000005614a0(0000)  GS:ffffffff8045bc40(0000)
knlGS:0000000000000000
CS:  0010 DS: 0000 ES: 0000 CR0: 000000008005003b
CR2: 0000000000000000 CR3: 0000000000101000 CR4: 00000000000006a0
Process bash (pid: 2680, stackpage=10011cda280)
Stack:  0000002a95e59000  0000000000000002  ffffffff803a1390
000001001115b980
         0000000000000002  0000000000000001  0000002a95e59000
ffffffff8013a6e8
      0000000000000002 0000000000000000
Call          Trace:<ffffffff8013a6e8>{do_rw_proc+168}
<ffffffff8016baf4>{vfs_write+228}  <ffffffff8016bc09>{sys_write+73}
<ffffffff80111830>{system_call+124}

Code: c6 04 25 00 00 00 00 01 eb 23 66 90 0f be f2 48 c7 c7 c0 9f
RIP <ffffffff8013ae64>{proc_dointvec_trap_kernel+84} RSP
<00000100111c9ea8>
CR2: 0000000000000000
```

The dump was taken directly from /var/log/messages, and we manually removed the preceding `<timestamp>` `<hostname>` `kernel:` markings on each line for easier reading.

If you didn't skip the "Adding a Manual Kernel Trap" section, the problem shown by the Oops Report will probably seem pretty obvious. But let's pretend that we have no idea where this trap came from and it's something that needs to be fixed.

Let's first analyze the first line:

```
Oops: 0002 [1]
```

Initially, this looks really cryptic and useless, but it actually contains a great deal of information! To begin with, we know that we're in an oops situation, meaning that the kernel has encountered an unexpected problem. The "0002" that follows "Oops:" is a hexadecimal number that represents the *page fault error code*. By decoding this, we can determine exactly what the error condition was. To decode it, we first need to convert it to binary—hexadecimal 2 is binary 10. Now we need to compare this value against Table 7.1 to decode the meaning.

Bit	Value	
	0	**1**
0	No page found	Protection fault
1	Read	Write
2	Kernel-mode	User-mode
3[2]	Fault was not an instruction fetch	Fault was an instruction fetch

Table 7.1 Page Fault Error Codes.

Using Table 7.1, we know that binary 10 means that no page was found, a write was attempted in kernel-mode, and the fault was not due to an instruction fetch (remember that this Oops Report was taken from an AMD64 machine). So from this information we know that a page was not found when doing a write operation within the kernel.

The next piece of information on the first line is the [1]. This is the *die counter* that basically keeps track of the number of oopses that have occurred since the last reboot. In our case, this is the first oops we've encountered.

The next line is CPU 0 and indicates which CPU performed the instruction that caused the fault. In this case, my system only has one CPU, so 0 is the only possible value. The next line is:

```
Pid: 2680, comm: bash Not tainted
```

The Pid indicates which user-land process ID initiated the problem, and comm: tells us that the process name was bash. This makes sense because the command I issued was redirecting the output of an echo command, which is all handled by the shell. Not tainted tells us that our kernel has not been tainted by any modules not under the GPL and/or forcefully loaded. The next line in the oops dump is:

```
RIP:                          0010:[<ffffffff8013ae64>]
<ffffffff8013ae6>{proc_dointvec_trap_kernel+84}
```

RIP is the name of the instruction pointer on the AMD64 architecture. On 32-bit x86 systems, it is called the *EIP* instead and, of course, is 32 bits long rather than 64 bits long. (Though it somewhat fits in this situation to have RIP stand for *Rest In Peace*, this is *not* the intended meaning here.) The "0010" is a

[2] Bit 3 is defined on the x86-64 architecture but not on the i386 architecture.

dumping of the CS register. The dumping of the CS register shows us that the current privilege level (CPL) was 0. This number corresponds to which permission or *ring level* the trap occurred in.

Note: Ring level is a term used to refer to what permissions code has when running on a CPU. Ring 0 has unlimited access, therefore kernel mode runs at ring 0. Ring level 3 is for user mode processes. On Linux, ring levels 1 and 2 are unused.

The `[<ffffffff8013ae64>]` is a dumping of the RIP register. This means that the instruction pointer was pointing to the instruction at memory address `0xffffffff8013ae64` at the time the trap occurred. Note the RIP address is printed out again by another function, which the kernel calls to perform more work.

The `{proc_dointvec_trap_kernel+84}` is the result of the kernel translating the RIP address into a more human readable format. `proc_dointvec_trap_kernel` is the name of the function in which the RIP lies. The `+84` means that the RIP is at an offset of decimal 84 into the `proc_dointvec_trap_kernel` function. This value is extremely useful in determining exactly what caused the trap, as we shall see in the "Determining the Failing Line of Code" section.

The next several lines are a dumping of the registers and their contents:

```
RSP: 0018:00000100111c9ea8  EFLAGS: 00010216
RAX: 0000000000000031 RBX: 00000100111c8000 RCX: ffffffff80413210
RDX: 0000010011cd9280 RSI: ffffffff80413970 RDI: 0000000000000000
RBP: 0000002a95e59000 R08: 0000000000000033 R09: 000001001f57dbc0
R10: 0000000000000000 R11: 0000000000000175 R12: 0000000000000001
R13: 00000100111c9ee8 R14: 000001001115b980 R15: ffffffff803a1390
FS:     00000000005614a0(0000)   GS:ffffffff8045bc40(0000)
knlGS:0000000000000000
CS:  0010 DS: 0000 ES: 0000 CR0: 000000008005003b
CR2: 0000000000000000 CR3: 0000000000101000 CR4: 00000000000006a0
```

Describing each register in detail and what it is used for is beyond the scope of this book[3]. It suffices to say for now that the values stored in the registers could be very useful when examining the assembly code surrounding the trapping instruction.

The next line of interest is

---

[3] For detailed information on the registers, I recommend reading the AMD64 Architecture Manuals found at AMD's Web site. Similarly for other architectures, manuals describing detailed hardware information can usually be found at the vendor's Web site.

```
Process bash (pid: 2680, stackpage=10011cda280)
```

The `Process bash (pid: 2680` is a reiteration of what was dumped on the third line. `stackpage=10011cda280` shows us the kernel stack page that is involved in this process.

The next few lines dump out a predefined number of 64-bit words from the stack. In the case of AMD64, this number is set to 10.

```
Stack:  0000002a95e59000  0000000000000002  ffffffff803a1390
000001001115b980
            0000000000000002  0000000000000001  0000002a95e59000
ffffffff8013a6e8
          0000000000000002 0000000000000000
```

The values are not too important at first glance. Depending on the assembly instructions surrounding the trap and the context of the particular problem, the values shown here may be needed. They are basically dumped here with an "in case they're needed" purpose. The next lines in the oops dump that are of interest are:

```
Call          Trace:<ffffffff8013a6e8>{do_rw_proc+168}
<ffffffff8016baf4>{vfs_write+228}
                      <ffffffff8016bc09>{sys_write+73}
<ffffffff80111830>{system_call+124}
```

`Call Trace` shows a list of the last few functions that were called before the trap occurred. Now we know that the execution path looked like what is shown in Figure 7.1.

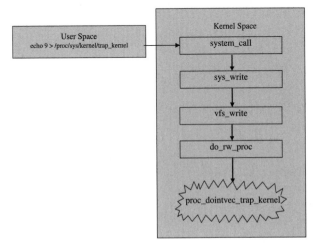

Fig. 7-1 Call trace in kernel.

7.2.9 Determining the Failing Line of Code

Now that we know a bit more about the trap and the characteristics of it, we need to know what actually caused it. In almost all cases, the cause is a programming error, so the key to answering that question is first knowing where in the source code the problem occurs. We know the function name, and we know the offset of assembly instructions into that function, so the first step is to find where the function `proc_dointvec_trap_kernel` is defined. Rather than scouring through the hundreds of source files that comprise the Linux kernel, using a tool called *cscope* is far easier (see the "Setting up cscope to Index Kernel Sources" section for more information). Plugging the trapping function name into `Find this C symbol:` we get the screen shown in Figure 7.2.

If you read the "Adding a Manual Kernel Trap" section, the results just shown will be very familiar. By typing "0," "1," or "2," the respective file will be loaded and the cursor position will be pointed directly at the proc_dointvec_trap_kernel symbol. For now, we just wanted to find out what source file the function appeared in. We now know that it is /usr/src/linux-2.6.2-2/kernel/sysctl.c.

Now we need to somehow translate the offset into the function of decimal 84 into a source line in the function in sysctl.c.

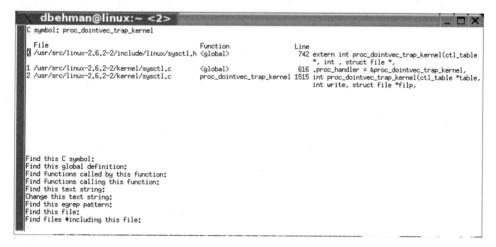

Fig. 7.2 cscope of kernel code.

First we have to get debug symbols built into the sysctl.o object. For the 2.6.x kernel source, do this with the following set of steps.

1. **cd /usr/src/linux-2.6.2**
   Everything we'll do here must be run out of the top level of the kernel source tree.

2. **rm kernel/sysctl.o**
   Removing this file forces it to be recompiled.

3. **export CONFIG_DEBUG_INFO=1**
   Searching /usr/src/linux-2.6.2/Makefile for CONFIG_DEBUG_INFO shows that if this is set, the `-g` compile flag will be added to the compilation.

4. **make kernel/sysctl.o**
   This will recompile the sysctl.c file with the `-g` parameter included.

5. If you happened to notice the size of sysctl.o before and after performing the steps here, you'll notice it's now much larger. This is expected because it should now contain several extra debug symbols.

6. Now for the critical part of converting the object file (sysctl.o) into a listing of assembly instructions mixed with the C source code. This is accomplished with the `objdump` command. Run it like this:

   ```
   objdump -d -S kernel/sysctl.o > kernel/sysctl.dump
   ```

   > **Note**: As documented in the `objdump(1)` manpage, the `-d` option will disassemble the object, and the `-s` option will intermix high-level source code with assembly if possible.

We're now ready to examine the assembly/source dump file and search for our decimal 84 offset. First open sysctl.dump created by the `objdump` command and search for the beginning of the `proc_dointvec_trap_kernel` function. It will look something like the following:

```
0000000000000fb0 <proc_dointvec_trap_kernel>:

int proc_dointvec_trap_kernel(ctl_table *table, int write, struct file
➡*filp,
                    void __user *buffer, size_t *lenp)
{
    fb0:        48 83 ec 38             sub     $0x38,%rsp
    char c;

    if ( write )
```

```
fb4:        85 f6                   test    %esi,%esi
fb6:        48 89 6c 24 10          mov     %rbp,0x10(%rsp,1)
fbb:        4c 89 64 24 18          mov     %r12,0x18(%rsp,1)
fc0:        4c 89 6c 24 20          mov     %r13,0x20(%rsp,1)
fc5:        4c 89 74 24 28          mov     %r14,0x28(%rsp,1)
```

As is shown here, the start of the function is at offset hexadecimal fb0. Because offsets are referenced in hex, we need to convert the decimal 84 to hex, which is 0x54. Next we add 0x54 to 0xfb0 to find the location reported in the oops dump. The offset we need to look for in sysctl.dump is 0x1004.

Tip: A quick way of doing calculations on a Linux machine is to run "gdb" and enter commands such as print 324 * 434. To do hex calculations, use a command such as print /x 0x54 + 0xfb0. Also note that print can be shortened to p.

Offset 0x1004 in sysctl.dump is shown as follows:

```
        {
            if ( ( get_user( c, (char *)buffer ) ) == 0 )
        fe5:        48 89 c8              mov     %rcx,%rax
        fe8:        e8 00 00 00 00       callq   fed
➡<proc_dointvec_trap_kernel+0x3d>
        fed:        85 c0                test    %eax,%eax
        fef:        75 32                jne     1023
➡<proc_dointvec_trap_kernel+0x73>
            {
                if ( c == '9' )
        ff1:        80 fa 39             cmp     $0x39,%dl
        ff4:        75 1a                jne     1010
➡<proc_dointvec_trap_kernel+0x60>
                {
                    printk( KERN_ERR "trap_kernel: got '9'; trapping the
➡kernel now\n" );
        ff6:        48 c7 c7 00 00 00 00 mov     $0x0,%rdi
        ffd:        31 c0                xor     %eax,%eax
        fff:        e8 00 00 00 00       callq   1004
➡<proc_dointvec_trap_kernel+0x54>
                    char *trap = NULL;
                    *trap = 1;
        1004:       c6 04 25 00 00 00 00 movb    $0x1,0x0
        100b:       01
        100c:       eb 23                jmp     1031
➡<proc_dointvec_trap_kernel+0x81>
        100e:       66                   data16
        100f:       90                   nop
                }
            else
```

```
            {
                printk( KERN_ERR "trap_kernel: ignoring '%c'\n", c );
     1010:          0f be f2                movsbl %dl,%esi
     1013:          48 c7 c7 00 00 00 00    mov    $0x0,%rdi
     101a:          31 c0                   xor    %eax,%eax
```

Looking at offset `0x1004`, we see the assembly instruction `movb $0x1, 0x0`, which means to store the value `1` into the memory address `0x0`. On x86 and AMD64 hardware, this produces a page fault that results in the trap we observed.

Immediately above the assembly instruction is the C source code that resulted in the generation of this assembly instruction.

```
     char *trap = NULL;
     *trap = 1;
```

This code is a blatant example of the classic NULL pointer dereferencing programming error. We've found the cause of the trap! Of course, this is the code I added as discussed in the "Adding a Manual Kernel Trap" section.

Determining the line of code does not always go this smoothly. Occasionally, the calculated offset is nowhere to be found in the disassembled object output. One of the main reasons for this is the use of a different version of the compiler to generate the listing than was used to originally compile the object in which the oops occurred. It is extremely important to use the exact same compiler version. Different versions of a compiler, even minor release changes, can and will change the ordering of the assembly instructions. Different optimization levels and/or options will also change the generated assembly, even when the same compiler level is used. At the assembly level, a single different or relocated instruction will make definitively locating the trapping instruction very difficult. With some ingenuity, though, even if the compiler levels are slightly different, one can get close enough to the trapping area of code to discover the fault.

7.2.9.1 2.4.x Kernel Oops Dumps

Analyzing kernel oops dumps in a Linux 2.4.x kernel is slightly different from doing so in a 2.6.x kernel. The main reason for this is the addition of the *kallsyms* feature/patch to the 2.6 mainline kernel source. The kallsyms feature provides a listing of all kernel symbols that the kernel itself can use to translate a hexadecimal address into a human readable symbol name.

Note that many 2.4-based distributions have backported the kallsyms feature to their customized 2.4-based kernels. This means that if an oops occurs in these distributions, the dumped data is automatically formatted. If your distribution does not have the kallsyms patch or you are running a 2.4.x kernel as downloaded from `kernel.org`, you will need to manually format the oops message before it is useful to anyone. To do this, run the utility *ksymoops* with the appropriate parameters as documented in the ksymoops(8) man page.

7.2.10 Kernel Oopses and Hardware

A kernel oops does not always mean that a software error was found in the kernel. In fact, hardware actually fails quite often, so it should never be ruled out as the possible cause of an oops. The question then becomes how does one determine if the oops is caused by faulty hardware. Here are some clues that can point to faulty hardware:

☞ Oopses occurring in places where it is almost impossible for them to occur in after examining the source code around the trap.

☞ Recurring oopses that don't always happen in the same place. Software bugs are almost always reproducible, but faulty hardware, especially bad RAM, can cause strange things to happen in seemingly random places.

☞ Sudden start of oopses. If the operating system has been running fine with little or no changes to it, and oopses all of a sudden start occurring.

☞ Hard machine lockups where nothing is displayed to the screen, SysRq magic hotkey does nothing, and only a hard reboot can be done.

If the hardware is suspected, tests should be performed immediately starting with the RAM, unless there is reason to suspect some other piece of hardware. Many servers have built in diagnostic programs that can be accessed from the BIOS menu. These should be run first. Soft ware testing programs such as memtest86 (available at `www.memtest86.org`) should also be run to examine the RAM.

Note: memtest86 is historically meant for 32-bit x86-based hardware. The need for the support of this software on AMD64 hardware was great, and this was one of the reasons for the spin-off creation of memtest86+ (available at `www.memtest.org`). memtest86+ fully supports all AMD Opteron chips.

The fsck (file system check) utility should also be run on all hard drive partitions to which the server has access. Sometimes a corruption can occur on a filesystem, which can lead to corruption in libraries or executables. This corruption can lead to instructions within the code becoming scrambled, therefore resulting in very bad things happening. The fsck utility will detect and fix any corruptions that may exist.

7.2.11 Setting up cscope to Index Kernel Sources

Most Linux distributions include the cscope package. If your distribution does not, you can easily locate it for download on the Internet. cscope is a utility that scans through a defined set of source code files and builds a single index file. You can then use the cscope interface to search for function, variable, and macro definitions, listings of which functions call a particular function, listings of what files include a particular header file, and more. It's an extremely useful tool, and we highly recommend setting it up if you plan on looking through any amount of kernel source. It isn't just limited to indexing kernel source; you can set it up to "scope" through any set of source files you wish!

Before running cscope to retrieve symbol information, a symbols database must be built. Assuming your kernel source tree is in /usr/src/linux-2.6.2, the following command will create the symbols database in the file /usr/src/linux-2.6.2/cscope.out:

```
find /usr/src/linux-2.6.2 \( -name "[A-Za-z]*.[CcHh]" -o -name "*.[ch]pp"
-o -name "*.[CH]PP" -o -name "*.skl"   -o -name "*.java" \) -print |
cscope -bku -f /usr/src/linux-2.6.2/cscope.out -i -
```

The cscope parameters to take note of are -b for build the symbol database (or *cross-reference* as it is referred to in the man page) and -k for "kernel mode," which ensures that the proper include files are scoured.

Once the database is built, searching it is simply a matter of running this command:

```
cscope -d -P /usr/src/linux-2.6.2 -p 20 -f /usr/src/linux-2.6.2/
↪cscope.out
```

The following simple Korn Shell script can be used to handle all of this for you.

```
#!/bin/ksh
#
# Simple script to handle building and querying a cscope database for
# kernel source with support for multiple databases.

build=0
dbpath="linux"
force=0

function usage {
   echo "Usage: kscope [-build [-force]] [-dbpath <path>]"
}

while [ $# -gt 0 ]; do
   if [ "$1" = "-build" ]; then
```

```
        build=1
    elif [ "$1" = "-dbpath" ]; then
        shift
        dbpath=$1
    elif [ "$1" = "-force" ]; then
        force=1
    else
        usage
        exit 1
    fi
    shift
done

if [ $build -eq 1 ]; then
    if [ -f "/usr/src/$dbpath/cscope.out" -a $force -ne 1 ]; then
        echo "cscope database already exists.  Use '-force' to overwrite."
        exit 1
    fi
    echo "Building /usr/src/$dbpath/cscope.out ..."
    find /usr/src/$dbpath \( -name "[A-Za-z]*.[CcHh]" -o -name "*.[ch]pp"
-o -name "*.[CH]PP" -o -name "*.skl"   -o -name "*.java" \) -print |
cscope -bku -f /usr/src/$dbpath/cscope.out -i -
    echo "Done."
else
    if [ ! -f "/usr/src/$dbpath/cscope.out" ]; then
        echo "cscope database (/usr/src/$dbpath/cscope.out) not found."
        exit 1
    fi
    cscope -d -P /usr/src/$dbpath -p 20 -f /usr/src/$dbpath/cscope.out
➡fi
```

7.3 CONCLUSION

Unfortunately, system crashes and hangs do happen. With the knowledge and tools presented in this chapter, you should be armed with the capability to at least know where to gather the diagnostic data needed for others to analyze and determine the cause of the problem. You can use the tips and suggestions presented in Chapter 1, "Best Practices and Initial Investigation" in conjunction with the information in this chapter to most efficiently and effectively get a solution to your problem.

For the more advanced or curious reader, this chapter presents sufficient information for one to dive deeply into the problem in an attempt to solve it without help from others. This is not always the best approach depending on your situation, so caution should be exercised. In either case, with the right tools and knowledge, dealing with system problems on Linux can be much easier than on other operating systems.

Kernel Debugging with KDB

8.1 INTRODUCTION

Having the ability to examine kernel processes and memory in real-time is extremely important to a kernel developer. It isn't quite as important to application developers or system administrators, but there are occasions when obtaining specific kernel data can be critical to resolving difficult problems. For this reason, this section offers an introduction to the basics of how to get KDB installed and running and the very basics of using it. It is an extremely powerful tool, and in-depth information on it is beyond the scope of this book. There are many resources available on the Internet and in print that can be referred to for further information.

KDB is not the only kernel debugger available for Linux—KGDB is also commonly used. Each has its own strengths and weaknesses, and many people prefer one over the other. The main difference is that KGDB actually uses GDB to debug the kernel; however, it must be done from a remote computer and cannot be done on the live machine. KDB provides kernel debugging capabilities directly on the live kernel while it is running and can also be used remotely. Given that using KGDB is the same as GDB, one can learn how to use it by referring to Chapter 6, "The GNU Debugger."

8.2 ENABLING KDB

KDB is not part of the mainstream kernel source code found at `kernel.org`. It is, however, included in the kernels that come with some of the major distributions. If you are not using a distribution kernel, the patch for KDB can be obtained from the KDB homepage at `http://oss.sgi.com/projects/kdb/`. Even though KDB is included in some distributions, it is very likely not enabled by default and requires a kernel rebuild. It is quite easy to enable—simply set the CONFIG_KDB configuration option manually or through your favorite `make config` interface and rebuild the kernel. Figure 8.1 shows the option highlighted and enabled in the "Kernel hacking" menu when using the `make menuconfig` interface.

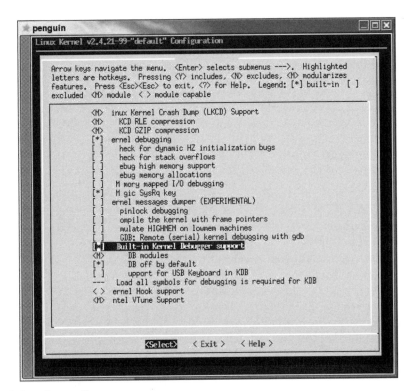

Fig. 8.1 make config menu.

Another option of interest is KDB off by default. The help text for this option documents what it does:

CONFIG_KDB_OFF:
Normally kdb is activated by default, as long as CONFIG_KDB is set. If you want to ship a kernel with kdb support but only have kdb turned on when the user requests it then select this option. When compiled with CONFIG_KDB_OFF, kdb ignores all events unless you boot with kdb=on or you echo "1" > /proc/sys/kernel/kdb. This option also works in reverse;, if kdb is normally activated, you can boot with kdb=off or echo "0" > /proc/sys/kernel/kdb to deactivate kdb. If unsure, say N.

If you want to use KDB to debug a real problem or just experiment with it, enable CONFIG_KDB_OFF. This way, KDB will only be turned on when you explicitly want it.

8.3 USING KDB

The following sections give a very high-level overview of how to use KDB once
it is installed on your system.

> **Warning:** KDB should be thought of as "open-brain surgery." It
> basically lifts the hood off of your computer and gives you complete access
> and control of the brains of your operating system. Just as in open-brain
> surgery, any wrong move can kill the patient—in this case, the patient is
> your operating system. Please exercise caution.

8.3.1 Activating KDB

If you use the X Windows system, be sure to first switch to a text virtual console
by using the CTRL-ALT-Fn key sequence. Once at a text virtual console, log in
as root and enable KDB by executing the following command:

```
echo 1 > /proc/sys/kernel/kdb
```

You are now ready to enter kernel debugging mode by pressing the hotkey
which is the *Pause / Break* key.

> **Note**: When KDB is enabled it will automatically be invoked during
> a system panic.

When you press the hotkey, you will see the following:

```
penguin:/proc/sys/kernel #
Entering kdb (current=0xc03dc000, pid 0) due to Keyboard Entry
```

> **Note**: When you are in KDB you may notice that your caps and
> scroll lock LEDs flash rapidly. This is normal.
>
> **Note**: Interrupts and the machine clock tick are disabled while in
> KDB so your computer's system time will appear to have stopped for the
> time spent in KDB. This in itself shows how intrusive KDB really is to a
> system!

8.3.2 Resuming Normal Execution

Because being in KDB is such a sensitive mode, let's immediately document how to get out of KDB and return your computer back to normal operation. Use the `go` command for this. You may need to press the enter key a few times to get your shell prompt back.

> **Note**: After returning your computer to normal execution, you may notice that the caps and/or scroll lock LEDs mismatch what the kernel sees them as. Pressing the mismatched lock key one or two times should correct this.

8.3.3 Basic Commands

The first thing to familiarize yourself with in KDB is the Help screen. You can display this by entering either the `?` or `help` commands. The contents of the Help display are shown here:

```
kdb> ?
Command         Usage                   Description

md              <vaddr>                 Display Memory Contents,
                                        also mdWcN, e.g. md8c1
mdr             <vaddr> <bytes>         Display Raw Memory
mds             <vaddr>                 Display Memory Symbolically
mm              <vaddr> <contents>      Modify Memory Contents
id              <vaddr>                 Display Instructions
go              [<vaddr>]               Continue Execution
rd                                      Display Registers
rm              <reg> <contents>        Modify Registers
ef              <vaddr>                 Display exception frame
bt              [<vaddr>]               Stack traceback
btp             <pid>                   Display stack for process <pid>
bta                                     Display stack all processes
ll              <first-element>         <lin Execute cmd for each
                                        ↳element in linked list
env                                     Show environment variables
set                                     Set environment variables
help                                    Display Help Message
?                                       Display Help Message
cpu             <cpunum>                Switch to new cpu
ps                                      Display active task list
reboot                                  Reboot the machine immediately
sections                                List kernel and module sections
lsmod                                   List loaded kernel modules
rmmod           <modname>               Remove a kernel module
```

```
sr               <key>              Magic SysRq key
dmesg                               Display syslog buffer
bp               [<vaddr>]          Set/Display breakpoints
bl               [<vaddr>]          Display breakpoints
bpa              [<vaddr>]          Set/Display global breakpoints
bph              [<vaddr>]          Set hardware breakpoint
bpha             [<vaddr>]          Set global hardware breakpoint
bc               <bpnum>            Clear Breakpoint
be               <bpnum>            Enable Breakpoint
bd               <bpnum>            Disable Breakpoint
ss                                  Single Step
ssb                                 Single step to branch/call
```

KDB has a large command set and is capable of doing a great deal of valuable debugging operations. The intent here is not to go into detail on what everything does; rather the intent is to help you get KDB running and to give a quick overview on some of the more straightforward commands.

The ps command is similar to the user-land command; however, in KDB it displays the task list from the kernel's viewpoint rather than the process listing from a user's viewpoint.

```
kdb> ps
Task Addr   Pid        Parent      [*] cpu  State Thread      Command
0xcdfa2000  00000001   00000000    0   000  stop  0xcdfa2280  init
0xc1c14000  00000002   00000001    0   000  stop  0xc1c14280  keventd
0xc1c10000  00000003   00000001    0   000  stop  0xc1c10280  kapmd
0xcdffe000  00000004   00000001    0   000  stop  0xcdffe280  ksoftirqd_CPU0
0xcdffc000  00000005   00000001    0   000  stop  0xcdffc280  kswapd
0xcdf66000  00000006   00000001    0   000  stop  0xcdf66280  bdflush
0xcdf64000  00000007   00000001    0   000  stop  0xcdf64280  kupdated
0xcdf60000  00000008   00000001    0   000  stop  0xcdf60280  kinoded
0xcdf0a000  00000009   00000001    0   000  stop  0xcdf0a280  mdrecoveryd
0xc2284000  00000012   00000001    0   000  stop  0xc2284280  kreiserfsd
0xc2ae0000  00000869   00000001    0   000  stop  0xc2ae0280  dhcpcd
0xc2a70000  00001040   00000001    0   000  stop  0xc2a70280  syslogd
0xc2a6c000  00001043   00000001    0   000  stop  0xc2a6c280  klogd
0xc2992000  00001102   00000001    0   000  stop  0xc2992280  khubd
0xc2ffc000  00001268   00000001    0   000  stop  0xc2ffc280  resmgrd
0xc2dea000  00001335   00000001    0   000  stop  0xc2dea280  cardmgr
0xc2d7c000  00001435   00000001    0   000  stop  0xc2d7c280  portmap
0xc2d0c000  00001466   00000001    0   000  stop  0xc2d0c280  vmnet-bridge
0xc2cd8000  00001489   00000001    0   000  stop  0xc2cd8280  vmnet-natd
0xc33e6000  00001829   00000001    0   000  stop  0xc33e6280  smpppd
0xc2c9e000  00001831   00000001    0   000  stop  0xc2c9e280  sshd
```

I've truncated the output, as it will display all kernel and user tasks running on the system.

Notice how all Task Addr and Thread addresses are above the 0xc0000000 memory location. As was discussed in the "/proc/<pid>/maps" section of Chapter

3, "The /proc Filesystem," in a 3:1 split address space, the kernel resides at
`0xc0000000`. This proves to us that we are in fact seeing pointers to kernel data
structures.

Let's have a closer look at the main process of a Linux system - `init`.
First, let's take a look at its stack (the format of the output is slightly modified
for easier reading):

```
kdb> btp 1
0xcdfa2000 00000001 00000000   0   000   stop   0xcdfa2280 init
ESP        EIP          Function (args)
0xcdfa3ecc 0xc0119e62 do_schedule+0x192 (0xc0421bbc, 0xc0421bbc,0x8f5908,
➥0xcdfa2000, 0xc01258c0)
➥kernel .text 0xc0100000 0xc0119cd0
       0xc011a040
0xcdfa3ef0 0xc0125933 schedule_timeout+0x63 (0x104, 0xcdfa2000, 0x1388,
0x0, 0x0)
                kernel .text 0xc0100000 0xc01258d0
                        0xc0125980
0xcdfa3f1c 0xc01548e1 do_select+0x1e1 (0xb, 0xcdfa3f90, 0xcdfa3f8c,0x1,
0x4)
                kernel .text 0xc0100000 0xc0154700
                        0xc0154930
0xcdfa3f58 0xc0154c88 sys_select+0x328 (0xb, 0xbffff720, 0x0, 0x0,
0xbffff658)
                kernel .text 0xc0100000 0xc0154960
                        0xc0154e30
0xcdfa3fc4 0xc0108dd3 system_call+0x33
        kernel .text 0xc0100000 0xc0108da0
                0xc0108de0
```

All of the functions in the stack traceback are kernel functions. Without knowing
a great deal about kernel programming, we can see that at the time KDB was
invoked, init was in the middle of processing a `select()` system call from user-
land. This conclusion can be made because of the `do_select` stack frame. Most
system calls have a kernel worker routine named after the system call with
`do_` prefixed to it. The `schedule_timeout` and `do_schedule` stack frames are
functions that `do_select` called to have this process wait for communication to
occur.

Let's now see what init will do when KDB is resumed. To do this, we can
examine the assembly instructions starting at init's current eip of `0xc0119e62`:

```
kdb> id 0xc0119e62
0xc0119e62 do_schedule+0x192:   pop    %ebp
0xc0119e63 do_schedule+0x193:   pop    %edi
0xc0119e64 do_schedule+0x194:   pop    %esi
0xc0119e65 do_schedule+0x195:   push   %esi
0xc0119e66 do_schedule+0x196:   call   0xc0119790 schedule_tail
0xc0119e6b do_schedule+0x19b:   pop    %ebx
```

```
0xc0119e6c do_schedule+0x19c:    mov    $0xffffe000,%eax
0xc0119e71 do_schedule+0x1a1:    and    %esp,%eax
0xc0119e73 do_schedule+0x1a3:    mov    0x14(%eax),%eax
0xc0119e76 do_schedule+0x1a6:    test   %eax,%eax
0xc0119e78 do_schedule+0x1a8:    je     0xc0119fe7 do_schedule+0x317
0xc0119e7e do_schedule+0x1ae:    mov    0xc0422324,%eax
0xc0119e83 do_schedule+0x1b3:    mov    $0xffffe000,%esi
0xc0119e88 do_schedule+0x1b8:    and    %esp,%esi
0xc0119e8a do_schedule+0x1ba:    mov    %eax,0x3c(%esi)
0xc0119e8d do_schedule+0x1bd:    cli
kdb> go
```

The most interesting thing here is that there will be a call to `schedule_tail` very shortly. Looking directly at `do_schedule` in the kernel source, there is only one call to `schedule_tail` in it, so we can make a very good guess which source code init is executing. The `do_schedule` function is rather large, so only a snippet of it is shown with the call to `schedule_tail` bolded:

```
switch_tasks:
        prefetch(next);
        rq->quiescent++;
        clear_tsk_need_resched(prev);

        if (likely(prev != next)) {
          rq->nr_switches++;
                rq->curr = next;

                prepare_arch_switch(rq, next);
                prev = context_switch(rq, prev, next);
                barrier();
                /* from this point "rq" is invalid in the stack */
                schedule_tail(prev);
        } else
                spin_unlock_irq(&rq->lock);
```

So from some quick commands in KDB, we can very quickly see exactly what a process is doing in the kernel. We can also make a good guess as to what the user-land process was doing as well.

Let's take a quick look at one more process that is more familiar to every user—a bash process. The following is a stack traceback listing of a running bash shell. The format of the output is again modified for easier readability:

```
kdb> btp 2571
0xc5758000 00002571 00002419  0  000   stop  0xc5758280 bash
ESP        EIP        Function (args)
0xc5759eac 0xc0119e62 do_schedule+0x192
                kernel .text 0xc0100000 0xc0119cd0
                                  0xc011a040
0xc5759ed0 0xc012597a schedule_timeout+0xaa (0xc2c19800, 0x246, 0x0,
```

```
                          0x286, 0x0)
                              kernel .text 0xc0100000 0xc01258d0
                                        0xc0125980
0xc5759ed8 0xc01cbbb1 set_cursor+0x61 (0xc2791000, 0xc3167ba0,
                   0xbffff46b, 0x1, 0xc3167ba0)
                              kernel .text 0xc0100000 0xc01cbb50
                                        0xc01cbbd0
0xc5759f84 0xc01bea4f tty_read+0x8f (0xc3167ba0, 0xbffff46b, 0x1,
                   0xc3167bc0, 0xc5758000)
                              kernel .text 0xc0100000 0xc01be9c0
                                        0xc01bea70
0xc5759fa0 0xc0144b88 sys_read+0x88 (0x0, 0xbffff46b, 0x1,
                   0x401d2c20, 0xbffff46b)
                              kernel .text 0xc0100000 0xc0144b00
                                        0xc0144c00
0xc5759fc4 0xc0108dd3 system_call+0x33
                              kernel .text 0xc0100000 0xc0108da0
                                        0xc0108de0
```

From this we can tell that the shell was executing a read system call, which makes sense because the bash shell was simply sitting at a prompt when KDB was entered. This conclusion is drawn by seeing sys_read, which was called by system_call in the stack traceback.

Occasionally, user-land debugging and diagnostic tools are unable to provide sufficient information about a process that is experiencing difficulty. For example, sometimes attaching strace to a process that appears to be hung may not reveal anything. This can indicate that the process is stuck in the kernel, perhaps waiting for a resource or another process. This is where observing the stacktrace and assembly instructions of the process in KDB can be most useful.

Another task commonly performed in debuggers is to display the current contents of the registers. In KDB, this is done with the rd command as shown here:

```
kdb> rd
eax = 0x089b1430 ebx = 0x41513020 ecx = 0x41513860 edx = 0x41513758
esi = 0x0000000e edi = 0x00000011 esp = 0xbfffef40 eip = 0x085bdb3d
ebp = 0xbfffef88 xss = 0x0000002b xcs = 0x00000023 eflags = 0x00000202
xds = 0x0000002b xes = 0x0000002b origeax = 0xffffff01 &regs = 0xc346ffc4
```

These values are meaningful only to the process the kernel is currently executing. One interesting observation is that the instruction pointer, eip, contains a value that is relatively close to executables' base address of 0x08048000. This generally means that code from an executable rather than a library is currently being run.

8.4 CONCLUSION

KDB is not for the novice user—nor, however, is it exclusively for kernel developers and kernel experts. As demonstrated in this chapter, even without an in-depth understanding of the kernel, KDB can be useful in determining system problems. Great care, though, must be exercised when using it.

CHAPTER **9**

ELF: Executable and Linking Format

9.1 INTRODUCTION

The ELF file format is the default format for shared libraries and executables on today's Linux systems. ELF stands for Executable and Linking Format and is the most common file format for object files, executables, and shared libraries on Linux as well as some other popular operating systems. A good understanding of ELF will improve your overall knowledge of how the operating system works, which in turn will help you diagnose problems faster.

A good knowledge of ELF will also directly improve your diagnostic skills given that many in-depth problems require a reasonable knowledge of ELF. For example, in some cases, a program may have more than one global symbol (for example, a variable) with the same name. Different parts of the program may access the correct variable; whereas, other parts of the program may incorrectly access the other. This type of problem can be very difficult to diagnose without a basic understanding of ELF and the run time linker. There are also some useful debugging tricks that require a good understanding of ELF. One such trick is to build an interceptor library for operating system (or libc) functions such as `malloc` and `free`. The end of this chapter has some examples.

> **Note**: The purpose of this chapter is to provide enough knowledge about ELF to help you improve your diagnostic skills. This chapter is not meant to replace or supplement the ELF standard but rather provide practical knowledge about ELF on Linux. Instead of walking through the ELF standard, this chapter will provide real examples and explain how things work under the covers.

For this chapter, we will be using the source code listed here to illustrate the ELF standard and how it relates to the Linux operating system:

```
penguin> ls -l *.C *.h Makefile
-rw-r--r--   1 wilding  build           759 Jan 18 05:59 Makefile
-rw-r--r--   1 wilding  build           641 Jan  9 08:57 foo.C
-rw-r--r--   1 wilding  build           161 Jan  9 08:04 foo.h
-rw-r--r--   1 wilding  build           649 Jan 18 05:37 intercept.C
```

```
-rw-r--r--    1 wilding  build       275 Apr 15  2004 main.C
-rw-r--r--    1 wilding  build       276 Dec 28 17:37 pic.C
```

> **Note**: The source code in these files can be found at the end of
> the chapter under the heading "Source Files."
>   **Note**: The .C extension is used for C++ files, although .cc and
> .cpp will also work.

These objects are all compiled as C++ source files. Some of them contain simple
C++ objects that will be used to explain how ELF handles simple C++
functionality such as constructors and destructors.

The source file foo.C contains a number of global objects that have a
constructor, a number of global variables, and a number of functions. Source
file, file.h, contains the definition of the class used for the global objects in
foo.C. Source file, main.C, calls a function in foo.C and also instantiates a global
object. Source file pic.C is a smaller, less complex source file used to illustrate
relocation. Lastly, the make file, Makefile, serves to make it easier to compile
and link the source files using the make utility.

To compile and link the source files, simply run make in the directory
containing the files:

```
penguin> make
g++ -c  main.C
g++ -c -fPIC  foo.C
g++ -shared foo.o -o libfoo.so
g++ -o foo main.o -L. -Wl,-rpath,. -lfoo
g++ -c -fPIC  pic.C
g++ -o pic pic.o -L. -Wl,-rpath,.
g++ -c pic.C -o pic_nopic.o
g++ -o pic_nopic pic_nopic.o -L. -Wl,-rpath,.
gcc -c -fPIC  intercept.c
gcc -o intercept.so -shared intercept.o
```

> **Note**: The -fPIC option is used for some of the source files to create
> position independent object files. This is the preferred choice when
> creating shared libraries. Position-independent code is covered in more
> detail later in this chapter.
>   **Note**: The -L. switch is used for convenience. It tells the linker to
> look in the current directory (".") for shared libraries. Normally, a real
> shared library directory would be used, but this is convenient given that
> the shared libraries are in the same directory as the executables.

The source file, `foo.c`, is used to create `libfoo.so` and the source file, `main.c`, is used to build the executable `foo`.

Throughout this chapter, we will be using the g++ compiler. This compiler is installed on many/most Linux systems and will compile C++ code to help illustrate how ELF handles some basic C++ functionality.

9.2 CONCEPTS AND DEFINITIONS

Learning about ELF can be a challenge because the concepts are somewhat interdependent in that learning about one concept can require understanding another concept and vice versa. Thus, before diving into ELF details, we will introduce a few basic concepts and definitions without going into too much detail. The most basic of these concepts is the "symbol."

9.2.1 Symbol

A symbol is a description of a function or variable (or other) that is stored in an ELF file. A symbol is similar to an entry in a phone book. It contains brief information about a function or variable in an ELF file, but, like the phone book entry, it is certainly not the item it is describing. A symbol can describe many things, but they are mainly used for functions and variables, which for the time being, we'll focus on.

Symbols have a size, value, and name associated with them as well as a few other tidbits of information. The size is the actual size of the function or variable that the symbol represents. The value gives the location in the ELF file of the function/variable or the expected address of the function/variable (using the load address of the shared library or executable as a base). Symbol names are for the sole convenience of humans and are used so that human software developers can use descriptive names in their programs.

Consider the function `printf` in libc. This function is defined and stored in a library "/lib/libc.so.6" on the system used for this chapter. We can see the details of this "symbol" using the `nm` command (note that `<...>` represents uninteresting output that was not included):

```
penguin> nm -v -f s /lib/libc.so.6

Symbols from /lib/libc.so.6:

Name    Value       Class       Type      Size       Line    Section
<...>
printf|0004fc90|    T |         FUNC|     00000039|          |.text
<...>
```

> **Note:** Some distributions may strip the shared libraries, which removes the main symbol table and makes the `nm` command here not work as shown. In this case, choose a library on the system that has not been stripped. You can also use the `file` command on an ELF file to see whether it has been stripped (the term "stripped" will be displayed).
>
> **Note:** ELF uses the term "class" to describe the scope and/or category of a symbol. The ELF term class, when used to describe symbols, is not related to C++ classes.

The field "Value" is the offset in the library where the executable instructions for "`printf`" are found. The class is "T" meaning "text". Text in this context means read-only. The type is "FUNC" for function. The size is 0x39 bytes or 57 bytes in decimal notation, and lastly, the section that this function is stored in is the ".text" section, which contains all of the executable code for the library.

Symbols can have different "scope" such as global or local. A global variable in a shared library is exposed and available for other shared libraries or the executable itself to use. A local variable was originally defined as "static" in the original source file, making it local to the code in that source file. Static symbols are not available to other ELF files.

There are two variables defined in the source file foo.C that are meant for illustrating the concept of scope:

```
int globInt = 5 ;
static int staticInt = 5 ;
```

The first is a global variable, and the second is defined as "static." Using `nm` again, we can see how the "class" (that is, scope) of the type variables differs:

```
penguin> nm -v -f s foo.o | egrep "staticInt|globInt"
globInt   |00000000|   D  |           OBJECT|00000004|      |.data
staticInt |00000004|   d  |           OBJECT|00000004|      |.data
```

The output shows an uppercase `D` for global data variable and shows a lowercase `d` for local data variable. In the case of the text symbols, an upper case `T` refers to a global text symbol; whereas, a lower case `t` refers to a local text symbol.

Symbols can also be *defined* or *undefined*. A defined symbol means that an ELF file actually contains the contents of the associated function or variable. An undefined symbol means that the object file references the function/variable but does not contain its contents. For example, the source file "main.C" makes a call to `printf` but it does not contain the contents of the printf function. Using `nm` again, we can see that the "class" is "U" for "undefined":

```
penguin> nm -v -f s main.o |egrep printf
printf    |      |  U |      NOTYPE|        |   |*UND*
```

Other ELF symbols describe variables that are read-only or not initialized (these have a "class" of R and B, respectively, in nm output).

ELF also has absolute symbols (marked with an A by nm) that are used to mark an offset in a file. The following command shows a few examples:

```
penguin> nm -v -f s libfoo.so | egrep " A "
_DYNAMIC             |00001c48|   A  |   OBJECT|        |  |*ABS*
_GLOBAL_OFFSET_TABLE |00001d38|   A  |   OBJECT|        |  |*ABS*
_bss_start           |00001d74|   A  |   NOTYPE|        |  |*ABS*
_edata               |00001d74|   A  |   NOTYPE|        |  |*ABS*
_end                 |00001d84|   A  |   NOTYPE|        |  |*ABS*
```

Notice that the absolute symbols do not include a size because they are meant only to mark a location in an ELF file.

9.2.1.1 Symbols Names and C Versus C++ One of the unfortunate problems with C code is symbol name collisions. With so much software in the world, it is not uncommon for two developers to pick the same name for two different functions or variables. This is not handled well (as explained later in this chapter) by ELF or other executable file formats and has caused many problems over the years for large C-based software.

C++ aimed to solve this problem in two ways. The mangled names include a name space (that is, class name) and information about the function arguments. So function "foo(int bar)" will have a different C++ symbol name than "foo(char bar)." This is covered in Chapter 5, but it is worth a quick reminder here under the context of ELF. There are many examples with mangled C++ names in this chapter.

9.2.2 Object Files, Shared Libraries, Executables, and Core Files

Source files are meant for humans and cannot be efficiently interpreted by computers. Therefore, source code must be translated (human to computer) into a format that is easily and efficiently executed on a computer system. This is called "compiling." There is more information on compiling in Chapter 4, but stated simply, compiling is the process of turning a source file into an object file.

9.2.2.1 Object Files Even though an object file is the computer-readable version of a source file, it still has hints of the original source code. Function names as well as global and static variable names are the basis for the symbol names stored in the resulting object file. As mentioned earlier, the symbol names

are solely for humans and are actually a bit of an inconvenience for computer systems. A good example of an inconvenience is the hash table section in an ELF file, which is detailed later in this chapter. The hash table consumes disk space and memory and requires CPU resources to traverse—it is required because of the human-friendly symbol names.

The command to create an ELF object file is fairly straight forward as shown here:

```
penguin> g++ -c foo.C
penguin> ls -l foo.C foo.o
-rw-r—r—    1 wilding   build         641 Jan  9 08:57 foo.C
-rw-r—r—    1 wilding   build        2360 Jan  9 09:05 foo.o
penguin> file foo.C foo.o
foo.C: ASCII C program text
foo.o: ELF 32-bit LSB relocatable, Intel 80386, version 1 (SYSV), not
➡stripped
```

The foo.o file is the object file that contains the compiled version of the source code in the file foo.C. From the file foo.o command, we can see that this is indeed an ELF file. From the ls command, we can see that the size of the object file is much larger than the source file. In fact, it is about three and a half times larger. At first, this might seem strange. After all, shouldn't the computer-readable version be smaller?

> **Note**: For more information about creating small ELF files, see the following URL: http://www.muppetlabs.com/~breadbox/software/tiny/teensy.html.

The actual combined size of the compiled instructions and variables is 247 bytes (using nm to count the symbol sizes). This is about one-third of the size of the original source file and accounts for only about one-tenth of the object file size. The object file foo.o must contain more than just the machine instructions and variables of the source file foo.C. One example of something that takes up space is the ELF header, which is explained later in this chapter under the heading, "ELF Header."

These object files cannot be run directly because they do not contain information about how the object file should be loaded into memory. Further, the undefined symbols in the object files must eventually point to the corresponding defined symbols, or the code in the object files will not run. For example, a call to printf must be able to find the actual function printf in libc (for example, "/lib/libc.so.6"). Before any machine instructions in an ELF object file are executed, the object files must be combined ("linked") into a larger ELF file type called an *executable* or *shared library*. For shared libraries, there is an extra step where the run time linker/loader (explained later in this chapter) must dynamically load the shared libraries into the address space of an executable. In any case, the process of creating an executable or shared library from object files is called linking. And part of the responsibility of linking is to resolve some of the undefined symbols.

9.2.2.2 Shared Libraries A shared library is made up of the symbols from one or more object files and can be loaded anywhere in the address space. There are some architectural restrictions that limit or guide the actual load address of shared libraries in the address space, but this does not affect ELF (any address is okay). A shared library, like an object file, has a list of symbols that are either defined or undefined. However, any undefined symbols must be satisfied through other shared libraries.

9.2.2.3 Exectuables An executable is very similar to a shared library, although it must be loaded at a specific address in memory. An executable also has a function that is called when a program starts. For programmers, this function is called `main`; however, the actual function that is run first in an executable is called `_start` and is explained later in this chapter.

The most significant part of an executable or shared library is the information about how and where to load the files into memory so that the machine instructions can be run. This information is contained in a special part of the ELF file called the "program header table." This is also explained in more detail later in this chapter.

9.2.2.4 Core Files A core file is a special type of ELF file that is very different from shared libraries and executables. It is the memory image from a once-running process. Core files contain a number of memory segments that were originally used by the running process and that can be loaded into a debugger for subsequent diagnosis.

9.2.2.5 Static Libraries Archive files (files that end with .a), also known as static libraries, are not ELF files. Archive files are a convenient file format to store other files. Technically, you can store any type of file in an archive file, although in practice, object files are by far the most commonly stored file type. Archive files do contain an index of the symbols from each ELF object file contained within them (which crosses the boundary a bit as far as a generic storage format is concerned). A description of static libraries (and their format) is beyond the scope of this chapter (because they are not an ELF file type). However, their importance will be explained as part of the linking phase.

9.2.3 Linking

Linking takes the symbols from the object files, shuffles them into a specific order, and then combines them into either a shared library or executable. Linking also needs to resolve some of the undefined symbols, either using the functions and variables of the object files that it is combining or through symbols exported by other shared libraries. The linker must also create a program header that includes information about how the executable or shared library should be loaded into memory. Let's take a quick look at the process of linking using Figure 9.1.

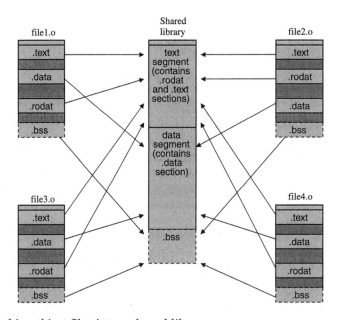

Fig. 9.1 Linking object files into a shared library.

The diagram shows four separate object files being combined into one shared library. Each object file contains a number of sections; only four are being shown here for simplicity:

☞ .text: contains functions
☞ .data: contains initialized writable (that is, not constant) variables
☞ .rodata: contains read-only (that is, constant) variables
☞ .bss: contains uninitialized and writable variables

Each of the sections from the four object files is merged in with a larger section in the shared library. The sections are also included in larger contiguous regions called "segments," which will eventually be loaded into memory with specific memory attributes such as read, write, and/or execute.

The order of information in an object file is not that important. However, the order of the information in a shared library or executable is very important because the goal is to move functions and variables that have similar properties into the specific loadable segments. The order of the segments in the shared library is:

1. text: read only
2. data: read/write

The segments of this shared library are loaded into memory in order, and space for the variables in the .bss section is also allocated. The .bss section is a special section that stores uninitialized variables and the space for them must be taken into account in the resulting shared library or executable.

The memory attributes for the text segment are read-only to protect the data from changing during run time. The memory attributes of the data segment are read and write because the contents will need to be modified at run time.

The order of the data and text section in a shared library or executable is important because the text section relies on the data segment being at a specific offset from the text segment—more on this later in the chapter as well.

Like an object file, a shared library or executable will have defined and undefined symbols. The difference is that the linker (the program which does the linking) will ensure that the unresolved symbols will be satisfied through other shared libraries. This is a protection mechanism to ensure that the shared library or executable will not run into any undefined symbols during run time. Here is an example of the error returned when trying to link an executable with an undefined symbol:

```
penguin> g++ main.o -o main
main.o: In function 'main':
main.o(.text+0x2b): undefined reference to 'baz(int)'
collect2: ld returned 1 exit status
```

The object file main.o references a function "baz(int)," but the linker cannot find this function. To successfully link this executable, we need to include a shared library that contains this function as follows:

```
g++ -o foo main.o -L. -Wl,-rpath, -lfoo
```

The -lfoo switch is a short form for libfoo.so. Because libfoo.so contains baz(int), the executable can be successfully linked. The -L. tells the linker to look in the current directory (".") for shared libraries.

> **Note**: The linking phase does not copy the contents of any undefined functions or variables from the shared libraries, but rather makes note of which libraries will be needed at run time to resolve the required symbols.

After the executable is linked, there are still no guarantees. The library libfoo.so could be removed, modified, switched for another library, and so on. The linker doesn't guarantee a perfect run with no undefined symbols; it just tries to protect against such a situation by requiring a shared library during link time so that it can embed the names of the required shared libraries into the executable (or shared library) that is being built.

Consider Figure 9.2 in which the executable is dependent on two shared libraries: #1 and #2. The reason the executable has a dependency on these shared libraries is that they contain one or more of the undefined symbols required by the executable. Likewise, shared libraries #1 and #2 are also dependent on other shared libraries for the same reason.

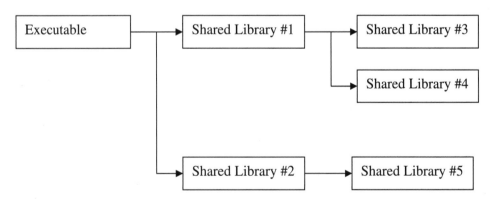

Fig. 9.2 Shared libraries and undefined symbols.

There are two good methods to find the dependent shared libraries. The first outlined here is to use the readelf command with the -d switch.

```
penguin> readelf -d foo

Dynamic segment at offset 0x810 contains 25 entries:
  Tag        Type                      Name/Value
  0x00000001 (NEEDED)          Shared library: [libfoo.so]
  0x00000001 (NEEDED)          Shared library: [libstdc++.so.5]
  0x00000001 (NEEDED)          Shared library: [libm.so.6]
  0x00000001 (NEEDED)          Shared library: [libgcc_s.so.1]
  0x00000001 (NEEDED)          Shared library: [libc.so.6]
  0x0000000f (RPATH)           Library rpath: [.]
  <...>
```

This `readelf` command here lists the shared libraries that are required by
executable foo. It does not however, list where this executable will get these
libraries at run time. This is what the second method, `ldd` can be used for:

```
penguin> ldd foo
        libfoo.so => ./libfoo.so (0x40014000)
        libstdc++.so.5 => /usr/lib/libstdc++.so.5 (0x40016000)
        libm.so.6 => /lib/libm.so.6 (0x400da000)
        libgcc_s.so.1 => /lib/libgcc_s.so.1 (0x400fd000)
        libc.so.6 => /lib/libc.so.6 (0x40105000)
        /lib/ld-linux.so.2 => /lib/ld-linux.so.2 (0x40000000)
```

The `ldd` command is actually a wrapper for a special environment variable
called LD_TRACE_LOADED_OBJECTS that works with the run time linker/
loader to trace the loading of the various libraries. You can use this directly,
although any command run off of the command line will only display a trace of
the shared libraries:

```
penguin> export LD_TRACE_LOADED_OBJECTS=true
penguin> foo
        libfoo.so => ./libfoo.so (0x40014000)
        libstdc++.so.5 => /usr/lib/libstdc++.so.5 (0x40016000)
        libm.so.6 => /lib/libm.so.6 (0x400da000)
        libgcc_s.so.1 => /lib/libgcc_s.so.1 (0x400fd000)
        libc.so.6 => /lib/libc.so.6 (0x40105000)
        /lib/ld-linux.so.2 => /lib/ld-linux.so.2 (0x40000000)
```

In general, it is best to use the `ldd` command. The run time loader that uses
the environment variable LD_TRACE_LOADED_OBJECTS also deserves a
quick overview.

9.2.3.1 Linking with Static Libraries Static libraries (archive files of
ELF object files) are a convenient method to store many object files. When
linking with a static library, the linker uses the symbol index stored in the
static library to find the symbols in the ELF object files. When linking with a

static library, the contents of the static library (the object files) are copied into the resulting executable or shared library.

9.2.4 Run Time Linking

Run time linking is the process of matching undefined symbols with defined symbols at run time (that is, when a program is starting up or while it is running). When a program is compiled, the linker leaves the undefined symbols to be resolved by the run time linker when the program is run. Another term for run time linking is *binding*.

Lazy binding is a term used to define a symbol resolution (linking of an undefined symbol with the corresponding defined symbol) the first time a function is actually called. This can improve the performance of program startup because only a few of the undefined symbols may ever be used.

9.2.5 Program Interpreter / Run Time Linker

The program interpreter or run time linker is a special library that has the responsibility of bringing a program up and eventually transferring control over to the program. This includes finding and loading all of the required libraries, potentially resolving some of the symbols for the executable or its shared libraries, running C++ global constructors, and so on. Eventually, the function `main()` is called, which transfers control over to the program source code.

> **Note**: On Linux, the program interpreter will be similar to /lib/ld-linux.so or /lib/linux-ld.so.2. There is a command that follows that will show the actual program interpreter as defined in the ELF file itself.

Now that some of the basic definitions and concepts are clear, let's take a look at the ELF format, starting with the ELF header.

9.3 ELF HEADER

The first part of any ELF file (including object files like foo.o) is the ELF header. There are several ways to look at the header. First, we'll use a program that dumps the raw data in hexadecimal and ascii (a text representation) for a file to see if there is anything that we can recognize.

```
penguin> hexdump -C foo.o | head
00000000  7f 45 4c 46 01 01 01 00  00 00 00 00 00 00 00 00
➥|.ELF............|
00000010  01 00 03 00 01 00 00 00  00 00 00 00 00 00 00 00
➥|................|
00000020  58 03 00 00 00 00 00 00  34 00 00 00 00 00 28 00
➥|X.......4.....(.|
00000030  12 00 0f 00 55 89 e5 83  ec 08 c7 45 fc 00 00 00
➥|....U......E....|
00000040  00 83 ec 0c ff 75 08 e8  fc ff ff ff 83 c4 10 03
➥|.....u..........|
00000050  05 00 00 00 00 89 45 fc  8b 15 04 00 00 00 8d 45
➥|......E........E|
00000060  fc 01 10 8d 45 fc 83 00  05 8b 45 fc c9 c3 55 89
➥|....E.....E...U.|
00000070  e5 83 ec 08 83 ec 0c ff  75 08 e8 b5 ff ff ff 83
➥|........u.......|
00000080  c4 10 83 ec 0c 68 20 00  00 00 e8 fc ff ff ff 83
➥|.....h..........|
00000090  c4 10 b8 00 00 00 00 c9  c3 90 55 89 e5 83 ec 08
➥|..........U.....|
```

> **Note**: hexdump is used in this chapter to show a raw hex dump of ELF files. The od tool can also be used.

At first glance, the only thing recognizable is the "ELF" text at the beginning of the file in the ascii part of the output. We can confirm visually that this is an ELF file, but in order to understand the rest, we need to look at the structure of the ELF header.

The structure for the ELF header is contained in various papers on the ELF specification as well as the /usr/include/elf.h file on Linux. The structure listed here is for 32-bit ELF files (refer to the elf.h header file to see the 64-bit version):

```
#define EI_NIDENT       16

typedef struct {
        unsigned char   e_ident[EI_NIDENT]; /* ident bytes */
        Elf32_Half      e_type;             /* file type */
        Elf32_Half      e_machine;          /* target machine */
        Elf32_Word      e_version;          /* file version */
        Elf32_Addr      e_entry;            /* start address */
        Elf32_Off       e_phoff;            /* phdr file offset */
        Elf32_Off       e_shoff;            /* shdr file offset */
        Elf32_Word      e_flags;            /* file flags */
        Elf32_Half      e_ehsize;           /* sizeof ehdr */
        Elf32_Half      e_phentsize;        /* sizeof phdr */
        Elf32_Half      e_phnum;            /* number phdrs */
```

```
            Elf32_Half      e_shentsize;        /* sizeof shdr */
            Elf32_Half      e_shnum;            /* number shdrs */
            Elf32_Half      e_shstrndx;         /* shdr string index */
    } Elf32_Ehdr;
```

If we map this structure to the raw output from the hex dump, we see that the
first 16 bytes is for the e_ident field, and the first four bytes include the text
"ELF." In fact, every ELF file contains the first four bytes 0x7f, E, L, and F to
identify the file type as ELF. This is called a *magic number*. Magic numbers
are used in many file formats, and the command file foo.o (referenced earlier
in the chapter) used this magic number to identify the object file as an ELF file
(see the /etc/magic file or read the man page for magic for more information on
magic numbers).

Here are the fields in the ident array (one byte per field) of the ELF
header:

```
0. 0x7f
1. E
2. L
3. F
4. EI_CLASS        : ELF Class
5. EI_DATA         : Data encoding: big or little endian
6. EI_VERSION      : Must be EV_CURRENT (value of 1)
7. EI_OSABI        : Application binary interface (ABI) type
8. EI_ABIVERSION   : ABI version
9. EI_PAD          : Start of padding bytes (continues until end of
➥array)
```

From /usr/include/elf.h, we have:

```
#define ELFCLASSNONE     0                   /* EI_CLASS */
#define ELFCLASS32       1
#define ELFCLASS64       2
#define ELFCLASSNUM      3

#define ELFDATANONE      0                   /* e_ident[EI_DATA] */
#define ELFDATA2LSB      1
#define ELFDATA2MSB      2

#define EV_NONE          0                   /* e_version, EI_VERSION */
#define EV_CURRENT       1
```

Let's use the data from a hex dump to map these three values from the ELF
file foo.o:

```
penguin> hexdump -C foo.o | head -1
00000000  7f 45 4c 46 01 01 01 00  00 00 00 00 00 00 00 00
➥|.ELF...........|
```

According to the hex dump, the "class" field byte at offset 4 (starting from 0x0) is 1, the data encoding field (byte at offset 5) is 1, and the version (byte at offset 6) is 1.

Thus, the class is 32-bit (ELFCLASS32), the data encoding is LSB (Least Significant Bit) (ELFDATA2LSB) or "little endian," and the version is EV_CURRENT (which it must be).

We can also map the next couple of fields in the ELF header structure using the raw output. The next two fields of e_type and e_machine are 16 bytes (EI_NIDENT) and 18 (EI_NIDENT + 2) bytes past the beginning of the file (at offset 0x10 in hexadecimal):

```
penguin> hexdump -C foo.o |head -2
00000000  7f 45 4c 46 01 01 01 00  00 00 00 00 00 00 00 00  |.ELF............|
00000010  01 00 03 00 01 00 00 00  00 00 00 00 00 00 00 00  |................|
```

From the output, the e_type field is 0x1 (elf.h: ET_REL), which is used for relocatable files. The e_machine field is 0x3 (elf.h: EM_386), which is used for executables that run on the x86 architecture.

Note: Because this platform is little endian, the byte order must be reversed to be translated into the big endian format—the format that humans are generally more comfortable with. For little endian, a hex dumped value of 0100 is actually 0001 or 0x1 (little endian is covered in more detail in the GDB chapter of this book).

Mapping the ELF structure to the raw hex and ASCII output certainly works, but it is inconvenient and shows that there is no real magic or mystery behind the ELF object types. Fortunately, Linux provides a much easier way to display the ELF header:

```
penguin> readelf -h foo.o
ELF Header:
  Magic:   7f 45 4c 46 01 01 01 00 00 00 00 00 00 00 00 00
  Class:                             ELF32
  Data:                              2's complement, little endian
  Version:                           1 (current)
  OS/ABI:                            UNIX - System V
  ABI Version:                       0
  Type:                              REL (Relocatable file)
  Machine:                           Intel 80386
  Version:                           0x1
  Entry point address:               0x0
  Start of program headers:          0 (bytes into file)
  Start of section headers:          856 (bytes into file)
  Flags:                             0x0
```

```
Size of this header:                 52 (bytes)
Size of program headers:             0 (bytes)
Number of program headers:           0
Size of section headers:             40 (bytes)
Number of section headers:           18
Section header string table index: 15
```

The last 10 values in the output correspond directly to the last 10 fields in the ELF header structure but without the work of having to find and format the information by hand.

First let's take a look at the difference between the ELF header for different ELF file types. We'll look at object files (which we just looked at), shared libraries, executables, and core files.

Here is the ELF header for an executable:

```
penguin> readelf -h foo
ELF Header:
    Magic:   7f 45 4c 46 01 01 01 00 00 00 00 00 00 00 00 00
    Class:                             ELF32
    Data:                              2's complement, little endian
    Version:                           1 (current)
    OS/ABI:                            UNIX - System V
    ABI Version:                       0
    Type:                              EXEC (Executable file)
    Machine:                           Intel 80386
    Version:                           0x1
    Entry point address:               0x8048540
    Start of program headers:          52 (bytes into file)
    Start of section headers:          9292 (bytes into file)
    Flags:                             0x0
    Size of this header:               52 (bytes)
    Size of program headers:           32 (bytes)
    Number of program headers:         7
    Size of section headers:           40 (bytes)
    Number of section headers:         35
    Section header string table index: 32
```

Besides the obvious difference that the e_type is EXEC and not REL, as it was for the object file, the e_entry and e_phoff fields are also defined for the executable. This is the information needed to load the executable into memory and start it running. This information is missing from object files, which is one of the reasons they cannot be run directly.

The e_entry (entry point) field contains the virtual address of the starting function for an ELF file. This field is usually only used for executable files. For executable files on Linux, this field contains the address of the _start() function, which runs before main() and ensures the proper start up of the executable. Eventually, _start() calls main() to hand control over to the user written code.

Using the nm utility, we can display the symbol table and confirm that the
_start function is at 0x08048540. When the executable first starts up, this is the
first function that is called in the executable.

```
penguin> ls -l foo
-rwxr-xr-x    1 wilding  build        12609 Jan  9 11:30 foo
penguin> nm foo | egrep ' _start$'
08048540 T _start
```

> **Note**: _start is a special function that initializes a new running
> process. It is run before main().

One thing worth noting is that the "offset" (first field) in the nm output is
larger than the file itself. The foo executable is only 12609 (0x3141) bytes,
although nm is suggesting that _start() is at offset 0x08048540. The reason for
this is that ELF provides the ability to specify a load address for a segment of
an ELF file. The load address is the address where a segment should be loaded
into memory. On Linux (x86 architecture), the load address for the segment
that contains the machine instructions of a 32-bit executable is 0x08048000.
This address is platform-specific and defined as part of the ABI (application
binary interface). This value is added to the offsets of the symbols to provide
the value displayed by nm. For more information on the load address, refer to
the heading, "Segments and the Program Header Table," later in the chapter.

The e_phoff ("start of program headers") field contains the file offset for
the program header table. The program header table is required for executables
and shared libraries and defines the various *segments* in an ELF file. A segment
is a contiguous part or range of an ELF object and has specific memory
attributes such as read, write, and execute. A segment is meant to be loaded
into memory with the corresponding memory attributes. The e_phentsize ("size
of program headers") field defines the size of an entry in the program header
table. The e_phnum ("number of program headers") field defines the number
of entries in the program header table. All entries in the program header table
have the same fixed size.

> **Note**: The only part of an ELF file that has a fixed location is the
> ELF header. All other parts of an ELF header are referenced by offset
> starting with the offsets listed in the ELF header.

The ELF header for a shared library is similar to that of an executable, and in
fact, the two file types are almost identical. A core file, on the other hand, has
some significant differences. A core file is the memory image of a once-running
process. Because there is no need to execute it, there is no need for sections of

the core file to contain machine instructions. There *is* a need, however, to load parts of a core file into memory (for example, when using a debugger), and thus there are some program headers (segments).

```
penguin> ls -l core
-rw——    1 wilding  build      184320 Oct 14 16:36 core
penguin> file core
core: ELF 32-bit LSB core file of 'excp' (signal 6), Intel 80386,
version 1 (SYSV), from 'excp'
penguin> readelf -h core |tail
  Entry point address:              0x0
  Start of program headers:         52 (bytes into file)
  Start of section headers:         0 (bytes into file)
  Flags:                            0x0
  Size of this header:              52 (bytes)
  Size of program headers:          32 (bytes)
  Number of program headers:        17
  Size of section headers:          0 (bytes)
  Number of section headers:        0
  Section header string table index: 0
```

Notice that there is no entry point and no section headers. Sections and segments are two different types of ELF file parts and really deserve a good explanation.

9.4 OVERVIEW OF SEGMENTS AND SECTIONS

An ELF file can be interpreted in two ways: as a set of segments or as a set of sections. Sections are smaller pieces of an ELF file that contain very specific information, such as the machine instructions or the symbol table. Segments are larger groupings of one or more sections, all of which have the same memory attributes.

Using an analogy of a car, the "sections" of the car would be the undeniable features of that car such as seats, the glove compartment, the gas petal, the steering wheel, the rear window, and the dash board controls. Regardless of how these are grouped, they exist and can be separated from the car if needed. Segments, on the other hand, are not as concrete or real but rather are more like a grouping of sections. For example, we could have front and back segments. The front segment would contain the steering wheel, the front seats, and so on. The back segment would contain the rear window, the back seat, etc. We could also split the car into left and right segments. Or we could create overlapping segments such as a front segment and a left segment. In fact, one segment could completely contain another segment. Regardless of how we group the "sections" of the car into segments, the sections remain the same. The location

of the sections in the car is important, however; the car wouldn't be very practical
with the steering wheel in the back seat!

The grouping of sections into segments for executable `foo` is shown in the
following command:

```
penguin> readelf -l foo

Elf file type is EXEC (Executable file)
Entry point 0x8048540
There are 7 program headers, starting at offset 52

Program Headers:
  Type      Offset   VirtAddr   PhysAddr   FileSiz MemSiz  Flg Align
  PHDR      0x000034 0x08048034 0x08048034 0x000e0 0x000e0 R E 0x4
  INTERP    0x000114 0x08048114 0x08048114 0x00013 0x00013 R   0x1
      [Requesting program interpreter: /lib/ld-linux.so.2]
  LOAD      0x000000 0x08048000 0x08048000 0x0076c 0x0076c R E 0x1000
  LOAD      0x00076c 0x0804976c 0x0804976c 0x001d4 0x001dc RW  0x1000
  DYNAMIC   0x000810 0x08049810 0x08049810 0x000f0 0x000f0 RW  0x4
  NOTE      0x000128 0x08048128 0x08048128 0x00020 0x00020 R   0x4
  GNU_EH_FRAME 0x000748 0x08048748 0x08048748 0x00024 0x00024 R
➡0x4

 Section to Segment mapping:
  Segment Sections...
  00
  01     .interp
  02     .interp .note.ABI-tag .hash .dynsym .dynstr .gnu.version
➡.gnu.version_r .rel.dyn .rel.plt .init .plt .text .fini .rodata
➡.eh_frame_hdr
  03     .data .eh_frame .dynamic .ctors .dtors .jcr .got .bss
  04     .dynamic
  05     .note.ABI-tag
  06     .eh_frame_hdr
```

The second part of the output shows which sections are contained in which
segments. Notice that the ".interp" section is contained by both segment 1 and
segment 2. The first part of the output, "Program Headers," will be explained
in more detail next.

9.5 SEGMENTS AND THE PROGRAM HEADER TABLE

The program header table is only used for executables, shared libraries, and
core files. It contains information about the segments in an ELF file and how
to load them into memory. As discussed earlier, the segments are contiguous
ranges of an ELF file that have the same memory attributes when loaded into
memory.

The elements in the 32-bit program header table have the following structure:

```
typedef struct elf32_phdr{
    Elf32_Word    p_type;
    Elf32_Off     p_offset;
    Elf32_Addr    p_vaddr;
    Elf32_Addr    p_paddr;
    Elf32_Word    p_filesz;
    Elf32_Word    p_memsz;
    Elf32_Word    p_flags;
    Elf32_Word    p_align;
} Elf32_Phdr;
```

p_type	The type of segment (types are listed below)
p_offset	The file offset of the segment
p_vaddr	The virtual load address for the segment
p_paddr	The physical load address for the segment (for platforms that use physical addresses)
p_filesz	The file-based size of this segment
p_memsz	The size of this segment when loaded into memory
p_flags	Read/Write/Execute attributes for the section (PF_R, PF_W, PF_X)
p_align	Alignment requirements for the segment

There are several types of segments, each with a different purpose and function. The valid values for `p_type` can be found in /usr/include/elf.h:

```
#define PT_NULL          0            /* Program header table entry
➥unused */
#define PT_LOAD          1            /* Loadable program segment */
#define PT_DYNAMIC       2            /* Dynamic linking information
➥*/
#define PT_INTERP        3            /* Program interpreter */
#define PT_NOTE          4            /* Auxiliary information */
#define PT_SHLIB         5            /* Reserved */
#define PT_PHDR          6            /* Entry for header table itself
➥*/
#define PT_TLS           7            /* Thread-local storage segment
➥*/
#define PT_NUM           8            /* Number of defined types */
#define PT_LOOS          0x60000000   /* Start of OS-specific */
#define PT_GNU_EH_FRAME  0x6474e550   /* GCC .eh_frame_hdr segment */
#define PT_HIOS          0x6fffffff   /* End of OS-specific */
#define PT_LOPROC        0x70000000   /* Start of processor-specific
➥*/
#define PT_HIPROC        0x7fffffff   /* End of processor-specific */
```

The most "interesting" segment types are:

☞ PT_LOAD
☞ PT_DYNAMIC
☞ PT_INTERP

The PT_LOAD type is a "loadable" segment meaning that it can be loaded into memory. Loadable segments contain everything needed by a program to run the executable code.

The PT_DYNAMIC type is for dynamic linking information. This is used by run time linker to find all of the required shared libraries and to perform run time linking.

The PT_INTERP segment points to the ".interp" section that lists the name of the program interpreter for an executable. The program interpreter is responsible for getting a program up and running under its own executable code. In other words, it takes care of the process initialization from the point of view of the dynamic loading, linking, and so on. See the section later in this chapter titled "Program Interpreter" for more information.

Let's take a closer look at the program header and segments for the executable `foo`:

```
penguin> readelf -l foo

Elf file type is EXEC (Executable file)
Entry point 0x8048540
There are 7 program headers, starting at offset 52

Program Headers:
  Type         Offset   VirtAddr   PhysAddr   FileSiz MemSiz  Flg Align
  PHDR         0x000034 0x08048034 0x08048034 0x000e0 0x000e0 R E 0x4
  INTERP       0x000114 0x08048114 0x08048114 0x00013 0x00013 R   0x1
      [Requesting program interpreter: /lib/ld-linux.so.2]
  LOAD         0x000000 0x08048000 0x08048000 0x0076c 0x0076c R E
➥0x1000
  LOAD         0x00076c 0x0804976c 0x0804976c 0x001d4 0x001dc RW
➥0x1000
  DYNAMIC      0x000810 0x08049810 0x08049810 0x000f0 0x000f0 RW  0x4
  NOTE         0x000128 0x08048128 0x08048128 0x00020 0x00020 R   0x4
  GNU_EH_FRAME     0x000748 0x08048748 0x08048748 0x00024 0x00024 R
➥0x4

<...>
```

The first program header (segment) is always the program header itself. The second program header entry describes an "INTERP" segment. This is a special segment that only includes the name of the program interpreter (more on this segment later in the chapter). The third and fourth program headers entry segment describes LOAD segments (more on these later). The fifth segment is the dynamic segment used for dynamic linking. The last two are special segments for vendor-specific information and exception handling and are not covered in this chapter.

The offset of a segment (program header) refers to the actual offset in the ELF file. For example, we can find the program interpreter (INTERP) by looking at offset `0x114` in the executable `foo`:

```
penquin> hexdump -C foo | less
<...>
00000100   48 87 04 08 24 00 00 00   24 00 00 00 04 00 00 00
|H...$...$.......|
00000110   04 00 00 00 2f 6c 69 62   2f 6c 64 2d 6c 69 6e 75  |..../lib/
ld-linu|
00000120   78 2e 73 6f 2e 32 00 00   04 00 00 00 10 00 00 00
|x.so.2..........|
00000130   01 00 00 00 47 4e 55 00   00 00 00 00 02 00 00 00
|....GNU.........|
```

At offset `0x114` (from the readelf output), the executable contains the name of the program interpreter: /lib/ld-linux.so.2.

The virtual address (VirtAddr) is the address at which each segment would be loaded into memory. The physical address (PhysAddr) is only used for platforms that use actual physical addresses (that is, that do not use virtual memory). With some rare exceptions, Linux uses virtual addresses so that the "physical address" field can be ignored by Linux users. The file size field (FileSiz) is the size of the segment on disk. The memory size (MemSiz) is the size of the segment after it has been loaded into memory. The distinction between the file size and memory size is important. Some segments (such as the second LOAD segment listed in the output) are larger in memory than on disk. This is where very specific sections go, such as the .bss section, which does not occupy any space in the ELF file.

The .bss section, located at the end of the data segment (the second LOAD segment in the output above), contains uninitialized variables. Allocating space in the ELF file for variables that have not been initialized is pointless because there are no values to store. However, when the data segment is loaded into memory, the additional space is allocated, making room for the uninitialized variables. The uninitialized variables will always be initialized with zeros when a shared library or executable is loaded for the first time.

The flags field (Flg) is the memory attributes used when the segment is loaded into memory. Lastly, the alignment field (Align) is the required byte alignment for the segment. An alignment of `0x1` means that there are no alignment requirements. An alignment of `0x4` means that the segment must start on an address that is on a 4-byte boundary.

Of particular importance are the two LOAD segment addresses. In order, these are the text and data segments, explained in more detail next.

9.5.1 Text and Data Segments

Every executable and shared library has one "text" segment (Note: *segment*, not section) and one "data" segment. The term "text" in this context refers to sections (contained in the text segment) that should have read-only access when loaded into memory. Examples of the sections that may be in the text segment include the ELF header, the text *section* (with executable code), string tables, and read only data symbols (the .rodata section). The data segment will contain sections that need to be written to during the process' life time and hence will be writable in memory. Examples of the sections in the data segment include writeable data symbols that are initialized (the .data section), the global offset table, and the uninitialized memory (the .bss section).

The text and data segments are both "load" segments because they are loaded into memory and used by a process.

```
penguin> readelf -l foo |egrep LOAD
  LOAD           0x000000 0x08048000 0x08048000 0x0076c 0x0076c R E
➡0x1000          .
  LOAD           0x00076c 0x0804976c 0x0804976c 0x001d4 0x001dc RW
➡0x1000
```

After running the program `foo`, the address space looks like this (Note: Only the first part of the output is displayed.):

```
penguin> head -4 /proc/4893/maps
08048000-08049000 r-xp 00000000 08:13 2044467     /home/wilding/src/
➡Linuxbook/ELF/foo
08049000-0804a000 rw-p 00000000 08:13 2044467     /home/wilding/src/
➡Linuxbook/ELF/foo
40000000-40012000 r-xp 00000000 08:13 1144740   /lib/ld-2.2.5.so
40012000-40013000 rw-p 00011000 08:13 1144740   /lib/ld-2.2.5.so
<...>
```

Notice the addresses of the two loaded segments for the executable `foo` (/home/wilding/src/Linuxbook/foo). The first segment starts exactly at the "virtual address" defined for the first load segment from the program headers. The second load segment is loaded at a different address than what is specified in the ELF file, `foo`. The reason for this is the alignment restrictions for the second segment, which are `0x1000` or on a 4KB boundary. This boundary is due to the underlying hardware and virtual address translation mechanisms. The in-memory segment starts at a lower memory address that is aligned according to the alignment restrictions. The actual important contents are still located at the original address of `0x0804976c`.

> **Note**: For an executable or shared library, the term *base address* is defined as the actual address at which a segment is loaded in the address space. This takes into account any address rounding to meet alignment restrictions, and so on.

We can see the system calls involved in loading a library into memory by using the `strace` command:

```
penguin> strace -o foo.st foo
This is a printf format string in baz
This is a printf format string in main
penguin> less foo.st
<...>
open("./i686/mmx/libfoo.so", O_RDONLY)   = -1 ENOENT (No such file or
➥directory)
open("./i686/libfoo.so", O_RDONLY)       = -1 ENOENT (No such file or
➥directory)
open("./mmx/libfoo.so", O_RDONLY)        = -1 ENOENT (No such file or
➥directory)
open("./libfoo.so", O_RDONLY)            = 3
read(3, "\177ELF\1\1\1\0\0\0\0\0\0\0\0\0\3\0\3\0\1\0\0\0\340\7\0"...,
➥1024) = 1024
fstat64(3, {st_mode=S_IFREG|0755, st_size=7301, ...}) = 0
getcwd("/home/wilding/src/Linuxbook/ELF", 128) = 32
mmap2(NULL, 7556, PROT_READ|PROT_EXEC, MAP_PRIVATE, 3, 0) = 0x40014000
mprotect(0x40015000, 3460, PROT_NONE)    = 0
mmap2(0x40015000, 4096, PROT_READ|PROT_WRITE, MAP_PRIVATE|MAP_FIXED,
3, 0) = 0x40015000
close(3)                                 = 0
<...>
```

The `strace` output shows several open system calls in the effort to locate the library called `libfoo.so`. The first 1024 bytes of the file are read, and then the contents are mapped into memory using mmap2. Notice that the mmap is loaded with the contents of the file with memory attributes, READ and EXEC, but not

write. Later, another memory map is used to load in the data segment with
memory attributes, READ and WRITE.

Segments are important for loading ELF files into memory, but the real
functionality and contents are in the ELF sections. Let's take a closer look at
ELF sections next.

9.6 SECTIONS AND THE SECTION HEADER TABLE

The section header table contains information about every part of an ELF file
except the ELF header, the program header table, and the section header table
itself. The section header table is a list (or array) of section header structures,
each defining a different section in the ELF file.

The following is the structure of a section header table entry for a 32-bit
ELF file. Refer to the /usr/include/elf.h file for the 64-bit version.

```
typedef struct {
    Elf32_Word    sh_name;
    Elf32_Word    sh_type;
    Elf32_Word    sh_flags;
    Elf32_Addr    sh_addr;
    Elf32_Off     sh_offset;
    Elf32_Word    sh_size;
    Elf32_Word    sh_link;
    Elf32_Word    sh_info;
    Elf32_Word    sh_addralign;
    Elf32_Word    sh_entsize;
} Elf32_Shdr;
```

sh_name   The numeric offset into the string table for the section name.

sh_type   The type of section.

sh_flags   A bit mask of miscellaneous attributes.

sh_addr   The memory address at which this section should reside in a
                 process. The value will be zero if the section will not appear
                 in a process memory image.

sh_offset   Contains the file offset of the actual section data. If the
                 section type is SHT_NOBITS the section occupies no space in
                 the file although the offset may still exist and will represent
                 the offset as if the section was loaded in memory.

sh_size   The size of the actual section data.

sh_link   The meaning of this field depends on the section type.

sh_info   Contains extra information that depends on the section type.

sh_addralign   The alignment requirements for the section.

sh_entsize   The size of fix-sized elements for sections that use them.
                 Example is a symbol table.

The ELF header contains the file offset of the section header table (e_shoff), the size of an entry in the table (e_shentsize), and the number of entries in the table (e_shnum). This is everything needed to find and sift through the contents of the section header table:

```
penguin> readelf -h foo |egrep section
   Start of section headers:          9292 (bytes into file)
   Size of section headers:           40 (bytes)
Number of section headers:            35
```

Let's take a look at the details behind the scenes again in the same way we did for the ELF header. This is useful to understand how the section header table and ELF string tables work.

According to the ELF header for the executable foo, the section header table offset is 9292 bytes, the size of a section header is 40 bytes, and there are 35 section headers. A hex dump of the file at the offset for the section header table shows (note that the "*" in the output denotes an identical row to the previous):

```
penguin> hexdump -C -s 9292 -n 160 foo
0000244c   00 00 00 00 00 00 00 00   00 00 00 00 00 00 00 00
➥|...............|
*
0000246c   00 00 00 00 00 00 00 00   1b 00 00 00 01 00 00 00
➥|...............|
0000247c   02 00 00 00 14 81 04 08   14 01 00 00 13 00 00 00
➥|...............|
```

The first section header (at file offset 0x244c for foo) always has a NULL type and can be ignored. Because the 32-bit section header structure is 40 (0x28) bytes, the next section header starts at 40 bytes after the first at 0x2474:

```
penguin> hexdump -C -s 0x2474 -n 40 foo
00002474   1b 00 00 00 01 00 00 00   02 00 00 00 14 81 04 08
➥|...............|
00002484   14 01 00 00 13 00 00 00   00 00 00 00 00 00 00 00
➥|...............|
00002494   01 00 00 00 00 00 00 00                            |........|
0000249c
```

We can get the values of the section header structure by mapping it onto the raw data at 0x2474:

```
sh_name:  0x1b    (section name is at offset 0x1b in string table)
sh_type:  0x1     (SHT_PROGBITS)
sh_flags: 0x2     (SHF_ALLOC)
sh_addr:  0x08048114 (virtual address)
sh_offset:        0x114  (file offset)
```

```
sh_size:  0x13    (total size in bytes)
sh_link:  0x0
sh_info:  0x0
sh_addralign:    0x1    (needs to be aligned in a single byte boundary)
sh_entsize:      0x0    (does not use fixed size elements)
```

The first field is the offset into the string table for the section name. To get the
section name, we first have to find the string table and then look at offset `0x1b`
in it. There should be a NULL terminated string at offset 0x1b in the string
table that is the name of this first section. According to the ELF header, the
section header table index for the section header string table is 32:

```
penguin> readelf -h foo | tail -2
   Number of section headers:         35
   Section header string table index: 32
```

To find the string table, we need to use the size of an element in the section
header table (40 bytes), multiply it by 32 (the section header table index of the
string table), and add the result to `0x244c`, which is the file offset of the start of
the section header table.

```
32 x 40 = 1280 = 0x500
0x500 + 0x244C = 0x294C
```

This offset in the file is only the entry in the section header table for the string
table and is not the string table itself.

```
penguin> hexdump -C -s 0x294C -n 40 foo
0000294c   11 00 00 00 03 00 00 00   00 00 00 00 00 00 00 00
➡|................|
0000295c   13 23 00 00 39 01 00 00   00 00 00 00 00 00 00 00
➡|.#..9...........|
0000296c   01 00 00 00 00 00 00 00                            |........|
00002974
```

Mapping the section header structure onto this raw data (sh_offset is at offset
16, and sh_size is at offset 20 in the section header structure) shows us that
the offset to the string table section is `0x2313` (as shown at offset `0x295c`), and
the size is `0x139` (directly after the sh_offset field). Remember that this platform
is little endian, so a hexdump of `1323` is actually a value of `0x2313`. A hex dump
of this file offset shows:

```
penguin> hexdump -C -s 0x2313 foo |head
00002313   00 2e 73 79 6d 74 61 62   00 2e 73 74 72 74 61 62
➡|..symtab..strtab|
00002323   00 2e 73 68 73 74 72 74   61 62 00 2e 69 6e 74 65
➡|..shstrtab..inte|
```

```
00002333  72 70 00 2e 6e 6f 74 65  2e 41 42 49 2d 74 61 67  |rp..note.ABI-
➥tag|
00002343     00 2e 68 61 73 68 00 2e     64 79 6e 73 79 6d 00 2e
➥|..hash..dynsym..|
```

Now we need to add the offset (`0x1b`) of the section name in the string table to
the offset of the string table itself (`0x2313`) to get `0x232e`. The section name at
this offset can be found with yet another hexdump:

```
penguin> hexdump -C -s 0x232e foo | head -2
0000232e     2e 69 6e 74 65 72 70 00     2e 6e 6f 74 65 2e 41 42
➥|.interp..note.AB|
0000233e  49 2d 74 61 67 00 2e 68  61 73 68 00 2e 64 79 6e  |I-
➥tag..hash..dyn|
```

This offset contains the string `.interp`, which is the name of the first useful
section. Whew! This is a lot of work, but again, the point is to show that there
is no magic in an ELF file format.

After all of this work, we know that the first useful section header (the
first actual section is a NULL section) is for the name of the program interpreter.
Other sections can include global variables, the machine instructions, and many
other types of data. The contents of a section depend entirely on its type and
purpose.

Of course, there is a much easier way to view the section headers using
`realelf` (don't discount the importance of understanding how this really works,
though).

```
penguin> readelf -S foo | head
There are 35 section headers, starting at offset 0x244c:

Section Headers:
  [Nr] Name           Type     Addr     Off    Size   ES Flg Lk Inf Al
  [ 0]                NULL     00000000 000000 000000 00   0  0   0
  [ 1] .interp        PROGBITS 08048114 000114 000013 00 A  0   0  1
  [ 2] .note.ABI-tag  NOTE     08048128 000128 000020 00 A  0   0  4
  [ 3] .hash          HASH     08048148 000148 000094 04 A  4   0  4
  [ 4] .dynsym        DYNSYM   080481dc 0001dc 000120 10 A  1  4
  [ 5] .dynstr        STRTAB   080482fc 0002fc 00011a 00 A  0   0  1
<...>
```

The ELF specification contains a full list of section types. Only the most common
and important ones are covered in detail next. We'll start with two common
section formats, symbol table and string table, because there is more than one
of these section types described.

9.6.1 String Table Format

The string table contains a list of all strings that are used by the ELF specification. The string table is very simple. It is a range of space that contains a list of NULL terminated strings, one after the other. The strings are indexed by offset from the beginning of the file, the same offset as from base address for the shared library or executable.

There can be a number of string tables in an ELF file, including one for the dynamic symbol table, one for the main symbol table, and one for the section header names. String tables all have the same simple format:

```
<string1>\0<string2>\0<string3>\0...<stringN>\0\0
```

An index into a string table will point to the start of a string.

9.6.2 Symbol Table Format

A symbol table is an array of ELF symbol structures that describe a function, variable, or other type of symbol. As discussed at the beginning of this chapter, a symbol table is like a phone book for functions and variables in an ELF file.

There are actually two symbol tables for an ELF file. One is called the dynamic symbol table and is used at run time to find the various symbols in the ELF object. The other is the main symbol table and contains all of the symbols for an ELF object, including static symbol information that is not used at run time. The main symbol table is used at link time to find all of the unresolved symbols.

Each element of the array has the following structure (from /usr/include/elf.h):

```
typedef struct
{
  Elf32_Word    st_name;     /* Symbol name (string tbl index) */
  Elf32_Addr    st_value;    /* Symbol value */
  Elf32_Word    st_size;     /* Symbol size */
  unsigned char st_info;     /* Symbol type and binding */
  unsigned char st_other;    /* Symbol visibility */
  Elf32_Section st_shndx;    /* Section index */
} Elf32_Sym;
```

The st_name field is the sting table index for the name of the symbol (Note: The dynamic and main symbol tables both have their own string table.). The "value" is either the offset in the ELF file, the address of the symbol when it will be loaded, or the offset in the section that contains the symbol. Executables will have values that are actual addresses; whereas, shared libraries will have offset into the ELF file. The difference is due to the fact that shared libraries do not have a specific load addresses for their memory segments. Executables, on the other hand, must be loaded at address 0x08048000 for 32-bit Linux. The st_size file is the actual size of the item described by the symbol entry. This could be a variable, function, or other. The st_info field describes the type of binding (local, global, and so on) and the type of symbol (variable, function, etc.). The st_other field contains information about the visibility of a symbol. The st_shndx describes which section contains the item described by the symbol entry.

The meaning of st_value field depends on the ELF type. For a relocatable object, the value is the offset within the section specific by the section index, st_shndx. For shared libraries and executables, the value in the symbol table structure is a virtual address. This additional complexity is to ensure efficient access by the tools and code that use these values.

Given what we've covered about symbols, let's see if we can find the global variable "list" in the object file foo.o. The variable "list" in foo.c is defined as follows:

```
int list[10] = { 0, 1, 2, 3, 4, 5, 6, 7, 8, 9 } ;
```

For the object file foo.o, the value in the symbol table for the global variable "list" is 0x20, which is the offset within the .data section for this global variable as shown here:

```
penguin> nm -v -f s foo.o | egrep list
list                |00000020|   D  |              OBJECT|00000028|   |.data
```

We can confirm this by adding the file offset of the .data section to the value of the symbol "list." We'll need to use readelf to get the offset of the .data section:

```
penguin> readelf -S foo.o | egrep "\.data "
[ 3] .data          PROGBITS       00000000 000140 000048 00  WA  0
0 32
```

From the file offset of the .data section listed in the output just listed, the global variable "list" should be at file offset 0x160 (0x140 + 0x20). We can use hexdump to confirm that the values for "list" are indeed at this offset in the file:

```
penguin> hexdump -C -s 0x160 foo.o | head -4
00000160  00 00 00 00 01 00 00 00  02 00 00 00 03 00 00 00
⮕|................|
00000170  04 00 00 00 05 00 00 00  06 00 00 00 07 00 00 00
⮕|................|
00000180  08 00 00 00 09 00 00 00  00 00 00 00 00 00 00 00
```

```
➥|...............|
00000190  00 00 00 00 00 00 00 00  00 00 00 00 00 00 00 00
➥|...............|
```

For a shared library, the meaning of the "value" field in a symbol entry
is a virtual address. In the case of libfoo.so, the value (virtual address)
of the "list" variable is 0x1b40:

```
penguin> nm -v -f s libfoo.so | egrep list
list  00001b40|   D  |              OBJECT|00000028|    |.data
```

This isn't the real virtual address when the shared library is loaded
into memory because shared libraries can be loaded anywhere. For
shared library files, the virtual address of the text segment starts at
0x0, and the virtual address of the data segment (which contains the
.data section) is set to some offset from the beginning of the text
segment. Looking at the .data section for libfoo.so reveals that its file
offset is 0xb00 and the virtual address is 0x1b00:

```
penguin> readelf -S libfoo.so | egrep "\.data "
[14] .data  PROGBITS  00001b00 000b00 000070 00  WA  0   0 32
```

Thus we can subtract 0x1000 (0x1b00 - 0xb00) from any value listed by
nm for libfoo.so to get the file offset of a symbol. This means that the
file offset of "list" in libfoo.so is 0xb40, as confirmed here:

```
penguin> hexdump -C -s 0xb40 libfoo.so | head -4
00000b40  00 00 00 00 01 00 00 00  02 00 00 00 03 00 00 00
➥|...............|
00000b50  04 00 00 00 05 00 00 00  06 00 00 00 07 00 00 00
➥|...............|
00000b60  08 00 00 00 09 00 00 00  80 0a 00 00 00 00 00 00
➥|...............|
00000b70  18 00 00 00 00 00 00 00  01 7a 50 52 00 01 7c 08
➥|........zPR..|.|
```

The binding of a symbol has an interesting feature worth mentioning.
As mentioned earlier in this chapter, symbols can be global or local
depending on their scope. Symbols can also be "weak," which is similar
to global—although a symbol with a global binding will be chosen over
a weak symbol of the same name. This can actually be very useful for
problem determination efforts because some system functions are
declared "weak," meaning that you can override them if needed. This is
covered in more detail with an example in the section titled "Use of
Weak Symbols for Problem Determination" later in this chapter.

9.6.3 Section Names and Types

The casual term "section type" has two different meanings in normal technical conversation. One refers to the section type as defined in the `sh_type` field of the section header structure. The other refers to the combination of name and type of a section. For example, a section can have a (`sh_type`) of PROGBITS, but that does not describe what is in the section. On the other hand, someone might ask "what type of section," and the response is usually the section name, such as ".rodata" or ".text."

The sections included in the shared library `libfoo.so` are listed here:

```
penguin> readelf -S libfoo.so
There are 30 section headers, starting at offset 0x1090:
```

Section Headers:

[Nr]	Name	Type	Addr	Off	Size	ES	Flg	Lk	Inf	Al
[0]		NULL	00000000	000000	000000	00		0	0	0
[1]	.hash	HASH	000000b4	0000b4	000158	04	A	2	0	4
[2]	.dynsym	DYNSYM	0000020c	00020c	0002f0	10	A	3	1b	4
[3]	.dynstr	STRTAB	000004fc	0004fc	000133	00	A	0	0	1
[4]	.gnu.version	VERSYM	00000630	000630	00005e	02	A	2	0	2
[5]	.gnu.version_r	VERNEED	00000690	000690	000050	00	A	3	2	4
[6]	.rel.dyn	REL	000006e0	0006e0	000060	08	A	2	0	4
[7]	.rel.plt	REL	00000740	000740	000028	08	A	2	9	4
[8]	.init	PROGBITS	00000768	000768	000018	00	AX	0	0	4
[9]	.plt	PROGBITS	00000780	000780	000060	04	AX	0	0	4
[10]	.text	PROGBITS	000007e0	0007e0	000280	00	AX	0	0	16
[11]	.fini	PROGBITS	00000a60	000a60	00001c	00	AX	0	0	4
[12]	.rodata	PROGBITS	00000a80	000a80	00004c	00	A	0	0	32
[13]	.eh_frame_hdr	PROGBITS	00000acc	000acc	00002c	00	A	0	0	4
[14]	.data	PROGBITS	00001b00	000b00	000070	00	WA	0	0	32
[15]	.eh_frame	PROGBITS	00001b70	000b70	0000d8	00	WA	0	0	4
[16]	.dynamic	DYNAMIC	00001c48	000c48	0000d8	08	WA	3	0	4
[17]	.ctors	PROGBITS	00001d20	000d20	00000c	00	WA	0	0	4
[18]	.dtors	PROGBITS	00001d2c	000d2c	000008	00	WA	0	0	4
[19]	.jcr	PROGBITS	00001d34	000d34	000004	00	WA	0	0	4
[20]	.got	PROGBITS	00001d38	000d38	00003c	04	WA	0	0	4
[21]	.bss	NOBITS	00001d74	000d74	000010	00	WA	0	0	4
[22]	.comment	PROGBITS	00000000	000d74	000050	00		0	0	1
[23]	.debug_aranges	PROGBITS	00000000	000dc8	000058	00		0	0	8
[24]	.debug_info	PROGBITS	00000000	000e20	000098	00		0	0	1
[25]	.debug_abbrev	PROGBITS	00000000	000eb8	00001c	00		0	0	1
[26]	.debug_line	PROGBITS	00000000	000ed4	0000bf	00		0	0	1
[27]	.shstrtab	STRTAB	00000000	000f93	0000fb	00		0	0	1
[28]	.symtab	SYMTAB	00000000	001540	0004d0	10		29	39	4
[29]	.strtab	STRTAB	00000000	001a10	000275	00		0	0	1

```
Key to Flags:
 W (write), A (alloc), X (execute), M (merge), S (strings)
 I (info), L (link order), G (group), x (unknown)
 O (extra OS processing required) o (OS specific), p (processor specific)
```

The first section is always NULL, although there are 29 other sections, each with its own purpose. The most interesting sections are listed as follows with more detail.

Before listing the details of each section, please note that we will be discussing the source file foo.c as listed later in this chapter under "Source Files." It includes a wide range of data types that will help to clarify the various sections.

Note: All sections start with a "." prefix in ELF.

9.6.3.1 .bss There is some debate about what the bss acronym actually stands for. The most likely origin is from Fortran compiler on the IBM 704. The acronym most likely stands for "Block Started by Symbol" and was adopted to describe the uninitialized data for an ELF object. The acronym bss is pretty much meaningless, so consider it a term, not a useful acronym.

The .bss section is used for global and file local variables that are not initialized with a specific value. It is zeroed out as the process starts up, which sets the initial value of any variables in it to zero. For example, the global variable noValueGlobInt in foo.c is stored in the bss section because it has no initial value.

```
penguin> readelf -S libfoo.so | egrep \.bss
[21] .bss      NOBITS      00001d74 000d74 000010 00  WA  0   0  4
penguin> nm libfoo.so |egrep noValueGlobInt
00001d80 B noValueGlobInt
```

According to nm, the value of the noValueGlobInt variable is 0x1d80. This value is right inside the .bss section as expected. Also notice that the section type (sh_type) is NOBITS, which indicates that this section takes up no space in the ELF file. We can confirm this by looking at the loadable program headers for this library:

```
penguin> readelf -l libfoo.so

Elf file type is DYN (Shared object file)
Entry point 0x7e0
There are 4 program headers, starting at offset 52
```

```
Program Headers:
  Type       Offset    VirtAddr   PhysAddr   FileSiz MemSiz  Flg Align
  LOAD       0x000000 0x00000000 0x00000000 0x00af8 0x00af8 R E 0x1000
  LOAD       0x000b00 0x00001b00 0x00001b00 0x00274 0x00284 RW  0x1000
<...>
```

The offset for the second load segment (the "data" segment) is `0x1b00`, and the
value listed from nm for `noValueGlobInt` is `0x1d80`. Therefore, the `noValueGlobInt`
is at offset `0x280` bytes (`0x1d80` - `0x1b00`) into the second load segment. The
value of `0x280` is larger than FileSiz but not larger than MemSiz. The FileSiz
field is the size of the load segment in the file. The MemSiz field is the size of
the load segment once it is loaded into memory. That confirms that the variable
really does not take any space in the file, but it will (obviously) require space
once loaded into memory.

9.6.3.2 .data This section contains initialized global and static, writable
variables. Looking at the details for this section brings to light a few interesting
things:

```
penguin> readelf -S libfoo.so | egrep '\.data'
 [14] .data    PROGBITS        00001b00 000b00 000070 00  WA  0   0 32
```

First, note that the .data section has the type PROGBITS, which means that it
does occupy space in the file. This is different than the .bss section, which had
type NOBITS. Another thing worth noting is that memory attributes WA are
the same as those for the .bss section. "WA" means that the section is writable
and will require memory in the program.

The source file `foo.c` contains two variables, `globInt` and `staticInt`, that
can illustrate how the .data section is used:

```
int globInt = 5 ;
static int staticInt = 5 ;
```

The variable `globInt` is a global, writable (non-constant) variable, and `staticInt`
is a static writable variable. Both should be in the .data section, but let's confirm
that here:

```
penguin> nm -v -f s libfoo.so | egrep globInt
globInt         |00001b20|   D |          OBJECT|00000004|     |.data
penguin> nm -v -f s libfoo.so | egrep staticInt
staticInt       |00001b24|   d |          OBJECT|00000004|     |.data
```

From the section information before, the .data section had a value ("address") of 0x1b00 and a size of 0x70. The two variables have values of 0x1b20 and 0x1b24 respectively, both of which are located in the range of the .data section and even have the .data section listed in the output.

9.6.3.3 .dynamic This section stores information about dynamic linking. This includes information about which libraries are required for a program or executable, where to look for these libraries (rpath), and the important sections of the ELF object needed to run the program. The DYNAMIC *segment* contains the .dynamic section (and contains only this one section). The readelf tool can be used to display the contents of the dynamic section/segment:

```
penquin> readelf -d foo

Dynamic segment at offset 0x830 contains 25 entries:
 Tag        Type             Name/Value
 0x00000001 (NEEDED)         Shared library: [libfoo.so]
 0x00000001 (NEEDED)         Shared library: [libstdc++.so.5]
 0x00000001 (NEEDED)         Shared library: [libm.so.6]
 0x00000001 (NEEDED)         Shared library: [libgcc_s.so.1]
 0x00000001 (NEEDED)         Shared library: [libc.so.6]
 0x0000000f (RPATH)          Library rpath: [.]
 0x0000000c (INIT)           0x80484c8
 0x0000000d (FINI)           0x80486f0
 0x00000004 (HASH)           0x8048148
 0x00000005 (STRTAB)         0x8048310
 0x00000006 (SYMTAB)         0x80481e0
 0x0000000a (STRSZ)          282 (bytes)
 0x0000000b (SYMENT)         16 (bytes)
 0x00000015 (DEBUG)          0x0
 0x00000003 (PLTGOT)         0x8049938
 0x00000002 (PLTRELSZ)       48 (bytes)
 0x00000014 (PLTREL)         REL
 0x00000017 (JMPREL)         0x8048498
 0x00000011 (REL)            0x8048490
 0x00000012 (RELSZ)          8 (bytes)
 0x00000013 (RELENT)         8 (bytes)
 0x6ffffffe (VERNEED)        0x8048450
 0x6fffffff (VERNEEDNUM)     2
 0x6ffffff0 (VERSYM)         0x804842a
 0x00000000 (NULL)           0x0
```

The key sections listed in the dynamic section are explained in this chapter. The entries that have a type of NEEDED are for the libraries required by the executable foo. The RPATH defines a search path for the libraries. The rest of the information in the dynamic section is a convenient way to locate the information needed to run this executable, including the address of other important sections such as .init, .fini, and others.

This section is mainly used by the program interpreter, covered in more detail later in this chapter.

9.6.3.4 .dynsym (symbol table) The dynamic symbol table is the smaller of the two symbol tables. It only contains symbols that are required for program execution, global symbols. The dynamic symbol table is required and cannot be stripped from an ELF object. The dynamic symbol table does not contain any static symbols because static symbol information is not needed at run time.

Static symbols are local to a file, and once a shared library or executable is linked, the offset of the static symbols are called directly through an offset that is known at link time. Dynamic symbols might be satisfied outside of the shared library and executable, and thus finding these symbols must be done at run time.

Consider the two variables again: staticInt and globInt, defined as:

```
int globInt = 5 ;
static int staticInt = 5 ;
```

The globInt variable should be in the dynamic symbol table, although the staticInt variable should only be in the main symbol table:

```
penguin> nm  libfoo.so | egrep staticInt
00001b24 d staticInt
penguin> nm -D libfoo.so |egrep staticInt
penguin> nm -D libfoo.so | egrep globInt
00001b20 D globInt
```

As expected, the static variable is not found in the dynamic symbol table. The main symbol table that contains all symbols is described as follows under the section heading, .symtab.

9.6.3.5 .dynstr (string table) This string table contains only the symbols that are required for dynamic linking. The majority of the content will be for the symbol names from the dynamic symbol table. The format is the standard ELF string table format.

9.6.3.6 .fini The .fini section contains the machine instructions for the function _fini. Notice that the file offset listed by nm for _fini, and the file offset for the .fini section match exactly:

```
penguin> nm foo | egrep _fini
080486e0 T _fini
penguin> readelf -S foo | egrep fini
   [13] .fini  PROGBITS      080486e0 0006e0 00001c 00  AX  0   0  4
```

The _fini function at 0x080486e0 calls the static (global) destructors for an executable or shared library. For an executable, _fini (and thus the destructors) is called when the program terminates. For shared libraries, the _fini function is called when a library is unloaded from memory. The _fini function has a counterpart function called _init that calls the global constructors.

There is more information on the .init section covered further on in the chapter.

9.6.3.7 .got (Global Offset Table) The Global Offset Table, known as GOT, is required for position-independent code. Position-independent code is compiled in such a way that it can be loaded and run from any address. This isn't as easy as it sounds. Code that needs to call a function has no idea where in the address space this function will be. The GOT solves this problem by providing a level of indirection between the code in an executable or shared library and the required functions and variables that may be in other shared libraries. Let's look at the GOT in more detail:

```
penguin> readelf -S libfoo.so | egrep .got
   [20] .got    PROGBITS      00001d38 000d38 00003c 04  WA  0   0  4
```

From the output, we know that the .got is of type PROGBITS, meaning that it does consume space in the ELF file itself (unlike the .bss section). The output also indicates that the file offset of the .got is 0x918 and that it has a size of 0x28 or 40 decimal. Let's look at the raw contents:

```
penguin> hexdump -s 0xd38 -C -n 60 libfoo.so
00000d38  48 1c 00  00 00  00 00 00   00 00 00 00 96 07 00 00
➡|H..............|
00000d48  a6 07 00  00 b6  07 00 00   c6 07 00 00 d6 07 00 00
➡|................|
00000d58  00 00 00  00 00  1b 00 00   00 00 00 00 00 00 00 00
➡|................|
00000d68  00 00 00 00 00 00 00 00  00 00 00 00          |............|
```

The GOT is an array of values that is stored in private memory. According to readelf, the size of this global offset table is 0x3c, which means that it has the following values:

Value number	GOT Address (File Offset)	Value
0	0x1d38 (0xd38)	0x1c48
1	0x1d3c (0xd3c)	0x0
2	0x1d40 (0xd40)	0x0
3	0x1d44 (0xd44)	0x796
4	0x1d48 (0xd48)	0x7a6
5	0x1d4c (0xd4c)	0x7b6
6	0x1d50 (0xd50)	0x7c6
7	0x1d54 (0xd54)	0x7d6
8	0x1d58 (0xd58)	0x0
9	0x1d5c (0xd5c)	0x1b00
10	0x1d60 (0xd60)	0x0
11	0x1d64 (0xd64)	0x0
12	0x1d68 (0xd68)	0x0
13	0x1d6c (0xd6c)	0x0
14	0x1d70 (0xd70)	0x0

The first value (0x1c48) is always the virtual address of a special global variable called _DYNAMIC. This is the address of the dynamic section (covered previously).

```
penguin> nm libfoo.so | egrep 1c48
00001c48 A _DYNAMIC
```

The next two values (1 and 2) are 0x0. Addresses 4 through 8 range in value from 0x796 to 0x07d6 and all point to addresses in the *Procedure Linkage Table* or PLT:

```
penguin> readelf -S foo
There are 30 section headers, starting at offset 0x1090:

Section Headers:
  [Nr] Name       Type       Addr     Off    Size   ES Flg Lk Inf Al
<...>
  [ 9] .plt       PROGBITS   00000780 000780 000060 04 AX  0   0  4
<...>
```

From the output, the PLT starts at 0x780 and has a size of 0x60. More information
on the PLT and how it relates to the GOT follows under the heading ".plt."

So what are the rest of the entries in the GOT for? The answer requires
some knowledge of relocation. Without going into too much detail here, some
of the GOT entries are used for global variables. The machine instructions in
the shared library will reference the GOT entries for the global variables, and
the relocation entries ensure that the GOT entries point to the correct address
at run time. The relocation entries are included here for the curious reader,
although relocation will be covered in much more detail later in this chapter.

```
penguin> readelf -r libfoo.so

Relocation section '.rel.dyn' at offset 0x6e0 contains 12 entries:
 Offset     Info    Type            Sym.Value  Sym. Name
00001b00  00000008 R_386_RELATIVE
00001b04  00000008 R_386_RELATIVE
00001b68  00000008 R_386_RELATIVE
00001d24  00000008 R_386_RELATIVE
00001d5c  00000008 R_386_RELATIVE
00001b6c  00002101 R_386_32        00000000   __gxx_personality_v0
00001d58  00001e06 R_386_GLOB_DAT  00001d80   noValueGlobInt
00001d60  00002006 R_386_GLOB_DAT  00001b20   globInt
00001d64  00002206 R_386_GLOB_DAT  00000000   __cxa_finalize
00001d68  00002c06 R_386_GLOB_DAT  00001d7c   myObj2
00001d6c  00002d06 R_386_GLOB_DAT  00000000   _Jv_RegisterClasses
00001d70  00002e06 R_386_GLOB_DAT  00000000   __gmon_start__

Relocation section '.rel.plt' at offset 0x740 contains 5 entries:
 Offset     Info    Type            Sym.Value  Sym. Name
00001d44  00001d07 R_386_JUMP_SLOT  000009d6   _Z3fooi
00001d48  00002407 R_386_JUMP_SLOT  00000000   printf
00001d4c  00002607 R_386_JUMP_SLOT  00000000   __cxa_finalize
00001d50  00002b07 R_386_JUMP_SLOT  000009c8   _ZN7myClassC1Ev
00001d54  00002d07 R_386_JUMP_SLOT  00000000   _Jv_RegisterClasses
```

Notice that offset of the relocation entry for globInt is 0x1d60, which is one of
the slots in the GOT.

Consider the following code from foo.c:

```
static int bar( int c )
{
   int d = 0;

   d = foo( c ) + globInt ;
   d += staticInt ;
   d += constInt ;

   return d ;
}
```

It references the global integer globInt. Let's see how it uses the GOT to find this variable by looking at the assembly language for this function:

```
penguin> objdump -d libfoo.so
<...>
000008c4 <_Z3bari>:
 8c4:   55                        push    %ebp
 8c5:   89 e5                     mov     %esp,%ebp
 8c7:   53                        push    %ebx
 8c8:   83 ec 04                  sub     $0x4,%esp
 8cb:   e8 00 00 00 00            call    8d0 <_Z3bari+0xc>
 8d0:   5b                        pop     %ebx
 8d1:   81 c3 68 14 00 00         add     $0x1468,%ebx
 8d7:   c7 45 f8 00 00 00 00      movl    $0x0,0xfffffff8(%ebp)
 8de:   83 ec 0c                  sub     $0xc,%esp
 8e1:   ff 75 08                  pushl   0x8(%ebp)
 8e4:   e8 a7 fe ff ff            call    790 <_init+0x28>
 8e9:   83 c4 10                  add     $0x10,%esp
 8ec:   89 c2                     mov     %eax,%edx
 8ee:   8b 83 28 00 00 00         mov     0x28(%ebx),%eax
 8f4:   8b 08                     mov     (%eax),%ecx
 8f6:   8d 04 11                  lea     (%ecx,%edx,1),%eax
 8f9:   89 45 f8                  mov     %eax,0xfffffff8(%ebp)
 8fc:   8b 93 ec fd ff ff         mov     0xfffffdec(%ebx),%edx
 902:   8d 45 f8                  lea     0xfffffff8(%ebp),%eax
 905:   01 10                     add     %edx,(%eax)
 907:   8d 45 f8                  lea     0xfffffff8(%ebp),%eax
 90a:   83 00 05                  addl    $0x5,(%eax)
 90d:   8b 45 f8                  mov     0xfffffff8(%ebp),%eax
 910:   8b 5d fc                  mov     0xfffffffc(%ebp),%ebx
 913:   c9                        leave
 914:   c3                        ret
 915:   90                        nop
<...>
```

> **Note**: In the assembly language here, the symbol name _Z3bari is the function bar. The name is a "mangled" C++ function name. The objdump tool accepts a -c switch to demangle the name, or alternatively you can use the command echo _Z3bari |c++filt.
>
> **Note**: In the assembly language just listed, the hex numbers to the left of the output are file offsets and not real memory addresses. However, the methods used by ELF to achieve position independence would work even if these were real addresses. When the library is loaded into memory, the real memory addresses would be used instead.

The instruction at 0x8cb makes a call to 0x8d0. This seems a bit strange because that is the next instruction to be run anyway—but this does have a purpose. The instruction at 0x8d0 puts the current instruction address into register EBX. The instruction at 0x8d1 then adds a hard-coded value 0x1468 to this.

```
0x8d0+0x1468 = 0x1d38.
```

This is where the GOT is located. For quick reference, here is the information for the GOT section again:

```
penguin> readelf -S libfoo.so | egrep .got
[20] .got      PROGBITS         00001d38 000d38 00003c 04  WA  0   0   4
```

Later in the assembly language, there is a call at 0x8ee that adds 0x28 to the value in EBX, which finds the offset for globInt.

```
EBX( 0x1d38) + 0x28 = 0x1d60
```

From the relocation information just listed, this matches the value of the relocation entry for globInt:

```
00001d60  00002006 R_386_GLOB_DAT    00001b20   globInt
```

The next instruction at 0x8f4 dereferences the value for globInt in the GOT to find the actual address of globInt.

Note: This is a very good example of how the text segment relies on the data segment being at a specific offset. In this case, it expects the GOT to be 0x1468 away from a particular instruction. If the data section (which contains the GOT) was ever loaded in the wrong place, the hard-coded reference to the GOT would be inaccurate.

9.6.3.8 .hash This is the symbol hash table. Because humans need to use symbol names (that is, function and variable names), ELF must implement a quick way to find the various symbol names to find the corresponding symbol.

We know that the symbol table in an ELF file is simply an array. Without a hash table of some sort, finding a symbol in this array would require a linear search of the array until the symbol is found or until the end of the symbol table is reached. This might not be too bad for a one-time search, but the typical ELF file contains many symbols (possibly many thousands). A linear search for each of these either during run time or for the linker (ld) would not be practical.

The hash mechanism in ELF is illustrated in Figure 9.3.

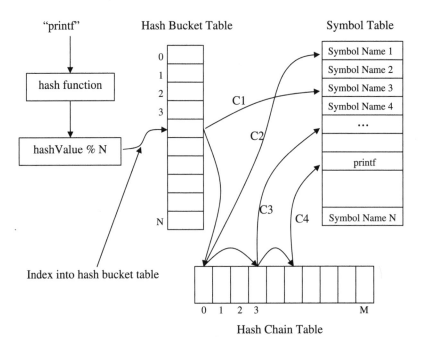

Fig. 9.3 ELF hash algorithm.

In the diagram, the function printf is run through the hash function to retrieve a numeric value. The modulus of this numeric value with the hash bucket table size provides an index into the hash bucket table. The hash bucket table contains an index into the symbol table as well as the hash chain table. At this point, the symbol name in the symbol table (pointed to by the hash bucket slot) is checked against printf ("C1" in the diagram). If the symbol name at this entry in the symbol table doesn't ARmatch, the index of the chain table is used.

Each chain table entry contains an index into the symbol table as well as the index of the next element in the chain if there are any. The symbol table entry from the first chain table entry is compared against printf ("C2" in the diagram). According to the diagram, there was no match, so the next element in the chain is used. This happens again until the function printf is found in the symbol table after four comparisons (the symbol is found in "C4" according to the diagram).

This is more complex but much more efficient than using a linear search in the symbol table, especially for large symbol tables.

For the interested reader, here is the hash algorithm as specified in the ELF standard:

```
unsigned long ElfHash(const unsigned char *name)
{
  unsigned long h=0, g;
  while (*name)
    {
      h = (h << 4) + *name++;
      if (g = h & 0xF0000000)
  h ^= g >> 24;
      h &= ~g;
    }
  return h;
}
```

9.6.3.9 .init This section contains executable instructions required for initialization of an ELF object. It is almost identical to the .fini section except that the information is for initialization, not finalization. The section .init contains a function called _init in the same way that the .fini section contains a function called _fini. The _init function is responsible for initializing global variables (including objects) for an ELF library or executable. Notice in the output that the address of the _init function matches the address of the .init section:

```
penguin> readelf -S foo |egrep "\.init"
  [10] .init    PROGBITS        080484b4 0004b4 000018 00  AX  0  0  4
penguin> nm foo |egrep 080484b4
080484b4 T _init
```

Let's dig a bit deeper to see how the .init section works (which is very similar to how the .fini section works). We'll start by looking at a global C++ object defined in main.c ,which eventually is compiled into the executable called foo:

```
myClass myObj3 ;
The class "myClass" is defined as follows:
class myClass
{
   public:

   int myVar ;

   myClass() {
      myVar = 5 ;
   }

};
```

Notice that it includes a constructor. This is what should eventually be called by `_init()`.

Disassembling the .init section using `objdump` shows us the following:

```
penguin> objdump -d foo | head -15

foo:    file format elf32-i386

Disassembly of section .init:

080484b4 <_init>:
 80484b4:       55                      push   %ebp
 80484b5:       89 e5                   mov    %esp,%ebp
 80484b7:       83 ec 08                sub    $0x8,%esp
 80484ba:       e8 a5 00 00 00          call   8048564 <call_gmon_start>
 80484bf:       90                      nop
 80484c0:       e8 0b 01 00 00          call   80485d0 <frame_dummy>
 80484c5:       e8 e6 01 00 00          call   80486b0 <__do_global_ctors_aux>
 80484ca:       c9                      leave
 80484cb:       c3                      ret
<...>
```

In the assembly listing, there is a call to `__do_global_ctors_aux`. Let's disassemble that function next (some output was excluded for simplicity):

```
penguin> objdump -d foo
<...>
080486b0 <__do_global_ctors_aux>:
 80486b0:       55                      push   %ebp
 80486b1:       89 e5                   mov    %esp,%ebp
 80486b3:       53                      push   %ebx
 80486b4:       52                      push   %edx
 80486b5:       a1 04 99 04 08          mov    0x8049904,%eax
 80486ba:       83 f8 ff                cmp    $0xffffffff,%eax
 80486bd:       bb 04 99 04 08          mov    $0x8049904,%ebx
 80486c2:       74 18                   je     80486dc <__do_global_ctors_aux+0x2c>
 80486c4:       8d b6 00 00 00 00       lea    0x0(%esi),%esi
 80486ca:       8d bf 00 00 00 00       lea    0x0(%edi),%edi
 80486d0:       83 eb 04                sub    $0x4,%ebx
 80486d3:       ff d0                   call   *%eax
 80486d5:       8b 03                   mov    (%ebx),%eax
 80486d7:       83 f8 ff                cmp    $0xffffffff,%eax
 80486da:       75 f4                   jne    80486d0 <__do_global_ctors_aux+0x20>
 80486dc:       58                      pop    %eax
 80486dd:       5b                      pop    %ebx
 80486de:       5d                      pop    %ebp
 80486df:       c3                      ret
<...>
```

The assembly listing shows the following instruction `call *%eax` at instruction `0x80486d3`. This takes the value of the EAX register, treats it as an address, dereferences the address and the calls function stored at the dereferenced address. From code above this call, we can see EAX being set with `mov 0x8049904,%eax` at instruction `0x8049904`. Let's take a look at what is located at that address:

```
penguin> nm -v -f s foo
<...>
__CTOR_LIST__       |08049900|   d |            OBJECT|        |  |.ctors
__CTOR_END__        |08049908|   d |            OBJECT|        |  |.ctors
<...>
```

According to `nm`, there are two variables `__CTOR_LIST` and `_CTOR_END`, which have addresses that surround the address `0x8049904` stored in register EAX. This is the address that eventually is dereferenced to get an address that is called.

We need to find the value stored at address `0x8049904` to see what address is eventually called. It is kind of a pain to do this, but we first need to find the difference between the virtual address and the file offset of the segment that contains this address. We know it will be in a LOAD segment because it contains information needed at run time:

```
penguin> readelf -l foo | egrep LOAD
  LOAD      0x000000 0x08048000 0x08048000 0x0076c 0x0076c R E 0x1000
  LOAD      0x00076c 0x0804976c 0x0804976c 0x001d4 0x001dc RW  0x1000
```

According to the output, the address `0x8049904` is in the second load segment (the data segment), and the difference between virtual address of the data segment and the file offsets in the data segment is `0x08049000` (`0x0804976c` - `0x76c`). This is the address that we need to subtract from `0x8049904` to get the file offset of `0x904`. Let's see the contents at that offset:

```
penguin> hexdump -C -s 0x904 -n 4 foo
00000904  7e 86 04 08                                       |~...|
00000908
```

According to the output, we have a value of `0x0804867e` at address `0x8049904` (file offset `0x904`). One more step is needed before we know what this address is for:

```
penguin> nm foo | egrep 0804867e
0804867e t _GLOBAL__I_myObj3
```

This is the global constructor of the myObj2 object, which is called, as expected, by functions under _init.

The __CTOR_LIST__ variable stores the list of global constructors for an executable or shared library. We can find all of the global constructors by listing the addresses between __CTOR_LIST and _CTOR_END. This can be useful if you need to know what will be run before the main() function of an executable or when a library is first loaded.

The .fini section has a very similar convention but uses the __DTOR_LIST__ and __DTOR_END variables to mark the addresses of the global destructors.

9.6.3.10 .interp This section contains the path name of the program interpreter. The program interpreter is used for executables and is responsible for getting a process up and running with all of its required libraries, and so on. A quick way to get the program interpreter is to use the readelf command as follows:

```
penguin> readelf -l foo
<...>
   INTERP          0x000114 0x08048114 0x08048114 0x00013 0x00013 R   0x1
        [Requesting program interpreter: /lib/ld-linux.so.2]
<...>
```

The program interpreter is described later in the chapter under the section heading, "Program Interpreter."

9.6.3.11 .plt (Procedure Linkage Table) The procedure linkage table is required by every shared library or executable that is dependent on shared libraries to satisfy an unresolved symbol. The PLT is also used to support "lazy binding," which means not resolving the address of a function until it is called for the first time.

The procedure linkage table contains a list of instructions that help functions find other functions in the address space. First, let's use the readelf tool to find the PLT for the executable named foo. It is always in the section named .plt.

```
penguin> readelf -S foo | egrep ' \.plt'
   [11] .plt     PROGBITS       080484cc 0004cc 000070 04  AX  0   0  4
```

The best way to look at the PLT is through the debugger. It starts at address 0x80484e0 and continues for 0x70 bytes:

```
(gdb) disass 0x080484cc
Dump of assembler code for function _init:
0x80484b4 <_init>:       push   %ebp
```

```
0x80484b5 <_init+1>:      mov      %esp,%ebp
0x80484b7 <_init+3>:      sub      $0x8,%esp
0x80484ba <_init+6>:      call     0x8048564 <call_gmon_start>
0x80484bf <_init+11>:     nop
0x80484c0 <_init+12>:     call     0x80485d0 <frame_dummy>
0x80484c5 <_init+17>:     call     0x80486b0 <__do_global_ctors_aux>
0x80484ca <_init+22>:     leave
0x80484cb <_init+23>:     ret
0x80484cc <_init+24>:     pushl    0x804991c
0x80484d2 <_init+30>:     jmp      *0x8049920
0x80484d8 <_init+36>:     add      %al,(%eax)
0x80484da <_init+38>:     add      %al,(%eax)
0x80484dc <sleep>:        jmp      *0x8049924
0x80484e2 <sleep+6>:      push     $0x0.
0x80484e7 <sleep+11>:     jmp      0x80484cc <_init+24>
0x80484ec <uname>:        jmp      *0x8049928
0x80484f2 <uname+6>:      push     $0x8
0x80484f7 <uname+11>:     jmp      0x80484cc <_init+24>
0x80484fc <__gxx_personality_v0>:        jmp      *0x804992c
0x8048502 <__gxx_personality_v0+6>:      push     $0x10
0x8048507 <__gxx_personality_v0+11>:     jmp      0x80484cc <_init+24>
0x804850c <__libc_start_main>:   jmp      *0x8049930
0x8048512 <__libc_start_main+6>:         push     $0x18
0x8048517 <__libc_start_main+11>:        jmp      0x80484cc <_init+24>
0x804851c <_Z3bazi>:     jmp      *0x8049934
0x8048522 <_Z3bazi+6>:   push     $0x20
0x8048527 <_Z3bazi+11>:  jmp      0x80484cc <_init+24>
0x804852c <printf>:      jmp      *0x8049938
0x8048532 <printf+6>:    push     $0x28
0x8048537 <printf+11>:   jmp      0x80484cc <_init+24>
End of assembler dump.
```

Disassemble the PLT? Yes, the PLT is executable, but it has very specific executable parts (one for each function in the PLT). We could have used objdump to disassemble the PLT, although objdump would not give any hints as to which parts of the PLT relate to which functions.

The location of the PLT is relative to functions that require other functions located somewhere in the address space. The relative offset from a function to the PLT is known at link time, so it is possible for the linker to specify a hard coded offset from an instruction address to the PLT. Because the location of the required/defined functions is not known at compile time or link time, the code instead makes a call directly to the appropriate slot in the PLT.

From the file main.C, the function main makes a call to sleep. The assembly language for this call from within gdb looks like this (some output skipped for simplicity):

```
(gdb) disass main
Dump of assembler code for function main:
0x80485fc <main>:        push     %ebp
```

```
0x80485fd <main+1>:      mov     %esp,%ebp
0x80485ff <main+3>:      sub     $0x198,%esp
<...>
0x8048641 <main+69>:     push    $0x3f2
0x8048646 <main+74>:     call    0x80484dc <sleep>
<...>
```

Note that the call to the sleep function is to the PLT slot for the sleep function
(compare the address used in the call instruction to the assembly listing for
the PLT above). Going back to the PLT slot for "sleep":

```
0x80484dc <sleep>:       jmp     *0x8049924
0x80484e2 <sleep+6>:     push    $0x0
0x80484e7 <sleep+11>:    jmp     0x80484cc <_init+24>
```

The first instruction is a jump to address 0x8049924. This is right inside the
Global Offset Table or GOT. To confirm, let's get the address of the GOT:

```
penguin> readelf -S foo | egrep ' \.got'
 [22] .got    PROGBITS         08049918 000918 000028 04  WA   0    0    4
```

Okay, so what's in the GOT that might be of interest to the PLT? That depends
on when you look. Before the program is run, the GOT looks like the following:

```
(gdb) x/40 0x08049918
0x8049918 <_JCR_LIST_+4>: 0x08049810 0x00000000 0x00000000
➥0x080484e2
0x8049928 <_JCR_LIST_+20>: 0x080484f2 0x08048502 0x08048512
➥0x08048522
0x8049938 <_JCR_LIST_+36>: 0x08048532 0x00000000 0x00000000
➥0x00000000
0x8049948:      Cannot access memory at address 0x8049948
```

The GOT slot for the sleep function (at 0x8049924) has a value of 0x080484e2.
This is the address of the second instruction in the PLT slot for the sleep
function.

```
0x80484e2 <sleep+6>:     push    $0x0
```

The instruction pushes a value of 0x0 onto the stack. The next instruction
jumps to 0x80484e0:

```
0x80484e7 <sleep+11>:    jmp     0x80484cc <_init+24>
```

It is worth noting that each of the PLT slots has a different value at offset 0x6:

```
0x80484e2 <sleep+6>:     push   $0x0
0x80484f2 <uname+6>:     push   $0x8
0x8048502 <__gxx_personality_v0+6>:      push   $0x10
0x8048512 <__libc_start_main+6>:         push   $0x18
0x8048522 <_Z3bazi+6>:   push   $0x20
0x8048532 <printf+6>:    push   $0x28
```

For example, the `uname` slot pushes a value of 0x8 onto the stack. This is a special marker used to find the PLT slot, used by the dynamic linking code. Dynamic linking is explained in more detail shortly.

Let's get back to the address of `0x80484cc`. This is the address of the beginning of the PLT and contains the following instructions (ignore the offset of `_init`):

```
0x80484cc <_init+24>:    pushl   0x804991c
0x80484d2 <_init+30>:    jmp     *0x8049920
0x80484d8 <_init+36>:    add     %al,(%eax)
0x80484da <_init+38>:    add     %al,(%eax)
```

The first instruction pushes a value onto the stack, while the second instruction jumps to the address stored in `0x8049920`. Let's see what value is at that address:

```
(gdb) break main
Breakpoint 1 at 0x8048605
(gdb) run
Starting program: /home/wilding/src/Linuxbook/ELF/foo

Breakpoint 1, 0x08048605 in main ()

(gdb) x 0x8049920
0x8049920 <__JCR_LIST__+12>:     0x40009c90
```

Okay, let's see what function is at `0x40009c90`:

```
(gdb) disass 0x40009c90 0x40009c94
Dump of assembler code from 0x40009c90 to 0x40009c94:
0x40009c90 <_dl_runtime_resolve>:        push   %eax
0x40009c91 <_dl_runtime_resolve+1>:      push   %ecx
0x40009c92 <_dl_runtime_resolve+2>:      push   %edx
0x40009c93 <_dl_runtime_resolve+3>:      mov    0x10(%esp,1),%edx
End of assembler dump.
```

So after all of this we know that the first call to "sleep" (or any function) will eventually call `_dl_runtime_resolve`. This is a special function that works to resolve the address of the function. The details of how this works are a bit beyond the scope of this chapter (and fairly lengthy to explain), but suffice it to say that this finds the address of the function whose slot was just executed. It then updates the GOT with the actual address of the function in the address space so that the second call to the function (that is, "sleep") will go directly to the address of the actual function itself.

Let's see what the GOT looks like after the function sleep is called:

```
(gdb) cont
Continuing.
This is a printf format string in baz
This is a printf format string in main

Program received signal SIGINT, Interrupt.
0x401a2d01 in nanosleep () from /lib/libc.so.6
(gdb) x/40 0x08049918
0x8049918 <_JCR_LIST_+4>: 0x08049810 0x40012fd0 0x40009c90
➥0x401a2ab0
0x8049928 <_JCR_LIST_+20>: 0x401a2750 0x08048502 0x4011d400
➥0x40014916
0x8049938 <_JCR_LIST_+36>: 0x40154c90 0x00000000 0x00000000
➥0x00000005
0x8049948: 0x00000000 0x00000019 0x7273752f 0x62696c2f
. . .
```

After the program is run and the sleep function is called, the slot for the sleep function in the GOT is `0x401a2ab0`. Let's confirm that this is the address of the actual sleep function.

```
(gdb) disass 0x401a2ab0
Dump of assembler code for function sleep:
0x401a2ab0 <sleep>:      push    %ebp
0x401a2ab1 <sleep+1>:    mov     %esp,%ebp
0x401a2ab3 <sleep+3>:    push    %edi
0x401a2ab4 <sleep+4>:    push    %esi
. . .
```

So the next time the function sleep is called, the GOT slot points directly to the actual sleep function, avoiding the need to resolve the function a second time (that is, find its address in memory).

9.6.3.12 .rodata This section contains read-only constant values, string literals, and other constant data such as the variable `constInt` from `foo.c` defined as:

```
const int constInt = 5 ;
```

This variable should be located in the .rodata section because it is read-only (that is, constant). Let's confirm by finding the location of the .rodata section and of this read-only (constant) variable.

```
penguin> readelf -S libfoo.so |egrep rodata
   [12] .rodata    PROGBITS    00000a80 000a80 00004c 00    A  0   0 32
penguin> nm libfoo.so |egrep constInt
00000ac8 r constant
```

As expected, `constInt` is contained within the .rodata segment, given the values of the preceding output. Let's see what else is in the .rodata section using the hexdump utility:

```
penguin> hexdump -C -s 0xa80 -n 76 libfoo.so
00000a80  54 68 69 73 20 69 73 20  61 20 63 6f 6e 73 74 61  |This
➥is a consta|
00000a90  6e 74 20 73 74 72 69 6e  67 21 00 00 00 00 00 00  |nt
➥string!......|
00000aa0  54 68 69 73 20 69 73 20  61 20 70 72 69 6e 74 66  |This
➥is a printf|
00000ab0  20 66 6f 72 6d 61 74 20  73 74 72 69 6e 67 20 69  |
➥format string i|
00000ac0  6e 20 62 61 7a 0a 00 00  05 00 00 00              |n
➥baz.......|
00000acc
```

This output shows that the .rodata section also contains constant strings, including those used in printf statements. Notice that such strings are *not* stored in any of the ELF string tables.

9.6.3.13 .shstrtab This section is the string table that contains the section names of the various sections:

```
penguin> hexdump -C libfoo.so -s0xffb -n 251
00000ffb  00 2e 73 79 6d 74 61 62  00 2e 73 74 72 74 61 62
➥|..symtab..strtab|
0000100b  00 2e 73 68 73 74 72 74  61 62 00 2e 68 61 73 68
➥|..shstrtab..hash|
0000101b  00 2e 64 79 6e 73 79 6d  00 2e 64 79 6e 73 74 72
➥|..dynsym..dynstr|
0000102b  00 2e 67 6e 75 2e 76 65  72 73 69 6f 6e 00 2e 67
➥|..gnu.version..g|
0000103b  6e 75 2e 76 65 72 73 69  6f 6e 5f 72 00 2e 72 65
➥|nu.version_r..re|
0000104b  6c 2e 64 79 6e 00 2e 72  65 6c 2e 70 6c 74 00 2e
➥|l.dyn..rel.plt..|
0000105b  69 6e 69 74 00 2e 74 65  78 74 00 2e 66 69 6e 69
➥|init..text..fini|
0000106b  00 2e 72 6f 64 61 74 61  00 2e 65 68 5f 66 72 61
```

```
➥|..rodata..eh_fra|
0000107b  6d 65 5f 68 64 72 00 2e  64 61 74 61 00 2e 65 68
➥|me_hdr..data..eh|
0000108b  5f 66 72 61 6d 65 00 2e  64 79 6e 61 6d 69 63 00
➥|_frame..dynamic.|
0000109b  2e 63 74 6f 72 73 00 2e  64 74 6f 72 73 00 2e 6a
➥|.ctors..dtors..j|
000010ab  63 72 00 2e 67 6f 74 00  2e 62 73 73 00 2e 63 6f
➥|cr..got..bss..co|
000010bb  6d 6d 65 6e 74 00 2e 64  65 62 75 67 5f 61 72 61
➥|mment..debug_ara|
000010cb  6e 67 65 73 00 2e 64 65  62 75 67 5f 69 6e 66 6f
➥|nges..debug_info|
000010db  00 2e 64 65 62 75 67 5f  61 62 62 72 65 76 00 2e
➥|..debug_abbrev..|
000010eb  64 65 62 75 67 5f 6c 69  6e 65 00 |debug_line.|000010f6
```

9.6.3.14 .strtab (string table) This string table stores symbol names for
the main symbol table. It uses the typical string table format described above
under "String Table Format." See the section, .dynsym, for the string table for
the dynamic symbol table.

9.6.3.15 .symtab (symbol table) This is the full (main) symbol table that
also includes all static functions and variables. This is used during the linking
phase when an executable or shared library is being built. This is not used
during run time. In fact, only part or none of this symbol table may be loaded
into the address space at run time.

In the executable foo, the offset of the .symtab section is 0x29c4 and is
0x51 0 bytes in size as shown here:

```
penguin> readelf -S foo | egrep symtab
   [33] .symtab  SYMTAB      00000000 0029c4 000510 10    34  3a  4
```

Using the readelf command, we can see that this section is contained by *none*
of the ELF segments:

```
penguin> readelf -l foo | head -16

Elf file type is EXEC (Executable file)
Entry point 0x8048540
There are 7 program headers, starting at offset 52

Program Headers:
  Type    Offset    VirtAddr    PhysAddr    FileSiz MemSiz Flg Align
  PHDR    0x000034  0x08048034  0x08048034  0x000e0 0x000e0 R E 0x4
  INTERP  0x000114  0x08048114  0x08048114  0x00013 0x00013 R   0x1
```

```
        [Requesting program interpreter: /lib/ld-linux.so.2]
  LOAD       0x000000 0x08048000 0x08048000 0x0076c 0x0076c R E 0x1000
  LOAD       0x00076c 0x0804976c 0x0804976c 0x001d4 0x001dc RW   0x1000
  DYNAMIC    0x000810 0x08049810 0x08049810 0x000f0 0x000f0 RW   0x4
  NOTE       0x000128 0x08048128 0x08048128 0x00020 0x00020 R    0x4
  GNU_EH_FRAME   0x000748 0x08048748 0x08048748 0x00024 0x00024 R 0x4
```

The fact that this symbol table is not loaded at run time makes it impossible to write a stack trace back function that can find and display the names of static functions from within the program itself.

Stack trace back functions are often called from within a signal handler to dump the stack trace to a file when a trap occurs. Some of the functions on the stack may be static, and the program's address space does not contain any symbol table that can be used to map the address of stack functions to function names.

9.6.3.16 .text This section contains the executable code of an ELF file. All of the compiled functions that an ELF file contains will be in this section. This is the most important part of an ELF file. The rest of the sections and all of the complexity of ELF serves to allow the executable instructions in this section to run. The file foo.c defines three functions:

```
penguin> nm libfoo.so |egrep " T "
00000916 T _Z3bazi
00000a60 T _fini
00000768 T _init
```

These functions are all within the range of the .text segment:

```
penguin> readelf -S libfoo.so | egrep text
[10] .text    PROGBITS    000007e0 0007e0 000280 00  AX  0   0 16
```

Because the .text section contains executable instructions, the best way to see the contents of the .text section is to disassemble an ELF file using the objdump tool and look for the .text section in the output:

```
penguin> objdump -d libfoo.so
<...>
Disassembly of section .text:
<...>
000009d6 <_Z3fooi>:
  9d6:   55                      push    %ebp
  9d7:   89 e5                   mov     %esp,%ebp
  9d9:   53                      push    %ebx
  9da:   83 ec 04                sub     $0x4,%esp
  9dd:   e8 00 00 00 00          call    9e2 <_Z3fooi+0xc>
```

```
9e2:    5b                              pop     %ebx
9e3:    81 c3 56 13 00 00               add     $0x1356,%ebx
9e9:    c7 45 f8 00 00 00 00            movl    $0x0,0xfffffff8(%ebp)
9f0:    8b 45 08                        mov     0x8(%ebp),%eax
9f3:    89 45 f8                        mov     %eax,0xfffffff8(%ebp)
9f6:    83 7d f8 63                     cmpl    $0x63,0xfffffff8(%ebp)
9fa:    7e 02                           jle     9fe <_Z3fooi+0x28>
9fc:    eb 07                           jmp     a05 <_Z3fooi+0x2f>
9fe:    8d 45 f8                        lea     0xfffffff8(%ebp),%eax
a01:    ff 00                           incl    (%eax)
a03:    eb f1                           jmp     9f6 <_Z3fooi+0x20>
a05:    8b 93 20 00 00 00               mov     0x20(%ebx),%edx
a0b:    8b 45 08                        mov     0x8(%ebp),%eax
a0e:    89 02                           mov     %eax,(%edx)
a10:    8b 45 08                        mov     0x8(%ebp),%eax
a13:    03 45 f8                        add     0xfffffff8(%ebp),%eax
a16:    83 c4 04                        add     $0x4,%esp
a19:    5b                              pop     %ebx
a1a:    5d                              pop     %ebp
a1b:    c3                              ret
```

All of the functions from the source files will be listed, as well as a few additional functions that support the inner workings of ELF.

9.6.3.17 .rel This is a relocation section. Relocation sections are prefixed by the section name that they will be operating on. For example, .rel.text is a relocation table that will work with the .text section. Relocation is a critical part of ELF because it allows shared libraries to be loaded anywhere in the address space.

Relocation is the process of changing an address in a loaded ELF section to the current address of a corresponding function or variable as illustrated in Figure 9.4.

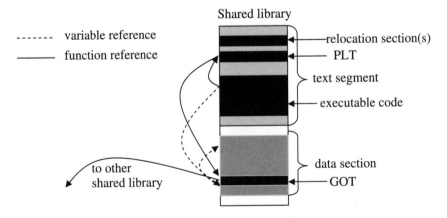

Fig. 9.4 Relocations.

Figure 9.4 shows the important sections that are needed to explain relocation. The text *segment* contains the procedure linkage table (PLT), relocation sections, and the executable code. The data *segment* contains the global and static variables as well as the global offset table (GOT).

A function reference first goes to the PLT to the appropriate slot. This then executes an address, which is stored in the corresponding slot in the GOT. The address in the GOT may point back to a function in the text segment, or it may point to a function in another shared library. In the diagram, this reference goes to another shared library.

A variable reference goes directly to the GOT and then to the address of the variable. The reference could go to another shared library (or executable) or to the data segment of the same shared library as it does in the diagram.

The relocation in this case can be as simple as changing the addresses stored in the GOT.

The `libfoo.so` shared library actually has two sections that are prefixed by .rel:

```
penguin> readelf -S libfoo.so | egrep rel
  [ 6] .rel.dyn   REL       000006e0 0006e0 000060 08   A  2   0  4
  [ 7] .rel.plt   REL       00000740 000740 000028 08   A  2   9  4
```

These are both relocation sections that contain entries of the form:

```
typedef struct
{
  Elf32_Addr   r_offset;   /* Address */
  Elf32_Word   r_info;     /* Relocation type and symbol index */
} Elf32_Rel;
```

Note: Other platforms may use .rela sections and the corresponding Elf32_Rela structure (see /usr/include/elf.h for this structure).

The r_offset field is the target address or offset that should be changed by the relocation. For object files, the offset is within the affected section. For shared libraries and executables, this is the "value" (address) of the symbol. The `r_info` field contains the relocation type and the symbol index. We can see the relocation information using `readelf`:

```
penguin> readelf -r libfoo.so

Relocation section '.rel.dyn' at offset 0x6e0 contains 12 entries:
 Offset     Info    Type            Sym.Value  Sym. Name
00001b00  00000008 R_386_RELATIVE
00001b04  00000008 R_386_RELATIVE
```

```
00001b68   00000008 R_386_RELATIVE
00001d24   00000008 R_386_RELATIVE
00001d5c   00000008 R_386_RELATIVE
00001b6c   00002101 R_386_32        00000000   __ gxx_personality_v0
00001d58   00001e06 R_386_GLOB_DAT  00001d80   noValueGlobInt
00001d60   00002006 R_386_GLOB_DAT  00001b20   globInt
00001d64   00002606 R_386_GLOB_DAT  00000000   cxa_finalize
00001d68   00002c06 R_386_GLOB_DAT  00001d7c   myObj2
00001d6c   00002d06 R_386_GLOB_DAT  00000000   Jv_RegisterClasses
00001d70   00002e06 R_386_GLOB_DAT  00000000   gmon_start__

Relocation section '.rel.plt' at offset 0x740 contains 5 entries:
 Offset     Info    Type          Sym.Value  Sym. Name
00001d44   00001d07 R_386_JUMP_SLOT  000009d6   Z3fooi
00001d48   00002407 R_386_JUMP_SLOT  00000000   printf
00001d4c   00002607 R_386_JUMP_SLOT  00000000   cxa_finalize
00001d50   00002b07 R_386_JUMP_SLOT  000009c8   ZN7myClassC1Ev
00001d54   00002d07 R_386_JUMP_SLOT  00000000   Jv_RegisterClasses
```

Notice that the variables are in one section, and all of the functions are in another section.

Static variables and functions do not need to be relocated because they will always reference using a relative offset from within the shared library. For executables, they will reference using absolute addresses.

The file foo.c defines two objects, one static and one global as follows:

```
static myClass myObj ;
myClass myObj2 ;
```

Only one variable, the global variable, will be in the relocation section:

```
penguin> readelf -r libfoo.so |egrep "globInt|staticInt"
00001d60   00002006 R_386_GLOB_DAT     00001b20   globInt
```

The type is R_386_GLOB_DAT and the symbol offset is 0x1b20, which is the value of the symbol in the symbol table. The relocation offset for globInt points to 0x1d60, which is the address of the globInt slot in the GOT. More information on relocations follows in the next section of this chapter.

9.7 RELOCATION AND POSITION INDEPENDENT CODE (PIC)

In this section we'll investigate the difference between position independent code (known as "PIC" from here on) and non-position-independent code and how both affect relocation.

9.7.1 PIC vs. non-PIC

Much of the complexity in the ELF standard is due to the need to load shared libraries at different locations in a process' address space. Objects built to be position-independent are specifically meant to be loaded anywhere in the address space. As discussed earlier, the code in ELF files contains relative references to data and relies on the PLT and GOT to resolve the symbols at run time. Let's take a look at position independent code in more detail, though, because it is an important concept for ELF.

Consider the following source code:

```
#include <stdio.h>

extern "C" int otherFunction( int val )
{
    return 23 ;
}

int myGlobInt = 12;

int buzz( void )
{
    int intVal ;

    intVal = myGlobInt + otherFunction( 5 ) ;

    return intVal ;
}

int main( )
{
    printf( "buzz: %d\n", buzz() ) ;

    return 0 ;
}
```

Make note that the source code shows a direct call to "buzz" as part of the call to the `printf` function. How the function is called is not important, but rather that it is called from within the scope of the main function.

This little code snippet contains a few functions and a global variable. Let's see how the resulting ELF object file differs when it is compiled as PIC or non-PIC. The `-fPIC` switch tells the g++ compiler to build with position-independent code.

```
penguin> g++ -c pic.C -o pic_nopic.o
penguin> g++ -fPIC -c pic.C -o pic.o
```

The first thing worth noting is that the resulting file sizes are different:

```
penguin> ls -l pic*.o
-rw-r-r-    1 wilding  build        1016 Dec 28 15:14 pic.o
-rw-r-r-    1 wilding  build         924 Dec 28 15:09 pic_nopic.o
```

The position-independent code is larger by 92 bytes. But what is different about the actual contents of the files? To find out, we need to look deeper. The first tool we'll use is nm:

```
penguin> nm -S pic.o
          U _GLOBAL_OFFSET_TABLE_
0000000a 00000036 T _Z4buzzv
00000040 00000045 T main
00000000 00000004 D myGlobInt
00000000 0000000a T otherFunction
          U printf

penguin> nm -S pic_nopic.o
0000000a 00000021 T _Z4buzzv
0000002c 00000033 T main
00000000 00000004 D myGlobInt
00000000 0000000a T otherFunction
          U printf
```

The PIC version includes the global offset table as a required symbol; whereas, the non-PIC version does not. We know that the GOT is used to support relocation, so this makes sense. The other important difference is that the functions have difference sizes. Let's take a look at the assembly instructions for function main using the objdump tool (only the output for the function main is shown here):

```
penguin> objdump -d pic.o
...
00000040 <main>:
  40:   55                      push    %ebp
  41:   89 e5                   mov     %esp,%ebp
  43:   53                      push    %ebx
  44:   83 ec 04                sub     $0x4,%esp
  47:   e8 00 00 00 00          call    4c <main+0xc>
  4c:   5b                      pop     %ebx
  4d:   81 c3 03 00 00 00       add     $0x3,%ebx
  53:   83 e4 f0                and     $0xfffffff0,%esp
  56:   b8 00 00 00 00          mov     $0x0,%eax
  5b:   29 c4                   sub     %eax,%esp
  5d:   83 ec 08                sub     $0x8,%esp
  60:   83 ec 08                sub     $0x8,%esp
  63:   e8 fc ff ff ff          call    64 <main+0x24>
```

```
   68:    83 c4 08              add     $0x8,%esp
   6b:    50                    push    %eax
   6c:    8d 83 00 00 00 00     lea     0x0(%ebx),%eax
   72:    50                    push    %eax
   73:    e8 fc ff ff ff        call    74 <main+0x34>
   78:    83 c4 10              add     $0x10,%esp
   7b:    b8 00 00 00 00        mov     $0x0,%eax
   80:    8b 5d fc              mov     0xfffffffc(%ebp),%ebx
   83:    c9                    leave
   84:    c3                    ret

penguin> objdump -d pic_nopic.o
...
0000002c <main>:
   2c:    55                    push    %ebp
   2d:    89 e5                 mov     %esp,%ebp
   2f:    83 ec 08              sub     $0x8,%esp
   32:    83 e4 f0              and     $0xfffffff0,%esp
   35:    b8 00 00 00 00        mov     $0x0,%eax
   3a:    29 c4                 sub     %eax,%esp
   3c:    83 ec 08              sub     $0x8,%esp
   3f:    83 ec 08              sub     $0x8,%esp
   42:    e8 fc ff ff ff        call    43 <main+0x17>
   47:    83 c4 08              add     $0x8,%esp
   4a:    50                    push    %eax
   4b:    68 00 00 00 00        push    $0x0
   50:    e8 fc ff ff ff        call    51 <main+0x25>
   55:    83 c4 10              add     $0x10,%esp
   58:    b8 00 00 00 00        mov     $0x0,%eax
   5d:    c9                    leave
   5e:    c3                    ret
```

The non-PIC version is certainly smaller, and there is a good reason for this. It is also interesting that neither version makes a direct call to the function buzz(). For that matter, there is no direct call to printf either. The secret here is relocation and how it works with PIC and non-PIC code.

The PIC code needs first to find the procedure linkage table before it can make a call to the function buzz(). This is because buzz() could be anywhere in the address space. The non-PIC code, on the other hand, can make some assumptions that the buzz() will eventually be at a predictable offset from any code that needs it. Well, sort of. There is an exception listed later under "Relocation and Linking." In any case, let's see how relocation is affected by position-independent code.

9.7.2 Relocation and Position Independent Code

As discussed before, relocation is a mechanism used to change values in a shared library or executable when it is loaded into a process' address space. As discussed earlier, calls to either `printf()` or `buzz()` at compile time would be premature because the compiler doesn't know where these functions will be located at run time.

For simplicity, let's look at the relocation information for the non-PIC version first:

```
penguin> readelf -r pic_nopic.o

Relocation section '.rel.text' at offset 0x378 contains 5 entries:
 Offset     Info    Type              Sym.Value  Sym. Name
00000016  00000702 R_386_PC32         00000000   otherFunction
0000001f  00000801 R_386_32           00000000   myGlobInt
00000043  00000902 R_386_PC32         0000000a   Z4buzzv
0000004c  00000501 R_386_32           00000000   .rodata
00000051  00000b02 R_386_PC32         00000000   printf
```

The relocations solve the mystery of the missing calls to `buzz()` and `printf()` in the previous section on PIC vs non-PIC. The relocation for `buzz()` instructs the run time linker to change the 32-bit value at offset `0x43` in the .text section to the eventual, run time location of the function `buzz()`. A quick look at the assembly language at `0x42` makes the purpose of this relocation even more clear:

```
   42:   e8 fc ff ff ff          call   43 <main+0x17>
```

The current instruction calls a false instruction at `0x43` because it will be relocated at a later time anyway. After the relocation, the 32-bit value at `0x43` will point to the address of `buzz`, so the call instruction at `0x42` will be correct. The same mechanism is used for `printf` at offset `0x51`.

Looking at the relocation information for the PIC object reveals some interesting differences:

```
penguin> readelf -r pic.o

Relocation section '.rel.text' at offset 0x3c8 contains 7 entries:
 Offset     Info    Type              Sym.Value  Sym. Name
0000001a  00000a0a R_386_GOTPC        00000000   _GLOBAL_OFFSET_TABLE_
00000020  00000803 R_386_GOT32        00000000    myGlobInt
0000002a  00000704 R_386_PLT32        00000000   otherFunction
0000004f  00000a0a R_386_GOTPC        00000000   GLOBAL_OFFSET_TABLE_
00000064  00000904 R_386_PLT32        0000000a   _Z4buzzv
0000006e  00000509 R_386_GOTOFF       00000000    .rodata
```

```
00000074   00000c04 R_386_PLT32   00000000    printf
```

Notice that the relocation entries for the PIC and non-PIC object files have different types for the functions and variables. In the PIC version, the relocation types are PLT32 and for the non-PIC version, the relocation types are PC32. The PLT32 is a type of relocation used with the procedure linkage table. A relocation of PC32 is a more primitive form of relocation.

There is an obvious performance impact when using position-independent code. A few years ago, a benchmark measured the impact at about 2 to 3%, although the actual percentage will depend on many factors (average size of functions, and so on). Regardless of the performance implications, position-independent code is required and effective and is used widely on Linux.

9.7.3 Relocation and Linking

As discussed earlier in the chapter, linking is the process of matching or binding undefined symbols to defined symbols of the same type and name. Linking can be done when a shared library or executable is actually created or at run time, although the mechanisms are very different. The relocation entries for object files are processed during the link phase, and relocation entries in executables and shared libraries are processed at run time.

When creating an executable or shared library, the linker (usually called "ld") will try to resolve undefined function symbols using the defined function symbols found in the constituent object files. This is where the main symbol table is used. Static functions are referenced through relative addressing, as are global functions. The main difference is that static functions will not be included in the dynamic symbol table.

Let's take a look at how the linker processes the relocation entries for pic.o. For quick reference, here are the relocation entries for pic.o from before:

```
penguin> readelf -r pic.o

Relocation section '.rel.text' at offset 0x3c8 contains 7 entries:
 Offset     Info    Type            Sym.Value  Sym. Name
0000001a  00000a0a R_386_GOTPC     00000000   GLOBAL_OFFSET_TABLE_
00000020  00000803 R_386_GOT32     00000000   myGlobInt
0000002a  00000704 R_386_PLT32     00000000   otherFunction
0000004f  00000a0a R_386_GOTPC     00000000   GLOBAL_OFFSET_TABLE_
00000064  00000904 R_386_PLT32     0000000a   Z4buzzv
0000006e  00000509 R_386_GOTOFF    00000000   .rodata
00000074  00000c04 R_386_PLT32     00000000   printf
```

Each of the function symbols, including the ones that could be satisfied locally by the function symbols in pic.o, have a relocation entry. The global variable myGlobInt also has a relocation entry. Let's see what happens when the linker links the object file pic.o and creates an executable.

> **Note**: The linker ld is called by g++. It is usually not a good idea to directly link an executable using ld. We could get away with it here because the source code does not include any C++ features. We will use g++ here as we have for the entire chapter because it allows us to show how ELF handles basic C++ features.

```
penguin> g++ -o pic pic.o
penguin> readelf -r pic

Relocation section '.rel.dyn' at offset 0x28c contains 2 entries:
 Offset     Info    Type             Sym.Value  Sym. Name
080495d4  00000106 R_386_GLOB_DAT    080494bc   myGlobInt
080495d8  00000606 R_386_GLOB_DAT    00000000   gmon_start__

Relocation section '.rel.plt' at offset 0x29c contains 2 entries:
 Offset     Info    Type             Sym.Value  Sym. Name
080495cc  00000207 R_386_JUMP_SLOT   080482d4   libc_start_main
080495d0  00000307 R_386_JUMP_SLOT   080482e4   printf
```

There are a few differences. The pic.o object file had one relocation section called .rel.text, and the executable "pic" contains two relocation sections called .rel.dyn and .rel.plt. The relocation for function buzz() is also missing from the executable. This is because the reference was satisfied by the function buzz() in the object file.

To see what these relocation entries really do, we need to find out which sections they belong to:

```
penguin> readelf -S pic |egrep "got|plt"
  [ 9] .rel.plt   REL       0804829c 00029c 000010 08   A  4   b  4
  [11] .plt       PROGBITS  080482c4 0002c4 000030 04   AX 0   0  4
  [21] .got       PROGBITS  080495c0 0005c0 00001c 04   WA 0   0  4
```

The GLOB_DAT entries have offsets of 0x80495d4 and 0x80495d8, both of which are in the global offset table. The purpose of these entries is to set the address of the symbol for this relocation entry in the corresponding slot of the global offset table. The executable code will be expecting it to be there when the program is loaded. The JUMP_SLOT relocation entries have offsets of 0x80495cc and 0x80495d0, and both of these are also in the GOT. These entries tell the run time linker to set entries in the GOT for the corresponding slots for the same symbol in the PLT. This is required for dynamic linking and in particular, lazy binding. See section ".plt" for more information.

If we link this object file as a shared library, the relocation entries are very different:

```
penguin> g++ -shared pic.o -o libpic.so
penguin> readelf -r libpic.so

Relocation section '.rel.dyn' at offset 0x5d0 contains 7 entries:
 Offset     Info    Type              Sym.Value  Sym. Name
00001888  00000008 R_386_RELATIVE
0000188c  00000008 R_386_RELATIVE
000019a4  00000008 R_386_RELATIVE
000019a8  00001d06 R_386_GLOB_DAT    00001890   myGlobInt
000019ac  00002206 R_386_GLOB_DAT    00000000   cxa_finalize
000019b0  00002706 R_386_GLOB_DAT    00000000   Jv_RegisterClasses
000019b4  00002806 R_386_GLOB_DAT    00000000   gmon_start__

Relocation section '.rel.plt' at offset 0x608 contains 5 entries:
 Offset     Info    Type              Sym.Value  Sym. Name
00001990  00001a07 R_386_JUMP_SLOT   0000079e   Z4buzzv
00001994  00002007 R_386_JUMP_SLOT   00000000   printf
00001998  00002207 R_386_JUMP_SLOT   00000000   cxa_finalize
0000199c  00002307 R_386_JUMP_SLOT   00000794   otherFunction
000019a0  00002707 R_386_JUMP_SLOT   00000000   Jv_RegisterClasses
```

There are quite a few more relocation entries for the shared library than for the executable. This includes the function buzz() because the reference for buzz() might not be satisfied by the buzz() contained in the shared library. See the section, "Symbol Resolution," for more details on how to force a shared library to use the symbols that it contains ("symbolic linking").

What if we try to create a shared library with the non-PIC object file?

```
penguin> g++ -shared pic_nopic.o -o libnopic.so
penguin> readelf -r libnopic.so

Relocation section '.rel.dyn' at offset 0x5d0 contains 11 entries:
 Offset     Info    Type              Sym.Value  Sym. Name
000007b0  00000008 R_386_RELATIVE
00001838  00000008 R_386_RELATIVE
0000183c  00000008 R_386_RELATIVE
00001950  00000008 R_386_RELATIVE
0000077a  00002302 R_386_PC32        00000764   otherFunction
00000783  00001d01 R_386_32          00001840   myGlobInt
000007a7  00001a02 R_386_PC32        0000076e   Z4buzzv
000007b5  00002002 R_386_PC32        00000000   printf
00001954  00002206 R_386_GLOB_DAT    00000000   cxa_finalize
00001958  00002706 R_386_GLOB_DAT    00000000   Jv_RegisterClasses
0000195c  00002806 R_386_GLOB_DAT    00000000   gmon_start__

Relocation section '.rel.plt' at offset 0x628 contains 2 entries:
 Offset     Info    Type              Sym.Value  Sym. Name
00001948  00002207 R_386_JUMP_SLOT   00000000   cxa_finalize
0000194c  00002707 R_386_JUMP_SLOT   00000000   Jv_RegisterClasses
```

The shared library is created, although the relocations are very different. The relocation type for the functions is PC32 and modifies the executable code. How does this work, though? The text segment is always loaded as read-only, and yet these relocations apparently change some values in the text segment. For a better understanding of this special type of relocation, let's build `libfoo.so` without using the `-fPIC` switch and then run the executable `foo`, seeing how it modifies the text segment of `libfoo.so`.

```
penguin> g++ -c foo.C
penguin> g++ -shared foo.o -o libfoo.so
penguin> g++ -o foo main.o -L. -Wl,-rpath,. -lfoo
```

Now to use `strace` to see how this works under the covers:

```
penguin> strace -o foo.st foo
This is a printf format string in baz
This is a printf format string in main

penguin> less foo.st
<...>
open("./libfoo.so", O_RDONLY)             = 3
read(3, "\177ELF\1\1\1\0\0\0\0\0\0\0\0\0\3\0\3\0\1\0\0\0\360\7\0"...,
➡1024) = 1024
fstat64(3, {st_mode=S_IFREG|0755, st_size=7113, ...}) = 0
getcwd("/home/wilding/src/Linuxbook/ELF", 128) = 32
mmap2(NULL, 7412, PROT_READ|PROT_EXEC, MAP_PRIVATE, 3, 0) = 0x40014000
mprotect(0x40015000, 3316, PROT_NONE)     = 0
mmap2(0x40015000, 4096, PROT_READ|PROT_WRITE, MAP_PRIVATE|MAP_FIXED,
➡3, 0) = 0x40015000
close(3)                                  = 0
<...>
mprotect(0x40014000, 4096, PROT_READ|PROT_WRITE) = 0
mprotect(0x40014000, 4096, PROT_READ|PROT_EXEC) = 0
<...>
```

The first part of the output shows where `libfoo.so` is loaded into the address space. It is loaded at address `0x40014000` as shown with the `mmap2` system call. Later on in the run, the program (the run time linker) uses `mprotect` to change the attributes of part of the text section to read/write and then back to read/exec. In between these two system calls is where the relocations take place in order to perform the relocations on the text file. These two calls to `mprotect` are not needed for the library that was built with a position-independent object because of the relocations action on the GOT, which is in the data segment.

Even though this special type of relocation works, it is not used much in practice. Non-PIC code is not meant to be position-independent, and forcing it to be part of a shared library is not standard and not recommended.

9.8 STRIPPING AN ELF OBJECT

ELF objects can be *stripped*, which is a phrase used to refer to the removal of the main symbol table and other sections that are not needed for run time. The main symbol table can consume quite a bit of space and can also give away information about how a program works. Because the main symbol table is not actually needed for program execution, it can be stripped away, leaving a smaller ELF object.

Let's use `libfoo.so` to show how strip works and the effects it has on an ELF file:

```
penguin> ls -l libfoo.so
-rwxr-xr-x    1 wilding   build        7301 Jan 16 11:00 libfoo.so
penguin> strip libfoo.so
penguin> ls -l libfoo.so
-rwxr-xr-x    1 wilding   build        4668 Jan 16 11:13 libfoo.so
```

Before stripping the shared library, it contained the following sections:

```
penguin> readelf -S libfoo.so | egrep "\[.*\] \." | awk -F. '{print
$2}' | awk '{print $1}' | sort | tr "\n" " "; echo "\n"
bss comment ctors data debug_abbrev debug_aranges debug_info debug_line
dtors dynamic dynstr dynsym eh_frame eh_frame_hdr fini gnu gnu got hash
init jcr plt rel rel rodata shstrtab strtab symtab text
```

After stripping the shared library, it contains the following sections.

```
penguin> strip libfoo.so
penguin> readelf -S libfoo.so | egrep "\[.*\] \." | awk -F. '{print
$2}' | awk '{print $1}' | sort | tr "\n" " " ; echo "\n"
bss comment ctors data dtors dynamic dynstr dynsym eh_frame eh_frame_hdr
fini gnu gnu got hash init jcr plt rel rel rodata shstrtab text
```

Therefore, stripping the shared library took out sections containing debug information: `debug_abbrev`, `debug_aranges`, `debug_info`, `debug_line` and the main symbol table with its string table: `strtab symtab`. Both types of information are not needed at run time.

The biggest problem with stripping an ELF object is that it removes some information that is very useful for debugging problems. Without the main symbol table, static symbols have no symbol name, and all debugging information (if the object was built with debug information) will be removed. This includes information that can help to match line number to function offsest, and so on.

The strip command is mildly beneficial for its ability to reduce the size of an ELF file and to protect intellectual property, but it can really hinder investigation efforts. Avoid it if possible.

> **Note**: You might find that some distributions have stripped libraries and executables. On these distributions, there should be debug libraries that contain the main symbol table. Consult your distribution documentation for more information.

9.9 PROGRAM INTERPRETER

The term "program interpreter" comes from the ELF standard. On Linux, the program interpreter is ld.so (/lib/ld-linux.so), the run time linker/loader. The program interpreter is responsible for bringing up an executable and getting it running. It is called by the kernel and is passed a special array of information called an *auxiliary vector*. This is shown as follows using the special environment variable LD_SHOW_AUXV:

```
penguin> export LD_SHOW_AUXV=true
penguin> foo
AT_HWCAP:    fpu vme de pse tsc msr pae mce cx8 apic sep mtrr pge
mca cmov pat pse36 19 21 22 mmx osfxsr xmm xmm2 27 28 29
AT_PAGESZ:   4096
AT_CLKTCK:   100
AT_PHDR:     0x8048034
AT_PHENT:    32
AT_PHNUM:    7
AT_BASE:     0x40000000
AT_FLAGS:    0x0
AT_ENTRY:    0x8048540
AT_UID:      7903
AT_EUID:     7903
AT_GID:      200
AT_EGID:     200
AT_PLATFORM: i686
This is a printf format string in baz
This is a printf format string in main
```

Brief definitions of the various fields can be found from /usr/åinclude/elf.h:

```
/* Legal values for a_type (entry type).  */

#define AT_NULL     0     /* End of vector */
#define AT_IGNORE   1     /* Entry should be ignored */
#define AT_EXECFD   2     /* File descriptor of program */
```

```
#define AT_PHDR      3         /* Program headers for program */
#define AT_PHENT     4         /* Size of program header entry */
#define AT_PHNUM     5         /* Number of program headers */
#define AT_PAGESZ    6         /* System page size */
#define AT_BASE      7         /* Base address of interpreter */
#define AT_FLAGS     8         /* Flags */
#define AT_ENTRY     9         /* Entry point of program */
#define AT_NOTELF   10         /* Program is not ELF */
#define AT_UID      11         /* Real uid */
#define AT_EUID     12         /* Effective uid */
#define AT_GID      13         /* Real gid */
#define AT_EGID     14         /* Effective gid */
#define AT_CLKTCK   17         /* Frequency of times() */

/* Some more special a_type values describing the hardware.  */
#define AT_PLATFORM 15         /* String identifying platform.  */
#define AT_HWCAP    16         /* Machine dependent hints about
➥processor capabilities.  */
```

Here is some additional information about the various fields:

AT_PAGESZ: The standard page size used on this operating system for normal memory regions. Other memory regions (such as shared memory) can have larger page sizes. It is assumed that normal memory regions are used when loading ELF objects into memory.

AT_PHDR: The address of the program header table for the executable.

AT_PHENT: The size of an entry in the program header table.

AT_PHNUM: The number of entries in the program header table. Note that with AT_PHDR, AT_PHENT and PHNUM, the program interpreter can find all of the loadable segments of an ELF object file.

AT_BASE: The address of the program interpreter (/lib/ld-linux.so.2 in this case) itself.

AT_ENTRY: Entry point of the program. This is the address of the execut able that the run time loader will hand control over to after finishing program initialization. This is usually the _start function.

AT_PLATFORM: The current hardware platform.

AT_UID, AT_EUID, AT_GID, AT_EGID: user ID, effective user ID, group ID and effective group ID respectively.

The kernel on some platforms that support ELF may choose not to load the program but instead pass an open file descriptor to the run time loader/linker so that it can load the program on its own. In this case, the auxiliary vector will include another field called AT_EXECFD.

It is the run time loader/linker's responsibility to load up the program if needed and perform all initialization. The initialization includes finding all required libraries, calling initialization functions, performing required relocations, and so on. However, before it initializes the program, it needs first to initialize itself. This is actually a fairly complex process that is beyond the scope of this chapter. The reason for its complexity is that the run time linker has to do this manually because the regular methods rely on some basic setup that does not exist when the run time linker starts.

The run time linker/loader ld.so also has a special environment variable to help debug it. This environment variable instructs ld.so to show all the main activity while it brings up a program. In other words, it is like a trace of the run time linker/loader. Here is an example of this special debug mode in action:

```
penguin> export LD_DEBUG=all
penguin> foo
27080:
27080:   file=libfoo.so;  needed by foo
27080:   find library=libfoo.so; searching
27080:    search path=./i686/mmx:./i686:./mmx:.  (RPATH from file foo)
27080:     trying file=./i686/mmx/libfoo.so
27080:     trying file=./i686/libfoo.so
27080:     trying file=./mmx/libfoo.so
27080:     trying file=./libfoo.so
27080:
27080:   file=libfoo.so;  generating link map
27080:     dynamic: 0x40015c48  base: 0x40014000   size: 0x00001d84
27080:      entry: 0x400147e0  phdr: 0x40014034  phnum:          4
27080:
27080:
27080:   file=libstdc++.so.5;  needed by foo
27080:   find library=libstdc++.so.5; searching
27080:    search path=./i686/mmx:./i686:./mmx:.  (RPATH from file foo)
27080:     trying file=./i686/mmx/libstdc++.so.5
27080:     trying file=./i686/libstdc++.so.5
27080:     trying file=./mmx/libstdc++.so.5
27080:     trying file=./libstdc++.so.5
27080:    search path=/usr/lib/i686/mmx:/usr/lib/i686:/usr/lib/mmx:/
          ➥usr/lib (system search path)
27080:     trying file=/usr/lib/i686/mmx/libstdc++.so.5
27080:     trying file=/usr/lib/i686/libstdc++.so.5
27080:     trying file=/usr/lib/mmx/libstdc++.so.5
27080:     trying file=/usr/lib/libstdc++.so.5
27080:
27080:   file=libstdc++.so.5;  generating link map
27080:     dynamic: 0x400c246c  base: 0x40016000   size: 0x000b23c0
27080:      entry: 0x40050700  phdr: 0x40016034  phnum:          4
<...>
```

This first part is called "loading" and involves finding and loading all required shared libraries. The search path (LD_LIBRARY_PATH) and the RPATH are searched as potential directories to find libraries. Make note of the following text in the output "generating link map." This is described in more detail shortly. Let's see what else is in this debug output:

```
<...>
27080:
27080:    calling init: ./libfoo.so
27080:
<...>
```

Here we see the init function in libfoo.so being called. This is before control has officially been handed over to the executable. The output continues...

```
<...>
27080:
27080:    initialize program: foo
27080:
27080:
27080:    transferring control: foo
27080:
<...>
```

This is where control is officially handed over to the executable foo. After this point, the contents of the debug output are for "late" or "lazy" binding:

```
<...>
27080:  symbol=_Z3bazi;  lookup in file=foo
27080:  symbol=_Z3bazi;  lookup in file=./libfoo.so
27080:  binding file foo to ./libfoo.so: normal symbol '_Z3bazi'
27080:  symbol=_Z3fooi;  lookup in file=foo
27080:  symbol=_Z3fooi;  lookup in file=./libfoo.so
27080:  symbol=_Z3fooi;  lookup in file=/usr/lib/libstdc++.so.5
27080:  symbol=_Z3fooi;  lookup in file=/lib/libm.so.6
27080:  symbol=_Z3fooi;  lookup in file=/lib/libgcc_s.so.1
27080:  symbol=_Z3fooi;  lookup in file=/lib/libc.so.6
27080:  symbol=_Z3fooi;  lookup in file=/lib/ld-linux.so.2
27080:  binding file ./libfoo.so to ./libfoo.so: normal symbol '_Z3fooi'
27080:  symbol=printf;  lookup in file=foo
27080:  symbol=printf;  lookup in file=./libfoo.so
27080:  symbol=printf;  lookup in file=/usr/lib/libstdc++.so.5
27080:  symbol=printf;  lookup in file=/lib/libm.so.6
27080:  symbol=printf;  lookup in file=/lib/libgcc_s.so.1
27080:  symbol=printf;  lookup in file=/lib/libc.so.6
27080:  binding file ./libfoo.so to /lib/libc.so.6: normal symbol
➡ 'printf' [GLIBC_2.0]
<...>
```

These binding actions are driven by the _dl_runtime_resolve function described back in the ".plt" section of this chapter.

9.9.1 Link Map

Remember that text, "generating link map," from the output from this special debug mode? A link map contains information about a shared library that has been loaded into the address space.

There is a special variable called _dl_main_searchlist that has the following structure:

```
struct
{
  /* Array of maps for the scope.  */
  struct link_map **r_list;
  /* Number of entries in the scope.  */
  unsigned int r_nlist;
};
```

From within GDB (the process has to be running for this to be useful), we can see the values of the two structure members:

```
(gdb) x/2x _dl_main_searchlist
0x400130c8:    0x40223030     0x00000007
```

The first value is the address of the list, and the second value is the number of elements in the list. Looking at the seven values in memory, we get the following:

```
(gdb) x/7 0x40223030
0x40223030:    0x40012fd0     0x40013590     0x400137f8     0x400139e8
0x40223040:    0x40013bd0     0x40013dc0     0x40012d80
```

Each of these values is a pointer to the following structure:

```
struct link_map
  {
    /* These first few members are part of the protocol with the
debugger.
       This is the same format used in SVR4.  */

    ElfW(Addr) l_addr; /* Base address shared object is loaded at.*/
    char *l_name;      /* Absolute file name object was found in. */
    ElfW(Dyn) *l_ld;   /* Dynamic section of the shared object.   */
    struct link_map *l_next, *l_prev; /* Chain of loaded objects.*/
  };
```

This is the link map that the `ld.so` output referred to. Let's look at the second address in the list:

```
(gdb) x/5x 0x40013590
0x40013590:   0x40014000     0x40013580     0x40015c48     0x400137f8
0x400135a0:   0x40012fd0
```

According to the `link_map` structure, the second value should be the path of a loaded library, confirmed below:

```
(gdb) x/s 0x40013580
0x40013580:      "./libfoo.so"
```

The next `link_map` value is another library:

```
(gdb) x/5x 0x400137f8
0x400137f8:     0x40016000     0x400137e0     0x400c246c  0x400139e8
0x40013808:     0x40013590
(gdb) x/s 0x400137e0
0x400137e0:     "/usr/lib/libstdc++.so.5"
```

Also notice that the fourth value in each `link_map` structure (`l_next`) points to the next link map structure. `l_prev` points to the previous structure. There is both a linked list and an array of pointers to these functions.

   The list of loaded libraries is used by the run time linker to keep track of the loaded libraries for a process.

9.10 SYMBOL RESOLUTION

We know that run time linking occurs, but what if there is more than one symbol with the same name? How does the order of dependencies affect which will be chosen at run time?

   To better understand this, we need a multi-layer dependency tree of shared libraries such as the one in Figure 9.5.

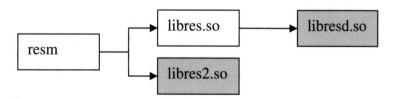

Fig. 9.5 Symbol Resolution with Shared Libraries.

The executable resm comes from a source file called resm.C. It was linked with two shared libraries, libres.so (res.C) and libres2.so (res2.C). libres.so also has a dependent library called libresd.so (resd.C, the d is for deeper). Lastly, libresd.so and libres2 export the same symbols.

Here are the contents of the various source files. The global integers globInt1 and globInt2 are defined in libres.so and resm but with different names. Both resm and libres.so contain the functions, function1 and function2:

```
resm.C
#include <stdio.h>

int globInt1 = 1 ;
int globInt2 = 2 ;

int function1( )
{
   printf( "function1: in resm.C\n" ) ;
}

int function2( )
{
   printf( "function2: in resm.C\n" ) ;
}

extern int function3( ) ;


int main( )
{
   printf( "calling function1 from resm.C\n" ) ;

   function1( ) ;

   printf( "value of globInt1: %u\n", globInt1 ) ;

   printf( "transfering control to shared library\n" ) ;

   function3( ) ;

}
res.C:
#include <stdio.h>

int globInt1 = 3 ;
int globInt2 = 4 ;

extern int function6( ) ;


int function1( )
```

```
{
    printf( "function1: in res.C\n" ) ;
}

int function2( )
{
    printf( "function2: in res.C\n" ) ;
}
int function3( )
{
    printf( "calling function2 from res.C\n" ) ;

    function2( ) ;

    printf( "value of globInt2: %u\n", globInt2 ) ;

    printf( "calling function6 from res.C\n" ) ;

    function6( ) ;

}
```

Here are the important symbols in each of these ELF files:

```
penguin> nm resm |egrep "globInt|function"
0804862c T _Z9function1v
08048656 T _Z9function2v
         U _Z9function3v
08049828 D globInt1
0804982c D globInt2

penguin> nm libres.so | egrep "globInt|function"
00000884 T _Z9function1v
000008ae T _Z9function2v
000008d8 T _Z9function3v
         U _Z9function6v
00001a38 D globInt1
00001a3c D globInt2
```

Now to run the executable `resm` to see the link resolution and order in action:

```
penguin> resm
main: calling function1 from resm.C
function1: in resm.C
main: value of globInt1: 1 in resm.C
main: transferring control to shared library
function3: calling function2 from res.C
function2: in resm.C
function3: value of globInt2: 2 in res.C
function3: calling function6 from res.C
function6: in res2.C
function6: value of globInt2: 2 in res2.C
```

The call from the function `main` in `resm.C` to `function1` called the version of `function1` in `resm.C`. A reference to `globInt1` from `resm.C` picked up the version of `globInt1` from `resm.C` (the executable) as well. Things get more interesting when the executable transfers control to the shared library `libres.so`. `libres.so` references `globInt2` and `function2`, which are defined in the executable as well as `libres.so` itself.

The `function3` in `res.C` calls `function2` although the version of `function2` in `resm.C` (the executable) is called and *not* the version in `res.C`. The resolution of the `function2` found the location in the executable, not the calling shared library. So imagine you're the owner of a shared library and someone adds a function or global variable with the same name as one defined in your shared library. This would almost certainly cause a problem.

The solution to this is symbolic linking. By using the `-Bsymbolic` switch, the linker will try to satisfy the undefined symbols using those in the immediate shared library.

```
penguin> g++ -shared res.o -o libres.so -L. -Wl,-rpath,. -lresd -
➥Wl,-Bsymbolic
```

Now to run `resm` again:

```
penguin> resm
main: calling function1 from resm.C
function1: in resm.C
main: value of globInt1: 1 in resm.C
main: transferring control to shared library
function3: calling function2 from res.C
function2: in res.C
function3: value of globInt2: 4 in res.C
function3: calling function6 from res.C
function6: in res2.C
function6: value of globInt2: 2 in res2.C
```

This time, we see that `function2` from `res.C` (`libres.so`) was called, and the value of `globInt2` is from `res.C`.

Another interesting link order problem is illustrated via `res2.C` and `resd.C`. Here are the almost identical source files, `res2.C` and `resd.C`:

```
res2.C
#include <stdio.h>

extern int globInt1 ;
extern int globInt2 ;

int function4( )
{
```

```
    printf( "function4: in res2.C\n" ) ;
}

int function5( )
{
    printf( "function5: in res2.C\n" ) ;
}

int function6( )
{
    printf( "function6: in res2.C\n" ) ;

    printf( "value of globInt2: %u\n", globInt2 ) ;

}
```

resd.C
```
#include <stdio.h>

extern int globInt1 ;
extern int globInt2 ;

int function4( )
{
    printf( "function4: in resd.C\n" ) ;
}

int function5( )
{
    printf( "function5: in resd.C\n" ) ;
}

int function6( )
{
    printf( "function6 in resd.C\n" ) ;

    printf( "value of globInt2: %u\n", globInt2 ) ;

}
```

The library `libres.so` requires a library `libresd.so` to satistfy a symbol `function6`, which is defined in both `libres2.so` and `libresd.so`. The executable has `libres2.so` as a dependency as well as `libres.so`. Now, the code in `libres.so` is probably expecting to use the symbols in `libresd.so` because that library was required at link time to satisfy the reference to `function6`. Let's see what happens in reality (here is the first output from the executable `resm` for quick reference):

```
penguin> resm
main: calling function1 from resm.C
function1: in resm.C
main: value of globInt1: 1 in resm.C
```

```
main: transferring control to shared library
function3: calling function2 from res.C
function2: in resm.C
function3: value of globInt2: 2 in res.C
function3: calling function6 from res.C
function6: in res2.C
function6: value of globInt2: 2 in res2.C
```

The call to function6 actually calls the version in res2.C instead! This would also cause unwanted results, although -Bsymbolic will not help in this situation because the values are outside of the shared library.

Some shared libraries support symbol versioning to reduce the chance of incompatible symbol collisions, although the details are quite complex and not covered here. Symbol versioning allows multiple, incompatible functions of the same name to exist in the same shared library. This allows older applications to continue to use the older versions of the function, while newer applications will use the newer functions. This is really meant for down-level compatibility, not necessarily unintentional duplicate symbols.

9.11 USE OF WEAK SYMBOLS FOR PROBLEM INVESTIGATIONS

Using weak symbols is a very powerful feature that every developer or senior service analyst should know about.

Step #1: Choose a weak symbol from libc.

```
penguin> nm /usr/lib/libc.so
nm: /usr/lib/libc.so: File format not recognized
penguin> cat /usr/lib/libc.so
/* GNU ld script
   Use the shared library, but some functions are only in
   the static library, so try that secondarily.  */
GROUP ( /lib/libc.so.6 /usr/lib/libc_nonshared.a )

penguin> nm -n /lib/libc.so.6 | egrep " W " | egrep -v _
<...>
0006dd70 W malloc
0006e570 W cfree
0006e570 W free
0006e940 W realloc
<...>
000bf930 W fchmod
000bf970 W mkdir
000bf9b0 W open
000bf9f0 W open64
000bfa40 W close
000bfa80 W read
```

```
000bfac0 W write
<...>
```

You can choose any weak symbol, but it is usually most useful to choose one of the standard system calls of `libc` functions. Some good examples are `malloc`, `free`, `realloc`, `mkdir`, `open`, `close`, `read`, and so on.

Step #2: Read the man page or header file for the function you want to intercept. You'll want to steal the exact function prototype. The header file is better because it will be more accurate. In any case, here are the function definitions for `malloc`, `realloc`, and `free`:

```
void *malloc(size_t size);
void free(void *ptr);
void *realloc(void *ptr, size_t size);
```

Step #3: Find the non-weak symbols (the real functions that get called). The easiest and most reliable way to find the non-weak symbols is to find strong symbols that have the same address as the weak symbols you are interested in.

```
penguin> nm -n /lib/libc.so.6 | egrep 'malloc$' | egrep " W "
0006dd70 W malloc
penguin> nm -n /lib/libc.so.6 | egrep 0006dd70
0006dd70 T __libc_malloc
0006dd70 t __malloc
0006dd70 W malloc
```

In the output here, we first find the address of the `malloc` symbol we're interested in and then look for symbols that have the same "value," meaning that they point to the same function. The matching symbol that has a class of "T," meaning defined, text (a real function) is that one we need and is called `__libc_malloc`. `__libc_` is the convention used for the real functions (also applicable to `realloc` and `free`).

Step #4: Build an interceptor library. You must define real functions using the prototypes from Step 1. We're using `malloc`, `free`, and `realloc` as examples here. You can do the same thing with any weak function in `libc`.

Building an interceptor library requires a special process. For example, you might not be able to include any system header files because of duplicate declarations. After all, you will be defining functions with the same definition as those in `libc`.

Another consideration is unwanted recursion. Some `libc` functions such as `fopen` will call other `libc` functions such as `malloc` under the covers. If we override `malloc`, we have to be aware that calling `fopen` from within `malloc` might eventually and recursively (because we're already in `malloc`) call `malloc`.

In any case, here is the source for an example interception library for `malloc`, `free`, and `realloc`:

```
intercept.c:
/* Here are the declarations needed to make all of this compile.
Copying these directly from a system header would normally be a very
bad idea. Here, we must do it to avoid any system headers */

typedef unsigned long int size_t;

/* Function definitions for the strong text symbols. The function
names should match that of their counterparts exactly with the
exception of having different function names. */

void *__libc_malloc(size_t size);
void *__libc_realloc(void *ptr, size_t size);
void __libc_free(void *ptr);

/* Actual function used to override malloc, free and realloc */

void *malloc(size_t size)
{
   void *rptr ;

   printf( "malloc  : Requested block size: %u\n", size ) ;

   rptr = __libc_malloc( size ) ;

   printf( "malloc  : ptr of allocated block: %p\n", rptr ) ;

   return rptr ;

}

void free(void *ptr)
{

   printf( "free    : freeing block: %p\n", ptr ) ;

   return __libc_free( ptr ) ;
}

void *realloc(void *ptr, size_t size)
{
   void *rptr ;
```

```
printf( "realloc : ptr of previous block: %p\n", ptr ) ;
printf( "realloc : Requested block size: %u\n", size ) ;

rptr = __libc_realloc( ptr, size ) ;

printf( "realloc : ptr of allocated block: %p\n", rptr ) ;

return rptr ;

}
```

The first part defines (and almost apologizes for doing so) some basic types used by the functions we're going to override. In this case, it defines size_t for malloc and realloc. The next section declares the strong text symbols for malloc, free, and realloc with the __libc_ prefix. The third and final section actually defines the functions we're going to override.

These overridden functions must eventually call the actual, matching libc functions, or any program run with this interceptor library will not run as expected. We also have to be careful not to change any behavior of the program we're investigating. For example, the program might (incorrectly) close and never reopen file descriptor 1, stdout, until a subsequent call to open() to open a real file. In this case, all of our printf text will go to this file instead of stdout, which could corrupt the file. Such interactions are rare, but it's good to keep them in mind.

Compiling the interceptor library is straightforward as shown here:

```
penguin> gcc intercept.c -fPIC -c
penguin> gcc -shared intercept.o -o intercept.so
```

Step #5: Use LD_PRELOAD (and possibly LD_DYNAMIC_WEAK).
For this interceptor library to work, we need to get it into the address space of a program. The LD_PRELOAD environment variable instructs the program interpreter to load a library before executing a program, ensuring that our interceptor library will be in the address space as needed.

```
penguin> export LD_PRELOAD=/home/wilding/src/Linuxbook/ELF/intercept.so
```

After this point, any program we run will call our versions of malloc and free. In the following example, we use the program ls to show how this works—with the resulting output:

```
penguin> ls
realloc : ptr of previous block: (nil)
realloc : Requested block size: 16
malloc  : Requested block size: 24
malloc  : ptr of allocated block: 0x8059850
```

```
realloc : ptr of allocated block: 0x8059870
free    : freeing block: 0x8059870
malloc  : Requested block size: 26
malloc  : ptr of allocated block: 0x8059870
malloc  : Requested block size: 10
malloc  : ptr of allocated block: 0x8059890
<...>
```

If this doesn't work, you may also need to set the LD_DYNAMIC_WEAK environment variable. See the man page for ld.so for more information.

This method of using weak symbols to override system functions can be very useful and can be used to:

☞ Trigger an action if a system call takes too long.

☞ Find difficult memory leaks when all else fails.

☞ Redirect system calls to do something else.

☞ Trigger an action when a very specific system call is made (for example, to a particular file).

☞ and so on...

Unless special circumstances dictate, this method should only be used to debug a problem and not to supplement the functionality of libc. The method works well, but any source code that copies definitions from system headers should be used with care.

9.12 ADVANCED INTERCEPTION USING GLOBAL OFFSET TABLE

The method of function interception described here (using weak symbols) is very powerful but requires starting the executable under the LD_PRELOAD environment variable. What if a process is already running?

Consider the following simple program:

```
#include <stdio.h>
#include <stdlib.h>
#include <unistd.h>


int main( )
{
   char *ptr ;

   while ( 1 )
   {
```

```
        ptr = (char *)malloc( 1024 ) ;
        sleep(5) ;

    }

    return 0 ;
}
```

Ignore the obvious memory leak. The purpose of this program is to illustrate a debugging technique. The program mimics a real program that may call `malloc` over and over again (as many/most programs do).

After the program is running, it is too late to start it under `LD_PRELOAD`; however, if the program was built with `-ldl` (i.e., it will load the `libdl` library), we can use gdb to dynamically load a shared library into the address space of the process and then redirect the entry in the global offset for `malloc` to a function in this new shared library.

```
penguin> g++ alloc.C -o alloc -ldl
penguin> gdb alloc
GNU gdb 5.2.1
Copyright 2002 Free Software Foundation, Inc.
GDB is free software, covered by the GNU General Public License, and
you are welcome to change it and/or distribute copies of it under
certain conditions.
Type "show copying" to see the conditions.
There is absolutely no warranty for GDB.  Type "show warranty" for
details.
This GDB was configured as "i586-suse-linux"...
(gdb) break main
Breakpoint 1 at 0x80483d2
(gdb) run
Starting program: /home/wilding/src/Linuxbook/ELF/alloc

Breakpoint 1, 0x080483d2 in main ()
```

In another window, we can use `readelf` to find the global offset table entry for `malloc`:

```
penguin> readelf -r alloc

Relocation section '.rel.dyn' at offset 0x290 contains 1 entries:
 Offset     Info    Type            Sym.Value  Sym. Name
08049578  00000606 R_386_GLOB_DAT    00000000   gmon_start__

Relocation section '.rel.plt' at offset 0x298 contains 3 entries:
 Offset     Info    Type            Sym.Value  Sym. Name
0804956c  00000107 R_386_JUMP_SLOT   080482d8   malloc
08049570  00000207 R_386_JUMP_SLOT   080482e8   sleep
08049574  00000307 R_386_JUMP_SLOT   080482f8   libc_start_main
```

From the output, we can see that the address of the GOT slot for `malloc` is
`0x0804956c`. We'll let the program handle the first call to `malloc` as normal (as it
would if we were attaching to it at some point in its lifetime).

```
(gdb) cont
Continuing.

Program received signal SIGINT, Interrupt.
0x401a3d01 in nanosleep () from /lib/libc.so.6
```

Okay, if the program is sleeping, it has made at least one call to `malloc`, resolving
the address of `malloc` and placing it into the GOT. Let's confirm by looking at
the value at the corresponding slot in the GOT:

```
(gdb) x/x 0x0804956c
0x804956c <_GLOBAL_OFFSET_TABLE_+12>:     0x40173d70
(gdb) disass 0x40173d70 0x40173d80
Dump of assembler code from 0x40173d70 to 0x40173d80:
0x40173d70 <malloc>:      push    %ebp
0x40173d71 <malloc+1>:    mov     %esp,%ebp
0x40173d73 <malloc+3>:    sub     $0x28,%esp
0x40173d76 <malloc+6>:    mov     %ebx,0xfffffff4(%ebp)
0x40173d79 <malloc+9>:    mov     %esi,0xfffffff8(%ebp)
0x40173d7c <malloc+12>:   mov     %edi,0xfffffffc(%ebp)
0x40173d7f <malloc+15>:   call    0x40177193 <malloc_extend_top+707>
End of assembler dump.
```

As expected, the `malloc` slot in the GOT is pointing to the function `malloc`. Now
let's proceed with the steps to redirect this call to a custom function in a shared
library that is not yet loaded into the address space. The first step is to get this
shared library into the address space.

```
(gdb) info func dlopen
All functions matching regular expression "dlopen":

Non-debugging symbols:
0x40025ec0  dlopen_doit
0x40025f10  dlopen_check
0x40025f10  dlopen@@GLIBC_2.1
0x400269f0  dlopen_doit
0x40026a40  dlopen_nocheck
0x40026a40  dlopen@GLIBC_2.0
0x401fdf40  do_dlopen
0x401fe010  libc_dlopen
```

There are a few functions that contain `dlopen`. The last one is the actual symbol
for `dlopen` (see previous section on weak and strong symbols in `libc`). We're
going to use this function to load a shared library into the address space:

```
(gdb) call __libc_dlopen( "/home/wilding/src/Linuxbook/ELF/intercept.so",
2 )
$1 = 134519336
(gdb) printf "0x%x\n", 134519336
0x8049a28
```

This call to `__libc_dlopen` uses the same arguments as defined in the main page for `dlopen`. For the second argument, we used the value for RTLD_NOW as defined in `dlfcn.h`:

```
penguin> egrep RTLD_NOW /usr/include/bits/dlfcn.h
#define RTLD_NOW       0x00002 /* Immediate function call binding. */
```

The return value from the `dlopen` function call is shown on the second line as $1 = 134519336$. This is the handle returned by `dlopen`, which we don't care about right now (as long as it is not NULL).

At this point, the shared library should be loaded into the address space. Let's confirm and get the address where it was loaded.

```
(gdb) info shared
From          To          Syms Read    Shared Object Library
0x40025dd0    0x40026ae0  Yes          /lib/libdl.so.2
0x40062700    0x400ba2c0  Yes          /usr/lib/libstdc++.so.5
0x400de740    0x400f6470  Yes          /lib/libm.so.6
0x400ff350    0x40104210  Yes          /lib/libgcc_s.so.1
0x4011e2e0    0x40200b94  Yes          /lib/libc.so.6
0x40001290    0x4000f12d  Yes          /lib/ld-linux.so.2
0x400146c0    0x400148f0  Yes           /home/wilding/src/Linuxbook/ELF/
intercept.so
```

The next step is to find the address of our `malloc` function in the shared library, `intercept.so`. In this example, the function we want to redirect `malloc` calls does not have to be called `malloc`. We're going to manually redirect calls to `malloc` so the target function could be named anything we want.

```
(gdb) info func malloc
All functions matching regular expression "malloc":

Non-debugging symbols:
0x080482d8  malloc
0x40172ec0  ptmalloc_lock_all
<...>
0x4000cbc0  malloc
0x400147a4  malloc
```

From the output, the last `malloc` function is the one we want. The address range for `intercept.so` is 0x400146c0 to 0x400148f0, and the address of the last `malloc` function, 0x400147a4, is in this range. Now we need to change the value of the GOT slot for `malloc` (in the executable `alloc`) to point to our function:

```
(gdb) set $a=0x0804956c
(gdb) set *($a) = 0x400147a4
(gdb) x 0x0804956c
0x804956c <_GLOBAL_OFFSET_TABLE_+12>:    0x400147a4
```

If we continue the process now, a call to malloc from the executable alloc should call our version of malloc. Let's confirm:

```
(gdb) cont
Continuing.
malloc   : Requested block size: 1024
malloc   : ptr of allocated block: 0x8049cb0
```

As expected, we're now in control of the malloc call. Every call to malloc made from the executable alloc will call our function because we changed the slot for malloc in the GOT to our own function.

Getting this to work without linking the executable with -ldl is possible but much more complicated. Fortunately, many programs are linked with -ldl, which makes this useful for those really challenging problems when all other methods fail.

9.13 SOURCE FILES

```
foo.C
#include <stdio.h>
#include "foo.h"

static myClass myObj ;
myClass myObj2 ;

int globInt = 5 ;
static int staticInt = 5 ;
const int constInt = 5 ;

int noValueGlobInt ;

const char *constString = "This is a constant string!";

int list[10] = { 0, 1, 2, 3, 4, 5, 6, 7, 8, 9 } ;

inline int foo( int a )
{
   int b = 0 ;

   for ( b = a ; b < 100 ; b ++ ) ;

   noValueGlobInt = a ;
   return b + a ;
}
```

```
static int bar( int c )
{
   int d = 0;

   d = foo( c ) + globInt ;
   d += staticInt ;
   d += constInt ;

   return d ;
}

int baz( int val)
{

   bar( val ) ;

   printf( "This is a printf format string in baz\n" ) ;

   return 0 ;
}
```
foo.h
```
class myClass
{
   public:

   int myVar ;

   myClass() {
      myVar = 5 ;
   }

};

extern int globInt;
extern myClass myObj2 ;

extern int baz( int val ) ;
```

main.C
```
#include <stdio.h>
#include <unistd.h>
#include <sys/utsname.h>

#include "foo.h"

myClass myObj3 ;

int main()
{
   struct utsname uInfo ;
```

```
        uname ( &uInfo ) ;

        baz ( 15 ) ;

        printf ( "This is a printf format string in main\n" ) ;

        sleep ( 1010 ) ;

        return 0 ;
    }
```

9.14 ELF APIs

The ELF APIs provide detailed functionality to read, create, and manipulate ELF files. Unfortunately, some distributions do not install the ELF library by default. Here is the URL for the ELF library on Linux in case you need it:
`http://www.stud.uni-hannover.de/~michael/software/english.html`.

9.15 OTHER INFORMATION

These will help you if you need to read or manipulate ELF files from a program.
`http://www.caldera.com/developers/gabi/`
`http://www.caldera.com/developers/devspecs/`
`http://www.x86-64.org/documentation/abi-0.96.pdf`
`http://www.muppetlabs.com/~breadbox/software/tiny/teensy.html`

9.16 CONCLUSION

ELF is one of those overlooked and under-appreciated aspects of the Linux operating system (as well as many other OSs). However, a solid understanding of ELF and how to use it to increase your debugging options is absolutely critical for any Linux expert. Hopefully this chapter provided an in-depth and useful look behind the scenes of the all-but-forgotten details of ELF.

The Toolbox

A.1 INTRODUCTION

This appendix contains a listing of the best problem determination tools available for Linux. The list is broken down by the categories of Process Information and Debugging, Network, System Information, Files and Object Files, Kernel, and Miscellaneous. Each tool listing includes a short description of the tool, where the tool can be obtained, the tool's usefulness, when generally to use the tool, and various notes and tips related to the tool. We recommend familiarizing yourself with each of these tools. You can then add them to your personal problem determination "toolbox," which will put you well on your way to solving some of the toughest problems with which Linux could present you. The listings do not get into a great deal of detail for each tool because the intent is more to make you aware of some of the best tools out there. For more information on each tool, the man pages, if applicable, will usually offer all the needed documentation. This book covers many of these in much more detail as well.

A.2 PROCESS INFORMATION AND DEBUGGING

A.2.1 Tool: GDB

Description: GNU project command line debugger.
Where to get: Included with most distributions or `http://www.gnu.org/software/gdb/`.
Usefulness: Very high
When to use: To debug a process using a command line debugger.
Notes: See Chapter 6, "The GNU Debugger," for more information.

A.2.2 Tool: ps

Description: Lists processes running on the system.
Where to get: Included with all major distributions.
Usefulness: Very high

When to use: Any time you need information about which processes are running on the system.
Notes: None.

A.2.3 Tool: strace (system call tracer)

Description: The strace tool traces all system calls that are called by a program.
Where to get: Included with most major distributions or `http://www.liacs.nl/~wichert/strace/`.
Usefulness: Very high
When to use: Any time a detailed process trace is required, especially when system call-level tracing is required. Very useful to see calls to system calls such as `open()`, `read()`, and `write()`.
Notes: A process will run slower when traced. See Chapter 2, "strace and System Call Tracing Explained" for more information.

A.2.4 Tool: /proc filesystem

Description: Not really a tool but is an alternative for many tools.
Where to get: Included with all major distributions.
Usefulness: Very high
When to use: Any time you need information about a process or the system.
Notes: See Chapter 3, "The /proc Filesystem" for more information.

A.2.5 Tool: DDD (Data Display Debugger)

Description: A graphical front-end to command-line debuggers such as GDB.
Where to get: Included with some distributions or `http://www.gnu.org/software/ddd/`.
Usefulness: High
When to use: To debug a process using a GUI.
Notes: See Chapter 6 for more information.

A.2.6 Tool: lsof (List Open Files)

Description: The lsof tool lists all open files on a system.
Where to get: Included with most major distributions or `ftp://lsof.itap.purdue.edu/pub/tools/unix/lsof`.
Usefulness: Very high

When to use: Any time you want to know which files are currently opened on the system and by which process(es).

Notes: To see files opened by root processes, you need to run this program as root. A suggestion to avoid the need to be root is to make the lsof executable setuid root.

A.2.7 Tool: ltrace (library call tracer)

Description: The ltrace tool traces all functions that are called by a program.

Where to get: Included with most major distributions or `http://www.cespedes.org/software/ltrace/`.

Usefulness: High

When to use: Any time a detailed process trace is required, especially when function-level tracing is required. Very useful to see calls to functions such as `malloc()`, `gethostbyname()`, `setenv()`, and so on.

Notes: Only works for functions called in shared libraries (which usually covers the majority of functions). A process will run slower when traced.

A.2.8 Tool: time

Description: This tool can time the run of a program.

Where to get: Included with all major distributions.

Usefulness: High

When to use: To time the run of a program or to find the percentage of system versus user time for a simple program.

Notes: The first run of a program may take longer than immediate subsequent runs due to file system caching. Ignore the time of the first run and use an immediate subsequent run to get a reasonable timing for the program.

A.2.9 Tool: top

Description: The top utility lists the "top" processes running on a system. Processes can be sorted by various metrics including top CPU consumers, memory consumers, and so on.

Where to get: Included with most major distributions or `http://www.unixtop.org`.

Usefulness: High

When to use: To get a "feeling" for what processes are consuming resources on a system.

Notes: The amount of "free" virtual memory may not always be 100% accurate.

A.2.10 Tool: pstree

Description: Lists processes running on the system in a tree format.
Where to get: Included with all major distributions.
Usefulness: Medium
When to use: Can be used to understand process' parent-child relationship.
Notes: None.

A.3 NETWORK

A.3.1 Tool: traceroute

Description: A utility that can trace network routes.
Where to get: Included with all major distributions or `http://freshmeat.net/`
`projects/net-tools/`.
Usefulness: Very high
When to use: To find the route or path between the local system and a remote system on the network.
Notes: Only finds the forward route (the route on the way to the remote host). There may also be several forward routes and several return routes.

A.3.2 File: /etc/hosts

Description: Configuration file used to define hostnames, IP addresses, and aliases.
Where to get: Included with all major distributions.
Usefulness: High
When to use: Examine when experiencing problems with resolving hostnames.
Notes: None.

A.3.3 File: /etc/services

Description: Configuration file used to define Internet network services.
Where to get: Included with all major distributions.
Usefulness: High
When to use: Examine when programs experience network difficulties.
Notes: None.

A.3.4 Tool: netstat

Description: Provides detailed statistics about network connections and interfaces.
Where to get: Included with all major distributions or `http://freshmeat.net/projects/net-tools/`.
Usefulness: High
When to use: To list the current connections on the system. To list the static network routes. To get detailed statistics for the various network protocols.
Notes: None.

A.3.5 Tool: ping

Description: A utility that can check the network between the local system and a remote system.
Where to get: Included with all major distributions.
Usefulness: High
When to use: To test the network between two systems.
Notes: ping has also been known to be used for malicious purposes, so many firewalls block ICMP packages (which ping uses). When this is the case, ping will not receive any response from the remote machine, giving the appearance that the remote machine is down when it is not.

A.3.6 Tool: telnet
Description: Connect to a remote system.
Where to get: Included with all major distributions.
Usefulness: Medium
When to use: To confirm that a remote server is up and running and that the network in between is functional.
Notes: Telnet is not meant to be a debugging utility, but it is very useful to test TCP servers. Telnet is also insecure, and SSH is preferred by many. To use telnet as a connection debugging tool, you need not send a username and password at all; if the connection is made and the remote machine provides a login prompt, the connection is successful and can be terminated at that point if desired.

A.3.7 Tool: host/nslookup

Description: Tools for testing DNS (Domain Name Service).
Where to get: Included with all major distributions.
Usefulness: Medium

When to use: Specifically to test DNS (for example, to look up host name and IP addresses).
Notes: This does not use /etc/hosts to look up host names.

A.3.8 Tool: ethtool

Description: Tool for displaying and changing the settings of an Ethernet device.
Where to get: Included with most major distributions or `http://sourceforge.net/projects/gkernel/`.
Usefulness: Medium
When to use: When an Ethernet card is not working as expected or as desired.
Notes: Exercise caution when using.

A.3.9 Tool: ethereal

Description: A network protocol analyzer.
Where to get: Included with most major distributions or `http://www.ethereal.com`.
Usefulness: High
When to use: To monitor (*sniff*) network and protocol activity.
Notes: It is an X11 GUI based application.

A.3.10 File: /etc/nsswitch.conf

Description: Configuration file used to specify user, group, and hostname "database" lookup order and configuration. The database can be facilities such as *shadow*, *netgroup*, or *dns*.
Where to get: Included with all major distributions.
Usefulness: Low
When to use: Examine when experiencing problems with user/group authentication or remote hostname lookup problems.
Notes: None.

A.3.11 File: /etc/resolv.conf

Description: Configuration file used to resolve network and Internet domain names.
Where to get: Included with all major distributions.
Usefulness: Low

When to use: Examine when experiencing problems with remote hostnames and domain names.
Notes: None.

A.4 SYSTEM INFORMATION

A.4.1 Tool: vmstat

Description: Display live statistics about the virtual memory on the system.
Where to get: Included with all major distributions or `http://procps.sourceforge.net/`.
Usefulness: Very high
When to use: When the system is not performing as expected.
Notes: Most of the useful statistics are measured between two points in time. Always run vmstat with a time interval even if you only want a single point in time result. The first stat line produced when running vmstat gives average statistics since the last reboot. No timestamp is associated with each report line, so if extended and vmstat collection is desired, it is recommended to run vmstat for short periods of time while displaying the current time in a script.

A.4.2 Tool: iostat

Description: Display live statistics about the input and output devices on the system.
Where to get: Included with all major distributions or `http://freshmeat.net/projects/sysstat/`.
Usefulness: High
When to use: When a file system or disk device is performing more slowly than expected or desired.
Notes: As with vmstat, most of the useful statistics are measured between two points in time. Always run iostat with a time interval, even if you only want a single point in time result.

A.4.3 Tool: nfsstat

Description: Display live statistics about the NFS client and server.
Where to get: Included with all major distributions or `http://sourceforge.net/projects/nfs/`.
Usefulness: High
When to use: When an NFS client or server is not performing as expected.
Notes: Not repeatable like vmstat and iostat.

A.4.4 Tool: sar

Description: Display saved system activity information.
Where to get: Included with all major distributions or `http://freshmeat.net/ projects/sysstat/`.
Usefulness: High
When to use: When the system is not performing or operating as expected. sar saves and archives system activity information when past system activity information is required.
Notes: Runs automatically on many systems by default to always capture and archive information. The information is archived by default in the /var/log/sa directory in binary and text formats.

A.4.5 Tool: syslogd

Description: System Log Daemon writes kernel messages to a log file.
Where to get: Included with all major distributions or `http://freshmeat.net/ projects/sysklogd/`.
Usefulness: High
When to use: When troubleshooting system problems. Some applications also log messages to the system log.
Notes: The name of the log file is defined in /etc/syslog.conf and is /var/log/ messages by default.

A.4.6 Tool: dmesg

Description: Display kernel messages still residing in kernel memory.
Where to get: Included with all major distributions or `http://freshmeat.net/ projects/util-linux/`.
Usefulness: Medium
When to use: When the system is not functioning correctly.
Notes: The syslog daemon process reads from the same kernel memory buffer that dmesg does and writes the messages to the system log file, usually /var/ log/messages. There may be situations where the syslog was unable to write the messages, so running `dmesg` could be very important.

A.4.7 Tool: mpstat

Description: Display live statistics about processor usage.
Where to get: Included with all major distributions or `http://freshmeat.net/ projects/sysstat/`.

Usefulness: Medium
When to use: When the system is not performing as expected.
Notes: Is repeatable like vmstat and iostat. vmstat reports include most of the info mpstat reports; however, mpstat report lines include a timestamp associated with statistics. Reports can be limited to a specific CPU in an MPP system.

A.4.8 Tool: procinfo

Description: Display system status in a nicely formatted output.
Where to get: Included with all major distributions or http://procps.sourceforge.net/.
Usefulness: Medium
When to use: When a quick snapshot of all major system resource usage is desired.
Notes: None.

A.4.9 Tool: xosview

Description: Graphical display and monitoring of system resources.
Where to get: Included with some distributions or http://sourceforge.net/projects/xosview/.
Usefulness: Medium
When to use: Great for watching system resource usage in a graphical format.
Notes: X11 GUI based application.

A.5 FILES AND OBJECT FILES

A.5.1 Tool: file

Description: Determine a particular file's type.
Where to get: Included with all major distributions.
Usefulness: High
When to use: When you have difficulties executing, viewing, or editing a particular file.
Notes: Use the -L parameter to resolve symbolic links.

A.5.2 Tool: ldd

Description: Display shared library dependencies.
Where to get: Included with all major distributions.
Usefulness: High

When to use: When a program complains of missing symbols or missing libraries.
Notes: Only works with dynamically linked objects.

A.5.3 Tool: nm

Description: View symbols in object files.
Where to get: Included with all major distributions.
Usefulness: Medium
When to use: If an object file complains about missing symbols, you can use nm to search through all libraries to find the missing symbol. Also useful to determine which functions a particular library provides.
Notes: None.

A.5.4 Tool: objdump

Description: Display detailed information about object files.
Where to get: Included with all major distributions.
Usefulness: Medium
When to use: Most useful for software development to analyze various sections and configuration data that comprise object files. Very useful to determine an object's *runtime path* with the -p option then examining the RPATH field.
Notes: See Chapter 9, "ELF: Executable and Linking Format" for more information.

A.5.5 Tool: od

Description: Dump files in octal, hexadecimal, or other format.
Where to get: Included with all major distributions.
Usefulness: Medium
When to use: When examining a file's raw data. This is a great utility for hex-dumping a file with the -x parameter.
Notes: None.

A.5.6 Tool: stat

Description: Display file or filesystem information.
Where to get: Included with all major distributions or http://freshmeat.net/projects/sysstat/.
Usefulness: Medium

When to use: When detailed information on a particular file or filesystem is desired.
Notes: None.

A.5.7 Tool: readelf

Description: Display detailed ELF information for a particular object file.
Where to get: Included with all major distributions.
Usefulness: Low
When to use: Most useful for software development to analyze ELF specific structures and function in a given library or executable.
Notes: See Chapter 9 for more information.

A.5.8 Tool: strings

Description: Display human readable characters and strings in object files.
Where to get: Included with all major distributions.
Usefulness: Low
When to use: When more information about an unknown file is desired.
Notes: None.

A.6 KERNEL

A.6.1 Tool: KDB

Description: Built-in kernel debugger.
Where to get: Included with some distributions or `http://oss.sgi.com/projects/kdb/`.
Usefulness: Medium
When to use: When debugging system problems or processes that appear to be experiencing problems in kernel mode.
Notes: Allows debugging the live kernel on the same machine. See Chapter 8, "Kernel Debugging With KDB," for more information.

A.6.2 Tool: KGDB

Description: Remote kernel debugger.
Where to get: Included with some distributions or `http://kgdb.linsyssoft.com/`
.

Usefulness: Medium
When to use: When debugging system problems or processes that appear to be experiencing problems in kernel mode.
Notes: Based on GDB. Requires a separate computer.

A.6.3 Tool: ksymoops

Description: Convert Oops Reports into a more readable format.
Where to get: Included with some distributions or `http://freshmeat.net/projects/ksymoops/`.
Usefulness: Medium
When to use: When the kernel produces an Oops Report that requires conversion.
Notes: Most major distributions have support built into their kernels, which generates readable Oops Reports that do not require conversion; therefore, ksymoops is not needed. See Chapter 7, "Linux System Crashes and Hangs" for more information.

A.7 MISCELLANEOUS

A.7.1 Tool: VMWare Workstation

Description: Create and use virtual machines to run Windows or Linux as a regular application within your existing operating system.
Where to get: `http://www.vmware.com`.
Usefulness: Medium
When to use: Useful for the following scenarios:

☞ Ability to run Windows within Linux

☞ Ability to run Linux within Windows

☞ Testing a Linux installation or application that may cause damage to the OS installation

☞ Kernel development work that may result in frequent crashes requiring reboot

Notes: It is a commercial application and is not free. A 30-day evaluation version is available.

A.7.2 Tool: VNC Server

Description: Remote system control server.
Where to get: Included in most distributions or `http://www.tightvnc.com` or `http://www.realvnc.com`.
Usefulness: Medium
When to use: Use to allow remote access to your X11 desktop.
Notes: By default, running `vncserver` starts up a new X11 server with the relatively useless MWM window manager. To use KDE in your vncserver, perform the following steps:

1. Kill the `vncserver` if it is running with `vncserver -kill:<display_number>`.
2. Remove the ~/.vnc/xstartup file (it gets automatically created if it doesn't exist)
3. Assuming KDE is installed in /opt, issue `ln -sf /opt/kde3/bin/startkde~/.vnc/xstartup`.
4. Restart the `vncserver`.

It is also useful to have the exact same desktop when using your desktop computer at the local console and from remote via the `vncviewer` program. To do this, perform the following steps on the local console:

1. Start the `vncserver` as your regular user ID (for example "joeblow").
2. Log into X Windows with a dummy user ID (for example "joeblow2").
3. Open an xterm and run the `vncviewer` program to connect to the `vncserver` started in Step 1.
4. Press the F8 key to display the `vncviewer` menu and choose "Switch to Full Screen."
5. With some versions of VNC, there is a bug that causes keyboard focus to be lost when switching to full screen mode. If this happens, add the following to the `vncviewer` command-line: `-xrm '*grabKeyboard: true'`
6. You can now use `vncviewer` from a remote computer to use the same desktop you use locally.

A.7.3 Tool: VNC Viewer

Description: Remote system control client.
Where to get: Included in most distributions or `http://www.tightvnc.com` or `http://www.realvnc.com`.
Usefulness: Medium

When to use: Use to control remote desktops.

Notes: Remote computer can be Linux, Windows, or any other platform supported by VNC. If you experience difficulties cutting and pasting to or from a `vncviewer` session connected to a Linux machine, ensure that you are using a real xterm window within `vncviewer`.

B

Data Collection Script

B.1 OVERVIEW

There are two main challenges for collecting data when a problem occurs. The first challenge is collecting the right data. This is a challenge because it is often hard to know what type of problem you've encountered and therefore what data to collect for it. The second challenge is to collect data quickly when you are under pressure to solve the problem immediately (or to get the system back up and running). Collecting all of the important information manually will lengthen the time to resolution and potentially increase the duration of an outage—and humans tend to make mistakes that can jeopardize the usefulness of the information. Addressing these two challenges is the purpose of a data collection tool or script.

As the name suggests, a *data collector* is a tool written for the purpose of collecting the right information quickly when a problem occurs. You can modify it when there isn't a desperate need to collect data—that is, when you have time to consider what data to collect for different problem types. Because it is a script or executable, it will run quickly when needed, potentially minimizing the duration of an outage (for example, with the right data collected, there is no need to keep the system in the same state).

Most of the information gathered by a thorough data collector will not be used for a specific problem investigation. The reason so much information is collected is that you often don't know what will be useful until you start investigating. It is best to collect everything you might need and then discard the output once you solve the problem.

The data collector, even though it is very useful as it is, is included as a sample for building something more elaborate that may include the ability to collect data for commercial products or other information relevant to the types of problems you encounter.

The data collector creates the directory structure outlined earlier in this chapter:

```
<problem number>          / inv.txt
                          / data /
                          / src /
```

It creates a new and unique directory under your home directory and puts all of the data it collects into the inv.txt (the investigation log). The output from various commands is placed directly in inv.txt, and the files collected are placed in the data directory. The src directory is created in case tools or specific scripts are needed as the investigation continues.

The script uses two simple bash subroutines to collect data: runCommand and collectFile. The runCommand subroutine, as expected, runs a command and captures the output in the investigation log. The collectFile subroutine collects the contents of a file in the data directory. The output of the runCommand looks like this (from the inv.txt file):

```
RUNCMD: /bin/netstat -i -n (Network Interface Information) ...
{
Kernel Interface table
Iface   MTU Met   RX-OK RX-ERR RX-DRP RX-OVR    TX-OK TX-ERR TX-DRP
➥TX-OVR Flg
eth0   1500   01287895866    14     0    01336107264    0    0    0
➥BMRU
lo     16436  0224593366     0     0    0224593366      0    0    0
➥LRU
}
```

The output is always prefixed with "RUNCMD" to make the output easy to find. The command itself is included on the same line to make it convenient for regular expressions. For example, searching for "RUNCMD.*netstat" will find all captured netstat commands.

The output from collectFile looks like this:

```
COLLECT: /etc/resolv.conf (DNS resolution configuration file) ...
➥success.

COLLECT: /etc/nsswitch.conf (Name service switch configuration file)
... success.

COLLECT: /etc/hosts (Static table lookup file) ... success.
```

The output is always prefixed with "COLLECT," again to make it easy to find. If the copy fails, the output of the copy command is included for convenience.

Collecting new files or the output from new commands is easy. Just add lines similar to the following:

```
runCommand   "Environment variables"                "/usr/bin/env"
collectFile "DNS resolution configuration file"      "/etc/resolv.conf"
```

The script is fairly simple, but do not underestimate its usefulness. It can reduce a lot of investigation time as it is, even without any modification. This is especially true if you work on problems for remote customers or users. A data collector can ensure you have the information needed to solve the problem and will dramatically reduce the need to iteratively request information as the investigation progresses.

There are seven options for the data collector script:

```
vacuum
vacuum - thorough
vacuum - hang
vacuum - trap
vacuum - perf
vacuum - error
```

Without any options, the data collector script collects information that does not take a long time to collect. Using the data collector without any option can be used for very basic problems or for when collection time is absolutely critical (that is, via a script when the script needs to finish immediately).

This mode takes approximately 10 seconds to run as shown in the following sample run:

```
penguin> time vacuum
Investigation directory: /home/wilding/investigations/131
0.340u 9.000s 0:09.42 99.1%    0+0k 0+0io 7551pf+0w
```

B.1.1 -thorough

This switch collects more information but takes more time to run (about 60 seconds). Use this switch to collect information when collection time is not an issue—for general system performance problems or for problems that involve a commercial product (for example, when the vendor doesn't provide a data collector tool).

B.1.2 -perf, -hang <pid>, -trap, -error <cmd>

These switches are left to the user to fill in. They are provided as part of the script for convenience. The one major caveat of the script is that it is written in bash, which lacks job control features that would make it easy to run and interact with a tool such as gdb. If the script is ported to ksh (Korn Shell), it will be possible to use more advanced job control.

These options also usually depend on the product or tool and/or situation. Because this is a script, the reader is free to modify these areas of the script as needed.

B.2 RUNNING THE SCRIPT

Running the script is straightforward as shown here:

```
penguin> vacuum
Investigation directory: /home/wilding/investigations/128
penguin> cd /home/wilding/investigations/128
penguin> ls -lR .
.:
total 456
drwxr-xr-x  2 wilding  build       4096 Jan 30 20:06 data
-rw-r--r--  1 wilding  build     453444 Jan 30 20:06 inv.txt
drwxr-xr-x  2 wilding  build       4096 Jan 30 20:06 src

./data:
total 1112
-r--r--r--  1 wilding  build        898 Jan 30 20:06 cpuinfo
-rw-r--r--  1 wilding  build        322 Jan 30 20:06 exports
-r--r--r--  1 wilding  build        187 Jan 30 20:06 filesystems
-rw-r--r--  1 wilding  build      26219 Jan 30 20:06 fstab
-rw-r--r--  1 wilding  build        707 Jan 30 20:06 hosts
-r--r--r--  1 wilding  build        505 Jan 30 20:06 ioports
-r--r--r--  1 wilding  build         27 Jan 30 20:06 loadavg
-r--r--r--  1 wilding  build        380 Jan 30 20:06 locks
-r--r--r--  1 wilding  build        555 Jan 30 20:06 meminfo
-rw-r--r--  1 wilding  build     718379 Jan 30 20:06 messages
-r--r--r--  1 wilding  build       1085 Jan 30 20:06 modules
-rw-r--r--  1 wilding  build       1346 Jan 30 20:06 nsswitch.conf
-r--r--r--  1 wilding  build        720 Jan 30 20:06 partitions
-r--r--r--  1 wilding  build       2899 Jan 30 20:06 pci
-rw-r--r--  1 wilding  build     306320 Jan 30 20:06 services
-rw-r--r--  1 wilding  build       4850 Jan 30 20:06 slabinfo
-r--r--r--  1 wilding  build        813 Jan 30 20:06 stat
-r--r--r--  1 wilding  build         96 Jan 30 20:06 swaps
-rw-r--r--  1 wilding  build       1204 Jan 30 20:06 syslog.conf
-r--r--r--  1 wilding  build        107 Jan 30 20:06 version

./src:
total 0
```

B.3 THE SCRIPT SOURCE

Here is the source code for the script. Again, this is provided as-is for the reader.

> **Note:** The source code for this script and the source code from the rest of the book is available at `http://www.phptr.com/title/013147751X`.

```bash
#!/bin/bash

################################################################################
#
#   This script captures basic information for when a problem occurs.
#   It   can be used any time a problem occurs, as root or as a
mortal user.
#
################################################################################

usage="Usage: vacuum [ -thorough | -perf | -hang <pid> | -trap | -
error <cmd> ]"
mode_thorough=0
mode_perf=0
mode_hang=0
mode_trap=0
mode_error=0
topdir=""              # The data collection directory

if [ -n $HOME ]
then
    topdir=$HOME/investigations
else
    topdir=~/investigations/$i
fi

if [ $# -gt 0 ]
then
    while true ; do
        case $1 in
            "-thorough" )
                mode_thorough=1
                shift
            ;;
            "-perf" )
                mode_perf=1
                mode="PERF"
                shift
            ;;
            "-hang" )
                mode_hang=1
                shift
                if [ $# -le 0 ]
                then
                    echo $usage
                    exit 2
                fi
                pid=$1
            shift
            ;;
            "-trap" )
                mode_trap=1
                shift
```

```
                  ;;
              "-error" )
                  mode_error=1
                  shift
                  if [ $# -le 0 ]
                  then
                      echo $usage
                      exit 2
                  fi
                  cmd=$1
                  shift
              ;;
              * )
                  echo $usage
                  exit 2
              ;;
          esac

          if [ $# -le 0 ]
          then
              break ;
          fi
      done
fi

if [ ! -n $USER ]
then
    USER=`whoami`
fi

##############################################################################
##  Create the appropriate directory for this problem
##############################################################################

i=0
invdir=$topdir/$i

while [ -d $invdir ]
do
    let "i = i + 1"
    invdir=$topdir/$i
done

echo Investigation directory: $invdir

##############################################################################
##  Create data directory, src directory and the investigation log
##############################################################################

mkdir $invdir
mkdir $invdir/src
datadir=$invdir/data
```

```
invlog=$invdir/log
mkdir $datadir
touch $invlog
echo
"##################################################################################"
>> $invlog
echo "##                                             Header
##" >> $invlog
echo
"##################################################################################"
>> $invlog
echo "Problem number                    : $i" >> $invlog
echo -n "Time of data collector run     : " >> $invlog
date >> $invlog
echo "Data collector run as             : \"$0 $1 $2\" " >> $invlog

##################################################################################
##   Ready to go...
##################################################################################
function collectFile
{
   local comment=$1
   local fileName=$2
   local output=""

   echo -n "COLLECT: $fileName ($comment) ... " >> $invlog

   output=`cp $fileName $datadir 2>&1`

   if [ $? -ne 0 ]
   then
      echo "failed." >> $invlog
      echo "output from copy:" >> $invlog
      echo '{' >> $invlog
      echo $output >> $invlog
      echo '}' >> $invlog

   else
      echo "success." >> $invlog
   fi

   echo >> $invlog

}

function runCommand
{
   local comment=$1
   local cmd=$2

   echo "RUNCMD: $cmd ($comment) ... " >> $invlog
```

```
    echo `{` >> $invlog
    $cmd 2>&1 >> $invlog 2>&1
    echo `}' >> $invlog
    echo >> $invlog

}

function doQuickCollect
{
    echo >> $invlog
    echo
"##########################################################################"
>> $invlog
    echo "##                              Quick Collect
##" >> $invlog
    echo
"##########################################################################"
>> $invlog

    #Environmental information
    runCommand  "Environment variables"                     "/usr/bin/
env"

    #Network information
    collectFile "DNS resolution configuration file"         "/etc/
resolv.conf"
    collectFile "Name service switch configuration file"  "/etc/
nsswitch.conf"
    collectFile "Static table lookup file"                  "/etc/
hosts"
    collectFile "TCP/IP services file"                      "/etc/
services"
    runCommand  "Interface information"                     "ifconfig -
a"
    runCommand  "Interface information (no DNS)"            "/bin/
netstat -i -n"
    runCommand  "Socket information"                        "/bin/
netstat -an"
    runCommand  "Extended socket information"               "/bin/
netstat -avn"
    runCommand  "Socket owner information"                  "/bin/
netstat -p"
    runCommand  "Network routing table"                     "/bin/
netstat -rn"
    runCommand  "Network statistics"                        "/bin/
netstat -s"
    runCommand  "Extended routing information"              "/bin/
netstat -rvn"
    ## the grep commands below look odd but it is a simple trick to
get the contents of
    ## everything under specific directories
```

```
    runCommand  "Network information from /proc" "/usr/bin/find /
proc/net -type f -exec /bin/grep -Hv '^$' {} "
    runCommand  "System information from /proc" "/usr/bin/find /proc/
sys -type f -exec /bin/grep -Hv '^$' {} "
    runCommand  "SYSV IPC info from /proc" '/usr/bin/find /proc/
sysvipc -type f -exec /bin/grep -Hv ^$ {} ;'

    #File system information
    runCommand  "Type information"                        "/bin/df -
lT"
    runCommand  "Usage information"                       "/bin/df -
lk"
    runCommand  "Inode information"                       "/bin/df -
li"
    runCommand  "Share information"                       "/usr/sbin/
showmount -e"
    runCommand  "SCSI and IDE disk partition tables"      "/sbin/
fdisk -l /dev/sd* /dev/hd*"
    runCommand  "NFS statistic"                           "/usr/sbin/
nfsstat -cnrs"
    collectFile "Filesystems supported by the kernel"     "/proc/
filesystems"
    collectFile "Export file"                             "/etc/
exports"
    collectFile "Mount file"                              "/etc/
fstab"
    collectFile "Partition information"                   "/proc/
partitions"

    #Kernel information
    runCommand "User (resource) limits"                   "ulimit -a"
    runCommand "IPC information"                           "/usr/bin/
ipcs -a"
    runCommand "Loaded module info"                       "/sbin/
lsmod"
    runCommand "IPC resource limits"                      "/usr/bin/
ipcs -l"
    runCommand "Kernel information"                       "/sbin/
sysctl -a"
    runCommand "Memory usage"                             "/usr/bin/
free"
    runCommand "Uptime"                                   "/usr/bin/
uptime"
    runCommand "System name, etc"                         "/bin/uname
-a"
    runCommand "Current users"                            "/usr/bin/w"
    runCommand "Process listing"                          "/bin/ps
auwx"
    runCommand "Recent users"                             "/usr/bin/
last|/usr/bin/head -100"
    runCommand "Contents of home directory"               "/bin/ls -
lda $HOME"
    runCommand "Host ID"                                  "/usr/bin/
```

```
hostid"
    collectFile "Kernel limits specified by the user"      "/etc/
sysctl.conf"
    collectFile "Load average"                              "/proc/
loadavg"
    collectFile "I/O memory map"                            "/proc/
iomap"
    collectFile "I/O port regions"                          "/proc/
ioports"
    collectFile "Interrupts per each IRQ"                   "/proc/
interupts"
    collectFile "CPU status"                                "/proc/
cpuinfo"
    collectFile "Memory usage"                              "/proc/
meminfo"
    collectFile "Swap partition information"          "/proc/swaps"
    collectFile "Slab information"                 "/proc/slabinfo"
    collectFile "Lock information"                    "/proc/locks"
    collectFile "Module information"                "/proc/modules"
    collectFile "Version information"               "/proc/version"
    collectFile "System status information"            "/proc/stat"
    collectFile "PCI information"                       "/proc/pci"

    #Version information
    runCommand "Package information"                  "/bin/rpm -qa"

    #Misc
  collectFile "Main syslog file"                "/var/log/messages"
    collectFile "Syslog configuration file"                "/etc/
syslog.conf"


}

function doThoroughCollect
{
    echo >> $invlog
                                                            echo
"###############################################################################"
>> $invlog
    echo "##                                    Thorough Collect
##" >> $invlog
                                                            echo
"###############################################################################"
>> $invlog

    runCommand "Virtual memory statistics"              "/usr/bin/
vmstat 2 5"
    runCommand "I/O statistics"                         "/usr/bin/
iostat 2 5"
    runCommand "Extended I/O statistics"                "/usr/bin/
iostat -x 2 5"
```

```
    runCommand "CPU statistics"                                    "/usr/bin/
mpstat -P ALL 2 5"
    runCommand "System activity"                                   "/usr/bin/
sar -A 2 5"

}

function doPerfCollect
{
    echo >> $invlog

                                                                        echo
"#######################################################################################"
>> $invlog
    echo "##                                             Performance Collect
##" >> $invlog
                                                                        echo
"#######################################################################################"
>> $invlog

    # Add specific commands here

}

function doHangCollect
{
    echo >> $invlog

                                                                        echo
"#######################################################################################"
>> $invlog
    echo "##                                                   Hang  Collect
##" >> $invlog
                                                                        echo
"#######################################################################################"
>> $invlog

    # NOTE: $pid contains the process ID of the process that is hanging

    ## check whether the process actually exists
    kill -0 $pid 2>/dev/null 1>/dev/null
    if [ ! $? -eq 0 ]
    then
        echo "Process ID \"$pid\" not found."
        exit 3
    fi

    # Add specific commands here

}

    function doErrorCollect
    {
        echo >> $invlog
```

```
    echo
"####################################################################"
>> $invlog
    echo "##                                         Error Collect
##" >> $invlog
    echo
"####################################################################"
>> $invlog

    # NOTE: $cmd contains the name of the command line that apparently
produces an error

    # Add specific commands here
}

function doTrapCollect
{
    echo >> $invlog
    echo
"####################################################################"
>> $invlog
    echo "##                                         Trap Collect
##" >> $invlog
    echo
"####################################################################"
>> $invlog

    # Add specific commands here
}

################################## MAIN SCRIPT BODY
#####################################

## Do the basics first, then anything else that might be needed
##
doQuickCollect

if [ $mode_thorough -eq 1 ]
then
    echo "Collecting thorough information"
    doThoroughCollect
fi

if [ $mode_perf -eq 1 ]
then
    echo "Collecting perf information"
    doPerfCollect
fi

if [ $mode_hang -eq 1 ]
then
    echo "Collecting hang information"
```

```
      doHangCollect
fi

if [ $mode_trap -eq 1 ]
then
    echo "Collecting trap information"
    doTrapCollect
fi

if [ $mode_error -eq 1 ]
then
    echo "Collecting error information"
    doErrorCollect
fi

echo >> $invlog
e                      c                    h                    o
"##############################################################################"
>> $invlog
echo "##              End of Data Collection (the rest is for user
investigation)     ##" >> $invlog
e                      c                    h                    o
"##############################################################################"
>> $invlog
```

B.4 DISCLAIMER

The script is provided as-is. It is an example of what you can do with a data collector script. The authors do not suggest or guarantee that it works or any fitness of purpose. Use it to build something useful for yourself.

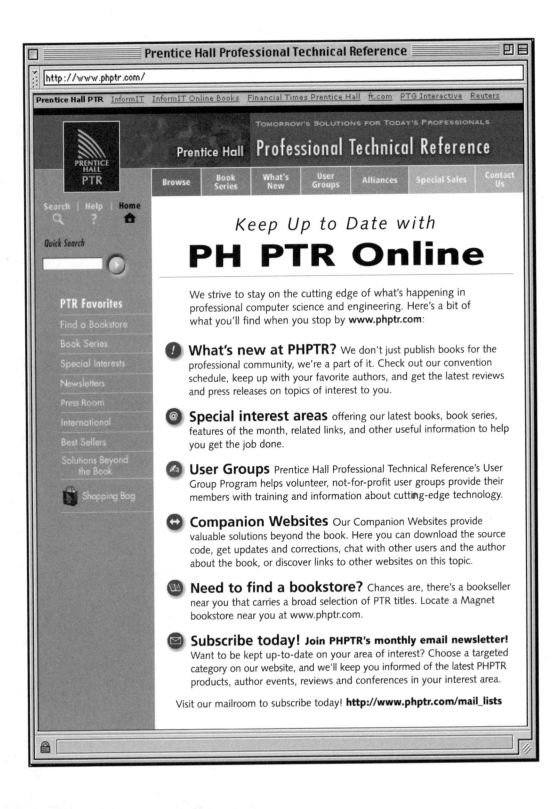

Prentice Hall Professional Technical Reference

http://www.phptr.com/

Prentice Hall PTR   InformIT   InformIT Online Books   Financial Times Prentice Hall   ft.com   PTG Interactive   Reuters

TOMORROW'S SOLUTIONS FOR TODAY'S PROFESSIONALS

Prentice Hall **Professional Technical Reference**

Browse | Book Series | What's New | User Groups | Alliances | Special Sales | Contact Us

Search | Help | Home

Quick Search

PTR Favorites

Find a Bookstore
Book Series
Special Interests
Newsletters
Press Room
International
Best Sellers
Solutions Beyond the Book

Shopping Bag

Keep Up to Date with
PH PTR Online

We strive to stay on the cutting edge of what's happening in professional computer science and engineering. Here's a bit of what you'll find when you stop by **www.phptr.com**:

What's new at PHPTR? We don't just publish books for the professional community, we're a part of it. Check out our convention schedule, keep up with your favorite authors, and get the latest reviews and press releases on topics of interest to you.

Special interest areas offering our latest books, book series, features of the month, related links, and other useful information to help you get the job done.

User Groups Prentice Hall Professional Technical Reference's User Group Program helps volunteer, not-for-profit user groups provide their members with training and information about cutting-edge technology.

Companion Websites Our Companion Websites provide valuable solutions beyond the book. Here you can download the source code, get updates and corrections, chat with other users and the author about the book, or discover links to other websites on this topic.

Need to find a bookstore? Chances are, there's a bookseller near you that carries a broad selection of PTR titles. Locate a Magnet bookstore near you at www.phptr.com.

Subscribe today! Join PHPTR's monthly email newsletter! Want to be kept up-to-date on your area of interest? Choose a targeted category on our website, and we'll keep you informed of the latest PHPTR products, author events, reviews and conferences in your interest area.

Visit our mailroom to subscribe today! **http://www.phptr.com/mail_lists**

informIT

YOUR GUIDE TO IT REFERENCE

Articles

Keep your edge with thousands of free articles, in-depth features, interviews, and IT reference recommendations – all written by experts you know and trust.

Online Books

Answers in an instant from **InformIT Online Book's** 600+ fully searchable on line books. For a limited time, you can get your first 14 days **free**.

POWERED BY

Safari
TECH BOOKS ONLINE®

Catalog

Review online sample chapters, author biographies and customer rankings and choose exactly the right book from a selection of over 5,000 titles.